D1602836

THE LAST BILLIONAIRE

THE LAST BILLIONAIRE

HENRY FORD

BY

WILLIAM C. RICHARDS

CHARLES SCRIBNER'S SONS · NEW YORK
CHARLES SCRIBNER'S SONS · LTD · LONDON
1948

PRINTED IN THE UNITED STATES OF AMERICA

The author wishes to express his profound thanks to a host of present and former Ford executives and newspapermen who were in position to study Mr. Ford at close range and in daily contact and who have contributed generously of their memories to this work.

An Explanation

TO ROSEMARY:

This book is written primarily for my own pleasure and not to shrink or stretch the stature of the late Henry Ford. It is doubtful if a single word of mine could add a brick or scratch to the incomparable monument he built to mass production. He confused the critics in life; there is no reason to suppose he will perplex the historians less, but the clay is now theirs.

This is no bilious exposé, no definitive biography, no honeyed hymn in his honor, but a series of reminiscences of mine, of men presently or past members of the Ford hierarchy and of others who knew him as a human being who was neither pristine saint nor as black as his traducers wanted to make out.

When I became acquainted with him he was a full-blown personality and the spotlight had disposed its silver shawl caressingly about his shoulders. Consequently I am concerned here with him *after* he became a controversial figure. These chapters have little to say of his heritage, his boyhood, his early struggles. Of such days I have only the enfeebled recollections of a corporal's guard of early playmates. I do not know if he was a good boy or bad boy, a trial to his folks, the despair of a father who preferred he stay on the farm.

Anyway, there is no intention here of building into significance a period when, if he made a screwdriver of his mother's darning needle, or kissed the butcher's daughter, or stuffed his blouse into a cap when he went swimming, or fixed a watch behind a geography, he only did what thousands of other boys did before him and have done since.

No one but he and Mrs. Ford attended in the kitchen of the home on the night when the first engine coughed for the first time. I was not a witness when they barged off to the probable mockery of those at the curb and the derision of those driving horses they met on the way. Personally I know only that the scoffers on the sidewalk and those who clucked along the roads as the Fords passed and reached for their carriage whips to quiet their perpendicular mares, showed up later in many an ingle-nook drawing painful comfort from stories they told of how near they came to buying stock in Ford's first motorized surrey and were deterred not by doubt—not at all—but by an unlucky lack of coppers at the time.

Completely unkind books were written of him with which I totally disagree and I have read a profusion of others which might be joined under the fair title *The Real Henry Ford*, but no one knew the entire truth about the motormaker, probably not he himself.

As a reporter, a little pompous in my nearnesss to the fountainhead, I imagined that I was riding some of the clouds with him, but they were filmy and insubstantial—and my edge always gave way, of course, tumbling me back to earth to watch Mr. Ford float majestically or awkwardly by, as the case might be.

It came as a shock at first to discover that when one was in the midst of exuberant applause, it was not unusual for Ford to turn his back abruptly and drift to the other side of the field and there begin the recitation of a sheer nonsense jingle. Thereupon you fell back upon your cheering section plank and waited, considerably let down, for him to stop making a ninny of himself and return to a clarity within your understanding.

You may remember that it was not long ago, in a time of ascending suicides and increasing applecarts, that he contributed to the public comfort such remarks as "These are really good times but only a few know it" and "The average man won't really do a day's work unless he is caught and can't get out of it" and "There's plenty of work to do if people will do it." I dumbly did not know what he was talking about. Those are the zany things I mean. There are a thousand other examples. Ford frequently did not add up.

Without empire and a billion dollars to validate each whim as world-wide news Ford might have died a nobody and been buried uncaroled in his cornfield. But in my opinion he would have been remembered by those who knew him if he had been a store-keeper, a foundry foreman or a mechanic in an obscure shop. People would have remembered him for four qualities. One was his belief that there was something holy in work—in this he bordered on fanaticism. On camping trips if he was not cleaning out springs he was chopping wood, and if he was not chopping wood he was showing children how an automobile engine ran. It always seemed a contradiction—urging the sanctity of work on one hand, and on the other shortening work hours and eliminating the drudgery.

Another characteristic he always expressed by maxim: "It is always too soon to quit."

His very doggedness produced results. A conversation with engineers might go like this:

"Have you done so and so?"

"Yes, we have, Mr. Ford."

"How about this combination?" No, they had not tried that. "Well, add that to it and see what you get."

What engineers discovered sometimes after trying five absolutely "crazy" ideas proposed by him was that the sixth might not prove as nonsensical as it first sounded. He was always stirring up people to do things he did not see clearly himself—or that they did not see clearly—and he did so not because he was sure what the answer was but because he was dissatisfied with things as they were. The principal thing was to learn by doing. He had an intensely inquisitive mind and the money to play with. If an idea did not work, no harm was done. "Let's see if we can do it!"

He had a notion he could build a dam of loose stones if he just threw in enough of them, but after hauling a great number of truck loads he finally agreed it might not be feasible. Once he staggered a county road commission. He urged that a road be paved and the engineers said the existing gravel was not too bad and the laying of concrete would cost more than the county could afford at the moment.

"All you've got to do," he floored the experts, "is to take the gravel that's there, run it through a mixer, add cement and make concrete."

He was put out and skeptical when the engineers assured him his way was no good and that sand and gravel had to be mixed in definite proportions to get a usable dense mass. The clay content by his method would have crumbled in no time.

"We could do as you say, Mr. Ford," said one commissioner, "but I'd want to leave the country after we did it."

He had the uncluttered imagination of a child and a bit of the attitude of a man who had been born at forty and who had said, "Nothing has happened before I arrived—all life begins here and now. Other men will tell me things which they will claim to be facts, but I must not believe them. I will not accept anything as true unless I, myself, prove they are true, and that goes for all subjects which these men call by such strange names as science, history, organized philanthropy, medicine, engineering formulae." School did no injury to his genius, someone once said of him, by giving him formulae that might have blocked his original thinking before he could pick the lock.

The fourth quality was a dynamism that got things done, that brought the spark and drive to the thing he set his mind upon. There were those who ranked Ford as an engineer not far beyond addition, but those about him agreed that when the chips were down he seemed to have the answer. On the idea he poured the warming sun of an exhaustless energy.

The car was really not the billion dollar idea. The billion lay in what he brought to it after the first explosion in the first cylinder—his notorious willingness to scrap, his constant search for the ultimate, the gospel of factory asepticism, a burning desire to explore and blaze new roads. Gamaliel Bradford struck it years ago in *Harper's Magazine,* when he said, substantially, "It was the infinite care and intelligence in detail, the extraordinary organization for efficiency, the economy of human effort in every possible way, the saving of time, of steps, of strength."

It has been popular in some quarters to say that Ford was progress-crazy—as the Aztecs a thousand years ago were blood crazy; that he made a gargantuan fortune without ever discovering that man works for the sake of life; that he would have immolated the entire population of the United States rather than let go of the hope of making two tons of fabricated steel grow where only one grew before and with the identical manpower; that his ideal man would do the work of the world in thirty minutes a day, pressing a button by the side of the bed and finding himelf automatically clad, fed, shaved, exercised and amused and put to bed again.

I do not believe he was the one virgin knight in a world of industrial footpads, always battling for the right against leagued contemporaries in the hire of Lucifer. He was no unarmed innocent in the rough market-place asking quarter of the burly boys he fought. I am sure I do not know, even after periodically reading the space-writers, if he belongs in a list of ten all-time immortals. I do not subscribe to a carefully nursed idea that he was another lodger on the third floor back, carrying a divine visa on a divine mission, and I consider a complete delusion a common belief that when a project went awry and repercussions were unpleasant, the responsibility lay not with him but with some tricky rascal who pursued a policy which Ford would have halted long before had he the least suspicion of what was going on. In passing the cemetery Ford would whistle as loudly as anybody, but if a ghost jumped out he could run as fast as the next man.

There always seemed to me a false ring to the lyric that work on an assembly line was as gay as a winning night at Monte Carlo and I never was able to understand how tightening 240 hub caps an hour was any less monotonous if a workman got $1 a day or $10 for doing it. The companion hoax, of course, is that before Ford appeared on the scene with conveyor belt and time studies, and succeeded in doing in a minute what old-time blacksmiths took a week to do, life was beatific, man did not have much to do but play the lyre in the berry patch and cool himself with a demijohn, and in the evening everyone wound up fresh as a daisy, only waiting the morrow to exultantly repeat the holiday.

But what happened? We are asked to believe that Ford was the base coxswain who chained man to the oar-lock and ran up the stroke until when day was gone, employes could only crawl home and to bed, having no spirit for fun left in them.

It probably will remain debatable whether man is closer Utopia or happier because of his ability to get from Buffalo to Harrisburg faster by automobile than he could behind a pair of horses or will fret less if the jet plane does to the motor car what the motor car did to the phaeton. The race may eventually go to those who learn to loaf again.

What am I proving by these reminiscences? Nothing at all. These chapters are a skylark which I dedicate to you—and I write them to amuse myself and because I like to remember Mr. Ford as the most human gentleman I ever knew. He wrote his name large in his world —and besides new trails he left, as all men do, an occasional muddy footprint on the carpet.

W. C. R.

CONTENTS

"Adventure is the vitaminizing element in histories. . . . Its adepts are rarely chaste, or merciful, or even law-abiding at all, and any moral peptonizing, or sugaring, takes out the interest, with the truth, of their lives. . . . No, the adventurer is an individualist and an egotist, a truant from obligations. His road is solitary, there is no room for company on it. What he does, he does for himself. His motive may be simple greed. It most often is, or that form of greed we call vanity. . . . But beware of underestimating this motive. . . . God help the ungreedy—that is, the Australian blacks, the poor Bushmen of South Africa, those angelic and virtuous Caribs, whom Columbus massacred in the earthly paradise of Haiti, and all other good primitives who, because they had no appetite, never grew."

THE LAST BILLIONAIRE

The world clamors for omniscience, and Ford, obliging, becomes an authority on what to wear, how to dance, where man came from, where he is going.

CHAPTER I

CLAIRVOYANT BY POPULAR DEMAND

THE New York *Herald* proposed in the administration of Woodrow Wilson that I ask Henry Ford ten questions. It was the first time I had talked to him and what I remember most was his candor in saying he did not know the answers to four of the questions and would not try to guess.

To four others he responded readily enough. The ninth he dismissed as a trick one—which it was—and over the last he paused, as if rolling around in his mouth a medicine of tart bite and could not make up his mind whether to swallow or spit it out. The editor apparently considered this one a capital fillip for the quiz.

"Lastly, Mr. Ford," I said, laying the onus squarely on the assigns of James Gordon Bennett, "the *Herald* wishes to know how you feel to be the world's first billionaire."

Mr. Ford was not a billionaire at the time but most people said he was, that being a round glamorous number, and, if he was not, the green was an easy chip shot away. He squirmed in his chair and twisted a leg over one arm of it, and then his eyes lost their equanimity and he exploded with an earthy vulgarism. I remember writing to the editor, "In answer to Question Ten Mr. Ford said, 'Oh, S--t!' Your problem is what to do with it."

What stuck in my memory in the intervening years was not so

much the expletive as his frank admission of ignorance, the fact he had no answers for four questions and would not talk—at least at the moment—of things he knew nothing about. "I pass that one," he responded to each, or just shook his head. The hour would come when he would tackle the toughest without awe or misgiving and often without knowledge. He would pass judgment quickly on world controversies, needing no more than a single sentence for the panacea.

He had days when you thought him an unqualified genius and more; there were other days when his mind seemed to give off strange emanations. Today you would say: "Those twenty words are it! Why hasn't anyone had enough sense to say it just that way before?" and the following day he would say something absurd and you would think you had not heard him aright. Later on, perhaps, you might become suspicious of your own wisdom, as some of his executives did of theirs when something he said, ridiculous on its face, turned out inconceivably well and proved you and them wrong and him exactly right.

Ford was a victim (if one can possibly use the word of one who worked so hard and did so much, and put a world on wheels instead of a mere privileged segment) of the reasoning that because a man piles up a vast fortune making a girdle or baking soda or tonic or flivver, the value of what he thinks improves with his net cash worth. Pre-eminence in one field, that is, guarantees capacity in all.

They asked him everything. All his life, or at least from the announcement of his $5 day on, they asked him everything. One does not go to the Ritz for hot dogs or to a ball park lunch stand for *entre côte* with good sauce Bearnaise, but those who poured into Dearborn seemed to expect some such all-inclusive buffet since Mr. Ford was fabulously rich and must be champion chef at all recipes. There were only some dishes, they learned in time, he whipped up superlatively well. Like all men he botched others, although his admissions of error were rare.

The last time I talked to him was in 1946 in front of Henry Ford Hospital. He was in the rear seat of an automobile near the main entrance. He was alone. I passed without seeing him and unaccountably turned in entering the hospital. I walked back to the sedan and he opened the door and extended his hand. During the First World War and through the twenties and early thirties it had been my assignment as a working newspaperman practically to live in Dearborn and be available when Ford had something to say which made copy. But I met him irregularly from then on, and exchanged only a few words with him after Pearl Harbor.

He said, "You don't look as if you needed to come to this place."

I said, "How's the skating at Wayside? Been down there lately?"

He was eighty-three and wore a shawl around his shoulders though the gentle warmth of a new spring was in the air. His expression took on remoteness as if he might have been visualizing his pond in Sudbury.

Edsel Ford had died and the passing of his only son wounded the elder Ford deeply. His memory was not as good as it had been. Radical shakeups had occurred in top company personnel. The therapeutic services of Harry Herbert Bennett, once head of the company police, had been dispensed with to an interesting melange of rumor. His power had been so tough and pervasive that Ford employees in a 1937 Labor Day parade marched in masks, and said on placards that they hid their faces to protect their jobs, their wives and children. Charles E. Sorensen, the celebrated head of the vast Rouge plant, was out. Other members of the inner coterie who had had their days of power were gone, fired or retired. He had signed a union contract more far-reaching than any in the industry.

His dancing instructor for twenty years had called at the estate to pay his respects and had not been remembered. The sands seemed running out. In the Rouge plant he had suddenly turned to his escort and asked where the reamer was that had been "right over there."

"Right there in that spot!" he said, apparently puzzled.

"Oh, we've moved that over to Department 46," the guide said—or whatever the department may have been.

The machine in question had been moved ten years before.

"You don't owe me any more money for golf balls, do you?" he asked me, sitting there in the car with his shawl about him, the old quizzical light returning to his eyes. He caught my astonishment and chuckled softly. The reference was to a deal we had eighteen years before and all I could manage was a remark that I was not into him for a penny and wished only that I was, and he'd "never get it." How he remembered the incident, or why, I will never know. He was often deft in recalling an event that others had long forgotten—and as conveniently forgetful about something which took place only yesterday.

John C. Manning, now a Hearst editor; A. M. Smith, another newspaperman, and I rode cross country with Ford in 1928 to preview a scaley tavern he bought and restored to its natural glow by paint and white pickets and period furniture and a cuisine which would have amazed the men who used to larrup their herds and flocks to Detroit along the toll pike in front of it and dropped in for a night's sleep and a quenching nightcap.

On the way we passed the golf club which Ford had built, and someone commented on the fine condition of the course and the seemly architecture of the rambling clubhouse.

Somebody asked him if he played golf. He snorted and said he didn't. They got him to take some practice swings at a half dozen balls once but one almost grazed a child's head and no one could get him to touch a club again. Edsel played left-handedly in the 80's. Ford asked if any of us played. "I luck around, but there never was a good southpaw," I answered.

"Don't let him get you into a bet," Manning cautioned gravely. "The present champion of New Zealand is a left hander, Mr. Ford."

This probably was pure fiction but New Zealand was far enough away to prevent any check on the statement. Mr. Ford nodded soberly over the hint I might be seducing him into a one-sided contest. He asked if I played at his club and I said no and he wanted to know why not.

"That's easy; I'm not a member," I said.

He said he'd see to that—come out any time; plenty of room, as we all could see. The property used to be part of the Ford farm.

"You like to play golf, eh?" He looked as if he had caught me in some unworthy sin, but he had the twinkle that was there when he was baiting you. Why didn't he get some clubs and take a whack at the game? Smith said he'd get him a cheap putter. Manning thought he had an extra No. 4 iron. I told him I'd give him some repainted balls.

"Energy should be spent on something useful." He broke in with a lecture. "Children ought to learn to swim in case a boat tips over. They ought to play games so they'll be strong enough to protect themselves. But golf——" his voice held disparagement. The only way to sell Ford was to prove a thing useful or educational.

"But I like holing a ten-foot putt and I don't need to be husky to do it," I protested. "You ought to take me on some time."

"See, Mr. Ford, he's after you; I warned you," Manning was saying from the front seat.

"I'll take him on at a schottische or I'll run him into the ground at fifty yards," Ford bragged and tapped my excess poundage.

Lilacs at a cross-roads set him on a new tangent. He said he had tried to buy them through an agent a while back.

"Stop the car, Burns, will you?" The car slowed. "The man found out I wanted them and how much do you think he wanted? Five hundred dollars! I'd say they were worth $100 at the best."

He hadn't quibbled over $175,000 for Wayside Inn or a half million for his peace ship; but while, as Henry Ford, he accepted some mark-up occasionally, he was stubborn at times when asked to pay a premium just because he was who he was—unless he wanted something so much he was willing to pay any price.

When we got back to the laboratory he wrote a few lines to the manager of the golf club saying I was to be allowed course courtesies at any time and signed it "Henry Ford" in the same Spencerian style of the letters blown up to eye-catching height on the stacks of his plant and on the hoods of the cars coming down to dump coffee at São Paulo and tulip bulbs at the Dutch ports.

The fourth or fifth time I played the course, my last ball disappeared in the rough off the ninth fairway, and I walked over to the pro shop, picking out four new balls and putting the cash on the counter.

"Sorry, we can't take money." The pro's young assistant pushed the bills back. "Just sign for them."

"But I'm not a member; I'm a guest."

"Whose?"

"Mr. Ford, senior."

"Well, sign his name to the tab."

"I don't want to sign his name," I answered irritably. "I want to buy the balls. There is no good reason why they should be going on Mr. Ford's bill."

"Sign it and give him the money when you see him." It was as simple as that to the caddymaster.

A few days later I met Mr. Ford and told him of the transaction.

He probably was about to buy a continent or run a sub-express to Calais, and probably telling me about it in the casual voice we use to say we must stop in for some razor blades.

"So," I concluded, "I owe you three dollars."

He said the cash would come in handy since he had left home without a dime that morning, and he put the bills in his pocket. He never seemed to have any money on him. Never gave money a thought, he'd say, ignoring the wince of a visitor who might be wondering from where the next payment on the mortgage was coming. Money had come to mean to Ford precisely what his coal heaps and scrap piles meant—material to keep the plant running.

He apparently frittered away the three dollars I gave him, for, several weeks later, I read in the papers he was broke again when the government issued a commemorative stamp in honor of Thomas Alva Edison, and Ford attended the ceremonies in Atlantic City incident to the first-day sale of the new postage. A two-column cut of Ford buying the first stamp carried lines which said he had to borrow two pennies from Mr. Russo, the mayor, to make the purchase.

Interpreters usually divided into three camps. Some joined in uncritical art work and brought forth a lacquered image. Others inferred he had debased the human race by strapping it to a machine and a sequence of repetitive back-breaking motions; and they, too, wound up with half the man. The third lot tried to strike a balance and met disbelief and were called straddlers since mankind wants its public men spotless or wholly base. Our celebrated ones must be Olympians or rogues from front bumper to tail-light.

In the beginning Ford was shy and a great part of the time apprehensive of the motley hegira of troubled peoples at his door—begging people, the princes and the pundits of press and pulpit poking questions at him when what he wanted was to be on with the manufacture of more and more Model T's, paying wages above the prevailing rate for the work on them, and finding ways to turn out more and better cars in less and less time to sell cheaper and cheaper. He accepted the visitors in those days not altogether as a compliment but as a phenomenon and a nuisance and ringed himself with men to sort the bell-ringers so he could get along with the things he knew about.

He had made a gas-propelled automobile—certainly not the first one—and if he could make enough and people would buy them, he obviously was by way of becoming an important figure in the world. Partly because of the first, but mainly drawn by his multiplying fortune, queues of people stretching out to every horizon came to ask the queerest questions about what he thought of transcendentalism, if there was a God, and about other mooted subjects to which he had given no, or small, thought. Seven gentlemen who said they were Jesus Christ presented themselves the year following World War I. Those to whom the secret of perpetual motion had been reputedly revealed came in gross lots. As a rule, those who wanted just unornamented cash asked for it in even numbers, obligingly. They invariably wanted $1,000 or $100,000 or $1,000,000.

He had in 1914 the manufacturing formula that was to pay off. A tiny model of his car stood under glass at one end of his Highland Park office, and Julian Street, a writer for a magazine of the day, asked how the company had managed to do a volume of $225,000,000 up to then.

"By getting one model of the right idea," Ford said promptly, pointing to the englassed miniature. "That's the secret of the whole dog-goned thing. There she is!"

All you had to do, he said, was to find something everybody wanted and make it and nothing else. In his case, a crony of his crisply put it, everybody "wanted to go from A to B sitting down."

"Shoemakers ought to settle on one shoe, stovemakers on one stove. Me? I like specialists." Ford leaned across the desk and shook his finger at the writer. It was why he was fond of Harry Lauder and Thomas Edison, he thought.

He was asked if his vaulting money had made a difference in his living.

"Well," he stewed, "my wife doesn't cook any more, or not much. We hire cooks but none can hold a candle to her." He said his streamlined kitchen staff tried to serve him a lot of fancy food and he wished they'd stop it.

Ford changed. It is hard to pin-point the exact time. In some ways he never changed, of course, but in the matter of extra-curricular adventure it was a slow evolution. If admiring mail does not abate and petitions for one's opinions steadily mount, a man may logically think he is wrong in his modesty and the questing crowd right. Perhaps he did know the answers, he may have decided one morning. Maybe there was in him the spark which privileged him not only to counsel on the grand scale but to impose counsel.

In subsequent years he was to take on a galaxy of foemen in defense of his views, and on myriads of gridirons he was to run with the ball with comfortable assurance. He thrust with aplomb into spheres where he had little experience and less information. He jousted with preparedness and the Jew, international bankers and Wall Street, cigarettes and alcohol and the Chicago *Tribune,* and he was to express his views stoutly on history, commodity money, medical ethics, short skirts, tariffs, the farm problem, food fads, old-fashioned dancing, reincarnation and what-not. He could be Pericles the wise and Throttlebottom the fumbler, all in the space of ten minutes.

He was never stopped by the possibility that some work he had in mind could not be done. A hundred errors simply meant he had learned one hundred things not to do again. If he ran the wrong way of the field he could rationalize it by saying it taught him not to run like that a second time. It was enough for him that what he wanted to do seemed the desirable thing. He was always looking for and putting men to work on the desirables. He had a superb confidence and one could not imagine his going home of an evening and saying in private: "Well, Henry, you certainly booted things around the plant today. You just didn't look too good."

His name entranced the great and the humble. In an obscure Italian hill town I once browsed in a linen shop. The goods had been wrapped, my *lire* were still on the counter and the proprietor was receipting a bill for customs. For some reason he asked if I was an American and where in America I lived.

"Detroit," I said.

"Henry Ford!" he exclaimed, instantly.

He asked if I knew Mr. Ford, and I said I did, and I was a half hour getting out of the establishment. What sort of a man, truly, was Mr. Ford? Did he really pay the men who swept his factories $6 or $7 a day? The dialogue was liberally dusted with many Tuscan Ah's and Oh's. When we had finished, the proprietor drew back the sales slip and rewrote the figures. Where a half hour earlier my bill had been 800 lire, it was now lowered to 600 and two 100 lire notes were pushed back at me across the counter.

"But I understood I owed you 800 lire," I said.

"You know Henry Ford," he beamed, and his black eyes could have held no more esteem if I had revealed an intimacy with St. Peter or Titian. "I could not take 800 lire from you. *Scusa!*"

Ford, as time wore on, did not content himself with empire building and his brimming chests, his famed mastery of mass production and his fatherhood of the rising day rate. He had confounded skeptics at more points than one in making motor cars and gauging the market. He had challenged and refuted some established canons of business regarded as sacred word. He socialized a billion dollars, one enthusiastic economist was to write, by "dedicating the output of his money to an indispensable use and rededicating the profits to an extension of that use."

He built 31,000,000 motor-propelled vehicles. He made fools of those who said originally there was only a class market for such a contrivance as a horseless carriage. He built a car in less time than you can get your shoes shined, and, while you were in a barber chair for a shave and a haircut, Ford could turn out fifteen or twenty complete automobiles.

The synchronization was such that on a peak day of two shifts Ford workers put together in all assembly plants just slightly less than 10,000 cars in sixteen hours, or at a rate of a finished car in slightly under a minute. Willow Run turned out B-24 bombers of 1,500,000 parts at a top speed of seventeen in a two-day shift, or just shy of one an hour. But all this was not enough.

Ford wanted to be Nostradamus and Cassandra and Joel Kupperman—or people insisted he be—and he allowed himself to pontificate like most men, however unqualified. The difference was that other men did not get headlines; if Mr. Ford said off-handedly he liked deviled crabs or pork chops it was wired and cabled to the world.

He was hard and gentle, straightforward and devious. Men who made any flat statement about him usually found they had to hedge. He was this or that but invariably he was the antithesis, too. Men would cite his gentleness and then think right away of a hundred incidents where he was not. They would say he was ruthless—and then could disprove it with a long list of kindnesses.

He had the lucidity of a clear thinking, profound man at times. And again, a critic said, he seemed to be "trying to bring up a large family of words on a small income of ideas." He rid himself of partners and executives—the conveyor never dropped a stitch. He had a naïve trust in human nature, mixed with a deep suspicion that the most honorable gesture of a competitor was designed to dupe him and do him in. When the directors of his principal rival met, he was sure they just sat about the table hollering "Get Ford!" and he knew they met for no other purpose.

He had an expert sense of materials and mechanical processes. There is a story, perhaps fictional, that some wag brought a common washer to him and asked where it belonged on a Ford car, and that he flung it out a window with the remark that it didn't belong to a Ford at all.

He considered a full day's work holy and he had exhaustless zeal. Attacked on every side save that of his private life, no scandal brushed Fair Lane. He did not believe in set hours of work but thought a man ought to work as long as he was able, and should enjoy his work so much that he would almost count the time lost when he was not working. Unfortunately he had no prescription as to how this could be realized for his men in the foundry, for instance, who may have thought, also, the matter of choice would be nice. Ford himself would have been no one to last on an assembly line. Team work was not his dish.

A magazine analyst got the impression that Ford was a man who had somehow outgrown himself, his brain "reaching into a region far different from that touched by his manipulating hands and trodden by his feet," and Dean Samuel S. Marquis, an Episcopal divine who quit his pulpit to head Ford's sociological department and quit Ford in disgust five years later to re-enter the church, exclaimed: "If only Mr. Ford was properly assembled! He has in him the makings of a great man but the parts are lying about in more or less disorder."

It was all part of a Brobdingnagian script to which Ford contributed heavily of punch and feat and failure. In the final totals overwhelming balance was on his side. His failures never got the space of his successes, and what he did industrially to transform a world of watering troughs and hitching posts dwarfed whatever he said. Someone may be able in time to find and confidently fit together all the pieces of the jigsaw puzzle. The writer does not pretend to do it here. The masks were so many it was hard at times to distinguish the man behind them.

An industrial infidel voluntarily doubles the pay of those who work for him and a divided world wrangles over whether he's a new holy child —or an idiot.

CHAPTER II

GOLDEN CORNUCOPIA

HENRY FORD shook the precious American economy from its capstans in 1914 by announcing he would share with his employees a minimum of $10,000,000 of his succeeding year's profits, dating from right then, and would pay every worker who qualified a minimum of $5 a day, including sweepers.

It landed him on the front page and there he was to stay until his death.

The first piece of publicity involving him appeared May 10, 1883. He was twenty. In the same paper appeared an account of two Mid-west gentlemen dueling with broadswords.

Ford was an obscure farmboy driving a wagon out a dusty road to home. He was nobody one second—but when he came to he was on Page One, painfully, for the first time. He was not to move up there permanently until thirty years later, when he would claim a thousand headlines, but it was a start. After reciting the general damage done by a violent gale the previous day, the Detroit *Free Press* particularized about the most serious accident of the day:

> The main storm cloud burst within four or five feet of the ground at a railroad crossing on Grand River avenue at the time that Henry Ford, a young farmer who lives in Dearborn township, nine miles out the road, was driving a team attached to a lumber wagon upon which was an empty hay-rack.
>
> The whirlwind caught Ford's wagon and whirling it several

> feet above the ground overturned it. When Ford was picked up it was thought he was dead and he was carried into the toll-house nearby where he remained unconscious until City Physician Chaney arrived. An examination showed no bones broken but it is feared that serious internal injuries were sustained.
>
> After restoratives were applied he recovered slightly, and after being made as comfortable as possible, an ambulance took him home. At the breaking of the storm Ford's horses took fright and ran nearly a mile beyond the toll-gate before captured.

There was no follow-up to tell how the patient was making out the next day, no hourly bulletins. The newspaper did run his full name in the third deck of the head: "Henry Ford Seriously Hurt; His Horses and Wagon Demoralized." The newspapers forgot him thereafter. Later headlines would come less arduously.

The New York *Times* index of 1913 contained no mention of him. *Who's Who* did not list him. After 1913 he was, like his car, ubiquitous.

No spotlight could shift fast enough thereafter to keep him out of it. Midnight did not strike again for Cinderella for a long time. The band played on, and when he wanted privacy, which he rarely did, he had to work for it.

A generation accustomed to spiraling prices may not grasp why a good 95 per cent of the world reacted to Ford's minimum-wage announcement as if a new holy child had been born, but a worker in manufacturing at the time got 22 cents an hour and weekly earnings averaged $11 though the Ford rate was slightly higher. Ford's program, like his manufacturing methods, was to change the face of the earth.

It was in the Ford tradition when Henry Ford II was first to reduce prices after World War II but his was the low pop of a cap-pistol compared to his grandfather's deafening blast of thirty-three years before.

The senior Ford's purposes were set down in a formal statement. It was polished off by someone who, searching for the ultimate in puffery, settled for "the greatest revolution ever known in the world in the matter of reward for workers." Briefly the plan was this:

1. He would divide with employees at least $10,000,000 of the 1914 profits. Actual distribution was $12,000,000.

2. Production would be continuous, giving employment to sev-

eral thousand more men through three shifts of eight hours instead of two shifts of nine.

3. Minimum wage under the plan would be $5 a day, even for sweepers.

The broom-pusher immediately became an acute worry of people who never had given the least thought to him. Tears were shed over his fate in this new affluence, and those who felt this over-night solicitude ticked off appalling pitfalls facing a man who got $5 a day instead of $2.34. Even Mr. Ford leaned to this philosophy and set up some rules of conduct.

The young man between eighteen and twenty-two had to show himself sober and saving, and satisfy the company that the money paid him would not be frittered on high living. "Riotous" was the word used. Determination of what "riotous" meant was vested in a sociological staff.

A married man had to live with and take care of his family, and single men over twenty-two were to be thrifty, likewise. A rule was sought by which all men could live comfortably and Ford arrogated to himself the right to impose on others the one he lived by as a rather nice model. Since employment by the company under the new arrangement would be pecuniarily desirable, he used profit-sharing as a lever by which to discipline rowdies who did not behave the way he thought they should.

Henry Ford, a boy off a farm with a useful idea, was about to go to town with it. It was an ironic twist that a man to whom money meant little should be headed for more than he could ever count or closely estimate. He said to me once, "I didn't know often if we'd have the rent," and in the next breath, as though the incongruity had just hit him, "I paid $79,000,000 in taxes last year."

Books about him were to appear in every European stall. He became a verb, "Fordize," which meant to do things the way he did them. "Fordism," which was his philosophy, was hotly debated. Wouldn't "Fordism," as some called it abroad, change the continent beyond all recognition? Germans lined up all night to buy securities when he built a plant in the Reich. Ford of England was a sensation on the London Bourse. A world wage survey was made. An Italian found a Ford worker in America could have five times as much food and as many rooms to live in as he, and wore clothes five times as expensive.

But now, in 1914, he was merely offering commerce a new philosophy. Profit had been based on payment of wages as low as a worker would take, and on pricing as high as the traffic would bear. Wages were kept down and history was bloodied by battles fought for another nickel an hour. Ford became a classic example of low pricing for the widest market and then trying to meet the price by volume and efficiency. He ran the other way to what the others were running, and the moans were heart breaking. Labor, he said, was a consumer to be paid well so it could consume more. But doubling wages voluntarily? There never had been such heresy.

The United States Junior Chamber of Commerce named Henry Ford II the young man of 1945 most likely to succeed. With the head start he had, this was a bet on Stymie to outrun Mr. Fred Allen over the Derby mile and a quarter, but there were no such kudos for his grandpa in 1914. He was bound straight for the toothy shallows, the dour said, if he did not get back on the proven course. Paying the rascals $5 a day was not the American way of life, circa 1914.

The assassination of Archduke Francis in June set the stage for the first World War. A sickly painter of business posters named Hitler was rejected by the Austrians as unfit for military service and goose-stepped off with one Rudolf Hess and the less exacting Sixteenth Bavarians to the first battle of Ypres.

A seven-year-old redhead played about a cottage in West Virginia and seemed infinitely remote from the affairs of Henry Ford, but as Walter Reuther, of the UAW-CIO, thirty years later, was to help spectacularly to prick the boast that no union ever would stick its unruly head in the doors of the Ford plant.

The press of New York gave Mr. Ford's announcement—the Manhattan project of the day—57 columns in a week and pundits praised and stoned him for his daring.

The ayes said it was magnificent generosity . . . a tidal push of civilization . . . a great Christian impulse which indicates the reign of a nobler conscience in industry.

The nays proclaimed it an economic blunder and foresaw unrest in the shops of other companies. Did Mr. Ford think industrial justice could be founded on such an uneconomic foundation? If the practice was extended, said one, people would not work for wages but offer good behavior in trade for gifts, largess or bonuses. The New York

Journal of Commerce suggested it was a form of advertising by which Ford meant to get rid of some of his "bothersome" millions.

A month before the announcement certain Ford executives answered their telephones one Sunday morning and heard his voice at the other end asking if they were doing anything in particular.

"I wish you'd come over to the plant," he said. He had something, he said, he wanted to talk over and didn't want to do it over the phone.

He had a worried talk with Couzens, his second in command, three weeks before over a scene in the shop. As he and an advertising man, with Edsel some yards in front of them, approached a drill press the operator glanced up and glowered at the boy. He wheeled back to his machine, seized a mallet and poised it as if about to smash the die and jig in front of him. The spasm passed, however. The machine hand wound up by giving the press a kick and tossing the hammer from him in a gesture of man embittered but not quite sure what to do about it.

Edsel was unaware of the angry show but the senior Ford saw it. "Did you see the hate in that fellow's face?" he asked his companion as they swung into another aisle. "Why should the sight of me and my boy affect him that way?"

He seemed to be pondering the age-old emotion of economic envy. "He was going to smash that press!" Ford was unacquainted with any temper which would purposely spend itself in breaking a good machine.

He claimed to be psychic and able to tell usually what a man was going to say to him before the words were out. "He was saying," he guessed this time, 'Look at Henry Ford's boy! What chance has mine beside him?'" But why should anyone begrudge him his enlarging kingdom? He had come by it the hard way. His was no willed fortune for which he had not worked. Of course there was an element of luck. It was true other men could sweat even more and never make the strike he had. But there was no silver spoon, no stock-jobbing in it, and it was not based on quackery or some gimcrack which the world would have been better without.

"I wonder," he said to Couzens, "what it would cost to change that fellow so he'd be glad to see us when we come along, or not resent us?"

Couzens thought higher wages might do it but had no other remedy.

The incident in the shop Ford kept to himself, except for Couzens, but he mentioned it this December morning and he asked the same question he had asked of his advertising manager when the workman had swung his hammer in his short-lived temper. Ford also relieved himself of some other tribulations.

The company had to hire 54,000 men in a year to maintain a 13,000 average. That was a 400 per cent turnover. He was sick of peanut raises doled out by foremen to the workers they liked or to those who asserted themselves. That way too many quiet fellows missed out.

He did not understand the floaters and the general instability. He was no worse off than competitors but this was no consolation. He genuinely wanted a big happy family.

He couldn't understand a fellow not always being on the job and giving the best he had. His own eyes glistened when he walked in a plant door, heard the octaves of sound, saw spread before him the vista of belts and cranes. The Hereafter was going to be like it or he would sell his stock in eternity.

He also was making what he called an "awful" profit. Not so many years before his New York manager occasionally would sell a car for what he could get and run with cash in hand to the Chemical National so it could telephone a Detroit bank to release the Ford payroll. Once he got a breathing spell by taking 50,000 orders for cars at the New York show and collecting a $50 deposit on each in advance. Now he was making too much. It used to be the problem of paucity; now it was plenty.

Nobody had used the word before in reference to profits. The men in the room gritted their teeth over the adjective. Profits were never "awful."

"I called you here this morning principally to talk about a wage raise," he sprang it finally. "How much now do you think the company can pay and needs to pay to satisfy the men?"

"Want some figures, Mr. Ford?"

He said he ought to have some and said for "Charlie" to give him some. Out in the shop they might have figured on a shingle. That was factory practice. He and Charles E. Sorensen, later power at the Rouge, were to use a shingle to rough-sketch layouts at the bomber plant in World War II, but now Charlie used a blackboard at one side of the private office. He picked up some chalk and wrote down the three standbys—materials, overhead, labor. The minimum plant wage went up on the board. It was $2.34.

"Now add a quarter," said Ford.

Well, that could be absorbed easily.

"Try another 25 cents."

He was adding quarters when the others in the room were content to stop, Now, they wagged their heads and questioned. Mr. Ford was a little daffy this morning. He had passed the point of feasibility—$3.50, $3.75, $4.00. Probably he was having a little joke. On the basis of their arithmetic it couldn't be done. The company could not stand the cost. They smiled uneasily, not sure where he was heading.

"Why not $6 a day," Sorensen said, breaking the tension. Well, they laughed at such an improbable notion.

"Add another 25 cents to that last figure, Charlie," Ford said and new calculations began. The total reached a point double the prevailing rate. "I guess that's it," the head of the company nodded over the last total.

All agreed a raise was in order and good business, but each saw a different virtue in it. No one but Ford thought the rate could be doubled.

"Well, keep this under your hats and we'll talk about it next Sunday." Ford dismissed them.

They went down the hall shaking their heads over the figure on the blackboard. Apparently the old man was not fooling. He'd lose his shirt. Always someone was saying Ford would lose his shirt although he always seemed to maintain a tight hold on it.

After the next week's discussion he saw Couzens. "He's for it—says if we're going to be fools let's be first-class fools and make it $5 a day," one of those present reported Ford saying of Couzens' reaction.

Another version is that Couzens forced the issue of the $5 day at sight of storming workers being hosed at the front gate on a wintry day when they demonstrated against a layoff. He was to say years later he never gave a thought to labor's welfare up to the moment of the icy rout of the men he saw from his office window.

"We lose good will by that," he told Ford, angrily. He led Ford to the window and pointed to water freezing on the retreating workers.

Ford agreed that those on both sides of the gate should have found a better way.

"I know we can't escape seasonal layoffs"—Couzens moderated his tone—"but we can pay workers more money to tide them over the slack periods."

Ford asked how much the men were being paid now. Couzens told him. Ford said other companies weren't paying more. Couzens said he missed the point. "We're also making a hell of a lot more than they are," he reminded.

Couzens argued that $5 a day would give employees a proper nest-egg, and Ford said he would see Pete Martin, the Highland Park superintendent. He reported back that Martin stuck out for a $3 minimum. Couzens said it wasn't enough, that Martin did not know what he was talking about. Well, Ford would see Martin again.

Couzens marshalled fresh arguments. The company was going places. The Selden patent case was out of the way—won—and the bonds posted to protect Ford buyers were no longer a sword over his head. The country had just spent a half billion on roads. Single handed, Ford had disproved the misgivings of a man named Woodrow Wilson, now in the White House, who seven years before had been shrilling from an ivory tower in Princeton that nothing was spreading socialism like the automobile—"new symbol of wealth's arrogance."

Ford had no competition worth the name. The car was no longer a dream in a woodshed. Of all automobiles sold 39 per cent were his. The road behind was strewn with luckless and misguided foes outdistanced. Chevrolet was a pasteup of a small company in Michigan and another in Jersey, making a couple of thousand cars, that's all, and asking $2,000 apiece for them. Ford made as many every day.

Martin said he would go for a raise to $4 a day. Couzens said Martin was a fathead.

"Five, or to hell with it!" He said give it or keep the minimum where it was.

"All right, I'll go for it," Ford assented.

Two weeks later the press was called in and Couzens talked while Ford tilted back in his chair with his head against the wall. The general manager was little known. Some of the newspapers called him "George" instead of James. No out-of-town journals were represented but in twenty-four hours they were there in droves.

Said Couzens: "We want those who have helped to produce this institution to have profits and future prospects. The movement toward a better society does not need to be started universally and simultaneously."

Said Ford: "We believe in making 20,000 prosperous instead of a few slave-drivers rich."

Instead of waiting until the end of the year to make a distribution he and Couzens had estimated the year's profits and had fixed upon a sum they thought was safe. It would be spread over the year and reach employees on the regular semi-monthly pay days.

A writer in *Everybody's,* prosperous monthly, guessed Ford had become bored by "the monotony of his own competence," and this was a bulletin on the factory wall to notify workers he was not a bronze statue but much like they were.

The rush to the gold fields began before the newspaper ink was dry. For a week there was no peace. A newspaper reporter warned that 5,000 would be pummeling at the gates at dawn. He was wrong. Twelve thousand descended afoot, by trail and trolley, bicycle and jalopy.

Regular employees formed a wedge to get in but rebounded off a wall of the early battalions.

The mob grew and it was necessary to unroll the hose to knock out a passage for those who had work to do inside the plant. Lunch carts were overturned. Stones sailed through plant windows. A false rumor circulated—Ford was firing all foreign born to make jobs for 100 per centers. Police reinforcements deployed. A fence in front of the employment office caved before the attack. A harried company spokesman climbed a packing box and raised a hand.

"We're not ready to take on extra men!" he bellowed. "No one will be hired today!" The crowd surged toward him. The herald fled. A placard was tacked up at 10 A.M. repeating his message and adding that applicants would not be interviewed until the middle of the month. Some who had accepted the company's telephone number, 50–50, as a lucky portent abandoned faith in it.

Job-hunters roughed the night, lit bonfires, still milled in the streets at daybreak. Steel chains replaced the leveled fence. The company announced it would not open the employment office until the crowd dispersed. Tumultuously the lobby was overrun.

Ford and Couzens were at the New York show. Photographers broke down palms in the lobby of the Belmont to get an unobstructed shot of them. A Jersey horticulturist named a new white orchid in Ford's honor.

Ford sat for a delighted Madison Avenue sculptor and a dubious Broadway barber. The sculptor said the sitter was an ideal husband since he talked all the time of how nice it would be if Mrs. Ford would consent to sit for a head and shoulders. The barber said he doubted greatly if that fellow Henry Ford out in Detroit intended to make good his fabulous promise.

"Sounds fishy to me," he said wisely. "What do you think?" He seemed agreeable to shifting sides if the customer had a different opinion.

"I work there," said his customer. "When he says he'll do something he will do it."

"You work there, eh?" The barber lost his cocksureness.

"And hard," Ford nodded.

The barber yelled over to a partner that here was a guy, Al, who worked at Ford's and who said Henry Ford's $5 a day was on the level.

"Get me a job there, Mister," the other barber came over to say.

Back from Manhattan Couzens denied that a strike victory of textile workers under I.W.W. leadership had anything to do with the Ford company's decision.

The besieging army, still bivouacked around the plant, worried him. Had everything been done to make clear that only unemployed workers who lived in the Detroit area would be considered? Hypnotized workers in other factories were assuming the names of relatives and posing as jobless at the Ford gates, although under the plan a worker had to be on the Ford payroll six months to qualify for a share in the profits.

Rivals moaned. Charles King, president of King Motor, advertised that the previous year every employee of his company had received virtually 10 per cent of his profits in addition to his regular pay, so that actually he was first at profit sharing, as well as first with "cantilever springs and left steer." Hugh Chalmers, another tycoon, said the Ford plan was too radical for the industry as a whole ever to adopt.

The warning of Couzens was wasted because of a fresh rumor—the company had fired 1200 Hungarians, Russians, Greeks and Rumanians for laying off two days to celebrate the Greek Christmas. The company denied the mass discharge and explained the boys had been sent home to sober up but their jobs were waiting for them.

On Saturday the crowd had thinned slightly and the poets massed. Editors were deluged with poesy:

Strive on, benevolent and kind,
Make needed, useful things
To ease the strain upon man's spirit.

And this:

Himself the fruit of creative genius
He saw in other men his own kind;
With quick arrest of thought he turned,
Brought from the largess of the years, the fruit
With outstretched hands; "Take of your own,"
He simply said.

Incense curled high Sunday in blessing of his works. City Hall steps crowded Monday with discouraged job-hunters come from afar with one-way tickets and beginning to feel the twin pangs of diminishing hope and empty stomachs. Ford phoned an offer of $50,000 for relief purposes—more if it was needed—and moved into his hospital some of those who had no beds. The sharing of $10,000,000 and 4,000 jobs proved not an easy division.

Newspapers had been swallowing hard over the load of copy from the new automobile industry and had been dumping most of it into waste baskets when unaccompanied by checks. The $5 day was a new poser. Was it news? Was it advertising to be billed accordingly? The Associated Press thought the latter. It did not put the story on its wires. Some of its subscribers bought special dispatches from newsmen on the ground, however, and then let go a blast at their news service for failure to distinguish between legitimate news and publicity blurbs. Utterances of Henry Ford, sacred or profane, were to rate thereafter with papal encyclicals.

Reporters fired more questions. What of the effect on other companies? "No factory is big enough to make two models of cars. Let them concentrate on one!" Ford also urged the press to get his idea before the public as he meant it.

"It's not a stated sum to be distributed—it's half the profit," he insisted. The more the company made the more the men made.

It figured this way. A man got a minimum wage which was about 15 per cent above what was being paid in the area for the kind of work he was doing. The minimum wage, PLUS the profit, made the $5. The hourly profit-sharing rate was graduated so as to give those receiving the lowest hourly rate the highest proportion of profits.

For example, a man receiving 34 cents an hour had a profit rate of 28½ cents an hour in addition. This gave him total income of $5 a day. A man getting 54 cents an hour had a profit-sharing rate of 21 cents an hour, or a total daily wage of $6.

What if profits went down?

"We'll consider that when we come to it."

Had his raise been reflected in production?

Some men had to be slowed down because they got ahead of the assembly line. No department could speed up independently without dislocating the timed lines.

A sub-foreman said it wasn't right that in his department he got $6 a day and a rank greenhorn $5.

"But it's something we're only trying. We ask you to co-operate."

"I don't like it. I've worked here a long time; this fellow's a newcomer. He gets only a dollar less than I do."

No, he wasn't satisfied with a reduction in work hours from nine to eight hours and a wage boost from $4.30 to $6. Look at the loss to his prestige if the wage differential between a green hand and him was only one dollar!"

"Turn in your badge!"

The critics left Ford, uncontested, the palm for originating the welfare program, and tore it to pieces. It was based on the premise that you could call the tune if you paid the piper. Many workers figured that since the sweat which earned the money was theirs, domestic brawling, overcrowded homes and Monday hangovers were their divine privilege. He did not have much luck with mass uplift. Workers didn't want a guardian angel in the spare bedroom.

He got an Episcopal dean to run the sociological department but old-stagers in high places often thumbed their noses at the "folderol" and sabotaged his program. They said too much time was lost from production in welfare interviewing. Some investigators turned jailers and meddled in matters that seemed none of their business. Some of the guinea pigs quit, and so did the dean eventually.

But eight thousand families moved to better quarters the first year. Rewards steadied the men. Labor turnover fell from 400 to 33 per cent. Accidents were cut 90 per cent. Insurance policies and bank deposits rose and investment in homes and real estate increased 85 per cent in 12 months.

When his welfare plan was criticized as paternalistic he told the Federal Commission on Industrial Relations he didn't want men working for him who shirked their family responsibilities. "I have conditions, not theories, to face," he said. He said theorists did not have to get along with 24,000 workers, all of a different stripe.

Ford straddled an old stump on the estate years later. The genesis of the $5 day had been so confused by loose guessing, contradictory yarns and what psychiatrists call the retrospective falsification of memory that I asked him about it. For instance, why the concern over the sweeper?

"The skilled man," he said, "got enough to raise his family but the unskilled man didn't and it was just as necessary for one as the other to provide for his household. Take the sweeper out of the shop and it would not be fit to work in. We get more than a sweeper's wages back in what he picks off the floor."

Of course there was more than one reason. If a man was paid well, he would work harder. Profits would rise and Ford could expand and there would be more jobs for more men. The company would be able to lower prices still farther and the public would benefit—the lower the price the wider the field of sale. It was a circle. It couldn't miss.

A month after the late President Roosevelt gave a Kansas governor a thumping at the polls, a social worker visiting the Ford home told the motormaker of her search for a Model T, despite the fact that he had ceased to manufacture that model ten years before. She wanted to buy one if she could find one that was not completely worn out and she had had no luck thus far, she said.

"There must be one around," he said.

"I wish I knew where."

Ford smiled broadly—"We made about as many of them as Landon got votes."

Ford mounts his first crusade and burns tobacco of his private golf club on a ceremonial bonfire to make clear his stand on cigarettes.

CHAPTER III

HE SADDLES A WHITE HORSE

UNTIL HIS fifties Henry Ford made no effort to cross the perimeter of his own shining genius and worry about the sins of the human race. No one remembers any mania for making bad men good or any concern if an early shopmate helled around. If Ford was concerned, no one recalls his saying so.

With the cheering section still on its feet, however, he decided to challenge evil, or evil as he conceived it, and reshape people more in his own image. It may have been that the rapid ascent to headlines on his private funicular made him slightly giddy or he may have mistaken the popular acclaim for a nomination to godhood. He became enamored, at any rate, of the show window and craved more limelight and authority. Years would pass before he would share or loan or give away either.

Father William Ford had remarked pessimistically to a friend, "John and William (Henry's brothers) are all right but Henry worries me. He doesn't seem to settle down and I don't know what will become of him." Henry was twenty at the time. His father also said morosely he would glut the market when production got to thirty-five cars a day.

The founder of Ford Motor built 10,000 a day in time and made more than 31,000,000 mechanical vehicles up to March of 1946, exclusive of bombers, amphibian jeeps, tank destroyers, Bren gun carriers and other upholstery of war. There also was a small item of a million tractors. Father William's son made hash of the adage "Father knows best." Father did not know what he was talking about.

Consumption was sixteen billion in 1914 when Ford sounded his first warning against cigarettes. By 1945 it had risen to 267,500,000,000, exclusive of a hundred million additional going to the armed forces outside the United States. His crusade against them, like his father's opposition to Henry becoming a machinist, had all the success of a butterfly trying to heel the *Queen Elizabeth* by doing handsprings on its stack deck.

Thomas Alva Edison gave the campaign the slap on the withers that got it out of the starting gate. Around a shore fire in Florida he told of testing a chemical known as acrolein when rummaging about for a filament to use in the incandescent light. Ford said he never heard of it. Edison said it was in cigarette paper.

"Rots the nerve centers," said Edison. "I don't employ anyone who smokes cigarettes."

"Young people shouldn't be taking that stuff into their lungs, should they?" Ford turned thoughtfully to his companions. Any threat to young people worried him.

"Not if they want to live long," Edison said.

The fact that Edison had spoken on the subject was good enough for Ford. He had said cigarettes were deadly injurious; Ford was for immediately nailing up danger signs for all to see and reroute themselves accordingly. Edison had once given him a helping hand when he needed it most; what Edison said thereafter was wisdom off Sinai.

In the years ahead Tom was to talk of building houses by pouring concrete into molds—Henry said he'd pour 400 as a starter. Tom said it might be practicable to extract rubber from goldenrod and alcohol from cantaloupe—the next thing Henry was buying acreage in Georgia and Pennsylvania to try it. Even when Edison said he would not support him for President but as manager of an industrial plant would vote for him—twice—Ford warmed to the praise and ignored the snub. Edison could do no wrong.

Ford hustled north, asking Edison before leaving to write him a letter on the ravaging effect of acrolein that would stand up scientifically, and pitched into the new found fray while the world was still babbling about his plan to share $10,000,000 with his employees and debating whether he was a sentimental no-account or a canny outrider for a new and disturbing order. Whichever it was, he had set up a frightening ferment in the status quo. People were talking of little else.

He launched the attack on cigarette smoking in a series of press interviews and followed with a brochure quoting miscellaneous persons who thought as he did, and containing the promised Edison warning:

"The injurious agent in cigarettes comes principally from the burning paper wrapper. It has a violent reaction on the nerve centers, producing degeneration of the brain-cells, quite rapid among boys. Unlike most narcotics this degeneracy is permanent and uncontrollable. I employ no one who smokes cigarettes."

And Ford himself told the press:

"Study the history of almost any criminal and you will find an inveterate cigarette-smoker."

He was not without allies. Reform was in the air. The General Federation of Women's Clubs was fearful of the dissolution of the republic through joy and saw the tango and hesitation waltz rotting away the nation's foundations. In 1904 a woman had been arrested on Fifth Avenue for smoking in an automobile. As late as 1914 an excited voice informed a Rochester, N. Y., newspaper that if a reporter would come with all speed he would see Irene Castle smoking a cigarette in the holy Pompeian Room of the Seneca Hotel, which never had been so desecrated, and reporters rushed to see the orgy of the *danseuse* who was the toast of the day.

Cigarette smokers drifted to saloons, espoused crime as a natural next step, wound up with lungs riddled—that was the majority thinking of the time. Many persons regarded cigarettes in much the way horses looked upon Mr. Ford's early cars. Ford not only gave heed to Edison's laboratory findings but he leaned to the view, and stressed it, that the boy who smoked not only fell to pieces prematurely but reached the unrelishable foldup by a standard route through poolroom, saloon, jailhouse and asylum, in that order.

He called to his troops such diverse bedfellows as Hudson Maxim, the munitions maker, who said cigarettes produced "invalids, criminals and fools" but omitted mention of graves dug by gunpowder; John Ruskin, who once observed that people erred in spending pains on the fallen instead of helping people not to fall; Marshall Field and John Wanamaker; a teacher of short-hand at Ann Arbor and a W. C. T. U. president in Georgia; a Pittsburgh company which said stoutly it would hire no cigarette "fiend"; the Larkin Soap Co. of Buffalo, employing no habitués, and an official of Cadillac Motor Car Co. who came up with the scientific statement that cigarette smokers were looser in morals and more apt to be untruthful than non-smokers.

Connie Mack of the Philadelphia Athletics and Grantland Rice, sports columnist, did testimonials intimating that the boy who used cigarettes hardly would live long enough to clear the bases with a lusty triple, and there must be some confusion today among those who accepted the theory at sight of Mr. Mize of the Giants and Mr. Ted Williams of the Boston Red Sox, holding packages of cigarettes aloft on a magazine cover as if they were baseballs and they were calling the ump's attention to the fact that someone had sneaked in a spitter—all in behalf of the right combination of the world's best tobacco.

"Let us see"—Ford sounded an economic threat as well—"whether an American boy can afford to ruin his prospects by doing those things which are disapproved by employers generally. If millions of American men have convinced themselves that cigarettes are good for them they have not succeeded in convincing employers of the fact."

His paternalism flexed its biceps. His $5 day was conditioned on certain behavior patterns. Now there was an indication that one who smoked cigarettes might be industrially ostracized and his bread and butter taken from him if he persisted. Seats on the bus to Valhalla were to be had but Ford fixed the rates and set the route. He did not spar with midgets. His opponents were usually full size. A very red Percival S. Hill, of the American Tobacco Co., was head of the cigarette interests and came out slugging.

"Our experiments," he said stiffly, "show the cigarette to be absolutely harmless."

Ernest G. Liebold, Ford's general secretary, salted Mr. Hill's wounds by retorting that if his scientists had failed to find an injurious substance in cigarettes Mr. Edison deserved the nation's thanks for being the first to discover it.

Mr. H. hinted darkly of a suit for slander. "The cigarette," he trumpeted, "contains less nicotine than any other tobacco product. Its temperate use is in no way hurtful to normal users."

Mr. Ford's friends considered "temperate" and normal" weasel words which admitted a doubt in Mr. Hill's own mind of the wisdom of excess.

The cigarette, the tobacco kingpin said, was a favorite smoke of doctors and he thought that common sense would convince any reasonable man that "cigarettes are not harmful or so many men of all types would not be smoking them."

"I ask you to point out what beneficial effect has come to anyone by indulgence in the habit," Liebold struck back tartly.

It was not unusual for Ford to fire the first arrow and then pass the bow and quiver to someone else. Mr. Ford was unfortunately absent from the city, his secretary wrote, and this and only this explained why Liebold wrote in his stead. As a matter of fact, Liebold spoke a sentence that was meant to be soothing. Wasn't Mr. Hill getting unwarrantedly excited since Mr. Ford was only interested, after all, in arresting the spread of cigarette-smoking among youth of the land? The day's youth being the morrow's market, Hill ground his teeth after that and in a dudgeon tossed cartons out his office window on the heads of delighted passersby.

Later Ford was to bring to his enterprises the better feathers of promotion and the zeal of an evangelist. He would be as sure of his virtue and motive as he was that no automobile compared with his and never would. In his brief bout with tobacco, of course, he may have been discouraged by an error in timing he could not foresee. A young Bosnian named Princips in Serajevo shot an archduke two months later; Wilhelm of the Germans was soon marching on Liége and Verdun, and no one cared if Henry Ford smoked cigarettes or not or whether they contained acrolein or mayonnaise. The anti-cigarette drive, after all, seemed no more than a range-finder for bigger things to come.

About all he had to show for it was an exhortative quatrain by one Captain Jack Crawford, "poet scout."

Arouse in the hearts of the masses a feeling;
'Twill stir them to action with never a stain
Of nicotine fingers our boys are revealing
As index to stunted tobacco-dulled brain.

"The Case of the Little White Slaver," his major work on the subject, gathered dust. Mr. Ford turned to a peace ship, Eagle boats, a joust with the Chicago *Tribune* for calling him an ignorant idealist, ran for the U. S. Senate, made the company all his own by buying out all the minority stockholders.

It never was safe to assume, however long the lull or whatever his new direction, that he had ever permanently pigeon-holed a preference to which he once committed himself. His memory was tenacious but it was easy to be misled by a surface indifference into thinking he had forgotten or to be deceived by a casual remark into believing he had changed his mind.

An absent-minded visitor took a cigarette from a case while talking to him some fifteen years later and put it between his lips. He snapped open his lighter and his hand was following the cigarette up when he stopped. There was an embarrassed pause. He removed the cigarette and closed the lighter.

"Sorry, Mr. Ford," he excused himself quickly. "I had forgotten you do not allow smoking in the plant."

Ford had the look of a man to whom this came as a tremendous surprise. He said it was news to him, in fact.

"We haven't issued any such order, have we?" He turned to a secretary in the room.

The secretary hardly could say anything to this but that he had not heard of any such rule. The guest lighted his cigarette. Mr. Ford merely may have been trying to put a visitor at ease; it could not have been that he did not know that smoking by employees in his plant was rigidly tabooed upon his orders.

A magazine writer brought up the subject another time but Ford disclaimed any desire to have people stop drinking or smoking on his say-so.

"I smoke," the writer announced, a little on the defiant side.

"Well, you don't look as if cigarettes hurt you," Ford conceded. "Some people don't get hurt. Take me—I don't smoke or drink but that doesn't mean I'm right," he said with beguiling humility. "If it doesn't hurt you why should you quit?"

Lightning struck the Highland Park plant without advance warning. Long after Ford's first outburst executives there continued to smoke. The boss gave most of his time to the Rouge and the tractor plant some miles away and appeared no more than twice a year at the scene of his early victories. The catch was that no one was sure when he would look in. Five years passed. Apparently the assumption was correct that cigars were not on the proscribed list. They had not been mentioned in the early philippics.

Lunch was finished and the air was thick with cigar smoke a dark noon when Mr. Ford appeared and shaded his eyes with his hand at the door, in an effort to see through the fog. He finally groped his way through the murk to a long table where his executives were sitting. He nodded without warmth and sat down. Occasionally he lifted a limp hand to fan away the haze. Some of the men at the table tried to tamp out their cigars but it seemed only to add to the stuffiness. Ford finally stirred and motioned to the manager of the cafeteria.

"Bring all the cigars you have," he ordered.

The boxes made a sizable stack in front of him. He pried open the lids and dipped in with his lean fingers. He put a handful of cigars in each pocket of the two men beside him. He got up and walked up and down both sides of the table, cramming the pockets of other executives until they were a lumpy and puzzled lot—cigars in side pockets, breast pockets, vest pockets, until the last box was emptied.

"Now"—he panted a little from the performance—"I hope you have enough cigars to last some time—there'll be no more smoking in this plant!"

Smoking stayed out until World War II and its influx of undisciplined labor. With the war, of course, one could walk into any rest room and find a score of employees dragging on cigarettes at any time of the day and invite a "wildcat" strike by mere mention of the plant rule against it.

The active drive against cigarettes was a dozen years behind when Ford made a piece of wheatland into a golf course for his Dearborn workers. The clubhouse was nearing completion and the question of supplies arose. How about cigars and cigarettes? Someone took up the question with Liebold who had charge of the club. He saw no objection. The country was legislatively dry so the question of potables at the club was settled for it. A decade had gone since Ford and Hill had traded punches over cigarettes, and Liebold considered it water over the dam, especially in stocking a country club for the usual mixed clientele which was seldom one except in search of par.

The course had a gala opening, duffers' tee shots began to find the creek on the tenth fairway, a good pro was on the job, members were getting the usual quota of eagles and 10's, and all seemed sportive and pleasing when male members voted to hold a smoker after a holiday tournament.

The manager had some qualms. "We'll never get the smoke out of the place," he was afraid, "and if Mr. Ford ever shows up next day and gets a smell of it"—he shivered at the prospect but gambled that the founder, only an occasional visitor, would not pay a visit until ventilation had done its work. By midnight of the smoker the interior of the clubhouse suggested that four destroyers had passed through the rambling rooms and laid a smoke screen.

Someone peeked in a window or a guest tattled. Ford had a limitless army of scouts, some hired for that purpose, some volunteers, who considered it to their advantage to keep him alerted. He always was turning up with information no one thought he had. Before noon next morning a truck from the engineering laboratory rolled up the club drive.

"I'm to pick up all the cigarettes and cigars in the place," the driver announced with just the right show of outraged virtue.

He delivered his load to Liebold's office.

"Mr. Ford said to put these in the vault," he said.

A dray-load of tobacco would not be carried down the long floor of the laboratory unnoticed and without word spreading. Certain executives had as big ears and as many pipe lines as the proprietor.

The vault doors hardly had swung shut when the secretary had a chance caller, Charles E. Sorensen, who bossed the Rouge and who after talking discursively for a few minutes got around to asking, with a slow wink, if it was true that Ernest had some cigars for sale.

Liebold could spare four boxes, yes. Six others to whom the underground had carried word of condemned cigars for sale depleted the supply further.

The chauffeur reappeared for the stored tobacco and brought word that Mr. Ford wished to see his executives out of doors. While they looked on with undetermined private emotions, the seized cigarettes and cigars from the golf club were tossed on a bonfire.

Only one person was missing. Ford suddenly thought of him. When Liebold did not appear, a special messenger was dispatched to say that Ford wanted him at once. Liebold was the malefactor, no doubt, who had condoned the infamous smoker.

"Mr. Liebold," the messenger reported back, "has four long-distance calls waiting and says he cannot possibly come."

Ford's lips thinned and he went on building his pyre of choice tobacco until all of it was consumed. For long thereafter if you played golf at Dearborn, you brought your own cigarettes or boned your partner and lit up when you were well down the second fairway and out of sight of the clubhouse.

It was always after such strictures that rumors began to circulate that Mr. Ford had suffered a change of heart about the club. The place probably was going to be transformed into a home for boys or re-planted to wheat. No one knew how the rumors came into being and none of them ever came true. It might have been a disciplinary device. He might say—or rather, he did say once—he only built the place to find out how many damned fools he had working for him. But what he actually said in driving across the field one day long before the course architects went to work was: "Going to build a golf club here. The boys need some exercise. It'll do them all good to get out and play."

But always in him was the conflict of the autocrat and democrat. It was possible for the one to provide the club and course; it was impossible for the autocrat to then give the membership *carte blanche* to use them as it wished. He had to impose don'ts.

A New York lawyer ran abaft the antipathy for cigarette smokers. He had been tentatively selected to head counsel for Ford in a $1,000,000 suit and came on for a conference. He happened to be smoking a cigarette and blowing shapely rings when Ford appeared at the door and peered in, motioning his secretary to come out into the hall. He asked who the smoker was.

"Get rid of him," said Mr. Ford. "I don't want him. Smokes like a fish!"

Of a top official who left him he was to say he wanted to get rich too soon—and could not stop smoking.

Two now famous medical men were among early members of the Ford Hospital staff. They had sleeping rooms in a building on the grounds above a small employee cafeteria. At the time, the establishment was run by a martinet to whom any Ford order was holy writ, but he found doctors on the non-conformist side and difficult as a class if anyone tried to dictate personal habits. In the privacy of their rooms the two paid no attention to the prohibition against smoking. They did not notice that stubs tossed from their windows landed in plain view on a small roof below, or if they saw it they did not care. The evidence caught the eye of the watchful myrmidon.

"Whose room is that?" He pointed to the windows from which the butts must have been thrown to land as they had. He stomped up the stairs to nip the insurrection in its incipience.

Did the doctors make a practice of smoking in their rooms? Yes. Didn't they know that smoking was tabooed on company property? This was not company property. The supervisor lifted an eye. What was it?

"This," said one physician, the slower-spoken, "is my home." He indicated his books and pictures, remembrances of medic days, family photographs. "I have smoked in my home since I was eighteen and"—he spooned out the words as if they were carbolic—"I expect to smoke in my home whenever I wish."

The rise of the masses was a little unsettling. Mr. Ford's spokesman could not think of an immediate or sufficient answer. He retreated and the doctors congratulated themselves on a blow struck for freedom.

Dinner in a lovely room was ending. Coffee was being served. The President of the United States turned his head and exchanged some pleasantry with an old man beside him, Thomas Alva Edison, about to speak at Dearborn on a national hook-up on the fiftieth anniversary of the birth of the electric light.

Army planes flew the night above the banqueters in tribute. The historic scene of a half century before was minutely reënacted in the original laboratory by the original workers with the original implements. Everything to the last fuse was the same except for the age of the participants, their hair grayed, their faces gullied by the years. It was Henry Ford's way of honoring the genius of Menlo Park who had so many inventive firsts to his credit.

The program missed at only one other point. Herbert Hoover was to have been driven behind a team of horses through Greenfield Village. The Secret Service thought the horses might run away and would not allow him to take the chance. Back in 1907 Theodore Roosevelt had wanted to ride in an automobile from railroad station to a Milwaukee hotel—and the Secret Service detail said no then—an automobile might explode!

Chairs were pushed back for the speaking. Through far doors

glided waiters bearing trays of cigarettes and cigars. They were heading for the tables when a horrified major domo, halfway down the floor, flew down.

"No, No, NO!" he hissed, interposing his bulk between the waiters and the speakers' table. He waved them back and they went, reddening. When the diners went for hats and sticks at the end of the evening's program, tobacco was stacked on side-tables and one could take his choice of cigarettes or cigars to smoke on the way home.

Mr. Ford had ordained, consistently, that there was to be no smoking at the anniversary celebration. Had not Mr. Edison told him around a Florida shore fire sixteen years before that acrolein lurked in cigarettes? Nothing had occurred in the meantime to make Ford change his hostility to them. If guests must smoke they could do so off the premises.

In one of the noble ventures of his age a mocked peace-maker sets out to end a war with cat-calls whistling in the rigging.

CHAPTER IV

THE LONELY BUGLER

HENRY FORD released a dove in the second year of World War I in the engaging belief that it might be able to fly and be seen above the sundering barrages of the Continent. It somehow might start men to thinking soberly in trench and chancellery on the superior boons of peace.

The voyage of the *Oscar II,* his peace ship, was an arresting idea but it violated all tradition. In war it was not permissive for an individual to so express himself. It brought down upon him the notable ferocity of non-combatants and the ragings of a press that by emphasis in wrong places made him out a mischievous witling. Naturally derisive were those who, if the United States was eventually embroiled, would participate only orally in what bayoneting had to be done.

Funnybones tickled, a great many people regarded as quixotic this Middle West archer, his arrows and his quaint idea that in a time of insanity and before being borne down by it, there might be a chance to do something and not wait until one side or the other lay decimated and unable to rise for another solitary shot.

He thought he could advertise a world into peace as others in years to come would try to advertise it into prosperity by glib talk of a multiplicity of chickens in a pot, a profusion of cars in every garage. He was less nonsensical than the Class of 1930 trying to make out there was no depression by merely repeating over and over that there wasn't and talking of good times around the corner.

There might have been no peace ship if a young newspaper man had not known a few things about Italian clocks and if a second had not been assigned to hunt up Ford and ask about rumored plant extensions.

Since the second young man never had met Ford, getting to him was supposed to take some doing, and since the expansion was in the whispering stage, the editor had little idea Mr. Ford would talk if seen. What he wanted mainly was to break up a poker game in a corner of the local room before someone walked in and asked if he did not have something better for his reporters to do, and if not had he not better fire some of them, and so on in the manner of periodically reformative publishers.

Instead of not finding Ford, the young reporter was knocking on his front door in no time, and a houseman was mumbling something about Mr. Ford not being home. The reporter said it was important that he see him, and the Filipino was repeating what he had said in the first place, and the reporter was asking, splenetically: "Are you sure, Bud?" when there were footsteps inside and a voice said. "I'll see the gentleman." It was easy as that.

Ford told what he had in mind at the Rouge and later suggested a turn in the garden. He did not say so at the time but somewhere along the way he decided to admit this new companion into his fold of favorites. It gave him two press protégés who quickly became known in the trade as Ford's white-haired boys because of the opportunities they had to talk to him when no one else could.

Their names were Ralph L. Yonker, now retired from the public relations field, and Theodore L. Delavigne, deceased, and their names are given here because in writing of the automobile magnate later, many writers lazily referred to the names of the pair as having been lost in history. For what they may mean to history the names are Yonker and Delavigne.

Ford talked to one today and the other tomorrow, and to each he might give an exclusive story which he would not mention to the other. He was long partial to this practice, as he was to playing company executives against one another, so that no reporter ever could be sure of waking in the morning and not finding a rival had skinned the pants off him.

When Ford completed the stroll in the garden and Yonker had

the story of the Rouge development buttoned up, his host said if the reporter wished to reach him in the future at odd hours here was his unlisted telephone number. For months he was the one street man in newspaper row who knew how to reach Ford directly at any time, a fact which was to play a part in the sailing of the *Oscar II* and the peace mission.

Delavigne first impressed Ford by remarking on a clock in the manufacturer's office.

"Lot of handwork; must be Italian," he ventured.

"How did you know?" Ford asked, surprised and noticing the newsman had called the make at thirty feet.

The reporter said he had known an Italian in Baltimore who ran a jewelry store and had a fine collection. He told Ford of the curiosa in the collection, and from then on enjoyed a special niche in Ford affection, tramping the fields with him, coming and going at the plant much as he pleased.

His editor suggested one August afternoon in 1915 that he drop in on his friend Ford and see if he could dig up a Sunday piece—and Delavigne obliged handsomely. The two prowled about the woods of the budding estate. Ford discoursed on the birds about them, then the war and the youth dying in it. News in 1915 had not been good—the torpedoed *Lusitania,* the first gas at Ypres, and the previous day the sinking of the *Arabic*.

"I'd give all my money—and my life—to stop it." Ford turned to the reporter.

"That is a lot of dough," estimated the reporter. He blithely devaluated the offer of his life which Ford made to boot. "How about quoting you?"

Ford said to go ahead.

"What shall I say?"

"You know how I feel," Ford said. "You say it for me—make it as strong as you like."

At his typewriter Delavigne took Ford at his word. Here was an incomparable liberty—to do a philippic on war and dedicate the tremendous Ford fortune to stamping it out. The reporter fell in love with his words, even with some flabby cliches, for five columns. It was red meat and anti-war. It appeared under his by-line on August 22, 1915, and was dressed up with a head which read:

HENRY FORD TO PUSH
WORLD-WIDE CAMPAIGN
FOR UNIVERSAL PEACE

Will Donate Life and Fortune to
Combat Spirit of Militarism
Now Rampant.

Scores Hypocrites Who Pretend to be Religious
Yet Foster War for Sordid Gain.

Ford's wealth was to be given to stamping out militarism "and to challenge the American who would cry for more armament for his country." From there on was a heavy top-dressing of such expressions as "wasteful war," "the spirit of militarism," "fake glory," "cloak of murder for centuries," "foul sustenance," "shot and shell," "vampire-like traders," "chains of greed," "damnable aims," and "suicidal militarism." Between the lead and concluding paragraph, Ford was quoted as saying:

"War is murder—desolating, destructive, cruel, heartless and unjustifiable.

"Paper invasions of the United States are high-sounding nonsense.

"If we had had an army equal in size to those of military Europe we would have been constantly at war.

"In all the history of civilization I find no man who has justified it or who did not publicly brand it as the work of Cain.

"If Germany wanted a place in the sun she could have bought colonies at a fraction of the cost in blood and treasure she is paying.

"The United States has spent a billion dollars on an army and navy to cope with an invasion that has never occurred and never will occur. The building of armament by the U. S. is wasteful and war-breeding.

"Nothing would give me more satisfaction than to bring to an end the 6,000 years of this unjustified hatred, ruthless waste and murder.

"If I can but see the world moving toward a day when wars shall cease, I will be ready to end my days where I began—a humble worker in a peaceful world.

"Millions of young men are being torn from a life that is theirs by right of birth and driven to slaughter by a system of murder.

"The advice of militarists as to the need of a vast army and navy is about the same as the advice of gamblers would be in framing civil law.

"We have 145,000 of our best men in the armed forces who produce nothing and who are as much a burden to the country as the insane and poor would be under national supervision. When forest fires were raging in Michigan a few years ago, none of them could be spared to save the region.

"Militarism draws its foul sustenance from the blood, labor and toil-earned goods of common people.

"The yells of the few who want war for their own gain seem to prevail merely because they make more noise than those who abhor it.

"It is a pity that most men who pose as standing for the best things and pray in the churches to God for peace on Sunday are busy Monday getting contracts to make shot and shell to destroy the loftiest things in the world—human life, happiness and prosperity."

A voice with some anguish in it spoke on Delavigne's phone a few days later.

"That you, Mr. Delavigne?" it asked. "This is Henry Ford. You had better come out here and see me."

Ford led the way when the reporter arrived. He opened a door and pointed a finger. "You got me into this—you'd better go back to your office and resign. Then come and get me out of it."

The room from floor to ceiling was packed with mail-bags.

"We've opened some of them," Ford frowned. "All tell me how to stop the war."

Delavigne quit his newspaper and went to burrow in the mounting mail and set aside for Ford's eye any ideas which seemed to have some reasonableness.

On an afternoon several weeks later the city desk yelled over to Yonker, of the Detroit *Journal,* that the Corner Room wanted to see him, and he walked into the managing editor's office to meet Mme. Rosika Schwimmer, European pacifist, pamphleteer and correspondent for several Continental newspapers. To Yonker the name meant next to nothing.

"Ralph," the editor said, "Madame Schwimmer needs some help

and I think she may have a case. Sit down and let her tell you about it."

Mme. Schwimmer had come to interest Ford in organizing a neutral conference for continuous mediation which would offer its offices to the belligerents. When she arrived he was on the West Coast. His local spokesmen were uncommunicative. Now she heard he was back and she had been told there was a *Journal* reporter who had access to him. Could he arrange a meeting?

Rosika Schwimmer was virtually unknown in Detroit. She was variously described in speaking appearances in the city as "Miss Schwimmer of Austro-Hungary" and "Mme. Schwimmer, a Budapest housewife." One paper, presumably to point up a homebody quality, said gracelessly that to see her was to be reminded of a "crock of cookies in the pantry." At least, there was nothing in her of a playgirl perched on starboard rail with skirt hitched up for cameras. She wore high-buttoned shoes, cotton stockings, and was the cartoonist's conception of the suffragette of the time, but she had not come to sell sex or feminism but a plan for peace.

The Budapest Jewess had lived a life remote from cookies in any pantry. She had been press secretary of the Woman Suffrage Alliance of London, lecturer for the International Malthusian League, editor of a political magazine, speaker before the International Congress of Women at The Hague, which had taken favorable action early in the spring on her mediatory proposal. Because she was an enemy alien the Congress named her to sound out neutrals and asked Chicago's Jane Addams to designate a group of women to see how belligerents responded to the idea.

She had pawned some personal ornaments to get passage money and had tried early in the year to see the President. So had David Starr Jordan, president emeritus of Stanford, and Louis P. Lochner, Middle West director of the American Peace Federation, with a plan similar to Mme. Schwimmer's—to invite reasonable peace proposals through a conference of neutrals. None of them had any success at the White House.

The Hungarian talked with force of what was going on in Europe. As she sat across the desk from Yonker she opened a long black bag in her lap and got out a handkerchief. If the contents of the bag had measured up to later guesses of romancing writers, it contained the secret plans of the Verdun fortifications, poison, hand grenades, drawings of the Paris siege gun and four German secret agents, but one who got a look into it said it held only the usual feminine miscellany, aside from a few papers.

"All the war-run nations have wanted to quit for some time," Mme. Schwimmer declared. "Because of the codes of military honor they cannot—they must go on blood-letting until one is exhausted."

She asked the reporter if he had seen a piece in this very day's paper. A clergyman was saying the war had brought out in men the ideal of Christ's teachings—death for a cause.

"To die for a cause, yes," she differed resolutely, "but not to kill for a cause."

"Hold it just a minute," Yonker went to an adjoining room and telephoned Ford of Madame, her background, briefly of her proposal.

"What do you think of her?" Ford asked, warily. He had been beleaguered by persons with sure-pop plans.

"I believe she knows what she's talking about, Mr. Ford," the reporter responded. "At least she has bona fides from good men abroad. She hasn't shown them to me but she wants to show them to you."

Ford said to bring her to the factory next day but Mme. Schwimmer sat down to a luncheon table of extremely skeptical and unsold senior executives of the company, except for the man who had invited her. They felt that running an automobile plant was a job in itself, with little left-over time for outside didoes. Schwimmer? Never heard of her. What was this—a touch? Why should Ford mix in it, anyhow? They were coldly polite.

She said she had come to lay her reports before Mr. Ford—what he did then was up to him. She described horrors she had seen, her visits to various chancelleries. One could not get the truth about the war except at first hand, she said, since one got only what the censors passed. Communiques were technical—ground lost or gained, prisoners or booty taken. If any nation said it was exhausted and wanted to quit, the others would smash it to bits. If any one said: "Look here! We have the means to continue indefinitely but we think the slaughter useless and we'll stop if you will," the others would say it was trying to dictate. Those fighting the war, Madame said, could not end it because of artificial obstacles they had raised in their own path.

She would place before Mr. Ford private memoranda of some

dozen statesmen, including Bethmann-Hollweg, the imperial German chancellor; Grey of England and Viviani, the French minister, as proof they were not averse to conciliatory efforts.

Ford's advisers still were wintry, although it did not matter much about them. Ford was the one whose "yes" or "no" would stick.

"I think I'd like my wife's judgment on this," he said.

He would give Mme. Schwimmer some more time next day but could the reporter arrange to bring her to Dearborn the day after that to talk to Mrs. Ford and also see his geraniums.

Less than three weeks later Ford sailed for Christiana but in the interim an opposition flung its sharpest knives at his head and swung on him its heaviest truncheons. His *beau geste* was blasted as though a major crime was to be done and Ford was made out a credulous rustic and enemy of the republic who was being misled into the most appalling of adventures. He thought the way to establish peace was to end war. He found that after a war started you couldn't call it on account of darkness, no matter how deep the darkness grew.

President Wilson refused to commit himself to neutral mediation. It would tie his hands if a better plan presented itself; glacially Ford announced he would go it alone without White House blessing.

Chartering a boat was not in his mind when he left home. The idea was tossed out by Lochner the day of his arrival in New York and it hardly hit the table before Ford caught it up.

"Just the idea," he greeted it. There was nothing abstruse about a transatlantic liner. It was quick action. It was dramatic. The proposed mediation might be nebulous, but a ship carrying a gallant company and defying torpedoes was meaty, and he could sink his teeth into it. "Get the steamship companies on the 'phone!"

He summoned the press. "I want to crush militarism and stop wars for all time," he announced. "I intend"—the slogan-writer in him coined a phrase which became celebrated—"to get the boys out of the trenches by Christmas."

He had been advised the warring nations were not unfriendly to the plan of a neutral parley. He had arranged for a ship to take plenipotentiaries to Europe. The Scandinavian-American Liner *Oscar II,* now west bound and 1,600 miles off Ambrose Light, had been engaged. It would be equipped with the longest gun in the world—Marconi wireless—so the world could be told of the ship's progress. Twenty thousand dollars had been set aside to inspire and reprint and circulate anti-preparedness speeches on the floor of Congress. Invitations were wired to a preliminary list of 125. The sailing date was only ten days away. It was short notice for those he invited, Ford apologized, but it could not be helped.

He set up his fiery cross against war and in no time the opposition was playing a powerful hose upon it. Trivia were blown into serious incidents. The extraneous was starred. He was peppered with loaded questions. The rumor mill ran twenty-four hours. The daffy gathered and many persons sympathetic to the expedition drew off, daunted by the bedlam. There was a tendency to judge the venture by the lunacy of the more pestiferous spectators.

It was reported that the State Department would refuse passports. It was said Copenhagen might not confirm the arrangements made for the ship by its Manhattan office. It was asserted the bar and smoking saloon of the *Oscar* would be boarded up because Ford did not smoke or drink and had ordered it done. Headquarters were dubbed the "Stop the War" suite. A crate of live squirrels arrived at the Hoboken pier where the peace ship had berthed. It was reported that William Jennings Bryan would be "first mate," although the Nebraskan did not make the voyage.

Ante-room loiterers who never got to see Ford were solemnly interviewed, including a lady who had inherited a medical formula of "great curative value" and who wanted to give it to passengers on the *Oscar,* soldiers in the trenches or just anyone—it was never wholly clear who was to get a shot of the miracle drug. A minor Sorbonne professor on a docking ship said he was sure none of the brave Allies would listen to Ford.

Special cables under London date said the American colony was "mortified." Precisely who was mortified was not plain, but among them was a "prominent" English peace advocate who apparently was calling that day on the American colony, an unidentified member of the American Society of London, who said he hoped the *Oscar* would meet a German sub, and a member of the American Luncheon Club, also unnamed. One was justified by the anonymity of the mortified in asking if an American editor, not quite in his right mind, was paying cable tolls for this truck or was saving the charges of transmission by inventing it in his home office.

An anonymous correspondent said no one could fool him. The peace ship was the brain child of Mme. Schwimmer and an unidentified teacher of German who was engaged to a German officer in active service. The New York *Times* reached back in the files and found, sure enough, that Mme. Schwimmer in an interview in March that did not stir a ripple had pleaded for a ship to be ready to sail in the spring of 1915. What this had to do with the merit or demerit of a Neutral Conference for Continuous Mediation was hazy.

A former pastor of the Fifth Avenue Baptist Church, New York, who had accepted an invitation to sail, was not recognized by a sentinel at a meeting room door and flounced off in a miff, declaring he did not care, really, if he went on the boat or not. Luckily he was overtaken and an apology offered but it made a merry stickful of type.

A Ford aide got beyond his depth. When Ford was asked if Mr. Bryan would be invited to sit in the peace congress if one was formed, an assistant intercepted the question and had an impolitic answer.

"Not if we can help it," he said, positively.

The next quarter hour was spent in explaining that the assistant had completely misspoken himself.

Actors wanted to ship and entertain the passengers. A solicitous Pennsylvania chief of police offered to finger-print the entire mission. Nice to have if the *Oscar* hit a mine. The Secretary of State, to purported queries from overseas, stated the pilgrims had no official status.

Theodore Roosevelt regarded the venture as "discreditable" but he also was punching William Howard Taft and the League to Enforce Peace and saying that most of its leaders were "foolish peace prattlers." A prime minister of Queen Victoria said there was about to sail for England "a vessel propelled by a gentleman named Ford, said to be a manufacturer of perambulators," and apparently considered himself a card. The London *Times* guessed the motormaker was making the trip to sell cars and regarded his followers as busybodies in search of notoriety.

The Logan Act was dusted off. Ford was not the first to distrust diplomats and heavy curtains on the windows. When a three-man commission visited France in 1798 to protest interference with American shipping by French privateers and it came back with a report that it could get no satisfaction, a Philadelphia Quaker, Dr. James Logan, determined son of a peace-loving father, cocked an eye and had an idea that the true views of the majority of people in the United States had not been properly set forth by its legates.

The clouds seemed to be darkening and Logan didn't like war in his day any more than Ford did in his. The Quaker certainly did not wish war with France but he thought some men in the United States did. So Logan had an unorthodox idea. He would go to Europe on his own hook and satisfy his suspicions. He sought out Thomas Jefferson and asked only a letter certifying to his own American citizenship, and Jefferson gave it to him.

"I want to know, Mr. Jefferson," he said, "if the attitude of the French had been misrepresented. I think the great majority of people in this country do not want a war with France and that France does not want war with us."

The Quaker physician had no such grandeur as a special ship. He bought his own ticket, traveled alone, went to Paris, saw Talleyrand without difficulty, and returned certain of the pacific intentions of the Directory.

Official Washington looked with dismay and shudderings on such impertinent meddling. It was a political trick, it said, to embarass the administration of John Quincy Adams. Logan called on George Washington and stated his case to a cold general. He found Federalist doors tightly closed but he was pertinacious and people outside Washington listened to him. Some historians credit him with reversing public opinion and averting a break with the French.

Congress took care of the upstart Logan. The one-man mission resulted in legislation making it a criminal offense, punishable by fine and imprisonment, for a private citizen to engage thereafter in diplomatic negotiations without official license. This may have satisfied political opponents and the traditionalists but it did not please the galvanized citizens of Pennsylvania. They proceeded to name Dr. Logan to represent them in the United States Senate.

By a singular coincidence newspapermen simultaneously stumbled at the same hour of the same day in 1915 on an unnamed authority who knew all about the Logan Act, and soon the public was led to infer that Henry Ford might be put in jail for several years and be fined if he transgressed the statute. Mention of the public support given Dr. Logan by wounded Pennsylvania citizenry and his subsequent election to the United States Senate was omitted, for some reason, from all predictions of Mr. Ford's possible fate.

Two Ford supernumeraries ran out of the base paths at this time. A cablegram over his name to the Vatican and bespeaking Papal good will was negligently addressed not to Benedictus XV but to Benedictus VII, dead some 900 years. A second headquarters man announced to the press that Belgium would prefer to see the war end than to have British and French armies travel its length in a liberating push, and that anyway Germany did not want Belgium.

"Who told you?" the Fourth Estate promptly asked.

The spokesman did not have a quick answer and shifted ground. He finally said he, for one, was for Germany getting a little chunk of Belgium if she wanted it and if it would bring the end of the war nearer.

"What chunk?" the reporters pressed, but at this point came some interruption in the quiz. What had been said, however, was enough to make front pages to the astonishment of a bewildered Ford, who knew nothing of the colloquy or of the misaddressed cable to Rome.

The Ford armor was thick. An occasional arrow found a chink but his spirit was unquenchable. His temper never seemed ruffled or his hospitality marred by all the punches thrown or the misplays of aides-de-camp. The chin squared a little more each time a blow shook him. He was just against this game of war the world had always played, and even when he turned out Eagle boats in World War I and bombers in World War II he remained unregenerate and unconvinced that war was not sanguine business, wasteful, corruptive.

He drew courage from thousands of letters whose writers saw inexpressibly high purpose in what he was doing. Consolingly, too, Commoner Bryan stiffened him, "If any of the people on the *Ark* had been making money from the flood, Mr. Ford, they would have ridiculed Noah for sending his ship out."

The sensations climaxed with a last-hour dispatch from Detroit which Ford repudiated but which could have been true in view of his love of staggering statement. It read:

"Henry Ford said today:

"The man in the trenches knows for what we are working. He is with us heart and soul. I have all faith that Christmas will see a general strike—that on that day war-worn men will climb out of the trenches, throw down their arms and start home. And the military will be dead—dead for evermore.

"A general strike on Christmas day is what we want—a general strike all over the world. I don't care what the critics say. I believe this is possible. I have believed other things possible—and they were.

"If men only will see, they can prepare for peace as easily by disarming as they prepare for war by arming. What we want is to get these men out of the murder ditches and home for Christmas. If the warring nations then go back to fighting they are fools."

The New York *Times* rated it a box on Page One. Repercussions were wide. Dutch "official circles," via London, were quoted as saying if Ford based on Holland and interfered with military operations of the warring countries he would be suppressed. Ford cabled the foreign office of the Netherlands: "The international peace pilgrims do not intend to foment any strike among soldiers in the trenches." His "strike" notice had served its purpose—it made the headlines.

Helen Keller, best known of the world's blind, did not join in the abuse. Contrarily, she wrote him: "If the expedition aids in bringing the logic of the general strike to the men in the trenches, if it makes them understand there can be no war without soldiers, no killing unless men will to kill, the great victory of the age is at hand."

Ford amended his statement about emptying the trenches by Christmas. He admitted he did not expect such luck—but there always was New Year's, Easter, Fourth of July.

"I realize now we may be staking out the impossible," he conceded, "but if we have a chance in a thousand we'll save thousands of boys for countless mothers."

On the eve of sailing Ford sat on a bed in his room in his shirtsleeves and listened to two men beg him to turn back. One was a hometown banker, the other was the Rev. Samuel S. Marquis, an Episcopal dean, who would go with him when he left but who was against going. They argued the trip was futile.

"We tried most of the night to prevail on him to abandon the trip," Marquis was to write later after making the crossing and eventually persuading Ford to quit the expedition. "His reply to me was, 'It is right to try to stop war, isn't it?' To this I could only say 'Yes.' 'Well,' he would go on, 'you have told me what is right cannot fail.' And the answer to that—that right things attempted the wrong way had no assurance of success—had no effect. He was following what he called a hunch, and when he got a hunch, he generally went through with it, wise or foolish, right or wrong."

Up to embarkation, headquarters typewriters batted out press copy—"First the European conflict must be stopped; then we must take up the fight against the reptile that is creeping through the country carrying the deceptive and dangerous word 'preparedness' on its back." It was not Ford but the Ford ghost wallowing in orchidaceous prose.

So the *Oscar* stood out on the forbidding Atlantic with a tough-minded man who had set himself a fantastic task of ending a war. His country had bade him goodby largely with hoots but it did not shrink his resolution. He had an idea that the way to establish peace was to put an end to war—to do something instead of trusting to elocution or annihilation.

The flood of fact and fable flowed on. An English correspondent reported Ford locked in his stateroom and chained to his bed. Fights, it was said, had broken out aboard. Ford was sick. Where there was no story one was manufactured. Before dawn and with his pastor at his elbow, he slipped down the back stairs of a Scandinavian hotel not long after arrival and shipped for home. His fellow passengers went on to The Hague but Ford, although paying the bills, was through. The dove of peace fell to earth with a badly broken wing.

When a magazine writer suggested to him in 1922 that Turkey and Great Britain were at odds and he might sound a warning against participation by Europe in any more wars, he said that of course there would be another European war and "the United States should get into it at the beginning and clean them all up," and his editor, on the air in '35, was to say, "This is the vigil of Armistice Day. Once again the fear of war is in the air. The pacifism of horror is sincere but makes a low appeal."

He never lost his hatred of war even when his factories were noisiest in building its weapons, but perversely he dulled in later years the high gloss of his abortive venture. I don't think he meant what he said. The idealist wanted to appear the canny business man.

"If we had tried to break in cold into the European market after the war it would have cost us $10,000,000," he said. "The peace ship cost a twentieth of that and made Ford a household word all over the Continent."

In *My Life and Work* he treated it almost as a youthful peccadillo. He allotted the Peace Ship eleven lines, but he said, wistfully. "I think everyone will agree that if it had been possible to end the war in 1916 the world would be better off than it is today."

They make Ford fork over $19,000,000 and rile him into buying out his shareholders so no one again can get in his way.

CHAPTER V

DODGE BROTHERS

A RENOWNED trial lawyer pawed the air when court recessed. He rumpled his hair, muttered fretfully to himself in the corridor, pursed his lips over the prospect of more trouble to come, and insisted to newspapermen that the witness with whom he had been having a trying time was really not Henry Ford, as everyone supposed, but Hans Christian Andersen, spinner of fairy stories.

"What you are listening to is an eight-cylinder fable," the wheelhorse of the bar mocked. "The witness and Mr. Andersen are one."

An attendant signalled that court was reconvening. Ford, passing the group, heard what was said and paused.

"Not Hans Christian Andersen, gentlemen," he said, his voice sandpaper, "but Santa Claus."

The lawyer returned to the plaintiffs' table and shuffled through some papers. Ford resumed the stand and abstractedly gazed out a window behind the jury as if he had closed one eye on the unpleasantry in court and with the other was counting the cars that gamboled out there, up and down the earth's highways, with his name stamped in their radiators. It was a good sight and made up for these minor tiffs.

John and Horace E. Dodge, manufacturers of automobiles themselves and owners of a tenth of Ford Motor Company, were trying to force Ford to disgorge at least 75 per cent of his accumulated surplus in dividends. They also prayed the honorable court to enjoin the rascally defendant from going forward with certain plant extensions, to order distribution of all earnings in the future above what might be reasonably required for emergencies and to appoint a receiver, if necessary, to manage the Ford business. It was 1917.

What Ford meant in comparing himself to Kris Kringle was that on a $10,000 investment in his company, paid not in cash but in machine work, the brothers Dodge had realized $6,600,000 in dividends, $10,000,000 in profits on work they had done for him in their shop, and still owned their original shares which they had offered to sell him for $15,000,000 in 1914, $25,000,000 in 1915, and $35,000,000 in 1916.

Largely on monies paid them by Ford, they had launched the Dodge Motor Company, reported making a million a month in net profit at the moment. On top of this, Ford was to pay the brothers $25,000,000 in 1920 for their stock interest, and the Dodge Company itself, four years after the death of the founders in 1921, was to be sold to Dillon, Read & Co., New York investment house, for $146,000,000.

Incidentally, Mrs. Alfred Wilson and Mrs. Hugh Dillman, widows of John and Horace Dodge, respectively, and Delphine Dodge Cromwell Baker Godde, daughter of John, were three of nineteen American women named twenty years later as in absolute possession of $25,000,000 or more and an annual income each of $1,000,000.

Ford considered the claims of the plaintiffs extraordinary. They had been made multi-millionaires by the management of which they now complained. The record hardly supported the contention, Ford thought, that he was a scatterbrain and did not know what he was up to.

What Elliott G. Stevenson, one of Michigan's outstanding trial lawyers, meant by reference to Hans Christian Andersen was that he personally disbelieved Mr. Ford's testimony on the stand and his answer to the bill of complaint to the effect that (1) his profits frightened him and were so enormous the public would not stand for them and (2) no one had the right to have so much money unless it was plowed back into improvement of the product, wage increases and a lowering of prices and (3) he had been fighting to hold down profits but it seemed to be a problem he could not lick.

The reaction of Dodge counsel was normal enough. Ford occupied an odd niche in the estimates of contemporaries. When he said he did some of the things he did because he loved mankind and wanted to share with it the benefits of his industrial system, critics asked for chapter and verse which said anything about a man being in business for any other reason than to make money for himself and his stockholders. If he said he did the same things because they seemed good business, skeptics asked what he knew about business and inferred that he was a success only because an inscrutable God held an umbrella over him. For anyone in a competitive economy to say, as Ford did on the stand, that he never gave much thought to money was insufferable fiction in Mr. Stevenson's book.

What Ford said at times was so opposed to accepted thinking and practice that one never was quite sure if here was not a man who dearly loved the grandiose and the startling and who, after picking one long-shot, had become a confirmed bettor on outsiders. Either that or he was a genius with a spark so rare it escaped persons attuned to other wave lengths.

Because he used to pop off strangely and occasionally talk nonsense on subjects about which he knew little did not invalidate his industrial theory, but a great number of people thought it did and were led to believe that because he had a periodical blind spot in non-manufacturing fields it followed that his excursions from the industrial norm also were due to defect in vision.

As the litigation progressed, however, some of what was said proved to be window-dressing. The Dodge brothers, wise and tough, were not at law wholly because of doubts of Mr. Ford's ability to do what he said he was going to do but because of an anxious belief that he might succeed. After all, they were manufacturing an automobile not quite in the Ford price class but close enough to be considered competition, and certainly they considered Ford competition. If Ford was allowed to put all those profits into fixed capital assets they were strengthening a business competitor.

Mr. Ford, it developed, was not running his business entirely on charitable lines, however much tinsel he sewed on the philosophy he modeled for the public, but the hardest nut to crack was his practice of cutting prices in face of rising demand, selling cars for less than he could get for them, and his most recent action of reducing his touring car from $440 to $360 after making $60,000,000 in one year at the former price and then saying in the press:

"We easily could have maintained our prices for this year and again cleaned up $60,000,000 to $75,000,000 (as against an estimated $35,000,000) but I do not think it would be right to do so. We cut prices and are now clearing $2,000,000 to $2,500,000 a month, which is all any firm ought to make—maybe more—unless the money is to be used for expansion. I have been fighting to hold down income right along. A man is not a success unless he can pay good wages and clear something for himself, but I think these wages should be paid without taking them out of the public."

If Mr. Ford stunned the courtroom at times, there were those who were bewildered by paradoxes in the Dodge allegations. They argued that Ford policy was dangerous—and asked the court to believe that if Mr. Ford was not stopped he was going to gobble all the business there was in the low-priced field. They argued, in one breath, for distribution of a succulent dividend of millions of dollars—and in the next contended that the company should keep a neat surplus as insurance against a post-war slump.

The suit was filed in November, 1916. Ostensibly it grew out of an announcement of vast contemplated expansions by Ford and a statement attributed to him that he had decided to stop distribution of lavish special dividends—$41,000,000 from December, 1911, to October, 1915—and stick to the regular dividend of 5 per cent a month on the capital stock of $2,000,000.

The decision which caused the first-degree burns was made at the end of the fiscal year 1916, when, after 500,000 cars were sold at a profit of $60,000,000, Ford then forced his directors, in the language of the Dodges, to cut the price of the car $80. At this scale-down the company would get $40,000,000 less in sales price the succeeding year for the same number of cars. He had done this, moreover, when an unsatisfied market was calling for cars and not price-cuts, they said, and was willing to pay the higher price without protest.

"You're not satisfied with producing a half-million cars a year?" Stevenson asked him.

"The demand was not satisfied," said Ford.

"So far as your experience of 1915–1916 is concerned, you had good reason to believe you could duplicate that production and sell it at the same price the next year, did you not?"

The witness said that was not Ford policy.

"You are satisfied you could do it, aren't you?" Stevenson insisted.

"No, we couldn't and keep the same price." Ford maintained that the old price was too high. What he called his policy, however, was a bit of a greased pig. Whether he raised or lowered prices depended, actually, on the exigencies of the times. The price was advanced from $360 to $450 in 1918, then to $525, later to $575, before he reversed the trend and cut back in November of 1920 to $440.

"The only thing that makes anything not sell is a too high price," he persisted.

"Yet you say you could not conscientiously think of making as much profit as you were making in 1916, didn't you?"

He had said in a newspaper interview that he didn't believe the company should make such "awful" profits. "Your conscience," Stevenson hammered away, "would not let you sell cars at the price you did last year and make such awful profits. Is that correct?"

"I don't know that my conscience had anything to do with it," snapped Ford. "It wasn't good business."

"You also said Dodge brothers claimed you ought to continue to ask $440 a car and that you did not believe in such exorbitant profits. Does that express your sentiments now?"

"Haven't thought of it since."

"You don't know now whether these are your sentiments?" Sarcasm crept into the examiner's voice.

"Not altogether."

"Don't you still think those profits were frightful and not right?"

"Well, I guess I do," Ford agreed. "We don't seem to be able to keep profits down."

Was he trying to keep them down? Was the Ford Motor Company organized for anything except profits? Ford had an answer for that—"organized to do as much good as we can for everybody."

Stevenson asked if Ford knew anything in law that said a word about doing good for people in connection with the making of automobiles or any other manufacturing business. The witness said he did not know anything about the law on many points.

"You did not object in the beginning to pretty satisfactory profits?"

"We needed them."

"You started in to make money, didn't you? That was why the company was organized?"

"I didn't give it much thought. The best way to make money in business is not to think too much about making it."

"But you got a lot of money out of it," Stevenson persisted, "and you still do, don't you?"

Ford said he thought it was just because he didn't have money in mind. He was asked for a definition of his business policy, why it was being continued, why the facilities were being enlarged. "To do as much good as possible for everybody." All right, what did he mean by that?

"Well," he broke it down, "to make money and use it, give employment, build factories, and send out the car where the people can use it."

"Is that all?" asked Dodge counsel. "Haven't you said you had enough money yourself and you were going to run the company hereafter to employ just as many people as you could and give them all the benefits of the high wages you pay, and give the public the benefit of a low-priced car?"

Ford said he supposed he had—"and incidentally to make money."

"Incidentally?" barked Stevenson.

"That's right," nodded Ford. "Business is a service, not a bonanza."

"Your controlling feature, since you have all the money you want, is to employ a great army of men at high wages, reduce the selling price so that a lot of people can buy your car cheap, and give everybody a car who wants one?"

If he did all that, Ford said, the money would fall into his lap—couldn't get away from it. Reduction of selling price would insure increased efficiency, he said.

"Just how?" Opposing counsel was at him. The whole factory would have to dig for profits, the manufacturer said. But what did the whole factory have to do with profits? The employees did not get any part of them, did they, so how were they affected by increased or decreased profits?

"They know we've got to have money," Ford responded.

"Did you tell them they had to hustle more because you had reduced the price of the car?"

He had done that, yes. Stevenson, truculent, said he was not satisfied with the answer. He would like an intelligent explanation of all this "mumbo jumbo."

"These men have been hustling all they could, haven't they?" The lawyer moved closer to the witness and pointed his bow glasses. "Didn't you state that five dollars a day and an eight-hour work day made them hustle so they did not have any more hustle left in them at the end of that time?"

Ford said he had not. "What do you know about how they hustle?" He turned on his examiner.

"I am asking you," the lawyer rejoined. "I am not on the witness stand. I am not a manufacturer."

The witness said that was easy to see.

"And I am not professing, like you, to take care of all the people in the world," Stevenson jabbed, ironically.

Alfred Lucking, Ford's attorney, accused Stevenson of sneering at a system that had produced unparalleled results. Stevenson said he was not sneering, that he believed Ford a very sincere man in his desire to improve the lot of men. Lucking said many people considered liberal treatment of public and workers an "enlightened selfishness." Did counsel want Ford to squeeze every last dime out of the public and his workers?

"I claim it is his duty," roared Stevenson, "to earn all the money he legitimately can for his stockholders." He said Ford had started on a hare-brained scheme to spend the money of stockholders in a plan that would ruin every man who had an investment in the company.

The year 1917, when the suit was tried, the Ford Company made more than $52,800,000 and surplus was $131,500,000. In 1925, when Stevenson died, the company had net income of $114,451,000, its second biggest year; surplus of $600,000,000 and paid $16,401,000 in dividends. The chimerical scheme was still going strong.

The Dodges, ex-bike-makers, decided to void their contract with Ford in 1913 and make their own cars. Their personal attorney had warned them they might be embarrassed if Ford decided to make the parts the brothers were manufacturing for him.

John Dodge laughed at the forebodings. "Don't believe in putting your eggs in one basket, eh?" he responded. "The basket is Ford's and the eggs yours," his lawyer countered. "If he tips over the basket, what becomes of your eggs?"

The Dodges took it to heart. They began making their own car. Then James Couzens, general manager and another Ford pioneer, walked out. The brothers considered him a balance wheel for an unpredictable Ford and were uneasy. The situation was not improved one morning when Ford visited them, accompanied by C. Harold Wills, in charge of manufacturing. The Dodges said it was too bad about Couzens quitting—Ford said it could not be better.

"Now we can do the things Couzens stopped us from doing—double output, halve prices," John Dodge quoted Ford as saying.

While the testimony was three to one against him, Ford denied on the witness stand he had said he did not intend to pay any more special dividends and was going to divert to expansion.

While the regular dividend of 60 per cent annually on the capital stock might appear large, the Dodges said it actually amounted to only a fraction over one per cent on total capital invested in the business. Assets of a company, representative of surplus, were as much the property of stockholders, they argued, as assets representing the capital stock, and stockholders were as much entitled to a dividend that would give them a return on their surplus investment as on their capital stock.

They had written two letters to Ford and the directors. The first suggested the appropriateness of a substantial special dividend. The second asked information on rumored expansion. Edsel Ford replied for his father that the first letter would be laid before the Board but that the answer was probably no, because money was needed to go ahead with long-considered developments.

When the Dodges received no answer to the second letter, they filed their complaint declaring the whole purpose of Ford's proposal was not to promote the financial advantage of the company but to increase the number of cars produced, the number of workers employed and furnish low-priced cars to a greater number of people—"worthy motives but not within the scope of the ordinary business corporation."

"These are ends to be prosecuted, if at all, by individuals associated for that purpose," the bill said. "The whole scheme is to bring about such a relationship of wages, revenue and car requirements as to preclude dividends of reasonable return on the face value of the stock."

It asked the court to order payment of a special dividend and stop all this risky expansion, since it merely siphoned off into fixed capital assets monies which rightfully belonged to stockholders. Ford was by way of becoming an octopus, it also was charged, since it was plain on the face of it that no competitor making 100,000 cars could hope to operate in the same market with a company making a million in the same price grouping. This may have been the kernel of the litigation—the threat to the Dodges' position in the trade.

Ford and his company said a great deal of this was silly posturing. They denied reckless planning and unlawful investment. No injury possibly could come to the Dodge brothers unless it came to Ford as well—and it was fatuous to say Ford would wreck himself. The Highland Park and Rouge expansion plans had been common property for a year and since they had raised no objection in all that time, Ford thought, the brothers had forfeited the right to object now. Expansion and distribution of profits were wholly a matter within the powers of the directors and it would be an unconstitutional assumption of authority for a court to intervene. As for the charge of monopoly, whoever heard of a monopolist, Ford asked, whose sole concern was to sell his product at a rock-bottom price?

Would it be serving the interests of Ford Motor Company to hold up its price because another automobile manufacturer wanted it to? His every cut, Ford said stoutly, forced competitors to their best efforts and highest efficiency and thus produced a competition healthy for his rivals and beneficial to the public.

The original price of the car had been $900. Now Ford had pared it down to $360 and up to mid-summer of 1916 the company had made and sold 1,272,000 cars. His salary was $150,000 as against $3,000 when the company was launched. His own dividends in five years had totaled $25,000,000. He and the whole industry had traveled far since President Teddy Roosevelt had been praised for bravery in riding a horseless carriage, and Chauncey M. Depew, lawyer-wit, advised a nephew not to put money into Ford's company: "Nothing has come along to beat the horse. Buy one and you'll have money left over to feed him until doomsday."

Ford had outrun all competitors by never taking his eyes from the target. Others could have the plush trade. Others had succeeded for a time in the lower-priced field and hashed up their careers when they got ambitious to make a more sumptuous car that would please Mrs. Astor and in which kings might deign to ride. Ford made cars for transportation and he did not care who rode in them.

As a witness he was stubborn, frank, forgetful, apathetic. He had a way some thought deliberate of testifying at times in a voice audible only to the court stenographer. His memory was not always good, although this was not surprising in one who had a mountain of detail to sift and purposely forgot as many things as he could, he said, to insure room for new business.

By his own testimony he added confusion. He did not like the witness box. It was said in legal circles in later years that the best way to win a case from him was to let it be known you would issue a subpoena and he would have to appear in person. Nimble-minded lawyers became his *bête noire.* He delighted in startling generalizations, but when he teed off on one in testifying, some stony lawyer was always pulling him back to the specific. The exchanges between counsel and witness were many and gusty.

A ledger was handed Ford to refresh his mind on a $35,000 real estate deal.

"I don't need it." He frowned at the book.

"Just take the book." It was handed to the witness.

"No, I don't need the book at all; just take it along with you." Ford put the ledger back on the stenographer's rail.

"I will get a direct answer from you and don't you forget it," Stevenson bristled.

Ford was unresponsive. He said he wouldn't be able to read it. Wouldn't be able to read? Couldn't he read? Certainly he was able to read—sometimes, he added.

"You can't always? You can read sometimes, you say?"

"Yes, but not in the dark."

"Do you consider it dark here now?"

"No, no." He never took the book.

His own lawyer would read something to which Ford would agree. Opposing counsel would read the same piece and Ford might say he did not understand it.

"Didn't you tell me this was your policy and that stockholders cheerfully acceded to your policy? Didn't you say that just a few minutes ago?"

"I think I did," Mr. Ford would hesitate.

"Is it true?"

"True if you want it so."

"Well," Stevenson glowered, "it is immaterial to me. You have put it so many ways I have lost all interest in which way you put it."

Ford asked the lawyer to stop "roaring." He also would say: "you've got the books; dig the answer out for yourself," or "separate the question so I can understand it."

"I'm not responsible for your understanding, Mr. Ford." Stevenson grew wintry. "You can understand plain English language, can you not?"

"You are the only one, I suppose, who can talk plain English," parried Ford.

"No, not the only one, but you seem to be the only one who is not willing to understand it," said Stevenson, taking the last poke.

He asked the witness if it was true that he did not put any more money into the company than the Dodges.

"You started with a model of a car, didn't you? A pretty poor model, too, wasn't it?"

Ford himself had been known to say it wasn't much of a car but that "the darned thing ran." This was his privilege but he did not like anyone else saying it.

"It seemed to sell all right and I put fifteen years of work into it," he said this time.

"And who made the first cars?"

"Dodge brothers made part of them." The first order was for 675 chassis. The Ford company at the start was almost exclusively an assembling operation.

"They made the motors and frames—they made the whole thing except tires and bodies. Isn't that right?" asked Stevenson.

"From our drawings," Ford flared. He added that the drawings were so good any able mechanics could have made the car.

"Mr. Ford"—the attorney addressed himself to the bench—"had a barn—a carpenter shop. The completed car was taken to the carpenter shop, wasn't it, Mr. Ford, and there the body was put on and you sold it? Dodge brothers spent $60,000 to $75,000 to re-equip their plant to do the work—to re-tool. They jeopardized everything they had."

"I don't know what," interposed Ford.

"Well, you didn't have anything to risk, did you?"

Ford said he gave up his drawings to be manufactured. "And the Dodges"—Stevenson pursued the subject—"gambled with their business to undertake the manufacture of an undeveloped car, didn't they?" Ford said he had forgotten quite a bit. "You have forgotten," rasped Stevenson, "that they produced the cars that brought the money to make you a success. There isn't a doubt of it, is there?"

"No," Ford conceded.

"You talk as if they were stealing something from you when they want a part of what belongs to them," the lawyer lectured the witness. "You make out they are ingrates."

The witness said Alex Y. Malcolmson, coal dealer whose original holdings in the Ford Motor Company equaled Ford's at the start, guaranteed the Dodges against loss. In the first manufacture of cars the Dodges were guaranteed payment by Malcolmson personally. As soon as the company was organized it took over this contract. The Dodges were not guaranteed against loss on their stock. They gave notes for it on which Ford made the payments when they came due and deducted the amount from the Dodge account owed by Ford for parts made by the brothers.

Ford said there were no better business men in Detroit than the Dodges and he said he would believe them as fast as he would himself.

"But didn't you mean them when you called stockholders parasites in an interview with a Dearborn editor?" he was asked.

He denied the imputation, "That's a word I picked up from John Dodge himself. He always called anyone who didn't work a parasite."

The Dodges reciprocated in a little stingier measure. They said they never had reason to complain about Ford until the last year or two. At the time of the suit the Dodge company needed sheet steel in a hurry, couldn't find any, and Ford permitted them to draw on his supply.

The industry was never daunted by the unexplored. The history of the motor car is one of new processes pulled out of a pond where the irresolute were sure you could fish for months without catching anything.

When Ford had his first blast furnace in mind, experts assured him it was absolutely necessary to have a first heating and then to reheat and remelt the product. That's the way it always had been done.

"Don't believe it," he frowned on these advisers in the steel areas. He told his own men that because it hadn't been done was a good reason the motor company should try it.

Ford told Stevenson confidently that it would be quite simple to make castings direct from the ore and save the expense of double melting, and Stevenson jumped on it as proof of Ford's wilfulness and erraticism.

"Who is doing this sort of thing now?" the lawyer asked.

"Nobody."

"And you are going to experiment with Ford Company money to do it, are you? You're going to undertake something nobody has even tried before?"

Ford said he certainly was.

"There wouldn't be any fun for us if we didn't try things people say we can't do," he smiled, broadly.

"At Ford Motor Company expense?"

"That's all I am working for at present—a little fun and to do the most good for the most people."

Ford had a comfortable assurance. He really knew nothing of his competitors or how many there were—that's what he said. He had all he could do to mind his own business. "The minutes spent on other people's business we lose on our own," he put it. Had he given thought to whether he could undersell these competitors he said he never considered? He didn't belong in business if he couldn't, he said blithely. Ford Motor could keep up with competition so long as it worked harder than others did.

If Ford saved some of the money going into fixed assets to meet post-war contingencies, that would be more the mark of a prudent operator, Dodge counsel suggested to the Court.

"Mr. Stevenson has forgotten to ask," Lucking donated ironically, "if you would or would not have money to face this danger he foresees if you paid it out in dividends instead of expansion."

"Maybe we could ask the stockholders to give the dividends

back if we needed them," Ford retorted. "How about it, John?" he called to the senior Dodge in a chair behind his counsel. Dodge did not answer.

It was from C. Harold Wills, chief of manufacturing, the Court got the backstage story of Ford Motor. Success was not merely a matter of streams of drive-aways leaving the back door and Ford, doubled up happily by the burden, running out the front hourly to bank another million.

Wills had worked with Ford in developing the car three years before the incorporation. They had shivered together in an unheated loft and when it got too bad they put on boxing gloves and slugged each other to keep warm. The trade understood what Wills said if it did not always know what Ford was driving at. He put no frosting of sentimental motive on the cake. He had advised an increase in facilities in order to make more money for the company—"that's what we are in business for," he flatly said. He dissuaded Ford from lopping $50 off the price recently—"we needed money for expansion." It netted $25,000,000 Ford wouldn't have had if he had pared down prices. Wills thought the success of the company lay in the price of the car.

His testimony was notable in disabusing the public mind of a notion that Ford Motor Company ran unoiled and without headache or was feverishly eleemosynary. If Ford made the teeth of "practical" men chatter, his production chief was no heretic. What was the reason for the price cuts that had been made when it had seemed all that was necessary was to show the car to sell it? He said:

1. The car did not have a self-starter and it was necessary to keep the price down to market it. If the starter was installed the shop would have to be shut down for months.

2. By keeping the price reasonably close and not earning too much the company put itself on a par with suppliers. The company could not buy so advantageously if it had excessive profits but asked people with whom it did business to trim to the bone.

"Is that why you lopped off $25,000,000 in profits deliberately as compared with the year before?" asked Stevenson.

"I think it is nearly that. I think it was deliberate if you want to call it that." Wills wagged his head affirmatively.

Expansion? More space to store and operate in? A huge surplus? Why not? Assembly was so integrated that if the company could not deliver completed cars for lack of one of the roughly 3,000 parts, it would be only thirty days from the end of its bank balance. Daily cash requirements were about $1,000,000.

If the dividend asked by the Dodges had been granted in the fall of 1916, Wills said, Ford would have been a borrower by March, 1917. Cash had shrunk $22,000,000 by that time.

Moreover, Ford dealt in cash. He bought at a better price because he paid cash. But since he did pay cash he needed a lot on hand. How much? Oh, a 50-day supply of $45,000,000 in cash and $35,000,000 in materials.

One reason for the shrinkage had been a change in models, of course. Everyone knew the first two or three months were a lose-your-shirt period and it was hard to get better than 50 per cent of normal production. The company made 3,000 cars a day, say—very well, 2,000 were needed to meet running expenses. There just had to be large output and good profit to overcome plant investment and general overhead.

Labor and materials were up. Pig iron, now $45, could be had last year for $18.90. The company had to take steel bars instead of sheet because of diversion of stocks to war uses. Ford also had insufficient storage space. You always could buy cheaper if you had a large reserve stock than by buying at random. The company had to go into the open market only recently, Wills mentioned, and pay 10 and 11 cents for steel against a former price of 4 cents a pound.

It had to shut down departments many times for lack of materials—the fender department for two days last week, for example. Fires in supplier plants had lost them precious stock and time, and it was necessary to send Ford crews to get the fire-struck suppliers on their feet and running again as fast as possible. The entire plant last winter was within a half hour of complete shutdown. In April it had only $19,000,000 in materials on hand.

The company wanted to build 100,000 trucks this year. It had been able to get material for only 10,000, really just a sample for each of 9,000-odd dealers. No use robbing car production to get truck production, or vice versa.

The sales department said last year it could sell 100,000 closed cars, but Ford had been able this year to get no more than 70 bodies a day, so the company had to go on making the cheaper car because facilities did not exist anywhere to provide bodies. The expansion program included a body plant.

The company was buying on the outside a lot of things it would make if it had space to manufacture them and a place to store them once they were manufactured. It ought to make its own bodies and windshields and steel frames, Wills thought. About 75 per cent of parts for each car were furnished by outside sources. If the Ford company could make more of these, it would save a lot of money.

When Dodge brothers stopped making transmissions for Ford, the Ford company manufactured them for itself at a saving of $9 to $10 each.

A special bolt for which the company had paid $41.70 a thousand, it now made itself for $8.70 a thousand, saving $582,000 this year.

The saving on push rods was $17.80, or $153,258 this year.

The company had saved $86,000 last year by building its own front springs.

Ford testified he paid no attention to competitors. Wills worried if Ford didn't.

"Anyone selling a car under $1,000 is considered competition," he said frankly. "People hesitate between buying a car at $360 and one at $1,000," he told Stevenson.

Between Ford, utopian, and Wills, materialist, one had a peek at a motor company behind the curtain.

The decision of the lower court was a sweeping victory for the Dodges. It ordered payment of a special dividend of $19,275,960 and enjoined the company from increasing its fixed capital assets and from going ahead with its proposed Rouge blast furnaces.

The Michigan Supreme Court reversed the decree in important particulars on February 7, 1919, except that it did not disturb the order as to the special dividend. It held that after earnings close to $60,000,000 in the fiscal year ending July 31, 1916, it was the "duty" of the directors to vote a distribution of "a very large sum of money" to stockholders and declared its failure to do so was arbitrary.

"A business corporation is organized and carried on primarily for profit of the stockholders," it held to be the rule. "Powers of directors are to be employed to that end. Their discretion does not extend to a change in the end itself, to the reduction of profits or non-distribution of them in order to devote them to other purposes."

The bench, with an eye on Ford's announcement that he had tried to limit profits, remarked there was a signal difference between incidental expenditure of corporate funds for the benefit of employees, like building a hospital or employment of agencies to better conditions of the workers, and a general purpose and plan to benefit mankind at the expense of others.

"It is not within the lawful powers of a corporation"—it waggled a finger reprovingly at Henry Ford—"to shape and conduct a company's affairs for the merely incidental benefit of shareholders and for the primary purpose of benefiting others."

On all other counts it reversed the lower court. The smelting of iron was not beyond the power of a corporation. It found no monopoly. The company legally might use unemployed capital for expansion. It would not intervene in an expansion program designed to add output and profits.

The company paid off in ten days. Of the $19,275,960, Henry Ford himself received $11,179,666 on 58 per cent of the stock, the Dodges $1,975,960 on their 10 per cent.

Ford was free to go back to his drawing board and proceed with his blueprints of empire—yet not quite. He had to prevent a repetition of this challenge to his authority. He tendered his resignation as president of the Ford Motor Company and went to California. While there he gave out an interview which scared the wits out of some stockholders. He would organize a new company and build a new car!

He didn't—but some of the original stockholders began to lose sleep. The Ford company without Ford was unthinkable and frightening. By sowing uneasiness he hoped to soften shareholders and then buy up their interests. He succeeded—they sold.

Being an account of those who never lost hold of the spun-gold coat-tails, and of how a bow to superstition cost a thirteenth man $1,755,000.

CHAPTER VI

TWELVE WHO CAUGHT A RIDE

TO A DOZEN men in a lamp-lit coal office in 1903 Henry Ford brought the philosopher's stone for which other alchemists had hunted in vain for centuries. It transmuted the base metal of a motor and an explosion in a small cylinder into a gusher of gold so swiftly that two or three later confessed they became slightly mad over the outpour.

Some placed their bets with confidence and some with hesitancy. Some misread the signposts and got out too soon. Some considered they were squeezed out. One died within three years and without realization of how good his gamble was. One got in to please his boss and out for the same reason. Others stuck until the last hand was dealt, or rather until Ford brought out their hats and helped them into their coats and said he had decided to play solitaire henceforward.

A woman with one $100 share was enriched by $95,000 in dividends and sold her holdings, multiplied by stock dispersals, for $260,000 sixteen years later. It cost a doctor $1,755,000 because the inventor of the Ford car thought thirteen incorporators would be unlucky and excluded him.

A depositor dropped into the German-American Bank of Detroit before the motor company was organized and John S. Gray, the president, said he had a good thing for the customer if he had time to sit down a minute and listen. The banker himself was putting in $10,000. He thought Dr. Frederick E. Zumstein could do worse than take a flyer in an automobile company of which a man named Henry Ford was to be chief engineer.

"Well, why not!" exclaimed the physician. "Put me down for five shares." He got out a blank check. "You know," he said, quizzically, "we doctors are invariably simpletons in investments."

The dozen pioneers met a week later and Gray announced that besides his own subscription he had $500 in his pocket for five shares for the physician. Ford counted those in the room and objected.

"There would be thirteen of us," he grumbled.

Enough shared the superstition and the check was declined. Gray said he'd explain to the doctor and return the money. They could put him down for the shares the physician wanted. The banker died three years later and heirs of the Gray estate, selling out in 1919 for $26,250,000, got the $1,755,000 the doctor would have received if there had been one more or less present at the accouchement in the coal office.

It is hard to figure how many men Ford made rich. To thousands all over the earth he brought food, homes, comforts of a wide variety, education for their children, jobs with him or in allied industries. He provided many executives with yachts and blooded herds and other prized paraphernalia of lively living. The seven stockholders who sold their holdings to him in 1919 received $105,816,858 to add to dividends of millions already paid. The five of the dozen stockholders who got off the train early got from 5 to 7 to 1.

Only two were considered moneyed men—Gray, the banker and first president of the company, and A. Y. Malcolmson, a coal dealer. James Couzens was an ex-railroad car checker and a bookkeeper in Malcolmson's office and he was in the picture in the beginning largely to keep an eye on the inventor, who might or might not prove as unstable as inventors were expected to be.

John F. and Horace E. Dodge paid for their shares in machine work. Albert Strelow, a carpenter, was largely noted for the fact that he owned the only hoisting equipment in Detroit at the time which would permit construction of a building higher than two stories. Charles H. Bennett, an inventor himself, was guiding the destinies of an iron wind-mill company that wasn't making wind-mills but air-rifles, and hadn't taken time to change its name. Horace H. Rackham and John Wendell Anderson were law partners of modest practice and Vernon J.

Fry had been head of the notions business of a department store for 13 years and was blossoming into real estate sub-dividing. C. J. Woodall, a clerk in the coal office, put in because his boss was so optimistic, borrowing $1,000 on a four-month note.

Of the seven of the dozen who went the route, most important was volatile James Couzens, later general manager, police commissioner, mayor of Detroit two terms, and later a member of the United States Senate and in the forefront of that chamber until his death in 1936.

Couzens was a pyrotechnical figure in the company's meteoric growth and some considered him responsible for a good half of it. In the main the majority of the stockholders picked the roses after the bush they helped to buy had been planted and came to bloom; for a dozen years, however, Couzens got out the spray morning and night, and saw that the garden gathered no rust or mildew.

The mortality rate of Ford executives was high. After periodical purges, the fact the ravenous conveyors and furnaces never stopped nor grew cool was accepted and promoted by the senior Ford's admirers as just one more proof that no one was important to the functioning of the incomparable machine but Ford himself.

The impression conveyed was that Couzens, C. Harold Wills, William S. Knudsen, Frank L. Klingensmith, Charles A. Brownell, William J. Cameron, Le Roy Pelletier, Hubert Hartman, Peter Martin, Alfred P. Lucking, Ernest R. Kanzler, Dean Samuel S. Marquis, A. M. Wibel, Norval Hawkins, Clarence W. Avery, Henry Bonner, the Lelands, William B. Stout, William B. Mayo, Charles E. Sorensen, Fred L. Black, John R. Lee, Charles Hartner, Lawrence P. Sheldrick, Ernest G. Liebold, Harry H. Bennett and others who quit or were decapitated were minor tracings in the blueprint of a genius—gentlemen who dropped in for a year or twenty-five and took up desk space as mere eyewitnesses of a rocket's flight.

Ford had shrewd strong men about him. The question always will remain unanswered in some minds whether he was a superman who could have carried the company in its formative years to its later high productive rhythm and technical perfectitude without some of those who walked the plank or banished themselves. Of these, one was Couzens, who had $900 in cash to start on, begged another $100 from a sister, and tossed in a $1500 note for the balance, and when he sold his stock to Ford for $29,308,858, got a higher per-share price, than other sellers—$13,444 as against $12,500 to the others. It was the only purchase Ford negotiated personally.

When Ford's chief aide-de-camp from 1903 to 1915 resigned, he left at a high boil and with trumpeting.

"I could not agree with Mr. Ford's public utterances on peace and preparedness," he came out shouting. "I disapproved of what he said. Disagreements have been more violent daily. I cannot be carried along on his kind of a kite. We started in the business 13 years ago and it was through my efforts the Ford Motor Co. was built up around the man Ford. I never worked for any man. Even as railroad car-checker in my early days I had no boss. I was, and am today, willing to work with any man; I'm willing to work with Ford but not for him."

For public consumption Ford guessed Couzens referred to Ford's opposition to piling up huge armament in the U.S. and to any Anglo-French loan. Privately he said the company couldn't be run from California or White Sulphur, and that a check showed Couzens had been away 180 days in the previous year. "I'd rather have Jim's judgment than anyone else's when he's here, but his judgment when he isn't here isn't as good as that of somebody who is."

He previously had decided, he said, to make the break with Couzens and the latter's ultimatum over an article in a plant paper gave an excuse. Couzens blue-penciled a piece against preparedness—Ford restored it.

"I want it killed or I quit!" rasped Couzens.

"You can't stop anything. I'm going to print it."

"Then count me out!" The general manager banged out.

The company had just paid dividends of $21,400,000 in the previous two years and Couzens held 11 per cent of the stock. He could pay his bets at Pinehurst with his share and have a balance—and was to be appointed some years later to the United States Senate, a seat for which Ford tried and failed.

The motormaker got a meed of revenge years later for the fiery retirement. Couzens arrived in Detroit during the banking crisis of 1933 and telephoned a lawyer close to Ford to see if a meeting couldn't be arranged. "Bring Jim along," Ford responded heartily. "Come on out to lunch."

Couzens found a buzzing table and a seat vacant for him across from Ford. Voices were loud, banter continuous, and no one could get in a serious word. When lunch was over the motormaker urged everyone to visit the laboratory dance floor and listen to his orchestra. It might have been that the orchestra was accidentally in a mood for deafening tunes that day or it could have been that Ford passed the word to play as noisily as it could, but loud it was and not even Couzens could make himself heard above it. The music finally ended and Ford rose briskly and shook hands with the Senator with that clasp which was always limp and seemed more a habit than a cordiality.

"Got to go now," he said, hurriedly. "Nice to have you at lunch, Jim. Come out again when you're in town."

He was off down the floor. Couzens called a few words after him but when Ford heard something he did not want to hear he ceased hearing it. The Senator never did get a chance to unburden his mind of what was on it.

The general manager did not resign merely because of Ford's pacifism or over whether a piece should be printed or not in a plant paper. No single friction causes divorce. There was an interesting untold reason. A distinguished Army engineer about that time innocently made over Couzens' philosophy, which was that money mattered more than anything else. The undesigning architect was the late George Washington Goethals, chief engineer of the Panama Canal, whose achievements in the Canal Zone Couzens had watched from afar with small boy adulation.

They met in Washington after the waterway was opened for world commerce and when Couzens' firm conviction still was that getting rich was the No. 1 design. He was pleased and a little abashed by the chance to talk to his hero. Eventually he got around to asking a question a money-mad man might ask.

"What did they pay you for that job?" he finally inquired of the man in uniform beside him.

The general looked as if he did not quite understand.

"Oh, my Army pay," he said. "As a lieutenant colonel for two years $4,500, as a colonel $5,000."

"A month?"

Goethals laughed. "No, a year. Of course now as the first civil governor I get $12,000."

For hewing in jungle conditions the big ditch which was one of the world's engineering wonders, Goethals had received $34,000 in salary in seven years. In automobile making and in the comfort of a modern malaria-free office, Couzens received $2,000,000 in dividends alone in the same period, and in the next two years added to it by $2,500,000.

"Why, man, your job should have paid $200,000 a year." The Ford general manager was indignant at such underpayment. It did not make sense to him.

"But Mr. Couzens, you miss two points," responded Goethals. "One is I loved every minute of it. The other is what could I do with $200,000, my tastes being what they are, that I couldn't do on the pay I get?"

Couzens turned that one over in his mind and found he had no ready answer. He discovered he did not have an answer considerably later, and what Goethals said stirred in him a little doubt of himself he never had before. The conversation had a part in changing his course. When he sold out of Ford he became police commissioner and then mayor of Detroit at $6,000 a year, was appointed to the United States Senate, turned into a soft touch in undertakings where children were involved, adopted the child of a Canadian soldier who had died at the Somme, and in 1929 set up a $10,000,000 foundation dedicated to the welfare of children everywhere, regardless of race or color or religion. He added two million later. He always said he would give another million to be able to make a speech like the late Senator William E. Borah.

The principal was enriched by income and up to April 1947 some $13,040,000 had been spent and the Children's Fund of Michigan of that date had the expenditure of $5,400,000 more ahead of it in the seven remaining years of its ordained life.

He had a great deal of Ford in him. That was why they were at opposite ends of the building—it was easier on plate glass. He, like Ford, thought the business sacred. Once he wrote an autocratic letter to a newspaper which had printed several flivver jokes, "forbidding" it ever to print the name of the company again. To show he meant business he cancelled some advertising. Ford cancelled the cancellation.

He, like Ford, thought he was born under a veil that gave him a sixth sense. Both trusted to hunches. Neither would hire a relative, though both had brothers. The two were alike in that they were apt to be right a good part of the time, but when they were wrong, wronger people would have been hard to find. Couzens said in later years after he tasted full power that he thought the best work he ever did was as railroad car checker—"Why, I could walk down a half mile of cars and when I came back write down the numbers from memory and tell where any car was." He had a prodigious memory and a cocksureness and temper no less big.

The common belief of Ford and Couzens in their infallibility is not hard to trace. In the case of Couzens he graduated from rail yards and coal-office ledgers to quick, big and irrevocable decisions as general manager for Ford. He spent nine months of the year on sleeping cars—more big deals, more quick decisions, self-assurance growing. He made millions, advanced fast politically—the rise cemented his confidence.

He campaigned as mayor for a municipally owned traction system—and got it. He was free with the word "liar" for opponents. When Detroit banks wanted RFC help in the financial crisis he told the White House he would denounce any such assistance from the housetops and incurred the animosity of his home town's financial interests. A special Senate investigating committee under his chairmanship climbed on Andrew Mellon, Secretary of the Treasury, for alleged favoritism in the bestowal of public funds "disguised as tax rebates." Mellon hit back with a suit against Couzens for $10,000,000 in taxes allegedly due on the sale of Couzens' Ford stock seven years previous—and it wound up in a rout for the greatest secretary of the treasury since Alexander Hamilton.

When his temper reached the bursting point and he was mad at all men, a trip in his car to two places caused him to forget adults he did not like. His first stop was a children's hospital which was one of his pet philanthropies and for which he built a 100-bed wing—his second a visit to a convalescent branch in the country.

"How a child can stay patiently on one of those boards for months upon end I'll never know," he said to me once on one of these inspections while watching young infantile patients strapped to Bradford frames. "If it was me, as you know"—his eyes twinkled—"I'd smash the thing to hell the first night."

He thought that children going under and coming out of an anaesthetic in an operating room were probably half scared to death, and he engaged an artist to fill the walls of surgery with capering dogs and elephants and other grotesques as an entertaining distraction and repeat the art work in the sunrooms.

It was never permissible to attribute a discharge order to Ford direct but Couzens broke the rule on one memorable occasion when he tired of the role of hatchet man.

One of the salesmen under Couzens was a personable Irishman who sold a lot of cars but who hung around such places as bars and liked good living and wanted no part of punctuality and time-clock. He never seemed to be around when Ford asked for him, and finally Ford told Couzens to get rid of him.

Couzens located the culprit eventually and told him he was through. The Irishman left the general manager's office irate and headed straight for Ford. Once in the office at the opposite end of the building he craftily introduced the reasons for his call by first relating some of the best stories he had picked up in disreputable haunts, and only then came to the point.

"By the way, Mr. Ford, I have just been told by Mr. Couzens I am finished."

Ford simulated agitation. The prelude of stories had put him in a good mood. He said he could not understand Mr. Couzens' astonishing actions at times. He was sure the general manager had used poor judgment in this case. He wound up by leading the ingratiating salesman to a small wall safe, throwing open the door and taking out a box heaped with watches.

"Here," he said, "take this watch to show you how I feel, and forget what Couzens said. I'll speak to him."

In all Ford told Couzens six times at various intervals to discharge the Irishman when the salesman was not on deck when wanted and six times the scenario was replayed. I do not know what eventually happened except that the salesman established a record of six absolutions and acquired the same number of silver and gold watches. He did get up courage to be rather brusque to the general manager in view of his winning streak—and finally Couzens blew up.

"I don't suppose it ever has occurred to you, you silly yap," he said, angrily, "that every time I have fired you it was Mr. Ford who ordered me to do it!"

"Well, what do you know?" The salesman sat catching his breath over the revelation for a full minute. He finally rallied to say, breezily, "He's a wonderful man, isn't he?"

Ford survived all but two of the original stockholders and outlived all who ran their fortunes into seven and eight figures under his golden burgee. Last to precede him in death was John Wendell Anderson, who bought in with $5,000 borrowed from his father, a Wisconsin doctor, and sold out for $12,500,000.

Anderson never owned a Ford car, got $25 for drawing up the incorporation papers, quit active practice in 1916 and decided to have fun.

Whether you were in Lucerne or the south of France or Rio thereafter, you would invariably run into the gay Andersons, not trying to run their profits into twice as much but enjoying the fruits of their luck. He withdrew from active legal practice even before he sold. He bought a summer place, "Moana," at Watch Hill, R. I., and his 80-foot yacht was christened the same and cruised ecstatically everywhere. When he got home from Europe one year, he wired the chef of his favorite San Francisco hotel what he wanted for dinner the night of his arrival. He picked up in Egypt and gave to the University of Michigan a collection of ancient papyri—a ten-foot legal document of the reign of Claudius, a wax tablet with Latin as legible as the day it was set down in Trajan's time, substantial portions of the *Shepherd of Hermas*, being the earliest known text of this Apocryphal writing, and a small portion on parchment of an oration of Demosthenes in the fourth century, a prayer to Isis, small bits of Homeric poems and a small fragment of the "Medea" of Euripides.

He had a small black book in which he kept a record from the time the miraculous client a young lawyer dreams of but who seldom arrives, walked into his office at 4 o'clock on a Saturday afternoon in 1902 with Alex Y. Malcolmson, a coal dealer, and outlined what he, Henry Ford, had in mind. Anderson called the book his memory booster and he once kept a Senate committee in gales of laughter by reading snatches of it.

Ford, the fabulous client, and Malcolmson wanted to talk over the organization of an automobile company. Malcolmson, who was driving a Winton, was going to put money into it and the company was called the Malcolmson-Ford Co., Ltd., in the first articles of incorporation. Anderson later used to define a corporation as "an impersonal person with no soul to damn and no tail to kick." He went home that night without realizing that lightning had struck. He was the last incorporator to sign, the last stockholder to sell.

He had a stroke at Watch Hill in 1933 which bothered his walking thereafter and disabled an arm but soon he was about and off for Honolulu and Mexico City and Bermuda with a wife who had the same *joie de vivre*.

In the very beginning he had gone with Ford to the Dodge machine shop where the brothers were turning out Ford engines, and Ford drove him home.

"It seems to me this automobile business is pretty complicated," Anderson had remarked when they were under way.

The way to really make cars, Ford simplified it, was not as they were doing at the time. That was only the best makeshift available.

"The real way," the budding magnate spelled it out, "is to make one like another, and as much alike as pins or matches."

Anderson thought of the relative sizes of a pin and an automobile and said it was still beyond him.

"The principle is just the same." Ford swung around the corner to Anderson's house. "All you need is more space."

The lawyer still had a picture of myriads of pins and asked how it was possible to sell automobiles turned out in the same profusion.

"Oh, the public will buy them," said Ford, unconcerned about any such bugaboo as saturation. "You can make them cheaper in a big factory and then people will buy them. Of course you've got to make them simple so people also will have no trouble driving them. The fewer parts the better. Make 'em like pins . . . one like the other."

Anderson was on the Continent in the spring of 1913. He and his wife got as far as Geneva. He had left word with his law partner, Clarence E. Wilcox, to cable the amount of any dividend that might be declared over the regular 5 per cent monthly.

"Never mind, Clarence, going into details," he said.

The family was dining in its Swiss hotel suite when the cable came. The lawyer did not believe it.

"Five hundred," it said.

"Probably an error in transmission," he said to his wife. "Must be," she agreed. They got the cable office and sent the Detroit partner a cable which read: "Your cable probably mistake. Say it over again." Wilcox repeated "500." Anderson's borrowed $5,000 had become a million.

"Put on your best hat"—he grabbed up his own—"and let's go and celebrate."

They went to the Kurtsall and broke champagne. They toasted Mr. and Mrs. Ford. They toasted Mr. and Mrs. Couzens. They drank to all the stockholders and to themselves.

"And," Anderson admitted, "if a Ford automobile had come into the square we would have dashed out and given it a respectful kiss."

He was a cagy man. When the minority stockholders were sounded out on their willingness to sell out to Ford their natural thought was what value the government would put on the stock for tax purposes and Daniel C. Roper, commissioner of internal revenue, estimated the value of the stock for them at $9,489.34 a share. When the estimate was accepted as a basis for the deal Anderson guarded his purse by a clause holding Ford liable for any future loss to him if the Roper appraisal did not stand up. He did not invoke the clause, however, when the government demanded millions more from the minority group eight years later and declared the earlier appraisal not binding.

Another time when a Detroit newspaper asked permission to reprint from a book, *The Amazing Story of Henry Ford,* an extract originating with the lawyer, Anderson displayed the same caution.

"This is to advise you," he responded, "that the transcription of the letter cited and appearing in the book was provided by me. Permission to publish said letter is hereby given—*providing* you agree to save me free and harmless from loss or expense to which, for any reason, I may be subjected hereafter from any source for having given you the above permission."

A quiet man who shrank from crowds and willed millions to improve the lot of those who form them, Horace H. Rackham, law partner of Anderson, ran away from the limelight as fast as the man who made him a multimillionaire galloped toward it.

When the incorporators put down their cash for stock in Ford Motor they produced only $28,000 in fresh money and $5,000 was Rackham's. He lived two houses away from Henry Ford. He and his wife Mamie had a sub-division and where it was not built up they grew vegetables and sold them on the market. They visited a bank and got a $5,000 mortgage on the property to go along with their neighbor.

Both were in their middle forties. He was the son of a sea captain but was no brash adventurer. He did not know Ford until the company was in formation but he could hear the sputtering of his neighbor's engine down the alley nearly every night and sometimes long after dark.

"Come on, Horace," urged his wife, "let's do it!"

C. C. Jenks, president of a bank who loaned him the funds, told his own wife that night he was sorry to see Horace sink his money in one of those wildcat automobile companies but his collateral was good and there seemed no chance of dissuading him.

The widow of Rackham said something unusual when her husband, leaving a $16,000,000 estate, and a will establishing the largest philanthropic trust in Michigan history up to the time, died thirty years later in Johns Hopkins. She gave out an interview.

"I can understand a hundred dollars but not a million," she remarked. She also said it was best that Horace had gone first. "I am better able to be alone than he."

It wasn't much she said but it was loquacity for a Rackham for they were indefatigably camera and publicity shy. He once threatened to stop his subscriptions when a community chest publicly identified a substantial gift as his against his express request that what he gave was to be treated anonymously.

After Ford paid him $12,500,000 for the stock he bought for $5,000 he continued to live much as he had, riding to his office in street cars so he could talk to fellow passengers, crossing the Detroit River to Canada on a Saturday to bowl on the green. Even in the rain he would walk to the corner, ignore taxis and wait for a trolley. At night he went home and told Mamie what some interesting passenger had said or of a baby he held on his lap. The Rackhams were childless themselves. To his employees he was scrupulously courteous, and at home he continued to carry out his own ashes, shovel his own snow, was a bit of a misanthrope, watched the pennies and was generous with dollars. His portfolio at his death contained nothing but blue chips.

He haggled with a lawyer over the unreasonableness of a $5 telegram in a bill for services totaling $204,000—but his check for the full amount was on the attorney's desk 15 minutes after the bill was presented. He lived close to the soil, as did Ford, and the minutes of the Ford company show they saw eye to eye.

As Ford voted Rackham voted. He never forgot who fished the murex up. It was Rackham who successfully proposed in 1907 they raise Ford's salary to $3,000 a month—in 1903 it had been $3,600 a year. When undercover overtures were made by a Boston trust company to acquire all minority stock, only Rackham, on Ford's orders, was told frankly by the intermediary that Ford was the bidder behind the scenes. He said on the stand he thought he loved Mr. Ford.

If it had not been for a golf game the philanthropic fund which for all practical purposes it now exhausted after expenditures of $13,-800,000 might never have been created. Rackham tired quickly in his later years, had to rest every second or third hole, found it hard to get golf partners for that reason. A judge, Arthur J. Lacey, met him in the clubhouse and asked if he'd care to go a few leisurely holes.

They teed off and loafed. Rackham began to talk of a desire to give poor boys an education and said he had fixed his will to give such help, but he was a little vague about the will's terms, said he "hadn't looked at the document in some time"; say, he said, he'd really like to make sure exactly what was in it. He managed the fourth hole in a pleasant 8 and as he dropped his putt he asked, "Let's get together tomorrow, eh?" A new will was drafted and signed. Thirty days later Rackham had a breakdown.

He was only five years younger than Ford and a bit George Apleyish. When the fabulous mine began to pay he did not buy a yacht or an ostentatious estate or covet social prestige. He built a modest house without battlements or swimming pool or crystal, and he died in it. To the fluxing population of a fermenting city about him he was a distant figure who had been an original lucky stockholder in the Ford company and gave a $200,000 tract of land to the city on which he built a $200,000 golf course which was named after him. Later the city opened a zoo adjacent and he became first president of its operating commission, donated $240,000 more for adequate parking space.

If people thought of him much beyond that, they were the golf players who may have wondered why he decided to give golf one nineteenth hole perpetually dry. The sale of liquor in the small refectory and locker-room was forbidden. It was an unexpected taboo for Rackham, who never drank, smoked or swore, never imposed his views on others or gave a cent to reform movements.

The interest in golf was accidental. He had been bothered by indigestion. He met another lawyer hurrying along the street who also bowled on the green, and he said he was hustling to get through with some errands so he could get away that afternoon.

"But this isn't Saturday," Rackham said. "There's no bowling."

"Going to play golf."

"Do you think I'd like it?"

"No harm in trying, is there?"

He got some sticks, become a rabid devotee and rid himself of his gastric worries. He was a charter member of the Detroit Golf Club, had a home at Pinehurst he occupied five months of the year, and wrote a clause in his will providing a $30,000 trust fund for his favorite pro, Alex Y. Ross, national open champion in 1907. Behind the scenes, unpublicized, he financed small colleges, set up scholarship trusts, dispatched a University of Michigan expedition to look for Egyptian tombs, never was entirely satisfied with what he did by conservative philanthropy.

The will left the bulk of a $16,000,000 estate to the "benefiting of humanity," specifically for "such benevolent, charitable, educational, scientific public purposes as in the judgment of the trustees will promote health, welfare, happiness, education, training and development of men, women and children, particularly the sick, aged, young, erring, poor, crippled, helpless, handicapped, unfortunate and underprivileged, regardless of race, color, religion or station primarily in Michigan but elsewhere in the world." No one in need was to be neglected.

The initial grant was $25,000 to the Warm Springs Foundation and the second another $25,000 to send infantile sufferers to the University of Michigan for treatment, but trustees chose to give the major portion to educational and scientific work. The University of Michigan was the principal beneficiary. Major items were a $2,500,000 Rackham School of Graduate Studies at Ann Arbor, Mich., a $1,500,000 Engineering Building in Detroit and $500,000 to Michigan State College for research designed to find industrial uses for agricultural products.

It may be significant or mean nothing that the only living stockholders of the original group, Bennett and Fry, did not stay to get rich under the Ford aegis. What became of the men who missed the rocket-ride? How did they come to miss? Did they play safe or were they frozen out as some of them protested?

Gray himself missed by death but Ford paid the banker's heirs $26,250,000 in 1919 for his holdings. Born in Scotland, Gray prospered in banking, lumber and a wholesale confectionery business before he met the motormaker. A brother, David, founded the Buffalo *Courier*. Their father opened a bazaar in Detroit when John was 14 and where he helped to sell toys and candy. His investment of $10,500 in Ford Motor Company was the perfect sure thing—his nephew Malcolmson promised him his money back within a year if he wanted to get out. He died at sixty-five before the incredible Model T even reached the designing board and his widow followed him a few months before Ford acquired the family's long held shares.

Gray had a daughter and three sons, but only the daughter survives. All died multimillionaires in the Twenties, one of them, David, banker and American art collector, at Grayholm in Santa Barbara, Calif., where the house telephone system had been out of commission two years because wrens had built a nest in the phone box in the grilled entrance door and he would not open the box for fear of destroying the roost.

Only two blocks of Ford stock were ever reported on the open market. Two months after Couzens quit the company, an offer by him of 500 shares at $13,500 a share was supposedly made, and the story is that a counter-offer was refused of five million cash, the balance in sixty days, and forfeiture of the deposit if the time limit was not met. The bidder did not improve on the offer and no one else was willing to go that high. A block of 1575 shares held by the Gray estate was reported for sale at one time but the best offer of $9,000 a share was declined.

Malcolmson sold his stock to Ford for $175,000 the year of Gray's death when the directors asked for his resignation as treasurer and director because of his interest in an air-cooled motor and on information that he was planning to manufacture automobiles powered by it.

The coal man died in 1923 after running his coal business, Ford profits and sewer and supplies business into an estimated $2,000,000. When his insurance policy for $633,500 was paid off, it was announced as the fifth largest paid in the United States and Canada that year.

The carpenter Strelow almost missed the boat in the first place because he did not like the way Ford dressed. He owned the building which housed the first Ford factory but when Malcolmson approached him in 1902 and said, "Albert, I want you to put up a shop for me back of your place—I want to build horseless carriages" and suggested that Albert risk some cash as well, Strelow asked who was in with him.

"A fellow named Ford," said Malcolmson. "Know him?"

The carpenter thought he did, vaguely, as a man around the Detroit Illuminating Company some 10 years before when he erected a building for the Edison people.

The coal man walked to a window and pointed to a man on the ground below. Strelow saw a seedy fellow in baggy pants and a yellow overcoat patched at the elbows.

"If you want me to put up a factory for him I won't do it," Strelow said, unimpressed.

He reconsidered and invested $5,000 the year of incorporation, however. When he sold out he tossed his profits into a gold mine in British Columbia and they stayed there.

It was funny about Charlie Bennett, who twice went around the world with a Daisy air-rifle as master salesman and is now president and a major shareholder of the company manufacturing that bellicose firearm of boyhood.

He still lives in the same home from which he commuted into Detroit one slushy February morning in 1903 with cash in his pocket to buy an Olds. Had he not stopped at his tailor's to try on a suit he probably would have gone on to the Oldsmobile salesroom and been just the first man in Plymouth, Mich., to own a horseless carriage. He is a little regretful at losing that honor.

The tailor had two curtained fitting rooms and he and the customer chaffed each other while Charlie was getting into his new wardrobe.

"If this suit doesn't fit better than the last I won't ride you around in my new car," he said.

"Going to buy a new one, Mr. Bennett?"

"Sure am! I'm on my way now." He said he and his wife, always had a nice span of horses because they always liked to be going somewhere but they had talked it over a week before and decided to tackle an automobile.

Charlie thought the next fitting room to his was empty but he had no more than walked out and the tailor was chalking here and there when another customer parted the other portieres—an architect whom Bennett knew casually from some work he had done in Plymouth a couple of years before. His name was Malcolmson and he was a cousin of A. Y. Malcolmson, Ford's coal-dealer partner.

"It's none of my business, Mr. Bennett," he remarked, "but I overheard you say you were on your way to buy a car." Charlie said he was. "I think," said the architect, "you're a man who likes the best and there's a man in town who's building a car with a horizontal engine. You don't get the jar from it that you do from most of these contraptions."

Charlie pondered as the architect continued enthusiastically and finally allowed it was true that since he had waited this long, there was no necessity of his buying a car that day. He would like to see the touted motor.

"I'd like you to take a ride with the man who made it. Let me telephone him—the name is Henry Ford." The name was new to Bennett. Malcolmson borrowed the tailor's phone.

"He says he will be in the alley behind this building in 25 minutes." Malcolmson turned around from the phone. Bennett signified he'd wait. "All right, Mr. Ford, he'll be there."

Ford arrived in the promised time and the two started in the rain and slush. The tires were hard rubber. The car steered by a tiller on the right-hand side.

"Would you like to run it?" Ford inquired after they had traveled several blocks.

"Think I could?"

Ford relinquished the tiller and Bennett thought he would insure himself against trouble by steering into the street car tracks. He was preening himself on his strategy when the quiet man beside him said something his passenger never forgot.

"It might help you in the future to know that driving on car tracks is not a good thing to do," Ford cautioned. "The car is likely to turn around."

At that precise moment the car went into a skid and wound up facing an oncoming trolley. The motorman stopped before he reached the stalled machine, but Bennett never drove an automobile on a street car track after that.

He liked the engine and asked when Ford was going to have an automobile he could buy.

"I don't know," hesitated the engineer. "That's really my partner's department. He is Mr. A. Y. Malcolmson."

"Well, I'm getting cold; let's go ask him."

"You liked it, did you?" said the coal dealer after the introductions.

"I don't know much about engines but it runs all right—it kept going. I want one if it doesn't cost too much.

Malcolmson showed the hesitancy of Ford. He said he didn't know when the car would be ready in quantity.

"Who does?" Bennett's voice had a little sand in it. "Mr. Ford says he doesn't—now you say you don't. What do I have to do to get one?"

Malcolmson was frank. He said he had ordered 250 engines and some bodies and a lot of other materials. There was no guaranteed date for delivery, however, and he admitted that while he had a good coal business, he and Ford didn't have much money to play with. Bennett examined some of the contracts.

"Would you be able to pay for all this stuff if it was dumped down in front tomorrow and cash demanded?"

The coal dealer said probably not. Did his banker know of all these contracts? Well, not exactly.

"I really think you ought to confide in your banker before the roof falls in." Bennett got ready to leave. He remembered with satisfaction, however, his ride with Ford. "When you're making cars," he warned, "be sure I get one."

Ford drove to Plymouth next morning with a proposal. He said his partner was a trifle uneasy after the previous day's talk. Would Bennett be interested in going into the automobile business?

Malcolmson already had put in $12,000 in cash. Ford would throw in his patents and services. In return he and the coal dealer would take half a stock issue of $100,000. Would Bennett put in $50,000 and cut himself in for half of Ford Motor Company? Also, would he run it?

"I've saved some money but not that much," said Bennett, promptly. "And I've got a business now."

But would Ford take E. C. Hough, his associate, for a ride in the car? An idea had struck Bennett. He did not have $50,000 but the Plymouth Iron Wind-Mill Company did. Would it be possible for the company, he reflected, to come in on the proposed deal? He put it up to Hough when Ford left.

"It's certainly a new one on me," said Hough. He agreed it might be well for Bennett to take the two good engineers to Detroit and get expert advice on the potentialities of the Ford engine.

"It's the best we've seen," the engineers reported after a day in the machine shop where the engines were being built. "We think it will pan out."

Lawyers were consulted. They said the Plymouth company was incorporated to manufacture wind-mills and air rifles. If Hough and Bennett exceeded that authority without consent of minor interests, they would have clear sailing—provided the speculation was successful—if it was not they would be liable for any losses. If they did not wish to take that risk it would be wise to secure the approval of other stockholders before any commitment was made. Bennett went to work and signed up four next day.

Later difficulties, unluckily, halted the deal and he had to report that purchase of a half-interest at the $50,000 figure could not be handled the way he hoped it might be. When Ford Motor was incorporated he put in $5,000 for 50 shares for himself and received what he remembers as the first stock certificate.

The elder statesman of Plymouth, Mich., now eighty-four, lives today in the same house from which he set out to buy the Olds automobile 45 years ago. We talked in a sumptuous recreation room over his garage. It has no telephone and when he wants privacy he goes there. The previous day he had been to Detroit to see the Tigers and the New York Yankees divide a double header. His cronies would meet in the same room the next night to play red-dog. The air-rifle plant around the corner employs ten times the fifty workers it did in 1903, although it has given up making wind-mills. Through three wars he has preached the beauty of a world of air-rifle sanity. When he sold a mill in the early days he gave the buyer's son a rifle as a bonus.

Men who invested the same amount as Bennett in Ford Motor

and stayed invested until Ford bought them out received an average of $12,500,000 for their holdings, exclusive of dividends.

"I sold my Ford stock for $35,000 and I had had two dividends of $5,000 each when I got out," Stockholder No. 1 said, gazing out on the tulips which colored one corner of his sloping lawn. Fry, now in Florida, and Strelow, who died in 1934, got the same. "I still consider those odds very good," he remarked. A few raindrops were falling upon the panes. "Probably just as well if that ball game today is rained out," he said. "Those Yankees look very strong this year, don't they?"

He cuts and thrusts at Jews but, on recanting, insists it wasn't he, really, who was to blame but an unmannerly subordinate or two who ran wild without his knowing it.

CHAPTER VII

PAPER POGROM

HENRY FORD became a storm trooper, American style, in the eyes of the Jewish people in 1920.

Week by week over a period of two years, irregularly thereafter and impotently opposed by members of his family and closest counsel, he caused to have published a series of articles in which he set up the major postulate that there was a Jewish plot to rule the world by control of the machinery of commerce and exchange—by a super-capitalism based wholly on the fiction that gold was wealth. The International Jew and his satellites had become, his editor said, a corruptive influence and the conscious enemy of all that Anglo-Saxons meant by civilization.

The paper pogrom—or school of instruction as he preferred to call it—ran seven years. Why? At the end of that time he retracted. Why? When he apologized he put the blame on others. Why? He said other men had abused his trust and it never would have happened if he had not been so busy. Why did he loose this force that added fury to similar forces already in existence?

To the Jewish people he appeared to be doing by the typed assault what Nazi Germany was to do a decade later with stones, yellow paint, Buchenwald and firing squads. To himself he was a man bent upon a desirable surgical operation for which he had no taste, awakening the public to a menace he professed to see and hoped to correct before it engulfed the United States.

Ford, according to him, was not anti-Semitic. The attack was not on Jews as Jews, he said—a distinction he found hard to maintain. The editor of his Dearborn *Independent* himself declared that Ford's weekly was merely a vehicle of unwelcome facts and he expressed a wish that some prophetic Jew would arise who would see that "the promises bestowed upon the Ancient People are not to be realized by Rothschild methods."

Twenty-six years later Henry Ford II, who had been three years old when his grandfather began his seminar, stood before leading Jews of the United States in New York at the beginning of the United Jewish Appeal and said, "The persecution of European Jews by Nazi Germany gave the whole world a horrible object lesson of what happens when prejudice and brute force destroy human freedom and the dignity of the individual."

At noon the same day I lunched with a high ex-member of Henry Ford's old guard. The former lieutenant had been reminiscing over early days. When he talked of Jews, what he said was interlarded with curbstone terms, and he snapped out the words as if banging a rifle over an inviting head. We finished our coffee and walked through the hotel lobby. Once when I turned to talk to him he was not beside me but bent over and picking up some object from the floor.

"What did you find?" I asked.

"A dime," he straightened and tucked the piece in a vest pocket. As we went on toward the door he said, "It's a wonder a Jew did not find it first."

The bygone days seemed back again when a Ford interviewer's ears rang with such remarks as, "When there's wrong in a country you'll find Jews," and, "The Jew is a huckster who doesn't want to produce but to make something of what somebody else produces." Did my luncheon host catch the disease from Ford or Ford from him? The behind-the-hand names he used seemed to make his own position clear.

No one knows when the seed was sown or who planted it. One explanation is that Ford was a country boy brought up in an area which knew no Jews and had a suspicion of races with which it was unfamiliar, but his plant abounded in nationalities and he found no cause to open a school of instruction for any other group.

It was said he had been duped by Mme. Rozika Schwimmer in

his peace ship adventure and hated the race responsible for her, but the Budapest Jewess who was one of the inspirations of that expedition is authority for the statement that as far back as 1914 he had said in conversation with her, "I know who started this war—the German-Jewish bankers," and had slapped a pocket of his coat where he said he had proof. "I have the evidence here—facts! I can't give them out yet because I haven't got them all. I'll have them soon!" Ford said she had more brains that all the others put together who sailed on the *Oscar II* and he went to her defense years later when she sued a columnist for saying Ford's Jewish bias was due to her mishandling of peace ship funds.

The actual inside story, another source has it, is that he called at a New York bank to cash a European draft and a teller directed him to an upstairs room. "There," he was to say later, "I found a lot of Jews sitting around smoking cigars as long as chimneys." Payment of the draft was not made promptly because of some technicality. For some time afterwards he spoke angrily of the experience.

Others disbelieved all these explanations and charged that his passage with Jewry stemmed from trouble in negotiating a loan in Eastern money markets, but if they had in mind $100,000,000 he borrowed to buy out his minority stockholders in 1919 that money was procured through a Boston house which scarcely could be described as a Semite institution. Moreover, if difficulties with Jewish financiers had kindled his ire, he would have been specific and named names. Those about him at the time do not remember his ever attributing his attack to any friction with Jewish banking circles.

World War I had been over only a year when a night worker at Dearborn bit into a candy bar and swiftly ran through his accumulated mail. He was just in from Washington and had taxied to the office on the way home to see if anything out of the ordinary had taken place in his absence. The train had been so crowded he had not been able to get into the diner. Along the way to the tractor plant he had picked up a couple of candy bars to tide him over until he got home for dinner. He had been sitting there only a few minutes when he noticed a face pressed against the glass panel of the outer door and the knob turned.

"What's up that you're here at this hour?" asked Ford, perching on a corner of the desk.

The executive said he was cleaning up odds and ends. He had been out of town and wanted to see what had piled up while he was away. Ford reached over and helped himself to a piece of candy. He munched on it and scowled a little.

"This stuff isn't as good as it used to be, is it?" he remarked. He put the untouched remainder back on the tinfoil.

The executive said, "Don't you think so?" perfunctorily, and added that he had noticed no particular change.

"The Jews have taken hold of it." Ford shook his head. He got up from the desk and walked around it to a chair. "They're cheapening it to make more money out of it."

The employee expressed polite interest but the remark nudged his memory. More and more of late he had heard Ford speak waspishly of Jews. Others had remarked on the drift. It might mean anything or nothing. The war had ended. The last Eagle boat had been launched, the final ambulance assembled, the last Liberty motor delivered. Was he looking for a new activity? Were the Jews to be it? It was hard to figure what was going on behind those blue eyes, or to tell in advance how he might jump. He would come galloping down to the takeoff in normal manner but instead of leaping straight ahead he might fling himself disconcertingly to right or left.

Exactly four years before Ford had sailed for Scandinavia in fruitless effort to stop World War I. He mentioned the anniversary—now that he had expressed himself on the mediocrity of the chocolate.

"So it is," the executive remembered. He said, "What did you get out of that trip, Mr. Ford? What did you learn?" They were variations of a question the motormaker always was putting to people.

"I know who makes wars," Ford responded quickly. "The International Jewish bankers arrange them so they can make money out of them. I know it's true because a Jew on the peace ship told me."

He said he got the whole dark story out of that one man. He had told Ford it was impossible to get peace his way. However good the intention, no argosy such as a peace ship could bring it off unless he saw the right people, and the "right people" were certain Jews in France and England.

"That man knew what he was talking about—gave me the whole story." Ford got up from his chair in the warm office. "We're going to tell the whole story one of these days and show them up!" He said it in the tone of one who had found an assailable evil worthy of his talent.

He went out into the hall and the executive returned to the reading of mail. It confirmed whispers he had heard before. A worried editor consulted him a few weeks later. William J. Cameron, Ford's writing chief, was unable or did not try to dissuade the motormaker from launching the attack but he was originally tepid about it himself. His predecessor, Edwin G. Pipp, quit because he did not want any part of it, or said it was one reason for his resignation. Cameron told his associate that Ford was harping on International Jewry and its alleged crimes and wanted a series of pieces written.

"He's making a lot of charges but offers no proof," the editor put it. "It's not enough to go on."

It is well established that when Cameron began writing about the Jews he did so with the same pseudo enthusiasm of an advertising man suddenly called upon to promote a toothpaste no different than a hundred others. It was an assignment, despite the fact it was said at the finish that he was the man culpable. Ford himself intimated as much and the editor's head was demanded as a peace-offering.

It was Ford's paper that printed the articles. It was his money paid for them. He was repeatedly advised by friends that he was wrong. He could have walked in any morning and laid low any headstrong scalawag who was doing anything against his wishes, a detail that seems to explode the theory that Ford had only a few articles in mind and that his editor, sold on the affray later, picked up the ball and ran away with it, Ford leaving the stadium and never looking back. No executive was so secure that he could safely do what Ford did not want done and go on doing it for seven years.

The Talmud was translated. European and domestic sources were tapped for information. He came into possession of the Protocols of Zion. Everyone who ever had been done a real or imaginary injustice by a Jew wrote to tell him about it. Articles were brought from special investigators. The ensuing 91 articles were issued in book form, 200,000 words to an edition, and widely distributed. A special printing in leather was prepared for a key list.

Ford found he had been slightly naive. He figured if he showed the Jews what was wrong with them in mannerism and habit, as he saw it, they'd mend their ways and everybody would be happy. He had a feeling, unbelievedly, that he was going to be of help and he was clearly disturbed when the Jews jumped on him. He felt the disciplining of a race was no different than that of an individual—that anyone of intelligence would welcome good advice. . . . You simply told a man what you considered wrong and he resolved to do better in the future.

The International Jew set the pattern of his articles. Ford's thesis was this:

The Jewish Question has been with the world for some time. It was the consequence of certain un-Jewish ideas held by Jews of the top flight.

The International Jew occupied literally every controlling level of power and nothing remained unvanquished but the Christian religion.

Russia had tried segregation. Germany attempted to vote Jewry out of political power only to find the roots deep in finance. England tried to work it out by absorption. Exasperated little countries turned to violence. None of this had worked.

He would try suasion and education in the belief that "the clear eye of the man who sees and understands is something that even the evil powers of Jewry cannot endure." His was no race hatred, race prejudice, persecution in the ordinary sense but a calm attempt to uncover the extent and causes of Jewish control in the United States and elsewhere. He was making the attempt himself because others seemed skittish about touching it.

"The idea seems to be," his paper said, "that any writing not simply cloying in sweetness toward things Jewish is born of lies, insult, insinuation and constitutes an instigation to massacre. It would seem to be necessary for our Jewish citizens to enlarge their classification of Gentiles to include the class which recognizes the existence of a Jewish question and which is still not anti-Semitic. The current press in general is open only to fulsome editorials in favor of everything Jewish while the Jewish press takes care of the vituperation."

All-Judaan, it was said, formed a state whose citizens, rich or poor, were unconditionally loyal.

Its means of power were capital and journalism.

Its fleet was the British fleet, guarding from hindrance the progress of all Jewish world economy, or that part which depended on the sea. In return, All-Judaan assured Britain an undisturbed political and territorial world rules.

All-Judaan's quarrel with any nation occurred only when All-Judaan could not control that nation's industrial and financial profits.

It could make war and peace, command anarchy in stubborn cases, or restore order. By the press it could always prepare the people for the next step.

When the powerful Jew was traced and his hand revealed, there came the ready cry of persecution. The real causes of the persecution, "which is the oppression of the people by the financial practices of the Jew," were never given publicity.

Having made his charges, Ford stated his remedies:

The old moral landmarks had been broken down by the Oriental Jewish invasion. The invincible course was to return to "the principles which made our race great."

Let businessmen go back to the old way when a man's word was his bond and when business was service and not exploitation.

Learn to test quality in fabric and food.

Re-examine so-called liberal ideas. "We have taken our amusements without thought and read our newspapers wholly innocent of the propaganda mixed with the news. We have been weaned from our natural leaders."

The solution of the problem lies in the United States. The work is to hold the world steady while the changes take place.

There is a serious snare in pleas for tolerance. Tolerance is first a tolerance of the truth. "Tolerance is urged today for the sake of suppression. Ignorance, suppression, silence and collusion are not tolerance."

For 91 weeks the Dearborn *Independent,* with what is called sanitary publicity, discussed the Jewish question. It predicted that swelling immigration of Jews who regarded the Gentile as an hereditary enemy would eventually bring matters to a head in the United States and outlined various steps by which resentment against the Jew in America would grow:

The first element here would be resentment against certain Jewish commercial success, and more particularly against "the united action by which it has been attained."

The second element would undoubtedly appear in prejudice and incitement. "The majority is not always right and it is not always initially reasonable."

The Jew will not be destroyed, but neither will he be permitted to maintain the yoke he has been so skillful in fastening on society. Jews are the beneficiaries of a system which itself will change, and they will be forced to other and higher devices to justify their place in the world.

The American mind will not rest with merely resenting certain individuals. It will probe deeper. It will get at the roots of the trouble and bare them to the light, to die as all roots do when deprived of the concealment of darkness.

Thus Ford set down his creed. The paper then turned from Jews in a world government to Jews in American finance, in copper, theater, motion pictures, baseball, bootlegging, song writing, with such enhancements as "The Jewish Associates of Benedict Arnold," "The Gentle Art of Changing Jewish Names," "What Jews Attempted When They Had Power," "The All-Jewish Mark on Red Russia," and "Taft Once Tried to Resist the Jews—And Failed."

The Middle Ages had their flare-ups. The Anti-Semitic League had been organized at Dresden. Hungary revived the Blood Accusation. Russia cooped the Jews in ghettos and sacked their towns. The story spread on the Continent that Jews were using Christian blood in baking Easter bread. France had the notorious Dreyfus case. Against the sanguinary past Ford promotion of a school of instruction was difficult. The articles touched off a conflagration, though mild.

Yet it was not that everyone Hebraic was *per se* an international plotter. No one stood higher in his esteem than his Jewish architect, who designed most of the buildings in which Ford processes were housed. No one had his respect more than a Jewish rabbi who later refused the usual automobile with which Ford presented him at Christmas. His payroll was not closed to Jews, although the industrial operations were not of a nature to attract the race in numbers and the ratio of Jews to the state's population was not what it was in respect to other nationalities. He did not employ them in his offices.

A boycott hit Ford sales. Most Jewish firms ceased buying his products. Individual Jews did the same. Gentile firms doing business with Jewish concerns and dependent on their good will followed suit to please their best customers. Ford competitors began to creep up. Branch managers complained bitterly of sales resistance in cities having large Jewish populations.

The articles began in May, 1920. The effect of the boycott was perceptible within a few months but was not strong enough to stagger in view of the potential post-war market. It was hard to measure how much the Ford fall-off was due to boycotting and how much to the fact that other makes of cars were being produced in greater quantities and a resentful prospect had the product of another company to turn to. More people were being influenced by competitive advertising. Another factor was that Ford held to his planetary transmission while other cars adopted standard gear shift. Former officials high in the company, however, agree that the company during the run of the articles lost business it did not regain.

Ford did not leave all the crusading to hired hands. When shown a cable that some of his tractors had been seized in Berlin, he told a Syracuse, N. Y. newsman, "I'll blame it on the Jewish business men—you blame it on anyone you want." To Judson C. Welliver for the *Review of Reviews* he said that while he had thousands of Jews working for him, he saw that they worked and didn't get into office jobs. On his way with Thomas Edison to inspect Muscle Shoals in 1921, an Alabama reporter got to him and he elaborated at length on his purposes. He said his "course of instruction on the Jews" would last five years. It contradicted the idea that Ford had only a few articles in mind and for the rest a runaway editor was responsible.

"It was the Jews themselves who convinced me of the direct relationship between the International Jew and war," he said to the Florence, Ala., correspondent of the New York *Times*. "In fact they went out of their way to convince me.

"On the peace ship were two very prominent Jews. We had not been at sea 200 miles before they began telling me of the power of the Jewish race, of how they controlled the world through their control of gold, and that the Jew and no one but the Jew could end the war. I was reluctant to believe it but they went into detail to convince me of the means by which the Jews controlled the war, how they had the money, how they had cornered all the basic materials, needed to fight the war and all that, and they talked so long and so well that they convinced me.

"They said, and they believed, that the Jews started the war, that they would continue it as long as they wished, and that until the Jew stopped the war it could not be stopped. I was so disgusted I would have liked to turn the ship back."

When he got back to the United States Ford said he began looking around for himself and claimed he found the proof he wanted.

He decided the situation should be made clear to the people of the country. But he could not get a single newspaper to touch the subject, he said. It seemed, he asserted, there was no paper which dared to print the truth.

Then a funny thing happened, he said. An old chap came to his office and wanted to sell a Dearborn newspaper. Ford bought it. The thought came to him in a flash, he told the Alabama correspondent, that if no publisher in the United States was strong or courageous enough to tell the truth about war, he'd do it.

"We'll show indisputably," he promised, "that one of the great factors that brought on the Civil War and made full settlement of the issues impossible was the Jew. And that is far from the whole story. There'll be more!"

Ford reversed himself in December of 1921 and ordered the Jewish articles stopped. He had soured on the gold standard and had a monetary reform of his own. He wanted the Jews to help him put it across.

"They won't do it," Cameron said flatly.

"Oh, yes, they will; we can work them," Ford said confidently.

The explanation of E. G. Pipp, Cameron's predecessor, for the turnabout was that Ford had his eye on the Presidential nomination. An adviser called his attention to the fact that no man ever had been elected President who did not carry the electoral votes of New York and Ohio—two states where his own Jewish campaign had been reflected in lowered popularity.

Ford ran for the United States Senate in 1918 at the reported request of Woodrow Wilson but was defeated by Truman H. Newberry, a Michigan Republican, but in defeat he had his eye on bigger game and began to build his fences.

"I believe he hoped to win votes by attacking the Jews," wrote Pipp in later years. "He knew there were about three million Jews in the United States and he figured he would gain three or four or five votes of non-Jews for every Jewish vote lost. He knew the feeling existent in thousands of small towns because he was a small town boy himself. From 1916 one could see his changing mind. At first he talked only about 'the big fellows' and said he had nothing against Jews in ordinary walks of life. Later he stated: 'They are all pretty much alike.' "

The articles ceased. They "ended" on a self-congratulatory note to the effect that Mr. Ford had provided a bunch of keys by which people might unlock doors and make further inquiries, and a further promise that the *Independent* would follow other aspects of the Question—the capital Q was the editor's—discussing them from time to time as circumstances warranted. It seemed that the intensive half of the lesson was over. It was not, however; but nothing would appear again until Ford had shaken off the Presidenial bee and announced himself for Calvin Coolidge. It was not until April 12, 1924, that he took wing again. This time it was a series of twenty articles under the general title "Jewish Exploitation of Farmer Organizations," and in them the name of Aaron Sapiro, Chicago attorney and organizer of co-operatives, was mentioned as an arch collusionist.

A million dollar suit of Sapiro against Ford went on trial in United States District Court, Detroit, in March of 1927. The defamation charged was that the *Independent* had painted him as leader of a Jewish ring bent upon obtaining control of the nation's agricultural interests.

The court refused to permit Ford's attitude toward the Jewish race in general to become part of the record. United States Senator James M. Reed of Missouri, chief of counsel for Ford, held that the Hebrew race was not bringing the suit and that Sapiro had no right to come into court, recover damages in the name of the race and put the money, if any, in his own pocket. Ford was only president, he said, of the Dearborn Publishing Co., a corporation. The corporation printed the charges. It wasn't the act of Ford. Besides, Ford had neither read nor seen the articles complained of.

William Henry Gallagher, counsel for Sapiro, argued that when Ford caused to be printed such headlines as "A Band of Jews Is on the Back of the American Farmer" and "Jewish Exploitation of Farmers' Organizations" and mentioned Sapiro as one of the back-climbers, the issue was bigger than a suit by his client against an incorporated publishing house. He asked that Ford be produced from behind the screen of legal fiction.

"There seems great fear in this lawsuit of mentioning a Jew, the Jewish question or the Jewish topic," he argued to the presiding judge. "The term seems taboo. The Jewish question? Oh, no, we can't discuss it. If there had been any misapprehension by Mr. Ford in the first instance such as his attorneys show now, there never would have been any reason for this lawsuit. There is no use trying to pull the wool over our eyes and tell ourselves this is only an attack on Aaron Sapiro and that he personally and individually is being libeled."

Counsel said about the only policy the Dearborn *Independent* had was to have a writer write an attack. A debate went on for days over the issue of whether Ford was an innocent bystander and not responsible for the declared libel or was the instigator and suable, despite the convenient corporate structure of the paper in which the purported calumny appeared.

Cameron, the editor, added slightly to the perplexity by testimony that he never had discussed with Ford any articles about any Jews. If there was onus it was probably his, the implication was, since Mr. Ford practically gave him freedom to go ahead and only insisted he be right. The editor said he never had seen Ford even read a copy of his paper. Everybody always said that. No one ever got around to ask if some of the articles in proof were read to him.

With the suit in progress only two weeks, a heavy closed car came up behind a coupe in which Ford was driving alone on a Sunday night near his home and sideswiped him. The coupe jumped a curbing, plunged down a fifteen-foot embankment and struck a tree a hundred feet from the Rouge River. A dazed Ford staggered to the gate house of his estate, and his wife was telephoned. Two days later the surgeon-in-chief of Ford Hospital decided to move him into the institution. He was reported suffering from a slight concussion, contusions over the ribs and some spitting of blood and passing of blood from the bladder.

The accident occurred on a Sunday. It did not become generally known until the following Wednesday when the company issued a statement explaining the secrecy by the lawsuit in progress and "unavoidable and unfounded inferences that might be drawn." A newspaper reported rumors of an attempted "death plot"; the company statement said "Mr. Ford strongly deprecates the suggestion that the accident was the result of intent on anyone's part." No proof was ever offered that the sideswiping was any more than a routine Sunday-traffic mishap.

Within another three weeks the Sapiro suit was declared a mistrial when a woman juror was accused by Ford detectives of accepting a package from a stranger, "presumably foreign," and an interview with the juror appeared in a newspaper. On July 7, about two months after the litigants had tentatively agreed to a date for a retrial, Henry Ford issued his apology to the Jewish people and the maneuverings behind the scenes were such that his editor, his counsel and other members of the Dearborn hierarchy learned first of the retraction in their newspapers.

The offer of the apology was his. The retraction would be acceptable, he was told, if certain conditions were met. There was to be no pussy-footing—it was to be complete. No more anti-Semitic articles were to be published. No more copies of the book, *The International Jew,* were to be circulated. Cameron and Ernest G. Liebold, general manager, were to be fired.

As peace envoys Ford sent Joseph A. Palma, head of the New York field force of the United States Secret Service, and Earl J. Davis, a former assistant United States attorney general, to Louis P. Marshall, head of the American Jewish Committee, and Nathan D. Perlman, former Congressman and a vice-president of the American Jewish Congress.

The story most often told is that on a visit of Palma to Dearborn Ford mentioned that he had been quietly investigating some statements made in the *Independent* and was shocked by what he found. Palma said he knew personally the offense Ford had given the Jewish people.

"I wish this wrong could be righted," Palma quoted Ford as saying.

The government agent said he would lend every assistance he could.

"Go to it," Ford said, according to Palma's story. "When my real views are explained to the proper people they will know I am prepared to act honorably and to repair the damage as far as I can."

Palma said Ford signed the retraction without reading it.

"This is pretty strong, Mr. Ford, and I suggest you go over it pretty carefully," Palma cautioned.

"Joe, no matter how strong it is it couldn't be too strong. Let the Jew judge me by my acts in the future."

In his three-quarter column retraction sent to Arthur Brisbane for release to the press as he saw fit, Ford said in part:

"In the multitude of my activities it has been impossible for me to devote personal attention to their management or to keep informed as to their contents. It has therefore inevitably followed that the conduct and policies of these publications had to be delegated to men whom I placed in charge of them and upon whom I relied implicitly.

"To my great regret I have learned that Jews generally, and particularly those of this country, not only resent these publications as promoting anti-Semitism, but regard me as their enemy. Trustworthy friends with whom I have conferred recently have assured me in all sincerity that in their opinion the character of the charges and insinuations against the Jews, both individually and collectively, contained in many of the articles which have been circulated periodically in the Dearborn *Independent,* and have been reprinted in the pamphlets mentioned, justifies the righteous indignation entertained by Jews everywhere toward me because of the mental anguish occasioned by the unprovoked reflections made upon them.

"This had led me to direct my personal attention to this subject in order to ascertain the exact nature of these articles. As a result of this survey I confess I am deeply mortified that this journal, which is intended to be constructive and not destructive, has been made the medium for resurrecting exploded fictions, for giving currency to the so-called protocols of the wise men of Zion which have been demonstrated, as I learn, to be gross forgeries, and for contending that the Jews have been engaged in conspiracy to control the capital and the industries of the world, besides laying at their door many offenses against decency, public order and good morals.

"Had I appreciated even the general nature, to say nothing of the details, of these utterances, I would have forbidden their circulation, without a moment's hesitation."

There was more but that was the general tenor. He said those who knew him would bear witness it was not in his nature to inflict insult or occasion pain. He was very sorry and he would not do it again. Thus Ford went to Canossa. He did in the end what the late President Harding, Thomas Edison, his family, many clergy, and thousands of others told him to do in the beginning, but for seven years he had thumped the tocsin or condoned it.

It broke as an utter surprise on those around him. He did not consult his son. Cameron learned of the apology first when he read it in a newspaper. Counsel for Sapiro received an important telephone call a few days before the announcement and sought out counsel for Ford. He said he had been reliably informed that Ford was prepared to make proper amends for his attack on the Jews. "Harry," said the Ford lawyer, "I have a feeling some one is spoofing you. I think I know Mr. Ford's attitude pretty well."

"Well maybe so, but wouldn't it be well to make certain?" Gallagher suggested. The lawyer thought it might.

"I guess you're right," Ford counsel reported on returning.

The senior senator from Missouri, chief of Ford attorneys in the Sapiro case, telephoned from Texas, irascibly unstatesmanlike, to say, "What in hell is this I see in the Dallas paper?"

The public proof of contrition evoked mixed sentiments. Some onlookers found hard to imagine the motormaker so wrapped in cotton wool that the major activity of his own magazine was unknown to him—as unaware of what the Dearborn *Independent* was doing as if he had been a Tibetan monk. Some considered unimpressive his willingness to try to hide behind subordinates. Certainly, said one editor, it was unpleasant to find the printing press "set up by men so ignorant as not to know or so callous as not to care" what a press they owned turned out. The *American Hebrew* credited him with a distinction—"he is the first man in history beguiled by anti-Semitism who has made public recantation." Some said it was a manly amend.

Ford apologized probably for a number of reasons. He was bringing out a new car. He wanted a clean slate. He did not relish the boycott. It struck at the car, and the car was all. He had no appetite for a siege on the witness stand in the Sapiro case, and one of the accepted conditions under which the offer of retraction was made was that the suit would be withdrawn. It was settled out of court. There was a shadow of fear that the automobile mishap might have been a little more than he made out publicly. He may have been in a transitory penitential mood. The Astrologers' Guild of New York said he apologized because he had Mercury in the Third House while Jupiter and Uranus were over his Neptune, and that this fact convinced him he should no longer insult people. Maybe the astrologers hit it.

Not only discontinuance of the hostile articles was ordered immediately but the Dearborn *Independent* ceased publication the first of the year. Neither Cameron nor Liebold was beheaded, however. The editor went to Ireland with a Lincoln and the general manager was soon busy selling the Ford railroad.

A month before the retraction Ford made up his mind definitely to wind up his assault. He called to Dearborn a Jewish lawyer with whom he had been long on good terms and announced his intention. He did not say why. He did say, however, that he proposed to burn a collection of anti-Semitic books, magazine articles and various clippings that had been acquired in the *Independent's* research. His visitor protested.

"Destruction isn't the answer," he said promptly. "You have a chance to do good with it."

"How do you mean?"

"I would say the collection is unique," the attorney said. "Why don't you present it to the Hebrew Union College at Cincinnati?"

He said the library was open to students and the public, and the material would give the former a chance, in their rabbinical studies, to acquaint themselves with some of the events in the history of Israel.

"Not a bad idea," said Ford. "Yes, a very good idea."

What disposal of the books and papers was made is not known, but they were not received in Cincinnati.

A good friend got Ford to one side at a golf club after the apology and asked him why he had printed the articles in the first place.

"I don't hate the Jews," he insisted; "I want to be their friend."

"Then why—"

"The Jews have gone along during the ages making themselves disliked." Ford nodded over the good point he thought he was making. "Right? They ignored their own splendid teachers and statesmen. Even they could not get their people to change some of their obnoxious habits."

"Well—?"

"I thought by taking a club to them I might be able to do it," said Ford.

He revives the polka and quadrille and old-time fiddlers come running around the mountain to saw out the tempting tunes of his teens.

CHAPTER VIII

THE BALLET-MASTER

HIS COMPEERS chose jade or racing stables, rugs or Raphaels; Henry Ford picked old-fashioned dancing as a relaxing interest.

At first thought it seemed an odd selection because on the dance floor he had earnestness but never abandon, suppleness and dignity but never ecstasy, and always he was Henry Ford and seemed to feel he was on exhibition. It was not the aloofness of a Lorenzo watching the capers of serving folk in a Medicean scullery. It was a normal reserve to be looked for in a man of sixty, which was his age when he started to exhume the old-time steps. A man of three score, full of fizz and sophomoric roughhouse would have seemed a ninny.

The Fords got to talking with old friends in their playroom one evening about the dances they did in their youth. The era's hi-de-ho drew indictment and laughter and someone asked if the schottische did not go this way, and did Henry recall the gavotte, and each got up and demonstrated what little he or she remembered. They guessed at the tunes and patterns and calls, and there hardly would have been more excitement if the host had tripled the production wage rate.

"Do you realize, Henry Ford, that we have danced very little since we were married?" reflected Mrs. Ford, as many a wife has said to a husband before her. The last guest had disappeared down the drive and they were alone and still in the grip of nostalgia—or at least she was. He said he missed it, too.

"It would do us both good," his wife suggested, "to take it up again," and Ford agreed it might be fun. But "might be fun" was far from any firm commitment to do anything about it.

Mrs. Ford's urging did bear fruit, however, for the telephone of Benjamin B. Lovett, in Hudson, Mass., rang some weeks later and Henry Ford wanted to know if Mr. Lovett, who had dance studios in Worcester and four other cities, could drop everything and come to Wayside Inn in Sudbury for a business talk. Inquiring about instructors familiar with period dancing, Ford had heard the name of Lovett mentioned and his talent commended.

"I have been after Mr. Ford for some time to take up dancing again," said Mrs. Ford, who was first to greet the teacher. "Now he's interested and I hope you'll help him."

Ford joined them and straightway wanted to know if Lovett knew the Ripple. He was sorry he did not, he said, and noticed his host was elated.

"Stuck him the first time." Ford turned to his wife and frowned mockingly.

Next morning Lovett went stalking the unfamiliar Ripple. He rode out of Massachusetts empty handed into New Hampshire, and out of that state without a clue into Vermont. Ford would have liked his persistence. A woman colleague there told Lovett she had taught it ten years before.

"Have you the calls?" he anxiously asked.

She had, but they were at her cottage twenty miles away. "Well, jump in my car, won't you, and we'll go there." Lovett had no time to waste. Unfortunately, she said, the cottage was on an island and the road there was torn up. There was no way but to walk. He dropped her with a groan but found a male teacher farther on who offered real help.

"That Ripple, Ben, is what we used to call the 'Newport, Down East,' " he said. "Remember?" He knew all about it. Lovett went back to Ford full of Ripples. A month later he went to Dearborn as the motormaker's private dance instructor for a week-end or two—and the week-ends stretched to twenty years.

Upon their return Mrs. Ford proposed a dance in the barn of the homestead, so with a Halloween party in 1924 a crusade was born. Lovett came on. The weather turned bitter but the host waved a wand

and a steam-heating plant, installed in a few hours, made the place comfortable.

Some say Ford set out to recapture the hour when his wife was a dark-eyed and graceful miss of eighteen and he had to outrun other beaux to her side when fiddles scraped and the grand march began. Others think his pick struck this new vein simply in his digging for McGuffey readers and antiques, and that all this was interrelated.

Actually Mrs. Ford was the propulsion. Whatever the impulse, however, it was different with the Fords than with most people. The idyll of long ago is usually lost for good; the pressed flower in the book remains powder, but Ford had a commingling of zeal and wealth that was a magic restorative. The idyll could be made to throb again, the perfume of the flower recaptured.

No narrow barn could contain any of his enthusiasms. If the idea was not contagious it could be made so. It would spread first to the near countryside, to the nation in a month and eventually to far places. Word of the fancy would be wired and radioed and cabled. Copyboys in distant newspaper offices would take a sheet of flimsy from a pneumatic tube and lay it on the news desk, men in green eyeshades would head it, presses would rumble and over their morning coffee a clerk in Capetown, a banker on the Paris Bourse and a sheepherder in Montana would read of and muse over Ford's new caprice. Yes, the germ would spread. He would see to it.

Four days later he sought a guinea pig and by great good luck found one right at hand. The pig may well have said, "Well, here we go again," but if it did, it took care to lower its voice and look over a shoulder to be sure no one was listening. Ford cleared appropriate space in his enormous engineering laboratory, signed up some musicians who knew the necessary melodies, invited Lovett to look on and get acquainted, and asked thirty of his staff and their wives to help in broadening the experiment by trying the steps.

Special flooring was laid. A craneway, installed against the day when Ford might want to build a locomotive, went into permanent eclipse. He wrote off the overhead machinery as something that seemed a good idea originally but was of no use to dancers of the lancers.

Guests were harrowingly confused the first night. The caller could not explain his own calls. The older people who knew one or two steps tried ineffectually to impart what they knew to those who remembered absolutely nothing of them, and finally a distressed Ford asked Lovett if he could straighten things out.

"If you can, then you and I will run the show," he volunteered.

They succeeded in unscrambling the tangle, and when the dance broke up Ford knew he had his man and Lovett wired Mrs. Lovett to sell their business and pack.

Possibly the executives were not bright, or it may have been they were unelated by their expanded chores, for improvement dragged and Mr. Ford, who could be flint, took steps to speed perfection.

"I tell you what we'll do," he announced, nice as pie, to the appalled group; "we'll have lessons every night until we get it right."

So for two solid weeks the top brass came to work wilted by nightly polkas and wondering if and when in all hell it would end. But they learned how many steps to pace off to left and right and rear in the mazurka, and all about balancing partners and the indubitable difference between the *chassé* of the dance floor and the chassis rolling on the No. 1 assembly line.

Ford treatment of the disinterred steps was characteristic. Histories were searched and a writer hired to discourse on the subject. An illustrated booklet appeared under the title "Good Morning" and subtitled, "After a sleep of 25 years old-fashioned dancing is being revived by Mr. and Mrs. Henry Ford." The first printing was 50,000. It was no shoestring crusade; it was to broaden and take in vast ground, and for his seat at the head of the captain's table Ford was to pay a huge cover charge said to have run into seven figures. His good wife may have started it but it was he who ran with the ball.

The editor of the manual's forepiece remarked that denunciation of dancing by protectors of public morals usually had been due to importation of dances "foreign to the expressional moods of the people." And he added, with some puffing up of fact and possibly hired tongue in cheek, that "the tide now has swung in favor of dances described in the book." If the tide was flowing in the direction of the quadrille, the usual measuring devices did not bear it out.

An orchestra skilled in the old tunes was organized. Dances were diagrammed and rules of conduct drafted. A person attending a dance was counselled to appear in the "neatest and cleanest possible condition"; courtesy was urged and defined not as the mere observance of set forms but as doing "the things a generous thoughtfulness would naturally suggest," and there were other sound words on manners which made anyone who read them realize how much had been sloughed off in the hasting of the race that might better have been retained. The manuals were largely, of course, to implement a plan which Ford had in mind for indoctrinating children.

A large space was fenced off with canvas as a temporary ballroom. Airplane motors stood high on the floor. A nearby press turned out the next issue of Ford's magazine. Men bent over blueprints of a dirigible a few yards from where the orchestra played *Pop Goes the Weasel*. The *Bible* said there was a time to dance. The time for Ford was any time he took it into his head.

The makeshift space was to serve for 13 years until Lovett Hall, paneled chastely, floored with costly teakwood, furnished in English colonial and reached by winding marble, was so christened in Edison Institute. It was an unprecedented tribute because the anonymity of Ford officials, outside the head of the dynasty, was as rigorously preserved as that of the writers of Dana's *Sun*.

Not more than nine months after the first party, Ford walked into the teacher's office and remained pensive for several minutes, looking out a window at nothing in particular.

"Mr. Lovett," he finally asked, "did you ever hear a saying: 'Courtesy makes friends and good manners keeps them?' "

"What's on your mind, Mr. Ford?"

"We did not get much social training when I was a boy," Ford confessed frankly. "I have been wondering if we could not organize a dancing school for boys and girls of Dearborn." He hastened to say there would be more to it than merely instilling knowledge of the quadrille. "I'm not thinking so much of teaching them how to dance," he mused aloud, "but of teaching children the courtesy and conduct that go with the dance."

Lovett saw possibilities. Yes, he had taught children. "All right," said Ford; "let's start a class at once."

A class of eight boys and eight girls was organized, and the small original group grew into a larger one and the larger one sub-divided. The mission field was broadened and pupils multiplied until there were 22,000 from the public schools in the area alone. Schools of higher learning added early American dancing to their curricula and offered them as credit courses—Temple, Michigan, Radcliffe, Stevens, North Carolina, Georgia, Missouri. Under Ford patronage the Lovetts taught in the physical training departments of thirty-four universities, colleges and normal schools.

Ford dancing parties were invariably on Friday nights and resulted from his walking into the dancing instructor's office several days in advance and delivering his orders in some such form as, "Mr. Lovett, do you suppose we could have a party next Friday?" This was a fiat, not a question; no one ever said there could not be a party when Ford asked if there could be.

If the host invited you to one of these events and you pleaded that dinner guests were coming to your home the same night—eighteen of them, in fact—and it was therefore impossible for you to attend, Ford would likely say, "Bring them out here. What time will you finish dinner? Nine o'clock? I'll send cars." At 9, wherever you lived, you would glance out the window and a train of Lincolns or station-wagons would be at the curb. If you had Mrs. Wilkes of Des Moines as a house guest, she would be most welcome, of course. If your daughter was home for the holidays, do bring her—and her young man, too, if she cared to invite him.

The host's hospitality was expansive and sincere. He would go out of his way to be gracious to the most obscure guest. When a father introduced his school-girl daughter, Ford would most probably say to her, "It would be an honor if you would grant me the pleasure of this dance."

A device seldom detected spared him discomfiture if he happened to draw a partner indescribably awkward. Take the case of Mrs. Wilkes or whoever she might be.

"Mrs. Wilkes, may I have the pleasure of the next dance?" he would say, old worldlike and a little stilted, unless one was born in the Lincoln administration, as he was.

You did not say, "Do you want to dance this one with me?" You did not applaud for encores unless reasonably sure that the partner wished to continue. You did not make a dash for the smoking room when the dance ended. When you retired after a dance you faced your lady, made a slight bow and stepped back two steps so as not to be seeming to turn your back on her. It was all set down in the manual and Ford not only sponsored the book but followed it.

"I'm sorry, Mr. Ford, but I don't know a thing, really, about these dances," Mrs. Wilkes might weakly plead.

"Don't mind that," he would say to stiffen her assurance; "I'll show you. It is quite simple."

If Mrs. Wilkes proved facile the dance continued to the end. If she was a thorough clodhopper and tripped over her feet and nearly dragged Ford down with her in her unsure gyrations, their circle of the floor was diplomatically interrupted more often than not by a third party who turned out to be—Ford's dancing master. The interception was welcome to Ford, who did not relish doing hand stands, and equally to the lady, no doubt, who probably was as much demoralized and sick of it all as he.

"I wonder if you will permit me to continue this dance with our guest, Mr. Ford?" the instructor would propose, as if he had just succeeded in getting up courage to cut in.

"Mrs. Wilkes," Ford would say, stepping back a pace or two, "will you allow me to present Mr. Lovett, our teacher here?" And then Mr. Ford, relinquishing Mrs. Wilkes, would act as though this interruption was a little disappointing to him and give the impression that apparently his teacher had become slightly inebriated by Mrs. Wilkes' beauty and nimbleness.

So shortly Mr. Lovett would be shepherding the relieved lady around the floor and she would calm down and get clear in her mind which foot was which because she was no longer the center of all eyes she thought she was as Mr. Ford's partner, and was dancing merely with an instructor who magically, the good fellow, seemed to accustom himself to her misdeeds.

Why old-time dances had been shelved in favor of such gymnastics as Ford saw on screen and stage and in private ballrooms of his friends he could not discover but he tried his best. He thought the modern dance failed largely because it began and ended with a single couple and there was no group fun in it.

Often when you were talking to him in office hours he would rise and stretch and suddenly shut out his empire, and he'd say, "Come on down to the dance floor—want to show you something I learned last night." At the two bays reserved for his parties and rehearsals he would consult the musicians who were always in attendance and they would start to play as directed. He'd say, "It goes like this—" and he would dance a few steps and ask what you thought of it.

A dance known as a galopade, a Hungarian prance to polka time, was tried at one party and a dejected Ford dropped into one of the laboratory offices to lodge a complaint next morning against the occupant.

"You didn't seem to get that step last night, Mr. Gray," he said, sorrowfully and shaking his head from side to side as if Mr. Gray had cracked a piece of machinery which could not be duplicated. The pupil admitted not getting the hang of it. "Watch now and I'll show you." Ford got up and moved rhythmically around the room, humming as he walked the measures. "Now you try it," he suggested.

The employee tried to synchronize his posturings with those of the boss but did not have success and he was also slightly dismayed by visitors and executives in adjoining offices who were watching the lesson through the glass partitions. To Mr. Ford, of course, the absorbed audience did not exist. His concern was in getting good Gray straightened out.

"Lovett is on the dance floor right now." Ford finally stopped him. "You see him and he'll clip off the rough edges."

At such a ukase you left your desk, whatever or however much was on it, and did as told, but you knew the step when you returned. The two, Ford and Lovett, were an unfailing partnership. Ford was always like this, an apostle of ceaseless industry one moment, ordering executives to the training camp five minutes after to brush up on a dance evolution.

He and Lovett did battle for years over how the Varsovienne and the five-step polka should be danced. They never did agree. The teacher stepped into the ballroom to find Ford demonstrating the French nougat for the benefit of Harry Bennett, head of his private police force.

"Mr. Lovett doesn't teach it right," he overheard Ford say as he parted the curtains.

The instructor made no comment but as the lesson proceeded he squirmed.

"Well, you're paying for it," he finally broke restraint, "and if you want it that way you shall have it." Lovett thought he might as well go all out. "Let me tell you I would hate to have a teacher who knows the dance see you doing it that way." The writhing artist was in full storm now. "Know what he'd say? He'd say, 'Why in the hell doesn't Mr. Ford hire a teacher who knows his business?' "

Ford laughingly threw up his hands and quit dancing. "Never

mind me, Harry; this Lovett knows his stuff. Do as he says," and he looked on meekly for another quarter hour while the teacher worked on the sweating gendarme.

He had a fascinating story, he said, for me one morning. That was his word for it. He had come upon a copy of *Harper's Weekly* of 1852—he was as excited as a boy who had found for the first time how to make a baseball dip—and there was a remarkable article in it. Remarkable was his word, too.

The French had invented a dance and called it the Varsovienne. Returning travelers apparently had told *Harper's* ship news men and said we ought to dance it over here. It was a standby at Ford parties but the country at large appeared to be unaware of it. He said I was to wait and he would send over to the house for the magazine so I could read the classic for myself. "A great story—the birth of the Varsovienne," he was muttering as he walked down the laboratory floor to tell a driver to go over home for it.

He took the magazine after I had read it and sped up the floor to the photographic department, and we walked back to the dance floor while photostats were being made.

"You remember it, don't you?" he asked. I knew the Astaires and the Castles, Pavlova and Doraldina, the first straw-skirt dancer, but I said unashamedly that I did not know the Varsovienne by that name but might if I ever saw it in front of me.

"I'll show you," my host offered, and he demonstrated the steps which Paris was dancing when Louis Napoleon set up the Second Empire.

I told him bluntly I still preferred Bill Robinson on a dance mat back in vaudeville's salad days but he only looked askance at me as if Robinson was a hula dancer and I a person of no taste.

The Fords were light on their feet and well mated for dancing except that he preferred a slow full-swaying rhythm for the waltz and she favored more ginger. Dancing together, they stopped in front of Lovett at one party and the chatelaine of Fair Lane asked for a faster tempo. Ford protested the music was fast enough. Such tight situations were handled by racing up the tempo for thirty bars and then dropping back to the slower pace.

"Are you trying to get me into trouble?" Lovett objected to the dilemma Ford put him in.

"I see you're a good strategist," was the answer, and that was all.

Privately, Ford could be as gusty as a teen-ager. A good friend who had been invited to see his antiques before his historical village was ready to receive them arrived one evening at the tractor plant with his wife. The watchman said if they walked down the hall over there they'd find both Mr. and Mrs. Ford waiting. "Can't miss them," he said confidently.

Part way down the jogging corridor the arrivals could hear strains of music they could not identify and a tapping of feet, and rounding a corner they came upon a room housing harmonicas and Sheffield tankards, Heppelwhite and countless blue pottery jugs of the same design—a phenomenon constantly recurring because Ford was always buying whole shops of antiques and snowed himself under with duplicates.

To one side was a refectory table and sitting on it was Mrs. Ford, clapping her hands in time and tapping the leg of the table with her foot while in the middle of the floor the master of the house jigged and got a lively accompaniment out of a jew's-harp.

"Come on along," he called as his guests hesitated at the door, taken slightly aback by the unexpected glimpse of domestic informality. The spell was broken. Mrs. Ford got off the table. Ford put his jew's-harp in its special rosewood box. Regulation masks were readjusted.

Nothing could have been more virginal than dancing at the Fords' but Isadora Duncan, international coryphee, rose up in Paris in the austerity of cheesecloth and sandals and laurel chaplet to point a finger and accuse Ford of surrendering to the sex instinct in reviving the old-time steps. The form might be different, she admitted, but she said sternly—and luckily in front of an American newspaper correspondent who may have hinted it might be a way to crash headlines—that the ancient steps were based as much on sex appeal as were the Charleston and the Black Bottom. She WAS surprised at Ford and she said she would as soon teach children foul words. She was surprised—for a whole column.

"I believe all these dances are inadvisable for children," her protest ran, "and I mean children of 1850 or children of today. The aim of educators should be to teach children movement based upon youthful heroic impulses, not upon sex impulses.

"You, Mr. Ford, would not teach children the dicta of Louis XV or George III. You should not teach them the servile courtesan movement of the minuet or the coquettish sex expression of the polka."

If Mr. Ford wanted her to teach real dancing to the children of America, all he had to do was send for her. She would come with joy and teach a dance which she said expressed the highest vision of the country as seen by the heroes of the Revolution and the great pioneers —"a dance which will be worthy of Abraham Lincoln."

Ford was busy with this and that and neglected to respond, failing even to cash his half of the publicity by a sharp rejoinder. He decided not to wind himself in tulle or put a rose in his lips and went right on with his libidinous gavottes.

He was a solicitous patron. If his dancing maestro made an error in calling a figure of the quadrille Ford would come to the rescue immediately and say to those nearby that Lovett actually had not called the number in a long time. Of older people he was thoughtful. When he invited them the calls were made simple, the music slow.

Ford talked little to his partner while dancing and seemed to carry his rectitude to the floor and make it part of his spinning. Mrs. Ford told you of the good book she had read, of the success of a new herb she had planted, of her roadside garden stands, of the goings and comings of familiar neighbors, or of an interesting house guest and what made him so. It might be Will Rogers or Louis Bromfield, David Lloyd-George or some princeling, but her dance floor chitchat did not encompass world affairs any more than any one else's.

He packed old dance orchestrations in his bags on Atlantic crossings, and one night on the *Majestic* when his host was breaking out champagne he left his glass untouched as usual and seized Mrs. Ford by the waist as the ship's band played a polka. On the *Bremen* when the orchestra struck up a melody several seasons later no one moved to dance but one couple.

"In einem Jahrtausend habe ich solche Musik nicht gehört," muttered a fellow passenger on the rail beside Oswald Garrison Villard, the editor, and began to hum softly.

"For a thousand years I would not know, *bitte,*" said Villard, "but it is sweet and good to hear again."

The only pair on the floor stood quietly for a moment getting into the swing of the music, and then the Fords were away in a mazurka, dancing as if they had the ship to themselves.

On the North German Lloyder he would dance every night and by day exclaim over the ship's bulbous underwater nose and sharp stern (the Germans got the idea by photographing a falling drop of water and Ford was intensely interested). He got the captain into a square dance, later sent him an automobile, and the captain wrote that he still thought running a ship was less a job than driving a car or stepping off the measures of a quadrille.

At his own parties he provided the dancing maestro occasionally with the names of women guests with whom he wished to dance, sometimes as many as a dozen, and in such cases a circle formation was arranged. His own favorite remained the quadrille. The dance manual had the same *leit-motif*—"Until one has known it, one has not known the most wholesome pleasure of dancing." He was first on the floor and last to leave.

Groups in Hawaii and Puerto Rico asked instruction. Children in Greenfield Village learned the minuet and Negro children on or near his Georgia plantation danced the polka and had fun. The dancing instructor's calendar spilled over with out-of-town engagements and the staff expanded. Young debs who danced at Dearborn returned to school in a glow, and soon disquieted managers of proms and cotillions decided to give the lancers a whirl and wrote in to learn how to manage it, half expecting Lovett to arrive in periwig by packet instead of bouncing in promptly on a plane to coach them in the steps.

Ford dances began at nine and ended at midnight. One had three hours of Ripple, Newport polka, valeta waltz, quadrilles and the rest of an assorted repertoire, and at 12 there were refreshments, with no double Martinis. There were no hat-check girls, no lushes in the lounge, no violets or kewpie dolls. No one rolled out a piano or bawled saffron lyrics, and no neckers ornamented the parked cars. The Fords preferred it that way, had it that way, and a lot of people were grateful for the nostalgic interlude.

Grace was necessary, but not athleticism; there was a dulcimer, but no trumpet. It was the quadrille that ruled, not the conga, and no one did bumps or turned cart-wheels. A Godey print became animated and swam before the eyes. It was fun. It was entertaining, at least, unless you were an executive and felt like homing in on a bad night. Wives of some officials got a little difficult occasionally after a siege of it. "But my dear" and "Don't dear me!" arguments developed over hints that it certainly was not mandatory, was it, to go to every party—they could not be all musts, could they?

Ford dancing ended at midnight and the orchestra played *Good Night, Ladies* and *Aunt Dinah's Quilting Party*. Usually the entire party circled round the host and hostess and sang the old songs, and you got into your car without benefit of supporting concierge or boys down from the campus and unsteady at the curb. The night was tranquil and the wind off the close-by woods clean and sweet, and it was all singularly disconnected, somehow, with the night shift under neons at the Rouge not far down the road.

It stopped as suddenly as it began. The Japs were at Pearl Harbor. Fourteen teachers enlisted or were drafted. A tired Lovett went back to New England on leave and quit for good the following year. The younger Ford died and a grieving father turned the key in the ballroom door. The boys who had danced swapped their slippers for combat boots and marched away to slog in the mud. Ford went into the plant to make the planes that gave them air cover.

Children and unknown soloists borrow from Ford's priceless collection, and acrobatic hillbillies bang famed Strads against knee and elbow.

CHAPTER IX

SAD ARE THE GHOSTS OF CREMONA

FORD ASSEMBLED one of the finest collections of violins in America and treated it with superb impiety as if the instruments were books in a drugstore library to be loaned to friend or stranger for a night or two years, dependent on his mood.

Shades of ancient masters may have held indignation meetings in the graveyards of Cremona and bewailed the irreverence; certainly there was bearishness over the practice where the buying and selling of such trophies are arranged today.

Ford might lend a fine, sensitive instrument to a musician more used to a fiddle he could bat across his knee. He would turn one over to a stranger to whose playing he took a fancy. He would lend one on the recommendation of a friend. He thought he heard genius in a child's fumbling bow and ordered she be given a Strad—a loan, of course—to see what she might do with a better instrument than her mail-order job.

I was barely seated with a Manhattan expert recently when he asked of the condition of the Ford collection. Distress was in his voice. "Tell me," he quavered, "in what shape is the Amati? Do you know?" The earliest purchase of the Dearborn *pukka sahib* was a fiddle of fabulously rich golden varnish and empyrean tone from the seventeenth century workshop of Stradivari's teacher. I had to say to the worried man I was wholly ignorant as an appraiser or reporter in the field.

"The last time I saw it"—the gentleman might have been the shocked curator of the Louvre who had come in some morning and found a toe off the Venus—"it was nicked and the varnish was badly chipped." The man before me shuddered. He scowled at the memory. He wished Ford had used more perception.

Unlike some collectors Ford had no desire to hoard or hide his acquisitions. He took no particular delight in getting them out in the quiet of home when he was alone and picking out a small melody for his own ear. With the main body of fanciers, too, he recognized that a violin was made to be played and not primarily to be looked at, and, since he did not play skillfully himself, he was quite willing to have them played by those who knew how.

Morgan the Elder paid $1,500 for his first painting when he was twenty-two; Ford put down $15,000 in his sixties for his first fiddle of note. His decision to collect dated to the '20's and the reasons were two. One propulsion was a summer neighbor on Lake Huron, the other a repentant thief who decided after forty years to return what he had stolen. The neighborly influence was Rudolph Wurlitzer, founder of the instrument house of that name. Ford said to him one day, "I wish you'd send out some good violins for me to look over."

The other event was more unusual. When Ford yielded to family entreaty—and a bribe of forty acres of wooded farmland—to stay home where he might amount to something and drop the preposterous idea of being a mechanic, he was twenty-one. He had gone into the shops of Detroit at sixteen and when he had first quit home he hung his violin on a hook in the barn. When he returned it was gone.

The disappearance was long a mystery. It was a mill-run instrument of no intrinsic value except in association and, if he had not had a prodigious memory for trifles, it probably would have been forgotten. In restoring the homestead of his birth, Ford remembered the name, make and model of a kitchen stove and the precise pattern of a parlor carpet. A lawyer would give him a curbstone opinion on some complex problem and be astounded a year later if he tried to reverse himself to get a quick "But a year ago you told me so-and-so," having almost his exact words flung back at him. A mind of that kind did not easily forget a vanished violin. A sweeper walked into Ford's private office with it two-score years later. He undid a bundle and sheepishly unwrapped the violin of Ford's youth. When I saw the motormaker the next day he was still enormously excited.

"What did happen to it?" I asked.

The sweeper, who had been a neighbor boy in the township at the time, merely had taken it from the shed and now had brought it back, an undistinguished instrument but prized more than any of Ford's nobler additions. He put it to his shoulder as we stood there, and fingered the strings happily. The tone seemed off to me but to him it was celestial.

"Mr. Ford," blurted the man who had brought it back, after an uneasy shifting from foot to foot for a few nervous seconds, "this thing has been preying on me." He took a deeper breath. "Years ago I was playing with some boys in your paw's barn." He interlaced his fingers. "I was ten then and I saw this fiddle on a nail, and I always wanted a fiddle. Well, sir; I wanted it bad and I swiped it."

Ford asked how he explained to his folks how he had come by the instrument, but didn't seem to be listening to the answer, being too busy examining what had been lost so long.

"Told them it must have fell off a wagon and I picked it up by the road," the sweeper said. "That's a long time back, ain't it?" he remarked, as if to himself. He also might have been reflecting on the financial gulf between two country boys who had started from the same county line. "Got five children now," he said irrelevantly.

Ford said he was sure glad to get it back and to hear about the children, and thanks.

"Oh, that's all right, Henry"—it was Henry now that the sin was absolved. "I'm certainly obliged for the loan." He turned and trudged out.

I wanted to telephone my photographer and perhaps have the return of the violin reënacted, but Ford said the story was just between us. Publicity might embarrass the employee.

In a playful moment a Detroit jurist, brought up in the Michigan copper country, asked an orchestra leader at a neighborhood club if he could borrow his violin for a moment. When he returned to his wife and other members of his party he played a jig or two on it. He played softly, or so he thought, so not to attract the attention of other guests, but when he had finished his impromptu concert an interested semicircle had formed behind him—among them an interested Ford.

"Where did you learn to play those, Judge?" he asked.

The jurist said that was the sort of music he danced to as a boy. Ford called another tune and asked if he knew it. Yes—he played it. Did he know this one? Ford took the fiddle and played a few bars. The judge named it quickly. In his mail a day or two later was an envelope containing a guest card to Ford's golf club and on it was, "To a first-class fiddler—better than H. Ford."

Beatrice Griffin, a pre-war violin soloist on continental stages and recently back from Sweden, was one of the earliest to whom Ford played patron. Ossip Gabrilowitsch, conductor of the Detroit Symphony Orchestra, engaged her as soloist while she was a pupil of his concertmaster, but the conductor was skeptical of the adequacy of the fiddle she played. It would redound to the girl's credit if Ford could be cajoled into loaning a violin for the debut—but could it be negotiated?

There was little on which to base hope. When Ford had been approached for a subscription to the orchestra he was curt in saying no.

"Any top organization of any kind ought to be able to get along on a self-supporting basis," he worded his refusal.

The conclusion was he had little interest in the music field, but still the hopeful Gabrilowitsch mentioned the need to a friend close to Ford. If he was cold to subscription campaigns, he was rarely indifferent to appeals for help in particular cases. Ford telephoned a few nights later and asked if it was possible for the conductor to drop out to his home either this night or the next. Gabrilowitsch said, "Right away," and started. Alone in his house, Ford talked a half hour of everything but what had brought the orchestra maestro, exhibited his Americana, told of a recent visit with Fritz Kreisler, put himself on record as bored and bewildered by some music and captivated by other melodies.

"Personally," he said, "I'm old-fashioned enough to like Stephen Foster's songs."

"Nobody," said the virtuoso, "is old-fashioned because he likes Foster. He's imperishable. His music will go on as long as Wagner's or Puccini's."

"They'll be singing his songs, Mr. Gabrilowitsch, long after automobiles are out of date," Ford predicted. "Oh, by the way—about that young girl of yours. Would you mind picking out a violin for her concert?"

He waved to a table on which a fortune in fiddles had been laid out.

The conductor examined the lot admiringly but suggested that it might be better for the concertist to choose for herself if Ford didn't mind. Ford said he thought that would be better, and so for a one-man audience Miss Griffin played a couple of nights later a concert of simple melodies at Fair Lane, but found when she concluded she could not make up her mind between a 1709 Strad and a Guarnerius. She finally settled on the first, after some wrestling with herself.

"It'll be delivered to you tomorrow," Ford promised; "and I'm grateful for a fine evening."

He decided to reduce the mental strain on his new acquaintance by sending her both violins over which she had been torn in making a choice. His messenger brought them with him. "There is no hurry, Mr. Ford says, about returning them," he assured her.

Miss Griffin retained the Siberian Strad for two years at Ford's urging. The violin took its name from the fact that in the 1870's it was owned in Ekaterinburg, close to the Siberian border, a little town which was to be in the cables a half century later when, in one of its cellars, a Bolshevik firing squad brought to an end the ruling house of Russia. The fiddle, its head and rich plum varnish considered exceptional, remained in the Urals until the '80's, when it reached a London dealer who sold it in Cairo. In 1910 it was held in England, and still later went to a Berlin collector.

The Guarnerius, product of Stradivari's most gifted pupil, Joseph Guarnerius del Jesu, and known as the ex-Doyen, previously belonged to a Paris amateur of that name who had owned at the same time the Kreutzer Strad, now at Oxford, and Ford was charmed the first time he ran a bow over it. Its varnish is rich golden red, its tone as robustious as Paganini proved the Guarnerius to be.

Violins were usually demonstrated in Ford's private office. The dealer's agent acquainted him with the fiddle's history. There were the customary holes in it. Violin biographies are notoriously fragmentary. The art in Cremona reached its peak more than two centuries ago and surviving examples naturally have passed through a host of hands. The situation is also complicated by those copied and mislabeled. Strads extant number about 400, and a few more than half are in American collections.

An offered instrument was played for an attentive satrap at Dearborn. Usually the music was a few bars from *Home, Sweet Home* and invariably there was a familiar jig. (Not long after the Ford Sunday Radio hour was launched, the motormaker felt that *Turkey in the Straw* should be sandwiched between *The Bartered Bride* and Beethoven's *Emperor* piano concerto, and from then on musicians accepted it as *de rigueur* since it was a sock hit with the sponsor.)

He might on occasion run a bow over the strings himself. He made up his mind quickly. There was no bargaining over price if he was taken by a fiddle. If he did not want what was shown him, no cut rate would make a difference. He did not want a violin because it was cheap but because it appealed to him—and he had a rare tonal sense.

"No, I just don't like it," he might say.

Or he might break in on a tune, carry a fiddle to a window to examine its varnish and design and state of preservation, or pick at the strings himself.

"It's a good job," he used to say when his mind was favorably made up. "Give him a check."

The description "good job" seemed to stick in the memory of the seller. No one heard any other collector put it quite that way and the trade smiled a little but said, why not? After all, that's what a violin was or wasn't. Ford had no time for studio patter.

The vault filled. Came the Bergonzi of 1746, a type considered distinctly unusual; the storied Maud Powell from the workshop of Guadagnini, a Strad of 1703 once owned by Sir William Curtis, mayor of London; several bows of Francine Tourte—$3,000 to $5,000 for these—with a particularly opulent example in original tortoise shell, precious stones to each side of a gold-mounted frog and in the end a rare pearl screw button, which had belonged to the Russian ambassador to France of the First Empire, and a viola of Jacob Stainer of the Tyrol.

Ford made concessions to orthodoxy. Since the collection was housed in a steel vault, the instruments were taken out and rubbed every ninety days with an olive oil and alcohol mixture. Each was contained in a silken bag and in each sack was a sliced potato to provide the necessary moisture. Every three months a symphony violinist came to exercise them and play first one and then another throughout the day.

Absent-minded at times, Ford might drop into the secretarial office and remark that he guessed he would take the Guarnerius home for the night. It might be gone a couple of months, and then one morning he would walk in and ask for it. "Don't you remember, Mr. Ford, that you got it some time ago and you said at the time you were taking it home?" It was no use mentioning that also at the time Ford said he would have it back next day.

"I did?" he would exclaim when reminded he had gone off with a violin a long time back. "Wonder what I did with it," he would say, surprised but seldom disputing.

He always seemed to find and return any missing violin or watch, but where he kept them in their absences from the regular depository no one ever knew except him. He seemed to be able to go straight to them when the subject was brought up. Once he had been using the side of a haystack as a pillow for a nap and left a fiddle in the field overnight.

If a guest, close or casual, happened to admire one of the Strads and show a glimmer of musicianship Ford was likely to say: "Want to take it home and try it? Go ahead." The visitor might think the magnanimity could not be true but soon would be walking out with the treasure.

A teacher in chapel might speak well of a child and confide that Harry, the boy in the third row, second seat in, seemed to have a soupçon of talent as a violinist. Ford might appear in the classroom doorway some morning later with a $5,000 to $20,000 violin in hand and suggest that Harry be allowed to try it for a day or a week or more to see what he could do on a good fiddle. It was a bounty appalling to those who looked upon the instruments as relics to be cosseted and handled gingerly against the inevitable day of final extinction.

I put the protest up to Ford once.

"Take that Messiah Strad in England," he retorted, rather pointlessly, it seemed. "It needs no more attention than occasional new strings and a little glue."

"But the Messiah," I suggested, "has careful museum attention and is not loaned to the first fellow who comes along."

"Playing on them doesn't hurt them," Ford persisted, sure of his ground here as he was sure of most things. "It's not playing on them that injures them."

Ford heard with appreciation a pupil of Jacques Thibaud who made his debut at the age of seven with the Los Angeles Philharmonic and came East in time and went on to Europe and Australia before the war, to concertize triumphantly. He was Grischa Goluboff, a Californian.

His radio debut in Detroit as a soloist with Victor Kolar conducting on the Ford Sunday Evening Hour in 1934 suggested a happy promotional idea. Would it not be splendid if Grischa, then twelve, would play one of Ford's own violins? The boy might be a child of destiny. There were some who thought the fact that Grischa was a young Jew and Ford had apologized profoundly only a few years before for a long attack on Grischa's people was not outside the calculations. Lending the boy one of his great violins might be considered a token gesture of continuing abnegation.

No critic failed to note that Master Goluboff had played the Tschaikowsky concerto and Sarasate's *Caprice Basque* on a $100,000 Stradivarius from the Ford collection, although the figure was publicity fiction. None of the instruments in the Dearborn vault approached that figure or came to half it. Some $35,000 was paid for one violin but that was approximately top.

The carping reviewers said the young prodigy played with obvious nervousness, which may have been natural in a twelve-year-old drawing a bow over a borrowed Strad, but Ford took the nettles out of the notices by going backstage to compliment the soloist and to tell him he was exceedingly good; and he offered more proof of his favor.

"Why don't you take the Strad along with you," he suggested, "and play it all season?"

Ford slapped the boy on the shoulder and said to go right ahead and use it by all means. Goluboff kept it for the season.

From time to time Ford seemed to surrender to the remonstrances of those about him and agree that his might not be the best way to preserve a collection. He would reform! Violins outstanding would be recalled and repaired when necessary, but the reformation was short-lived. The half-million collection would be back clandestinely on lend-lease in no time. The promise of restraint was largely made with mental reservations, even though the return of some prized fiddle in disreputable repair might annoy him temporarily and incline him to the idea that maybe he was too prodigal.

When the urge to munificence was stronger than his will to be stern he would circumvent the custodians and multiply secretarial fretting by going into the vault himself, without announcement, taking the violin he desired, and disappearing with it without record of the name of the man or woman, boy or girl, who next day would have it.

This easily could be managed by the ruse of dispatching secretaries on errands to distant points so he might rummage unseen in his own vault, or he might get the wanted violin during his nightly tours. It was never uncommon for a watchman to run into the boss in the plant at any hour of night, bent on some little task that had just occurred to him and which could not wait until morning, he thought; or it might be he was there for no other reason than to see how his Antaeus had made out in the day's grind.

Violins of lesser breed had a Renaissance of their humble own when Ford took to dancing. Fiddlers of hoary strains came out of their cracks everywhere. Instruments long stowed in garrets emerged in roughened hands of pleasant rustics and set up a national caterwauling. The revival produced, among others, a foeman who shamed Ford by the length of his press clippings. Name: A. Melanson Dunham. Age: seventy-two. Home: Norway, Maine. Mellie made snowshoes but his principal claim to stardom was that he was "champion" fiddler of his state. Ford asked him to perform at Dearborn, and Dunham, who looked every ruddy inch a Santa Claus, proceeded to make a novice of Ford at wangling headlines.

He was one of the numerous champs who bounced from caves and walked down the mountains when the countryside found the old dance steps not so stale and joyless as it may have thought them at first. A Tennessee gallant claimed to have won an old-time fiddling title in Texas and flung shrill challenge at pretenders. A Hopedale, Mass., contestant won a loving cup by beating 200 others in a radio tourney. Ford and Thomas Edison found and lionized a Jep Bisbee, of Michigan, being so captivated that he was hurried to Jersey to be recorded on platters, and Mr. Ford shipped him a sedan in admiration. Hundreds of others had their ringing say about their own merit.

Dunham was a wrinkled glamor boy and a Disney character, and Ford was only a member of the supporting cast from the hour that Mellie, on his way to Dearborn, stepped out of a weather-stained farmhouse in which he was born until he landed on the stage of the New York Hippodrome as a feature act next in billing to Miss Irene Franklin. He made only one concession to the gala journey. His wife helped him pick out a new ninety-cent cap before he set out for the empire of Ford in a private railroad car, handsomely bannered, on a honeymoon trip for which he and Ma had waited fifty years, and waved off by an exultant town.

The Boston *Post,* which seemed to have men stationed at every stop, reported him in khaki shirt open at the throat, no collar, tie or vest; a pair of homespun trousers slightly the worse for six years' wear and a pair of woodsman's heavy boots. Dunham was smart, had smart advice, or had no other pants. He never overdid his prominence.

Ford sent a personal representative in a Lincoln. Ralph O. Brewster, the present senior senator from Maine, then Governor, dispatched a colonel from his staff. Five thousand thronged the train shed. Placards shouted: *One of Nature's Noblemen* and *God Speed You, Merrie Gentleman* and *Mellie Will Fiddle and Henry Will Dance* and *Send Them Back Safely, Henry*. Movies shot them, the high sheriff rode a horse at the head of a police escort, Mellie doffed his cap and Ma waved her handkerchief, and guardsmen had to poke a lane through the jam to the coach steps.

Fred Sanborn, the town editor, gave $25 for tobacco money, though Mellie didn't smoke. The postmaster climbed aboard with a pouch of fan mail. A band played *Till We Meet Again* as the train pulled out, and the Dunhams cried a little in passing a cemetery where their only daughter was buried. The governor himself mounted a milk truck at South Paris and wished them well. Their nine children came aboard to be kissed.

"Now, listen," said Ma to the eldest, "look out for those kids. Send the papers to Rose. Send the baby his stockings and look out for everything I've told you to do."

They gave him a diary and at Island Pond he made his first entry: "Me and Emma are having the time of our lives." The train was off for Montreal.

"Nice seats; I like 'em," remarked Mellie. He found farther on that he could open a Pullman window and he stuck his head out to say hello at Berlin, New Hampshire. "Get his head in before he loses it!" shrieked Ma. "Give him a whack before I do." The Canadian Snowshoe Club tendered a dinner at Montreal. At midnight he was back on his first railroad sleeper. "Kind of a slimpy bed," he suggested, "But I suppose we got to try everything they put in front of us."

At Dearborn, Mr. Ford was also there. Mr. Dunham, the *bon vivant,* charmed the guests with his tunes and informality, his blue eyes and his unconcern over where he was and everything that had gone before.

Then, a little to Ford's secret admiration, Mel went back to Norway, mailed his recent host a laconic post-card: *Thanks for good time,* organized some townspeople into an act, and went trouping in vaudeville, giving an approximation of a New England barn dance.

"He did pretty good for himself, didn't he?" granted Ford afterward. It was understatement.

His experience with another violinist did not throw Ford off stride quite as much as his unsettling encounter with the champion of Maine. He bought Botsford Inn, a tavern where it was not uncommon in the old days to find a thousand Detroit-bound cattle in the yards while their owners relaxed at the bar.

Ford put in courting mirrors, colored prints that had tickled Grandpa into spasms, created an old-fashioned garden of sweet William and pinks and mignonette and lilacs, brought up a forest of pine from his own farm and replanted it to the rear of the tavern; on a nail in the hall hung a size 22 collar of John L. Sullivan. Long before a gentleman on a dance floor began to throw his lady the length of the hall, they used to find gayety here in the Flower Dance, the Prince of Wales schottische and the New York polka.

When he owned the inn he asked about musicians who used to play there. That is how Vaughnley Gunning came to be mentioned. He had a farm down the road a piece now. We started. I remember coming on a farmer along the way who was leaning on his plow handles and Ford saying: "We've too many farmers who plow with one-eighth of an eye on the plow and the other seven-eighths looking for a real-estate subdivider."

Gunning laughed as if he'd split at the idea he should come to the inn and play.

"Me?" He put down his milking pails. He was seventy-three. He extended his gnarled hands. "Look at them," he said. He was too sick, besides. He wasn't feeling pert at all. Not him, he said. "Glad to see you any time, Mr. Ford, but the answer as to whether I'll play at the tavern is no." He smiled ruefully, and picked up his pails again.

No one could lick the rock in Ford so easily. He was back in two weeks. Gunning apparently had been thinking over how good he used to be. He was not so obstinate this time. "I tell you," he finally said, "I'd kind of like to play my old violin again but it's out in Kansas City somewhere."

Telegrams flew to Ford dealers in the area. The boss wanted a certain violin. Drop everything! Maybe it was at the home of a Gunning relative. He had provided that frail clue, but Vaughnley had said he wasn't really sure where the fiddle was. It was located and flown to Dearborn for a test run and lubrication job.

Restoration of the tavern moved apace—mohair in the parlor, bedeviling pictures like "The Sailor's Adieu" and "Godey's Fashions of 1864" for the walls, yarn-winders and powder-horns, hot charcoal foot-warmers and a fire horn given to a long-dead and forgotten Captain Davock in 1846. Ford even got some gophering irons with which Grandma curled her bonnet ribbons. The bar was polished. Grandpa Botsford had once bought rye there, the books said, at sixteen cents a gallon wholesale and marked it up to twenty-five cents over the counter.

Ford packed the rejuvenated Gunning fiddle under his arm and went back to the farm.

"Well, here it is," he said. "Now how about playing?"

The man who used to play at the inn raised it to position. His unpracticed fingers fumbled at first, but the touch grew surer, the music jiggier. In a month, Mr. Gunning reported for duty and the Fords and their friends often danced late to his effervescent music.

An engine that conked out over the Atlantic brought pain to the collector of fiddles and fiddlers, however. The hobby threw Ford and a fine old player of *Money Musk* together, and the violinist told Ford one day that the song of the propeller seemed to be ringing in his young son's ears as other lads had listened to siren winds in the rigging of four-masters or watched an express train pass and felt a fierce urge to drive one.

"Send him to Dearborn and let me talk to him," Ford said helpfully.

Harry Brooks was nineteen. He put on overalls, worked as

riveter, learned designing, testing—in a year and a half was chief test pilot. He flew Lindbergh's mother to Mexico City. He winged back and forth from plant to nearby suburban home in what he and the man who worked with him called a flivver plane—twenty-five feet of wingspread, that's all—but Harry dreamed great dreams of it, one of breaking the world's record for distance. Ford said to Harry's father, "You know, he does to a plane what you do to a fiddle."

To see how much the bantam plane could take Brooks set out from Detroit for Florida. The pilot got to Titusville, Florida, and had to sit down to await a new propeller. He climbed for the last lap to Miami, when it arrived; set out over an upset ocean. Watchers followed him, a diminishing dot in a black sky. A battered plane was washed up on a littered beach next day. The sea had swallowed the fiddler's boy.

A billionaire applies spit and polish to a humpty-dumpty railroad, rides the swaying coal of the tender, promotes a crap game.

CHAPTER X

THE LITTLE TOY TRAIN

ONE IS undecided where to hang emphasis in a discussion of Henry Ford, railroader—on a crap game he maneuvered with an all-colored cast in the diner of his special train or on the fact he took a line which had one foot, or both, in the grave, made it the only American road in technicolor and after nine years sold it at a profit of $9,000,000.

Under his sponsorship, wherever the underscoring belongs, old No. 424 and her cronies in the roundhouse flounced around curves with coquettish and nickled swish as if they had just bounced out of Adrian's. A vacuuming of the road each morning hardly would produce a full dustpan. The almshouse atmosphere disappeared. The Detroit, Toledo & Ironton became a lady under his management and a respectable carrier which demanded and got value for her favors.

Admirers of Ford insisted at the time that those running other lines were slowpokes and even scoundrels and that he ought to be czar of the country's transportation. Perhaps, they said, the need of government financial help for railroads was less than the need of six Henry Fords to run them wisely.

Critics said his railroad was a plant facility, wondered if an ingenious way had not been found to evade the law on rebates, and asserted that under the same set of circumstances any road would pay. To rivals he was a crazy influence and they were not friendly to his entrance into the field. No one ran up to embrace him or to say, "Glad to have you with us, Mr. Ford."

It is sometimes wisdom to take second things first, despite the claim to the contrary, so the dice game is promoted to significance because it seemed so to those who saw it.

Ford headed an inspection tour south a few days after taking over the road. With him were a dozen members of his staff and two other consultants, Frederick Osborn, then president of the D. T. & I. and a major general on the Army General Staff in World War II, and Kenneth Chorley, division superintendent at the time and currently president of Colonial Williamsburg, Virginia restoration of the Rockefellers.

Ford and the two experienced railroaders were so absorbed that until they dispersed at midnight no one noticed that the rest of the party, together in the observation car earlier, had drifted off and apparently had gone to bed. As the remaining three broke up and walked through the train, they learned the true reason for the desertions. On a table in the diner the absconders were shooting dice and a player was trying to make a point of four against united opposition and the usual catcalls. Edsel Ford was among them but the senior Ford seemed tired and indifferent. He said good-night pleasantly enough and went on to his compartment.

Business discussions were resumed next morning. It was during a pause and without turning in his seat that Ford said to his son directly behind him, "Edsel, what was that game you were playing last night?"

"It was craps, Father," the son responded.

"I thought so," the senior Ford reached for the porters' bell. "George," he asked when one responded, "do you shoot dice?"

The attendant said he did not. "I got myself religion a while back, Mr. Ford," he reported, "and I'm through with gambling." The sinner who had quit the primrose path asked if there was anything else.

Ford asked about the other porters. A half dozen were rounded up. Did they shoot craps? They certainly did—yes, suh, Mr. Ford! This was apparently a new boss of delightful tastes. Did they roll dice? Man, oh man!

"Well that's fine," the man in the lounge chair said. "We're going to have a big game in the diner after lunch."

The porters withdrew, highly pleased. Executives on the side lines glanced at one another in some perplexity. Ford asked the conductor to stop the train at the next station and wire ahead for a half dozen Mason jars and $30 in nickels, and when the party went forward to the dining car in mid-afternoon he was sitting at a table and in front of him were the six glass jars, each holding five dollars in nickels.

Tables were moved to the far end of the car to provide a clear floor for play and the master of ceremonies announced the rules. It was to be freeze-out. Loss of all the coins in any jar eliminated the owner of the jar. Whoever won all the change was to be adjudged champion.

The start was quiet but the tempo picked up as first one player and then another dropped their stakes. When only three remained the fray took on the usual emotional overtones of a hard fought dice game, as points were thrown and made, tossed and lost.

The porters on the floor put in extra digs. They wriggled, exhorted, sweated, rolled their eyes, squirmed, talked to the tumbling ivories affectionately and not so affectionately and worked their wrists and elbows with flourish. In the end the steaming victor alone remained, flat on his stomach with arms about the stakes an hour's perspiring battle had won. If Ford wanted entertainment the porters gave a bang-up show.

"That was good work," he congratulated the winner, and he thanked the others for a fine if not as lucky an exhibition. The audience filed back into the observation car, still wondering slightly at the meaning of what they had seen, and got down to serious conversations again.

Another break occurred a couple of hours later and Ford made his point on the crap game he had staged. In a lull he said: "I THOUGHT, Edsel, that craps was a colored man's game." No more was said, but Ford had made clear by the histrionics of the diner he considered dice undignified for a member of his personal household. He still thought of the game in terms of his own youth before five million doughboys came back from the camps of Europe, schooled in it as well as in arms.

Ford and the D. T. & I. entered into wedlock over the opposition of almost his entire organization. His counsellors thought he was too deeply involved in other activities and said—this rather *sotto voce*—another good reason for leaving the deal alone was that he knew nothing about running a railroad.

But the road's light, twisting and senile rails ran south 380 miles from Detroit to the Ohio River and strategically crossed every main line railroad east and west. They offered access to coal fields of three states. Speed was essential to get his huge volume to assembly points and slash the time of inventory in transit. What he wanted most, however, was a continuous flow of coal to his voracious furnaces.

Osborn had a plan for a bond issue to develop a terminal serving industries in southwest Detroit. Rail congestion was bad at that point and companies were pretty much at the mercy of the Pennsylvania and New York Central. He got a good commitment from an alkali company and then went to Dearborn to see if Ford could be interested.

The road's inadequacies were not hidden and could not be. It had not paid a dividend in fifty years. It had been through one wringer after another. Tracks, cars and engines were largely worn out. Osborn drew an honest but hardly rosy picture for a prospective investor.

But the railroad's losses, he argued, were due primarily to a single cause. Since it controlled no traffic, the road received something less than a switching charge from big operators as its proportion of rates from Detroit to both seaboards.

He had a cure. "If we can go to main junction points and dicker on a basis of a large quantity of high-grade carload freight," he told Ford, "they'll be forced to grant the D. T. & I. a fairer division. Thus the road will jump into the black immediately."

Ford took Osborn out into the shop to see some experimental motors and invited him to come back next day when the senior Ford outlined the idea sketchily but enthusiastically to Edsel and other top executives.

"What about buying the road, Edsel?" he wound up.

The junior Ford said he liked the possibilities.

"How much can we have it for?" Ford turned on Osborn.

"Five million."

"We'll take it." Ford got up from the table. He paid 60 cents a dollar on the bonds, $5 a share for the preferred, $1 for the common, and assumed $1,800,000 in first mortgage and car trust bonds.

When Osborn returned in two weeks to close the sale a Ford lieutenant had engaged Ford, Bacon & Davis to report on the road and said Ford Motor could not go ahead with the purchase until the report was in. The proposed postponement was a surprise to Ford himself.

"Who are they?" he demanded.

"They" were engineering consultants who would prepare an inventory.

"Mr. Osborn has told us the engines are broken down, that the road has no cars to speak of and the rails are rusted out," broke in Ford, not one to be braked by cautious counsel if his mind was set. "All they have so far as I can see is a right of way to the Ohio River. They have been operating a hundred years and I guess they must own it."

He opposed delay. "Tell those engineers we don't need them," he ordered.

The bride came to him with hardly an unraveled stitch to her back. The D. T. & I. boasted no crack Pyrenees-Côte d'Azure Express or blue trains. It had no spas or scenery to charm travelers. An overall antiquity gave the impression that Jesse James or Geronimo lurked in the woods along the roadbed and was likely to ride down on engine and crew at any time. Scenario writers might glamorize the Union Pacific, but no one hurried down a plush hall to see Mr. Mayer or Mr. Goldwin to urge there was good movie material in the despondent D. T. & I. and its 26 reorganizations.

After the first inspection under his ownership I asked Ford if he still liked his buy and what kind of a trip he had.

"We weren't scalped," he shrugged, "but otherwise we were back in pioneer days. We can do a lot with it, though."

Osborn had been right. In three months an agreement was negotiated with intersecting main lines under which the D. T. & I. got an average rate boost of .018 cents per ton-mile as against six or seven mills per ton paid previously. Some carriers considered the percentage excessive but they knew Ford could divert his huge tonnage elsewhere if they balked.

He bought locomotives and flat cars and coal cars, and when he found new engines came to $60,000 apiece he rebuilt old ones for $35,000 and they turned out good as new. The glandular treatments kept many a locomotive on the tracks long after it was thought ready for the taxidermist. He loved to take the bones of old engines and fit them back snugly into their original sockets.

Maintenance costs seemed high and he approached his superintendent with a proposal to build track on steel ties laid in cement.

"It won't work, Mr. Ford," the seasoned railroader said. On curves he was sure it would be fatal.

"But why?"

"You cannot operate on a rigid rail," he demonstrated with pencil and paper how a track moved under a train.

Ford didn't believe it. He proceeded to construct a long stretch of track laid on steel sunk in concrete. He was fair about it, too—he put a curve in it—and the whole cost him several hundred thousand dollars.

The road done, he wanted a train run over it to see if he was right or wrong. A locomotive and two passenger cars were detached from regular service but it was not so easy to find an engineer and fireman who were willing to risk their necks. The hitch was overcome, however, when two fearless lads consented and Mr. Ford invited friends to see his vindication—or whatever might come.

The train clattered down the solid track to the curve and once on it, climbed the rail, as predicted, and ran off like a race-horse leaping the infield fence and quitting the track.

"Do it again." The boss man was unconvinced.

The second run was a repetition but Ford was still unsatisfied and demanded a third performance. It went no better than the other two.

"That'll do—tear up the track!" he turned away and said he guessed it wouldn't work. He had to see for himself. It was the way he learned his lessons.

Wages were rescaled. He sent for Chorley and wanted to know how much engineers, firemen, brakemen and lesser fry got and how many hours they worked. He wanted to change all that and named figures substantially above prevailing rates.

"Also"—he surprised Chorley—"I want to pay engineers as much as conductors."

The superintendent said this was a rude violation of practice, that the conductor was boss of the train. It was because he was in charge and responsible for the train's operation that he got more money than the engineer, but Ford, engineer himself, disputed the logic. With a head full of novel notions he quarreled with custom persistently.

"All a conductor does on a passenger train is to pick up a few tickets," he persisted, belittling that worthy's role. "And what does he do on a freight train? He sits pretty in a caboose." In his voice was triumph. No, sir, the responsibility was the engineer's. Pay him as much as the conductor!

He was reminded there was a little matter of wage arrangements with the railroad brotherhoods. What about existing agreements? It was a problem the superintendent thought well to discuss with Warren S. Stone, president of the Brotherhood of Locomotive Engineers. Stone was interested and reassuring.

"Put the rates into effect," he smiled, "and there'll be no difficulty."

Stone revealed a little more of what he was thinking when Chorley reached for his hat.

"You see where this puts me, Mr. Chorley," the union chief remarked. "I am now in stronger position to get increases from other roads."

Engineers and conductors on the Ford roster got $375 for 208 hours, their fellows on other lines $250 to $275 for the same time. In the lower brackets rates were proportionately higher than on other roads. The lowest-paid D. T. & I. employee received $1,872 for 2,496 hours a year. Employees of other lines in the same class averaged $1,538 for 2,584 hours.

Whole trains were bathed and scrubbed and varnished and tightened. Ballast was neatened, cutoffs built, curves and heavy grades eliminated. Industries along the line were asked to clean up and to move back in some cases to reduce the chance of sideswiping. Roundhouse walls were painted white and washed daily. Even the inside of desk drawers got the same color so any dirt would be sure to show. Out with all dinginess!

Aluminum floors were laid in cabs, fixtures were nickeled, chairs with nine-inch spring-cushion seats eased the rumps of engine crews. The countryside was dazzled by the make-up and took some time to become used to the new cosmetics.

For the dictatorship of precedent Ford substituted his own authoritarianism. He would have no smoking. He shut down Sundays. Engines had to be cleaned after each trip. Titles were out.

Claims for personal injury or freight claims were to be wound up in a week or less, but one wasn't. No. 5, south bound, sailed off the tracks and turned over near a small Ohio town, but only one person was seriously injured. Adjusters located all but a single passenger and he had been last seen zigzagging across a plowed field as if afraid the train behind him was about to explode. He was apparently going to be as far as possible from the blast when it happened.

A clue led to Kentucky. As a company adjuster plunged deeper into the hills, both they and the reputation of the runaway passenger got worse. A fellow at the gas station in the valley nodded over the description.

"Probably Joe Bent," he said. "Better let him alone." The agent asked why but the native would not say.

The man in the lean-to up the slope was not as talkative as the one in the valley but he asked more questions and seemed to know of Joe's unsettling train ride. Joe had said when he came back that he should have stuck to muleback.

"Does he farm around here?" asked the adjuster.

"Guess so, son," the hillman said, dryly. He glanced up the path and down. "Might be better if you didn't go up there, boy. You might be all right, as you say, but he wouldn't know that until it was too late." He spat four yards. "Joe doesn't like company." He added almost as an after-thought: "Had to shoot a couple of fellows once."

The agent looked up the path into the disquietude of the woods, too, and developed a distinct apathy over any shock Mr. Bent might have suffered in the railroad accident. He took the down path whistling feebly.

The name of Bent, the moonshiner, was carried a long time on the D. T. & I. books in case he ever bobbed up with wounds he might charge to the railroad, but he presumably thought that by diligence and his squirrel rifle he would last longer in the hills than by ever trusting a railroad again.

Long before he bought the D. T. & I., Ford was critical of railroad rolling stock. The heavy locomotives and the cars they pulled were the reason to him for the high expense of keeping roadbeds in shape.

He tried his hand with a light steel car. His secretary telephoned the railroad one morning to announce a new type of passenger car had been completed and that Mr. Ford wanted to take it out on the line for a test run. Would the superintendent make arrangements for right of way? The superintendent suggested, on his part, that it might be well for a motive power expert to look over the car before the run began.

Ford's secretary curtly asked why.

"We'll check for width and height to make sure we'll clear bridges and the like," the superintendent said. "The brakes ought to be tested by someone familiar with railroad needs."

The secretary said stiffly he did not think this would be at all necessary since Mr. Ford always knew what he was doing. However, there was an over-night change of heart. The head of motive power was instructed to look over the car.

"Say, Ken," that gentleman called a short time later, "this new car has NO brakes."

"Are you sure?"

"Come over and see for yourself."

Whoever was responsible had failed to provide the car with some means of stopping once it had started. The trial run was hastily cancelled, the oversight corrected, and on a later day the car rolled out for its experimental trip. Instructions were to secure right of way from Detroit to Springfield, Ohio, where the party would spend the night.

The car was shorter than the ordinary passenger car. It had the usual center aisle between two rows of wicker chairs and operated a good deal like an automobile except that no steering was necessary. The driver sat in a forward corner.

The coach bounded along nicely and the passengers were in a complimentary mood. Two or three hours out the younger Ford decided to try his hand at the tiller. On all roads—the D. T. & I. crossed the New York Central, Wabash, Nickel Plate, Pennsylvania, Erie and Big Four—a distance signal is set at varying distances from an intersection, a home signal closer to the crossing.

Roads are equipped with the further safeguard of a derail also in varying forms—in this case a rail sliced in two at an angle. When signals are against a train there is a break in the track; when all is clear a towerman closes it. The distance signal was against the test car approaching the main line of the Pennsylvania. They were traveling 60 miles an hour but the young president of Ford Motor made no move to slacken and the division head across the aisle assumed he had not seen the signal.

"Did you miss the warning, Mr. Ford?" He leaned across the aisle.

The junior Ford seemed absorbed in what he was doing. He made no answer and no move to apply any brakes. He apparently had ideas of his own of their power and the distance required to halt the car. The warning home signal and main line loomed! The derail was set!! A pile-up seemed inescapable.

"We're going off!" Chorley raised his voice and braced himself.

Edsel had misjudged the strength of the brakes. He cut speed but the car hit the derail and swung off on a jarring run over rough ground. An embankment would have been fatal but it was luckily flat at the point where the car left the tracks. It was a close call. The dynasty could easily have been snuffed out. Several passengers were pitched into the aisle but there were nothing worse than minor bruises and raised temperatures. The rail turned up and sheared the motors off the underside of the car.

Young Ford was not a man to dodge responsibility. He took the blame without hesitation when his father managed to get off his knees and lurch up forward to ask what had happened. He had been twice advised to slow down, Edsel said, but thought that in the intervening 5000 feet of track he had plenty of time to pull down if the home signal did not change in time to let him shoot through.

A freight locomotive on a passing track was cut off and got the experimental car back on the track but it would not operate under its own power and was towed to Springfield.

It had been impossible to hide the debut of the Ford experiment in railroading, if there ever was any desire, and the group had been advised of a welcoming party waiting to salute his new coach, but the accident dampened any fancy the senior Ford had for official handshaking. He did not relish a triumphal arrival behind a freight locomotive. Automobiles, ordered to meet the party at a belt line outside Springfield, conveyed the passengers from there to a hotel without drumbeat or bunting.

Ford would ride tenders on top of the coal in search of flaws and sometimes just for the sheer fun of it. He would have his chauffeur drive south some 30 miles and there flag a train. Ford would get aboard and the driver would continue on down the highway to some appointed place to pick him up later.

He usually chose the least populated areas for these joy rides and he seemed to have a stirring time perched on the rocking coal. Occasionally he would sit there playing a harmonica, listening closely as if trying to catch the rhythm of the car wheels and match it. Occasionally he'd crawl over the coal and into the cab, and you could tell when he took the throttle—the train flew as though off non-stop for the Aleutians.

He made a delightful acquaintance on one excursion. Strains of a fiddle drew him to a crossing-tender's shack. The occupant, at ease on an empty soapbox, did not recognize his visitor and went on with *Money Musk*.

"I like that," Ford complimented. "Y'mind?" He reached for the violin and played a little tune himself.

"That's good, too," the owner patronized, and said it would be better, of course, except the fiddle was not too good.

"It isn't, is it?" Ford agreed. "Too bad."

Well, it was the best a working man could do. After all, the man in the shack said, violins cost money. Ford showed up with a package the next week, said he had a fiddle he wanted his friend to try.

They sat down on the same box. The difference in music was quite noticeable. The crossing-tender hardly recognized what his bow brought forth.

"Say, that's good!" he said at the conclusion, scrutinizing the instrument. "Where did you get it?"

Ford said he just picked it up. It should have been good. It was an Amati which had cost him $35,000. He left it with the railroad hand for a month and when he went to get it back he was sorry he had to turn down a good offer. The crossing-tender said he thought he could get a loan of $75 on his insurance policy if Ford would sell.

In some way he found that merchants in an Ohio town were charging his workers one price and had another set of prices for other customers. The practice angered him.

"I want that situation cleaned up right away," he ordered, and a company executive reached for a telephone.

The business people of the Ohio town were thunderstruck one morning to see excavators on a site immediately in their midst and a sign on the property announcing that this was going to be the future home for a new large branch of a well-known chain. Ford had found a way of coping with gougers.

Ford climbed a ladder to a roof of the plant one morning when he saw a workman asleep on it.

"Why," he frowned when he had shaken the slumberer awake, "are you taking your sleep on our time?" In speaking of the company it was never "I" or "mine" but "we" and "our."

The worker said it was true he was napping on company property but on his own time. "I quit twenty minutes ago," he protested. He had resigned right up there on the roof. He was sick of washing windows. He had been doing that for two years without a raise in pay and since he was 20 he thought life was slipping away from him. Besides, he didn't like window-cleaning no matter what it paid—took it only because he needed work.

"What do you think you'd like to do?" Ford had taken a seat on the roof beside him.

As long as he could remember, he said, he had wanted to be a railroad engineer. Ford looked him up and down appraisingly and had one of his honored hunches. Individuals interested him more than man in the mass.

"Come over to the office with me." He led the way down the ladder and across the yard.

This was a rabbit he'd get out of Harry Bennett's sleeve. When the chief of his service department set traps for a miracle he usually came in with one on the fender like a buck in season. He had produced one only the previous day when Ford called Bennett's attention to a stretch of ballast that was brown.

"Know what that is?" he asked.

Bennett would not have known what it was if the color had been heliotrope or dusty pink. He had no interest in railroads, industrial processes and didn't even like to drive an automobile. Once he became so confused by horn-blowers at a five-way intersection that he abandoned his car in the middle of the road.

"There it is," he said to the cop on the corner, "you figure it out," and walked away.

No, Mr. Ford, he didn't know what the brown was, he said.

"Iron," Ford pronounced it, "and it shouldn't be there."

Two hours later it wasn't. Bennett didn't know what brown

ballast meant but he knew an order. In no time trucks were beside the rails and the slag was hauled off to be dumped by the Rouge furnaces with a message from Bennett that Mr. Ford did not like to see iron wasted on slag.

Ford telephoned Bennett about the boy on the roof.

"He wants to be a locomotive engineer." He pointed his finger at the speechless fledgling, now awake to the fact that something was happening to him that couldn't. "See what you can do, Harry."

"Come on, Kid." Bennett walked out. The young worker stumbled after.

Ford heard a hail from a yard locomotive a month later. "Hi-yah, Mr. Ford," a voice saluted and a hand waved.

The window-washer had not risen full distance to the throttle but he was wide awake this time and pitching coal. The moral, one of Ford's less serious aides said at the time, was that a good way to get ahead was to fall asleep on a roof and let Ford catch you at it.

Whether the motormaker was extraordinarily proficient as a railroad operator because of some sixth sense, as some said, or whether he made a white elephant fly and pay by the business which naturally flowed to the road from his ownership, I do not pretend to know. He not only got profit because he owned the road but also as the originator of volume. If he couldn't get equity from one connecting line he diverted business to another. In return for his traffic other roads cut in the D. T. & I. on their unrouted business in the opposite direction.

He quit railroading because he never was able to do with the road what he hoped. His first reason for buying it was to insure himself an unbroken flow of coal, and he didn't get it.

"They told me I had to own mines to get coal, so I bought mines," he said when he reached the end of the rope. "Then they told me that to haul it I really needed a railroad of my own, so I bought a railroad. Then I bought 2,000 cars to haul the coal in, and I still don't seem nearer the right answer than I was before."

He stood at the window mooning and rubbing his jaw with both hands.

"Sell the thing!" he said.

The Grand Monarch had been giving orders too long to take them. It wasn't the only reason. Edsel, in a later federal hearing, was to testify that the road in 1928 was taking up too much company time that could be better spent. Aviation was coming into the picture and Ford bought a small establishment. A minority stock interest sputtered because Ford didn't pay dividends on the D. T. & I. but diverted profit to profit-sharing schemes.

Always, too, there were rules that bothered him. He seemed to be constantly drawing a $1,000 fine for running a train without a caboose. Operating a railroad was not like running his plant which he could open and shut as he wished. He could raise wages, cut prices, tear apart, stick together, with no one to say he couldn't. With the railroad he couldn't. The government had too much to say to suit him.

Three roads were interested when the D. T. & I. went on the block. The Pennsylvania and the Baltimore & Ohio were two to whom the property looked good. The Michigan Central wanted a piece. Sale terms were developed after a year's negotiations with Pennroad. Details were put up to Ford in a long report. He dropped in on his secretary, Liebold, and asked him if he had read the terms. No? Well, get a copy and see what he thought of them.

"You've got a reputation as a smart man but you won't have it if you sign," the secretary reported after his study.

The proposal called for payment of $10,000,000 in cash and balance of $26,000,000 in 20 years. The clause to which major exception was taken gave the Pennsylvania first option on 70 per cent of total tonnage of the Rouge plant for 40 years. Also, was there any good reason Pennroad should not pay all cash?

"I won't sign it," Ford promised.

Edsel, sailing for Europe, dumped his bonds on the secretary's desk. The senior Ford did likewise. "Now you go out and sell it," the senior Ford said to the secretary.

Under the rewritten terms Pennroad paid $36,000,000 in cash and the option on Rouge freight was struck out. Ford was leaving the laboratory a month later as Liebold was arriving. They met in the lobby.

"How's the railroad coming?" Ford stopped to ask. It was the first time he had mentioned it since refusing to go through with the original deal.

"We closed today and the cash is in the bank," he was told.

In lieu of an actual cash transfer, the Ford company and Atterbury interests exchanged lists of depositaries. Pennroad banked with a dozen or so; Ford had accounts in some fifteen scattered banks. The two ran down their lists and checked nine institutions in which both had accounts.

The plan called for the holding company, on the closing date, merely to transfer from its account to Ford's in those banks a total of $36,000,000. An officer of each receiving bank was then to wire a Detroit bank the amount of the deposit.

Liebold, the secretary, gathered up a sheaf of telegrams just before closing time. They were from the named banks and announced fresh deposits to Ford account of the entire sales price of the D. T. & I. Ford would miss pulling the throttle and feeling the surge of old No. 424 as if it was going to take the whole state of Ohio in three good broad jumps. He would miss the crossing-tender who played bouncy jigs on the Amati. He was out of railroading.

Just when the nimbus seemed a perfect fit and what he should be wearing, he'd shake his head and it would slide rakishly down over one ear.

CHAPTER XI

HE WOULD NOT STAND STILL FOR HIS HALO

THE WORLD had no prior experience with a lord so talkative. No Astor or Morgan sat down with reporters for a chummy talk or challenged them to a foot-race or treated them to carrots from a hillock he tilled himself. Ford held a thousand midgets on his lap unabashed and even called in the photographers himself. Publicity was his pudding.

Many hundreds of trains going and coming in his twenty-track mind got through on schedule or ahead of time; some ran red lights, through open switches, down embankments, but the percentage of loss was light in relation to the traffic.

Ford won stature by some headlines because he was unorthodox and often ahead of the band, because he took ideas and walloped them an awesome country mile and because no one was ever sure he would not hit another home run into the same far tier of seats.

He lost size by other headlines because he often talked unguardedly and spectacularly for sheer talk's sake, purposely aiming to startle no matter how; because some hunches did not jell; because he did not think through all his enterprises, or thought them through but added wrong and got a bad answer, and because everything he said was magnified by men mesmerized by his possessions and his record as author of hit shows.

Rivals tried until red in the face to equal him in corraling news space. He made pygmies of them and towered over them. He was without a peer in maintaining his name in lights. In a measure it was because he had a sixth sense for right timing, a knowledge of what made news, and okayed his own copy.

He could be indifferent to veracity and consistency. It was less important that a thing be true than that it be exciting, stunning. To test its effect on a man to whom he was talking, Ford was quite capable of saying something he did not mean or say he was going to do a thing he did not intend to do. It could be pure blarney, but if the effect satisfied him he let the statement stand. A good effect on one guinea pig was a sign it might dazzle a much larger audience.

He had a bandaged ankle one fall. He had been playing football, he said, with the children. Of course he had not been playing football with the children but the report of an injury on the gridiron at seventy-one was more dramatic than the truth that he had a common blister.

He wore an old shoe one birthday that was not a mate of the other. Had he hurt his foot? Not at all, he said. Every birthday he put on an old shoe to remind him that he once had been poor and that there was no insurance he would not be poor again unless he watched his step. Nonsense! He had put on a wrong shoe in the dark but by a little imagination he made a piece of it that the press would print.

He was going to make cars of plastic and there was great to-do but he only made one, being photographed slamming it with an axe to show how tough it was. He had decided to build 400 houses for workmen by pouring concrete into molds, but he did not pour any. He may have had it in mind to do so when he mentioned it but no plan not under way was a binding contract. Moreover, he reserved the right to throw the helm over as he pleased and beat off on a new course.

His refusal to stay put agitated one newspaper exceedingly. He gave out an interview in support of municipal ownership of Detroit's traction system. He went sled length but the paper was suspicious. The editor called in his reporter. "Go out and get Ford to put his signature on this thing," he said, quite aware Mr. Ford might say one thing one day and back away the next. "I don't want him walking out on this."

The reporter got nowhere in obtaining the signature. A second tried and cooled his heels several days. The newspaper even recalled its

Washington correspondent and told him to see what he could do. Ford never signed. He did not repudiate the interview but up to the voting it was thought he might.

He was to under similar circumstances. This time he wanted to be against municipal operation of the surface lines, he told his editor.

"You can't do it," his editor said. "A little while back you applauded the idea."

"When? Where?" Ford demanded to know.

Date and place were furnished.

"I'm coming out against it anyway," he said, petulantly.

He was warned the public would not have forgotten. So he had one of his top executives damn the proposed acquisition of the surface lines as too costly. It could not have happened if Mr. Ford had not given the interview the nod.

Ford fretted under the surveillance of his own police. A press photographer tried to snap the motormaker on a new bicycle and almost had the camera snatched from his hands.

"None of that now," he was warned by plant police. "No pictures!"

The incident did not escape Ford. He sidled over to the camera man and whispered, "I'll slip away from these fellows and meet you at the back gate."

The photographer hid himself in bushes near the exit and Ford kept his word. He showed up alone and rode in circles while the pictures were taken. On the other hand when the pictures were published Ford called his police chief on the carpet.

"Can't I even be protected from the photographers when I want to be?" he reprimanded, acting out the part of a man who paid for protection and expected to get it or know why.

It got bruited about that Ford put on a red tie when he was fighting mad. He told a newsman so. I didn't believe it but he said he did when I asked. I still don't believe it.

"That's right," he said. "Makes me feel spunky. I put it on to match my temper."

When Ford was mad he did not think in terms of haberdashery. He did not go from the plant to the house to change his tie for battle. He fought as he was, any weight, any adversary, in silk, poplin or no tie at all if anyone caught him that way. His statement did not square, either, with the fact that on a very tranquil day he would appear in a red tie. What he said about red ties simply set people to talking and that was what he wanted. Publicity was the overriding reason for so many of his eccentric statements and actions that after a time you got to know that often what seemed spontaneous had been probably well thought out.

One day when he was in excellent humor and wore a red tie I asked what he was doing in it feeling as good as he was. He threw himself into a role of an angry man before my eyes. His eyes snapped, he clenched a fist—he slammed out, saying he had a few words to say to a fellow, and leaving the impression it was going to be pretty rough on the other man.

I followed him at a distance where he would not see me unless he turned around. He seemed to be pleased with himself. Out the door leading to the laboratory he wheeled right and retraced his steps, walked into the corridor and back, smiling, into his own office, giving the tie a jaunty pull as he went in. He apparently was trying to make good the myth of the red tie for my benefit.

His statement that the public could have any color in a Ford so long as it was black went so well he decided to have a fling at another color. When John S. Coppin, Detroit artist, was commissioned to do a portrait of Ford for a collection of scientists, business leaders and inventors being formed by Thomas J. Watson, of International Business Machines, the automobile tycoon told Coppin he couldn't see why he should pose after his last experience fifteen years before. He said Carl C. E. Lindin, New York artist, had worked on him then.

"Weeks it took!" Ford maddened at the memory. It might have been three or four days but as the irritated motormaker recalled the event it was weeks. "One afternoon he said to me, 'I guess that's all for today,' and said he'd make an appointment for another sitting. I said 'I'll make the next appointment.' " Ford looked at Coppin fiercely. "I never went back!"

He wanted to know why the painter could not get all he needed from photographs. Coppin said the results would be flat and generally unsatisfactory. Edsel put in a word. "No, I won't pose," said Ford, impervious, "I'll sit and talk and you can sketch or get some ideas. How's that?"

It had to do.

"There's another thing, Mr. Ford," the artist ventured. Ford wore a blue tie with white stripes. "To warm it up, if you don't mind, I'm going to put a red tie on you in the portrait."

"Why?"

"Well, you're wearing a cold colored suit or it will look cold on canvas."

Ford nodded.

"Ever wear a red tie?" the artist asked.

"Yep," said Ford, giving his old line a twist. "Put any color of tie on me as long as it's red."

Newspapermen assigned to him daily got to regard themselves as members of the kitchen cabinet—non-voting B members, it is true, but those who held cards found it easier to record the feats and let the follies alone. The home-town reporter rationalized his semi-surrender. He balanced the hypothetical value of a one-day sensation which might improve his status in the trade for a few hours against the tangible profit of being able to share in the solid run of news material Ford was forever creating, and he usually voted to take the long-term profit, whatever Greeley or Dana might have done.

Converted Navy blimps, at $19,000 a month rental, now cruise the sky spelling out in lights the superiorities of the Ford car. The company spent more than $800,000 for radio time last year on one network. In an earlier day Henry Ford just sat there in his office and blew off, and his name spread economically to every point of the compass. Books, magazines, newspapers were his dirigible and radio, and usually he had them free; and through all the powwows of analysts as to what kind of a man he was, the assembly lines moved without pause and thousands ate regularly, built homes, educated their young.

Ford would ramble along pleasantly about something he or the two of you were interested in. Sometimes he would answer your questions; sometimes he would say, "I don't want to talk about that right now," and launch into some subject he did want to talk about. Some days he was lucid and highly quotable, others, disjointed and obscure. He'd be tranquil; he'd be sulphurous.

When he became bored with the conversation, as he did with visitors, distinguished or undistinguished, he slouched lower. When his head on the back of his chair and his feet on a desk in front of him reached virtually the same level, this was the nadir of boredom, and you knew you were about to lose him. He'd be on his feet in a jiffy and practically run out of the room taking no sociable leave—just getting out.

He was always alerted to the machines beyond the door, though.

A mechanic appeared in oily overalls; Ford turned his head and said, "Yes, Joe?"

"That machine is going, Mr. Ford." Some called him "Henry" but they were not many.

"I'll be right there." He rose and broke up the interview. "Sorry I've got to go." He hurried after the workman.

At times he was not the Presence at all, with plants girdling the planet and pockets full of millions, but a neighbor on whom you were paying a pleasant call—one friend talking casually and unguardedly to another with no thought that a palpitant populace might be at the keyhole. He never said such talks were not for publication but instinctively one sensed when the conversation went off the record and the jury was out of the room. Then a new question was asked, formalism returned and you knew he was talking again for world consumption.

He had many moments of extravagant speaking. An Associated Press writer was fanning with him when conversation swung to the Bible.

"There are only two things in the Book worth a damn," Ford remarked.

It was a flat generalization of the type mankind is given to. He was asked what passages he had in mind. One was from Paul's declaration of faith to the Romans:

> Dearly beloved, avenge not yourselves but
> rather give place unto wrath, for it is
> written, Vengeance is mine; I will repay,
> saith the Lord.

The other was from the eleventh chapter of *Hebrews:*

> Now faith is the substance of things hoped
> for, the evidence of things not seen.

At this point the correspondent noted with some surprise what looked an abnormality on Ford's left hand. He dropped Biblical texts without asking the reason for the preference and looked closer. Four fingernails were trimmed but the nail of the little finger extended a half inch beyond the tip.

"Wondering about the nail?" Ford realized his visitor's attention was on something besides the Bible. "I've been letting it grow to show Eleanor [his daughter-in-law] how silly women look with nails like that." He glanced, slightly dubious, at his own experiment. "I guess I'll spray it with paint after a while," he observed, chuckling at the fancy.

In writing of the day, the reporter had an eye on the clerical rumpus which might result if Ford was quoted in endorsement of only two things in the Bible, so the texts were offered inoffensively as Ford's "favorite" passages. The fingernail went unchronicled and if there was later merriment over the promised duco job, it was enjoyed privately around one dinner table and not around the world.

Occasionally when Ford was in an outlandish mood and saying things which did not square with known fact, a listener at one side of the room would hunch forward and slip into the conversation, "What Mr. Ford means is—" William J. Cameron, Ford editor, would say and would proceed from there to file down edges and touch up the cadence with an adroit carpentry.

Another sub-editor had a different approach. When Ford was lost in an undertow and no one except him was quite sure what he was driving at, Fred L. Black would remark: "You see, Mr. Ford often speaks in parables," and he would point to the particular parable at bat at the moment, distilling what you had been hearing to what he said was the essence.

These analyses must have been competent for I remember few if any times when Ford repudiated them. He would nod pleasantly as if he was listening to his own thought repeated merely in dressier words. When the fog settled deep, one somehow had a notion that what he was thinking was perfectly plain to him but he was without the necessary fund of words to tell others.

Talking through an interpreter to a visitor whose language he did not speak and whose English he might not recognize, he had a standard cure-all for the problems of foreign states in which he had no direct interest but whose envoys found relief in telling him what little Ruritania was up against. When he was clearly over his head and had not even begun to get straight in his mind what an earnest gesticulating caller had said, he fell back on the stock recipe.

"Well, there is only one cure for that," he would remark, cheerfully, "and that is Hard Work."

It was on this note the audience usually broke up.

The Ku Klux Klan entered the mayoralty election in Detroit in 1925 by backing Charles E. Bowles, a political nobody and a Protestant, against John W. Smith, the incumbent, and a Catholic.

Mr. Smith, a Bull Moose Progressive, who reveled in most of the pleasant laxities of mankind, was a connoisseur of Rhine wine, Bokharas, good music and troubadours. He either owned a piece of a Canadian race-track or was said to have lost enough in wagering to have bought the controlling stock. He came near to acquiring a *weinstube* in Heidelberg in a sentimental moment, and periodically turned over his home to members of a symphony orchestra and the press for what presumably would be known in today's argot as a jam session.

Around a guitarist introduced as the world's last surviving troubadour, political writers and others used to gather and sing *Abdul Abulbul Amir,* the only familiar piece the troubadour knew in a long repertoire of fine Hungarian folksongs. The parties were quite memorable, with perhaps *Traviata* in the study, the violin section at Nevin or Liszt or Victor Herbert in the living room, the surrounded troubadour strumming in an upstairs bedroom, Budweiser in the basement and a crap game on a plaid blanket of the tribe of Bruce on the kitchen floor. The host had picked up the plaid in Scotland and thought it was lucky for him.

Against these allurements, Mr. Bowles pitted unknown but considerable virtues—custard bowls for women voters and a chaste Protestantism—and hooded tribesmen burned crosses in the outer purlieus of the city. Mr. Bowles disowned the demonstrators, but intolerance had a vivid inning.

As the campaign took on vitriolic touches Smith said "Get me Henry Ford's endorsement if you can" and was off to bet a race at Devonshire. Smith had been an early circulation manager of the Dearborn *Independent* but his political enemies told Ford that Smith had quietly joined in criticism of Edsel Ford for his exemption from military service in World War I. When the senior Ford was in a barber shop one day, a subscription-taker for the *Independent* came in. The next day he announced he was thoroughly dissatisfied with the sales talk of the agent, and the entire Smith organization was out.

His steering committee thought a Ford endorsement might do its candidate more harm than good since many Ford employees disagreed with the national estimate of their boss and often voted obstinately against what he was for, but I was told several days later that Ford would stand up and be counted for Smith if I would see him.

He kept his word. He put Smith midway between Bismarck and Disraeli.

"That does it, doesn't it?" he observed. Cameron and Sir Percival Perry, president of Ford of England, were present and merely listened. Unfortunately I ran the wrong way of the field at this point. As he got up to go I asked how he sized up the Klan movement. This proved not at all the right thing to have said. When a fly was cast in these waters no one could tell what would rise to it. Ford reseated himself and said he was glad to kill two birds with one stone.

"I think the Klan, the Knights of Columbus and Masons can be traced back to Wall Street," he asserted. "Yes, sir!" He shook his head gravely. "Now there you have it," he exclaimed and looked around as if for a seconding nod. He did not get it. The room was quite still.

"No child ever went to church and came out the worse for it," he said. "These organizations will get us into war if we don't watch out."

He seemed to tire of the theme, and walked out, leaving those behind slightly bemused.

"How about lunch?" someone asked. The Englishman said that would be nice, indeed. We crossed the laboratory to the pine-paneled restaurant.

"How about forgetting that last statement?" a nervous Ford representative asked.

The Briton said it was quite extraordinary. I certainly did not want any piece of the bomb, which was so far just a dud in the family. It would ruin the endorsement. I was interested exclusively in touting the statesmanship of Mr. Smith. Moreover, Ford and my publisher were Masons. Smith was one of the Knights.

Standard practice at the time was to submit for check before publication articles in which Ford was directly quoted, so after lunch the Smith endorsement was written on a company typewriter and mention was omitted of the Klan, the Knights and the Masons being mere speaking tubes of Wall Street.

In midafternoon Ford was back and it was read to him. He nodded approvingly but appeared not wholly satisfied.

"Isn't there any more?" he asked.

The secretary said there was not.

"You forgot to say," Ford shook an admonishing finger, "that the Klan, the Knights of Columbus and the Masons can be traced to Wall Street." He took the pages from the editor and passed them to me.

"What Mr. Ford really means," said the editor, after the door closed behind his liege lord, "is something he expressed in other words to me a few days ago."

"Well, what did he mean?" I asked, a little crabbedly. "You write it if he has left something out that should be in or if he misstated something he has in mind."

The spokesman turned to his typewriter and batted out in three paragraphs an amended Ford answer to the question of what he thought of the Klan movement. It came out this way:

"There is an epidemic of organizations in America engaged in church-baiting or interfering in devious ways with the peaceful progressive life of the race. I am NOT mentioning the Klan or the Masons or the Knights of Columbus but I am including them all.

"A majority of them are breeding spots that may involve us in another war. The leaders of them and Wall Street get the profit. I am referring to organizations which directly or indirectly seek to criticize the church. No child ever went to church and came out the worse for it. People who fight against religion haven't any religion to fight about.

"We will be saddled with them until intelligence prevails and the public cannot be herded like sheep. Many of these organizations, I repeat, are agents of Wall Street and are composed of the harebrained who only lose the fees they pay in."

Ford returned in ten minutes and the ghosted statement was read to him in its revamped form.

"Now that's just right." He gleefully slapped his leg with his hand and was out the door again.

The Klan, Knights and Masons were still in it but were no

longer tied to Wall Street with a fast knot. The ghost succeeded in including and excluding them by a little dexterous double talk. I remember the New York *Times* editorial when the statement reached it, "The sweet influence of Dearborn will continue to reign upon the peaceful progressive life of the Nordic race." It said Ford talked too rarely and that "the words of the wise were as goads."

As proof of Ford's variability, Mr. Bowles beat off opposition when he ran again for mayor two years later and when he was recalled, Ford's lawyer joined counsel for the anti-recall forces.

On the basis of what was laid to him there were those who thought Ford was misquoted but it only seemed he must have been. He was safer in the hands of reporters than stenographers. What he actually said was often stranger, in full context, than what, in skeleton, he was credited with saying. Many caught him in inspired moments when he seemed to possess an extra gadget in his head which others lacked and which turned him into a superior oracle. Many heard him say things which made them distrust their ears.

Of those who came and went none was more diligent in the vineyard than a clergyman who doubled as a Ford interviewer for a news syndicate. He was a staunch laborer and slaved hard to make an often reluctant Ford see life as he saw it. The motormaker's editorial janizaries had to read him closely because of the license he took.

The clergyman had a happy device. He would deliver 200 or 300-word sermonettes to Mr. Ford in the form of questions, full of metaphysics, polysyllables and poetical allusions, and ask if Ford agreed. If Ford said no, he was worked over. If he said "I guess you're right there," the words were taken out of the clergyman's mouth and put into Mr. Ford's as a statement coming from him when they appeared in type. It was a simple trick but not new.

Discussion centered one morning on the company's coal properties. The pastor thought company houses a devil's device and wanted Ford to say so.

"What's wrong with them?" Ford interrupted sharply.

"The monotony of the architecture, the denial of man's right to express his individuality—"

"People live in apartments all alike and are happy in them, aren't they?" he argued. "I don't see anything wrong with our company houses."

"But—"

"Rent is reasonable, they have every improvement and we keep them in good shape," Ford ran right on. "Moreover, the families take pride in them and keep them clean."

He wandered out of the room without waiting for an answer. The clergyman was distressed. He said to the official spokesman, "He won't say what I want him to say."

"He often won't," the spokesman said laconically.

The pastor bested Ford in the end. Instead of reporting the negative, he got the answer he wanted into the article by omitting it and giving the impression Ford had said yes when he had said no. The article ended, "You don't believe then in the company house, do you, Mr. Ford." He put a period at that point as if merely confirming a statement that had come from Ford originally. The pastor got Ford against company houses, willy-nilly.

The head of Ford Motor complained to me of two stories I wrote of him in thirteen years and asked suppression of only one, and that an item of small account. He said he did not like a feature article I had done on an old violinist who had visited him. I ran into Ford the morning it appeared.

"Didn't like that story this morning," he said and moved on without explanation.

At least it was a refutation of a rumor that he never bothered to read the papers. The story in question did not seem to be the sort to which he would pay any attention. He never said why he objected to it. He asked me not to publish the fact that a violin stolen from him as a boy had been returned years later by a neighbor boy who had taken it.

About half an hour after the criticism of the story of the violinist I felt a hand at my elbow.

"Forget what I said about that story," he apologized. "You write them the way you see them."

When Allan Benson, magazine writer and Ford biographer, disagreed with him about the Jewish campaign, Ford offered him some bound volumes of the Dearborn *Independent* to read but Benson said he knew what was in them and still was critical of the attack.

"Read them again," Ford said, petulantly, "and then if you don't agree with me don't ever come to see me any more."

Benson continued talking as if the conditional sentence had not been passed, and a few minutes later Ford got up from his chair and put a penitent hand on Benson's shoulder.

"Guess I'm out of sorts this morning." He was all excuses. "You come to see me any time you want."

A reporter was talking to a bank official of odds and ends and the latter happened to mention a new game played at his room the previous night. Among the guests were Mr. and Mrs. Edsel Ford and the game was called "Murder." It was one of those short-lived parlor diversions and he described the way it was played and the fun the party had.

"Who were killed off?" The newsman had in mind a feature supplement his paper was publishing. It contained all sorts of succulent tidbits about sea serpents, maharajahs, flights to the moon, and how far everything would reach if put end to end. The banker mentioned some nice people who had been histrionically done in—among them his own wife and Ford's daughter-in-law—and how it was accomplished. The reporter pieced together a splash page on murder in the drawing room.

The promotion department of the newspaper unhappily ran a three-column teaser ad to boost Sunday sales and mentioned as a forthcoming salty attraction a story on the "murder" of Mrs. Edsel Ford without explanation that the homicide was all in fun and between good friends.

Several hours later Dearborn telephoned. What was this promised story of homicide?

"A parlor game they've been playing on Long Island," he was told. "It was tried out at Grosse Pointe the other night and went very well."

There was a large hieroglyphic grunt at the other end.

"No chance to kill it, I suppose," he ventured.

"Went to press last night," he was told.

"Of course. Well, much obliged," the weary voice at Dearborn said. "People are on my neck out here."

The advertising manager of the newspaper involved said in an equally tired tone Monday morning: "Ford advertising is off the schedule." For the intrusion on Ford privacy the paper did ten-day penance before going back on the list of those sharing its lineage.

Talks with other members of the high command in industry

might be couched in sedate language, dried to the last comma and certainly in line with a holy thing known as policy. Mr. Ford, of Greenfield township, never had to worry about such trifles. HE was policy. He had a roundtable where miscellaneous matters were discussed and decisions made, but if the vote was eight to one and he was the one, the single vote prevailed. Whether what he said was good or bad it was right from the barn and you were privileged to use it if you could escape the clutches of the man who said, "What Mr. Ford really means is—," and his confederate who said "Mr. Ford often speaks in parables."

Since the senior Ford was top source no one had to write "on good authority it was learned" when he handed out news. Often he tried to make out that something sublime was crazy, or the other way around. He said in 1919 that history was the bunk, but other gentlemen of substance had expressed the same thought before he did and created no such furore; "capital punishment is being promoted by international financiers" in 1927; "the average daily wage in 1950 will be $27," at about the same time; "liquor is as dead as slavery" in 1928, and he erroneously predicted there would be no World War II because America had two million veterans of World War I who would not let it happen. But what he said was IT and called for no qualification.

His more discreet competitors were at a disadvantage against such independence. The president of a competing company was asked to pose with two young boys who had won a company contest and had come from their respective towns to claim their trophies. A press photographer said he would like to get a little human interest into the picture and would the executive kindly stand between the boys with a hand on the shoulder of each.

"Sorry, but not that," the president said, curtly. The children stood there not knowing what to make of his reluctance. "I'll just stand between them—nothing else."

He explained it later. He remembered, he said, a much discussed picture of the gangster Dillinger taken at an Indiana jail from which he subsequently escaped. Dillinger was posed arm in arm with the sheriff, and after the jail-break and the genial snap-shot was found the public asked questions.

"You can see for yourself the spot I'd be in," the cagy auto executive said, "if those two young boys turned out badly and a picture was found with my arms about them." He said he was sorry but that's the way it was. He seemed pleased by his talent for taking the long view.

Public Enemy John Dillinger, slain by Federal Agents in Chicago in 1934, wrote Ford a letter before he was silenced. Ford gave it to newsmen after the hoodlum met FBI men outside a Chicago theater and was through with killing and running away. It read:

"I want to thank you for making an excellent car. If I am ever captured it will have to be someone in another Ford."

Ford developed attachments for certain newsmen in Boston and Atlanta and was likely to talk with abandon in those two cities. He was free there from those subordinates who liked to use a sieve on what he said and pick out the clinkers. It was in Boston he said there would be no war—that Europe did not dare launch its armies—and four days later the Nazis moved into Silesia and across the Polish frontier. Within a week Chamberlain told Parliament a state of war existed between His Majesty's Government and Hitler's Germany.

It seemed that nearly always when Ford went to Wayside Inn he got in touch with some favored one in a Boston newspaper office and said, "Come on out." It was in Boston in '26 he said the British general strike was "put over" by the same interests responsible for wars. "The British people don't know it," he assured the Boston *Globe,* "but the strike was jockeyed by the very same people—the people back of the statesmen, who manufacture wars." He could name the people, he said, but the *Globe* would not print them if he did.

It was in Atlanta in the spring of '44 that he said the war would be finished in two months. If he had been in Dearborn it is probable that all these bad guesses would have been waylaid long before they got through the plant gates. Maybe they wouldn't—holding in leash his urge to startle and play prophet was never easy labor.

He early developed the habit of playing favorites among writers. The confidant of the moment sat on his lap, as the saying is, for an uncertain time and then for no apparent reason would be cast out and replaced by another writer. There was no hard feeling about it. It was one of the occupational hazards of "covering" Ford. Many reporters enjoyed an inside track and his private telephone number for a spell and were then traded in for new models but were philosophical about it.

They were not unlike a contractor who did a great many jobs for him. Then he bid on a new job and waited and didn't hear from it and got a little nervous. He ran into Ford one day in the building, asked how his work was going. Were there any complaints?

"No complaint. Why?" asked Ford.

The contractor said he had asked because he had not received any yes or no on his last bid and wondered if it had been lost in the mail or if there was some fault with work he had done. They walked out to Ford's car.

"Let's see—how long have you been doing work for us?" Ford asked.

The contractor said three years.

"Well, three years is long enough, don't you think?" said Ford, very friendly, as he stepped on the starter and drove off. This simply was the end of relations—the bid had not gone astray in the mail. Terminations happened that suddenly.

Long ago he was particularly partial to one of the New York papers. His office was in the tractor plant at the time and one of his myrmidons was a gentleman who was anathema to the press but in whose duplicities Ford may well have had a hand. After all, his job was to make it hard, not easy, for people to see the head of the company.

Reporters descended to question Ford on some subject that was hot at the moment. They idled all day without seeing him. The watchdog said he did not know where Mr. Ford was or when he would appear, and after a fruitless wait of hours the gentlemen of the press returned to town.

"Mr. Ford still is not here and I don't know when he will be," they were assured by the same secretary when they reappeared next morning.

A latecomer produced a lethal blow. He arrived with a copy of the favored newspaper and it contained an exclusive interview with Mr. Ford given the previous day on the very subject which had brought the local press trooping to his door. The reporters read it and went out to the front lawn to let off steam and some racy profanity.

They were standing there when one noticed an extraordinary sight at the far end of the building. Ford was climbing out his office window, the sill of which was only a foot or so off the ground, and apparently was about to leave the premises. The reporters charged down on him and Ford straightened his coat and tie and was as bland as the man who had said he was not there.

"Good morning," he said as if the visit was an entire and agreeable surprise and he had not been called on the telephone only a few minutes before and told that a reportorial battalion was on his track and he'd better be off if he did not wish to be bothered. After all, he had used the cellar door of the White House in the Harding administration to duck correspondents. Leaving by a window was no trick.

"That son of a bitch of a man of yours said yesterday you weren't here and he said the same thing this morning," said a forthright reporter whose boiling point had been reached by the delaying tactics.

"What did you call him?" Ford asked as though he could not believe he had heard correctly.

All right, Ford had asked for it. "I said," remarked the reporter with rising choler and chucking in extra castigation, "that he was a no good son of a bitch."

Mr. Ford smiled amiably, almost shyly, and made a motion with his hand as if he had heard something which confirmed a belief of his own.

"You know, gentlemen," he said, "in an organization as big as ours we must have an occasional son of a bitch." He looked from one man to the next as one reasonable man discussing a problem with other reasonable men. "Naturally," he added, "we are so big we must have the very best in certain positions that we can get."

He rebuilds the school where the lamb made a fool of Mary, and is offered the reputed mummy of Lincoln's assassin to prove history the bunk he said it was.

CHAPTER XII

NOSTALGIC JOURNEY INTO YESTERDAY

WHEN AN ordinary man has an extraordinary dream he usually forgets it between home and the office; an idea swimming in the Ford sub-conscious was likely to find itself an heroic project next day. He would rub the lamp and call up a thousand genii, and soon they would be galloping the roads so that the effendi might have his wish.

Instead of striking a gong for servingmen he even might turn expediter himself and set out alone on a mission, as he rode bareback as a boy to some distant farm to fix a clock. Most of them were no shoe-string undertakings and in them he had an edge on contemporary dreamers. At the point where they might turn back after counting their cash and estimating the danger, he could plunge on indifferent to both.

The expense of some enterprises was quite nominal—but one stood him $25,000,000. To each he gave unflagging attention. That one cost more did not mean stinting of the one that cost less. Both were equally compelling in his mind and expense was not the determinant. As a result, when an undertaking was done he had a work as perfect as hands and money could make it. The manufacture of cars got to be routine—he had to have diversion, and his diversion was on no pocket scale.

If some wanted original could not be found the replica was exact, even to the errors. When it was the remembered tone of sleighbells worn by his father's horses when he was a boy, and he wished to hear them again, no bells of other pitch would do and he personally hunted months for bells that rang as they did.

"Got any ideas about a museum to house my Americana?" he asked an architect on an Atlantic crossing.

"If it were mine"—the architect knew he had to think fast and engagingly—"I'd do a reproduction of Independence Hall."

On the tender into Cherbourg in the morning Ford told the architect to think over that idea and so would he, and "come to see me when you get back."

Architectural errors in the Philadelphia original were apparent in the measured drawings if they were not visible to the naked eye. Pilasters were off center an inch or so. Upstairs windows did not line up exactly over windows on the lower floor. Workmen of the period apparently had not worked to close current exactness. The architect was pleased with himself at catching the mistakes; being forewarned, he would be sure they did not creep into the reproduction.

"No, I don't want you to do that," Ford said flatly. The errors were to be repeated in the facsimile. He wanted validity, not correctives.

Historians might play fast and loose with events in the world's past, as he believed they did, so one hardly could tell what was what; he wanted no one taking architectural liberties, even remedial, with his carbon copy of the meeting house of the first Continental Congress, even if he shook up the interior to serve his needs.

A book on John Wilkes Booth led Ford into fourteen states in a year's investigation of its claim that the actor-assassin of Lincoln did not perish shortly after the crime, as history said, but escaped and died of poison in Oklahoma thirty-eight years later.

When he reconstructed the Sterling, Mass., schoolhouse to which the lamb followed Mary, he innocently found himself involved in a long-standing controversy over whether Mary and her ewe actually lived, and were put out of school for making the children laugh and play, or whether the stanzas were unalloyed fiction.

I have before me a copy of a twenty-two-page report made at his instigation and as serious in tenor as though it dealt with a Nuremberg war criminal. It begins with the conclusion, "There WAS a Mary and there WAS a lamb," and then, going back to the earliest beginning, it works forward, weighs each pro and con as a court might charge a jury and comes at last to the researcher's confident judgment that Mary was a living child and her lamb no less genuine.

Besides money, Ford had tenacity and long memory to call upon in this hunt for basic truth. He occasionally knotted the chain of his watch to remind him, he said, of something he might forget, but his household said a little suspiciously that he had "a good forgetter," and it meant "convenient" when it said "good." He could forget what he wanted to but some of his memory feats were a little staggering.

The mysterious actions of a pair of men digging in a sand dune on a Michigan bay some years ago might have puzzled anyone who happened to see them. Their car stopped a few yards from the shore line and backed a little. One of them got a shovel out of the back of the car, and the two walked over to a half buried object which a half hour's digging revealed as a discarded stove.

"No, not it," said the older man, disappointedly, and rested his spade.

"Sure? It seems to be a Starlight." The younger man got to his knees and studied the nameplate.

"Oh, it's a Starlight, all right, but a smaller model than the one we used to have," said the first man, resignedly.

They got back into their car. Henry Ford and his son Edsel were on a strange search. The treasure sought was a duplicate of the stove which warmed Ford's living room when he was boy. The make and model he had remembered for forty years. Eighteen months passed before the search ended.

A small-town doctor answered a knock at his door one hot summer morning and found a stranger who looked like someone he should know, but he couldn't place him at the minute.

"I'm told you have an old stove, an old Starlight stove," the man on the step said.

"Why yes, I have."

"I wonder if I could see it?"

The doctor preceded his caller into a back room. There it was—a companion piece of the stove in the Ford homestead, and they made a deal for $25. The doctor could have had ten times the price. He even helped his smiling buyer to lug and shove and carry it out and lift it into the visitor's automobile. The purchaser seemed hardly able to resist kindling a fire in it this roasting day. The anxiety to take immediate possession was beyond the town physician, but, after all, he was satisfied with the money he got and never did learn the identity of the palpitant buyer.

It took almost as long to find a duplicate of the Brussels carpet which had covered the homestead floor and which Ford remembered by the repeated urns of roses in the pattern. That quest ended in New York State after the country had been combed from coast to coast and many a defeated automobile dealer had embarrassedly reported failure—and lost his chance to win knighthood from the home office.

Mrs. Ford quoted a line from a schoolbook in 1913 and it set her husband off on a long and costly journey into lost country. She heard children laughing in the street in passing their home and she said to him, "Hear the children gayly shout," and he took it on from there and finished the couplet, "Half past four and school is out."

"That's from McGuffey's reader, but which one, Henry?" she asked. He said he wasn't sure but thought it was the first. The domestic banter launched him on his first serious collecting. The search for McGuffey readers led to the restoration of his birthplace . . . to the purchase of the Wayside Inn of Longfellow . . . to a passion for antiques . . . to the acquisition of not only single pieces of colonial and post-colonial *objets d'art* but of whole shops . . . to bulging warehouses and eventually to the building of Greenfield Village, where one could see how people lived and worked for 250 years, changing tools, methods, customs and environment. To some he seemed a man going furiously about with a basket trying to pick up pieces of a civilization he had done much to destroy.

He bought with profligacy, at times, as if he had been a poor man just advised of a winning sweepstakes ticket, but he got off to a modest enough start, and with no thought of the interminable road before him, in a search for the many editions of the school-readers of William Holmes McGuffey on which he and his wife and most Americans of their day had been suckled. They browsed in second-hand bookshops. They knew best what they wanted and at the time he was more inclined to do things for himself than trust to hired agents. He could do his own reconnoitering then without drawing a crowd or needing a police detail.

The eclectic readers were literary digests of their day. They contained, in capsuled form, those things that McGuffey regarded as classic—the soliloquy of Hamlet, the Elegy of Gray, "Death of Little Nell," "The Raven," "Evangeline"—his choice of the best from the whole body of English literature. McGuffey, the Indian fighter's son, had not written them; he merely assembled the material for the readers. Miami University made Ford a copy of the six-sided pedestal desk at which he did it. The six small books put out in endless editions gave the youth of America its first taste of world literature.

Ford wound up with a collection of readers second only to that of the university where McGuffey once taught. He reprinted them, made them must reading in his own schools, became a devoted member of the Federation of McGuffey Societies, made friends with whom he would trade duplicates and a blissful tip at times such as, "If you are short a third reader of 1844, write Anthony Harrendon, Pueblo, Col."

He acquired and moved to Dearborn the cabin in Pennsylvania where the teacher was born, its flintlocks and powder horns, Ma's candle molds and Pa's shaving mug, and even a covered bridge over a country creek that barefoot McGuffey walked as a boy.

He and Hamlin Garland, the author, not only shared a common resentment against theoretical farm lovers who painted rural life in rosy color as if cows milked themselves and crops were self-harvesting, but both were McGuffey alumni. Ford would sit on one side of a desk and Garland on the other and try each other's memory on what McGuffey had put in his books. One would recite a line, the other would follow with a second, and they'd go on until one or the other was stumped—then start afresh on other stanzas.

Restoration of Ford's birthplace took on some of the complexion of a Nile archaeological party burrowing for a lost Ptolemy but, instead of a king, the excavators came on a prize just as good—a broken piece of a dinner plate which provided a needed clue to the pattern of the china which William and Mary Ford had set upon the table before the problem boy, Henry, aged twelve and daft over machines. With it to go by, the cupboard was restocked to the last egg-cup.

The house had memories missing from the later and larger establishment called Fair Lane. Here Ford was born and his mother died. From its windows he could see the church where he had been christened and down the road a piece had lived the girl he married. Beyond those fences he cleared timber when that happened and built a house with his own hands, felling the trees and sawing them into the proper lengths.

Not that Fair Lane was regal. It had no gold-fitted baths or sky-lighted ballrooms such as 1945 GI's found when they clumped into the Villa Hugel of the Krupps at Essen. There were a half dozen rooms down, another six up, a billiard room, swimming pool, a bowling alley in the basement, and at one corner of the estate stood a bungalow where Ford used to entertain favored dealers in the halcyon days. As he got older he was more for and by himself. Other people usually wanted something, or he thought they did.

Not a specimen of the original family china could be found when Ford got to the restoration. Not a relative—and relatives were a dime a dozen—had a cup or plate, but one had an ingenious idea.

"Why don't you tear up some of the ground around the place?" this one suggested. "I'll bet some of them were broken at one time or other and they probably buried themselves."

A crew with spades and sieves was at the exhumation next morning and each night one of their number would go to his office or home to show the rewards of the digging. They not only brought up shards by which the design of the old china was determined, as had been guessed, but a pair of blackened skates on which Ford used to travel the Detroit River in the winter.

And then he came to the Red Horse Tavern, or Wayside Inn, immortalized by Henry Wadsworth Longfellow and run by four generations of Howes at Sudbury, Mass., since David put it up in 1686. Here many a dressy blade of history slept and swigged. Here Hawthorne's Molyneaux scratched on a window glass:

Who do you think
Here is good drink
Perhaps you may not know it;
If not in haste
Do stop and taste
You merry folk will show it.

Longfellow had found the hostelry the right muse for his *Tales of a Wayside Inn,* despite his reference to a "kind of Hobgoblin Hall now somewhat fallen to decay." Ford put the hobgoblin in sequins and gave it a renovating hair-do. Bostonians tried to raise money to do the same thing but failed, and asked the Fords to join them. But the Fords did not take in partners; they took over. They paid $175,000 for the inn and got free and clear control. As soon as the déclassé structure took on some of its original glory the waitresses struck—the heartbreak of ladies who said their wages and tips ran to $15 a day before Ford decided to turn back the clock and install a tipless day rate of $6. But despite the moans of the stricken ladies picketing on the turnpike, that's the way it stayed.

Ford loved the inn. He skated often on its pond and roamed its meadows and the country about it. Wayside came to be a must in the guide-books. He was there when I spent a night at the tavern, and I joked with him about the ropes curled at the upper windows as emergency exits in case of fire. How was anyone to slide out those narrow windows and get to the ground?

"You don't think they could?" he asked.

I said I was positive they couldn't. Ropes might be germane to the period, but not practical.

"Wait here." He was off.

He vanished in the house and appeared a few seconds later at a second-story window. He was sixty then. He allowed the rope to play out to the ground, and then climbed out and slid easily down without bothering to loop the rope about him.

"Easy as that," he said, as he wiped his hands with a handkerchief and asked one of the surprised hotel staff to go upstairs and roll up the fire-escape again.

His avidity for accuracy was applied to the tavern. A Sudbury woman with whom he danced said she did not think the floor of the ballroom on the second floor had the spring it did when she was a girl. In the remodeling, stout supporting posts had been erected under the floor. Ford put back the bounce she missed. A month later large car springs were installed in the tops of the two pillars and the wainscoting was made to slide.

He said once that the inn was his way of saying thanks to Longfellow for his "Psalm of Life," and one expected him to mention great men's footprints in the sands of time but he didn't. He had in mind, he said, four other verses—those that began "Tell me not in mournful numbers life is but an empty dream" and "Life is real! Life is earnest!" and the beginning of the sixth, "Trust no future, howe'er pleasant" and finally the ninth, "Let us then be up and doing."

The remark of a transient at Wayside hoisted Ford to the saddle of another hobbyhorse—a wooly one. The visitor said it probably was not generally known that in nearby Sterling was what was left of the school to which the lamb followed Mary in the jingle of school days, and that a descendant of the embarrassed Mary occupied now the same house Mary did then. Was not this Americana? Was he not custodian of good portions of Americana? His head on the pillow that night, he considered if he should bring to active functioning again the school of Mary and the lamb and put it into shape so children might sit in its seats again. It would delight them, wouldn't it? There was the possibility, of course, that the guest had been gulled by irresponsible hearsay. Well, he closed his eyes—he'd see to it in the morning.

Within seven months the foundations and framework of the original school, transferred to a side road between Wayside and a farm Babe Ruth used to own, had been worked into a replica of the old one. It was reborn and reoccupied, and early-rising Ford was at the door the wintry morning when the first sixteen pupils arrived and took their inkwells out of the niches in the warm chimney where Mary and her friends also kept theirs from freezing.

Information on the school was gathered in box-car lots. A collection of 200 manuscripts on the incident was acquired. Mrs. Christopher Tyler, *née* Sawyer, a matron of a Somerville, Mass. asylum and the Mary of the doggerel, had died in 1889 and was buried in Boston. She had soured pretty thoroughly over the publicity the verses got her and politely avoided the subject in later years as much as she could.

John Roulstone, author of the original three stanzas, had died at seventeen, a divinity freshman at Harvard. Aged twelve, he had been amused by eleven-year-old Mary's embarrassment that day in 1817 when she walked up the aisle to recite and the lamb clumped up after her, and next morning he rode across his father's fields and gave her a sheet of paper with the three verses upon it.

The lamb was gored by a cow and died in Mary's arms shortly

after the scandal at the schoolhouse, and the only surviving reminders of the ewe's ever being real, aside from the poem and what people said, were two pairs of stockings the mother of Mary knitted from the wool of its first shearing. They were unraveled and snips of them sold, with Mary's autograph, when Boston raised money to save old South Church.

The primitive school itself was opened in 1796, sold in 1856 for $35.50 and eventually became part of a church garage in Sterling, with of course no thought it would ever rise to the distinction of bronze tablets and cars with foreign licenses at its doors.

It is considered part of good husbandry to remove the tails of lambs but it wasn't safe practice when Ford's head was spinning with such staves as "Bah, bah, black sheep, have you any wool?" and particularly the one about those who'd come home dragging their "tails behind them."

I came upon a red-faced farm superintendent one morning who had seen no relation between the boss's current hobby and standard sanitary procedure of the time. While Ford was out of town, the shepherd had been struck with the idea that the lambs looked shabby and he cut off their tails. It turned out to be the wrong thing to do when an owner was carrying a torch for lambs *with* tails. Ford had been thunderstruck when he saw his own lambs.

"He is back and he just fined me $200." The farm manager paused as though reflecting on the crime that no agricultural college would have thought a crime at all. The angry flush deepened. "I've got to give the two hundred bucks to the Community Fund, he says." The tail-clipper groaned and drew his hand over his eyes as if to shut out the whole matter.

Nor was the filming of Mary and the lamb without incident.

"We'll do it ourselves," said Ford confidently, and started casting at once. "Your daughter will be Mary," he said to the executive across the desk. "You go ahead with the whole thing."

The official was a good bit busy at the time. He was buying property for railroad yards, had his fingers deep in three other company pies, and he found he was not always able to give the necessary time to the proposed film, in which first rehearsals centered on creation of a cordial alliance between his daughter and a chosen lamb from the Ford farm, so she could handle it and the animal would follow her. As often as he could, however, the father would deliver the young lady to the pasture and she would lean over the fence or go into the field and try to make friends with the lamb. But whether the animal was shy or had no acting sense, the progress was slow. Besides, as other work pressed on him, the father of the actress, Mary, was not always able to deliver her on location, and it seemed her courtship of the lamb took a lot of time from her regular school work.

"I see you weren't with us last night," Ford said one morning. The executive explained the difficulty of synchronizing business calls with the movie schedule.

"Yes, I know," Ford could see the trouble and had hit upon a way to overcome it. "I was thinking we would send over a lamb and a pen and put them in your back yard," he said. He looked for an assent that was hard to withhold. In that way, he said, the twilight trips to the farm could be by-passed.

When the official reached home the same night he found a stockade and a doghouse, an uncooperative lamb, some straw to bed it down and neighborhood kids lined along the fences shouting "Ba-a-a!" and the lamb, interested in the phenomenon, spiritedly yelling "Ba-a-a!" right back. A farm truck delivered milk each morning for the animal. At least the backward lamb had a star's perquisites.

About dawn it would wake before the neighborhood and have a spree of bleating. Occasionally it would break out of the corral and a volunteer posse would take after it. Household life was further complicated by the fact that even after the children of the town had been persuaded not to engage in their face-to-face contest, they would let out cries in passing on the far side of the street and the challenged captive would give ear and bleat defiance.

The daily exchange between lamb and children became such a fixture that even when the shooting of scenes finally was transferred east and the executive's back lawn was emptied of lamb, pen, milk and straw, the kids continued to "Baa" members of the family. They were able to go off barbitols, however, and get some welcome sleep.

None of the three lambs drafted ever seemed able to get it through its skull that it was supposed to follow Mary adoringly and lie down and be tended by her. That was the way it had to be. Mary had saved the original lamb by careful nursing and catnip tea; it thus became devoted to her and trotted after her to school. It was not possible to doctor fact. If it was not catnip for the lamb, Mary was getting clover tops for the horses, and on all the evidence it was only a matter of time before a horse would have followed her to school, if it had not been for the ewe making a show of her.

Just when the movie lamb was up in its lines it had fattened so much in long rehearsal that a smaller lamb, with fresh obstinacy and no idea of what was wanted, had to be substituted and the grind begun again. The second had to be let out for the same reasons: swelling girth and failure to snap into the role. A third appeared.

With that the troup moved to location on Redstone Hill, Mass., scene of the original episode, and eventually the project was turned over to professionals. Somewhere they got a lamb who recognized the story possibilities and the rare chance to get its name into lights.

Ford listened in wonder to one enchanting story which took a great deal of labor and travel to fit together and had him on the edge of his chair for a year. Voltaire, Plutarch, Goethe and Thomas Jefferson said, in so many words, that history was bunk, but when Ford testified he thought so, too, in a libel suit against the Chicago *Tribune,* there was much excited slavering and pointing of fingers in his direction. He was scoffed at by those who scoff easily, but as a poultice for his sores, if he needed any, he had many letters from people who said he was right and offered proof of what they thought historical misstatements—a list of dark spots in the past which later-day bookkeepers had whitewashed, and stories which seemed to bear out the thesis that recorded history was a cracked and convex looking-glass.

Among the miscellany were two copies of the same book. Ford tossed one of them on the desk of Fred L. Black, one of his Warwicks, and said he had been awake with the other until 4 o'clock that morning.

"Quite a tale," he admitted.

The book was *The Escape and Suicide of John Wilkes Booth,* and the pretentious sub-title was: *The First True Account of Lincoln's Assassination.* The author was Finis L. Bates, a lawyer of Memphis, Tenn., the publication date 1907.

"Read it over," Ford suggested as his subordinate thumbed through the pages, "and let me know tomorrow what you think of it."

He was back and seated across the desk again as soon as Black hung up his hat next day. Well, what was his opinion?

Black said it was a whopping tale—fascinating. Ford agreed it sure was, but was it true.

"I'd want to see a number of statements checked before I could swallow it," Black turned skeptic. He thought some of the purported evidence weak, some too pat and seemingly scissored to order.

The Bates contention: The actor Booth had not been shot to death under the locusts of the Richard H. Garrett farm south of Washington, eleven days after the murder of Lincoln, but took poison in his bed, as David George, house painter, thirty-eight years later in Enid, Oklahoma. Bates professed to have in his garage the remains of the assassin.

"Let's get this fellow up here and see what he has to say for himself," Ford recommended.

The Memphis lawyer admitted the need of caulking some of the holes in his narrative. If Ford would put up $8,000 he'd do a more intensive investigation to fortify the weak spots. His home was mortgaged and otherwise he just couldn't afford to drop his law practice to scuttle around the country clearing up the disputed points. The resultant new book he would write, he was sure, would have tremendous sales, and he and Ford would share the applause for correcting a palpable historical untruth.

"I'll put the mummy in your hands as collateral," the lawyer offered.

But Ford did not want any mummy put in his hands for $8,000 —or $1,000, the rock-bottom price it was reduced to. (The carcass later had an unreal career, being sold dissected in Chicago, seized for debt in Omaha, threatened with hanging by Civil War veterans in Pennsylvania, exciting the bug-eyed who paid their dimes to see it on carnival circuits.) Bates was put off and he returned to Memphis.

"You nose out the truth." Ford turned to Black. The project thus set afoot belonged by its twists and thoroughness of execution and *dramatis personae* with the pukka sahib's best. The trail ran long and led through fourteen states and to crossroads never heard of. Stories told were as dissimilar as the dissimilar people who told them.

The cast included Lincoln and Booth, a Zouave suspect plummeting from a cliff to escape pursuers, a leathery mummy in a Tennessee barn when not rented out to tent shows, an ex-New York *Sun* reporter, who had discovered an embalming secret of the Egyptians, a fugitive hidden in Ceylon, a Texas saloonkeeper claiming a decade after the assassination that he was Booth, an Oklahoma morphine addict dying a suicide in 1903 and confessing he killed Lincoln, and an Atlanta clergyman, the Rev. J. G. Armstrong, who did not say he was or wasn't the murderer of the President but about whom the myth-makers of his parish had ideas.

There was such furniture of drama as derringers and drugs and deathbed confessions, doctors' affidavits and secret remittances, horses driven into quicksand and shot, a body buried headless, the rusty threat of "Tell a word of this and I'll slit your throat."

Black spent a tireless twelve months groping methodically and persistently in the misty labyrinth of this cloak-and-dagger classic.

The official version of Booth's flight and death eleven days after the assassination is familiar—the concealment of the body for fear hotheads might make off with it and use it to inflame Southern sympathizers to new revolt, the later ample identification by scars and jewelry and diary, the trial and hanging of four conspirators, subsequent exhumation of the remains and burial in the family plot at Baltimore. But the romancers would not be denied. It was said the body had been buried headless . . . it had been taken to sea on a gunboat, weighted and sunk . . . two years after the slaying a sea captain wrote that Booth was in hiding on the island of Ceylon. Others insisted Booth never died as the government said.

Bates set up two major claims: (1) A saloonkeeper client, John St. Helen, had sworn him to secrecy in Granbury, Texas, in 1876 and then announced he was Booth. (2) A house painter named David E. George died of self-administered poison in Enid, Okla., in 1903, saving his last whispered words for a similar confession. Bates had gone to Enid, professed to see in George his old friend St. Helen, and claimed the remains. The implication was that the government had paid $75,000 in rewards for a man not Booth.

Ford's investigator, Black, found that the alleged St. Helen confession, moreover, was no skin-and-bones affair. It embodied the generally known facts published in many newspapers up to the now questioned capture, and thus known to many people, but Bates had Booth or St. Helen leaving the Garretts, taking to the underbrush when told of approaching troops, posing as a Rebel soldier by day, sleeping in creek bottoms by night, making his way unrecognized and unsuspected across an alerted continent afoot, by horse and as driver of a wagon train, until he joined up with his mother and brother, Junius, on the West Coast. Then Mexico and finally to harbor in Granbury.

Why had he killed Lincoln? St. Helen was quoted as saying he did it at the instigation of the vice-president of the United States, Andrew Johnson, so the Tennessean might become president and make reconstruction easier on the beaten South. The exact dying words of the man, who did not die, were:

"I am dying. I am not John St. Helen but John Wilkes Booth. I am the assassin of Lincoln. There is a tintype under my pillow. I leave it with you for future identification. Notify my brother Edwin Booth in New York."

And followed the windy tale of flight from the rail of Lincoln's box at the theatre to the Pacific Coast, the haze increasing as the Garrett farm and the substantiated events receded. Black quickly discovered that two main points conflicted with established fact:

In the Bates report of St. Helen's "confession," Booth and a collusionist had stayed at a tavern ten miles out of Washington and did not reach the city until 3 o'clock the afternoon of the assassination. Yet it had been established that Booth got a haircut in a Washington barbershop at 9 A.M. the same day; and he called at Ford's theatre for mail about noon, being seen by five persons.

St. Helen exhibited to Bates, the lawyer said, scars on his right leg which he attributed to his jump from the theatre box to the stage in his flight. Yet at the conspiracy trial the doctor who taped the fugitive Booth swore it was the left foot which was fractured and from which he had to slit a shoe.

Between what Bates wrote and old settlers remembered in the Ford agent's inquiry was a considerable gulf. Bates described the saloonkeeper as constantly reciting Shakespeare, making fine speeches, appearing at public entertainments—a social favorite "who held all men to polite behavior" and a leader in amusing games.

Men still living recalled St. Helen as a "typical saloon desperado, who kept away from social gatherings, never was seen to read a book, was hardly able to make a speech because of asthma, became dramatic only when warmed by whiskey, received a deep cut from a half-breed's knife in a bloody scuffle."

After Bates had done with the known published facts in the reputed disclosures, he was vague as to dates, names and places. He hinted of secret remittances that kept St. Helen going, but old-timers told Ford's investigator the saloonkeeper never had more money than he normally could earn out of his business. He packed one day and left Granbury and no one there saw him again.

On the night of April 13, 1903, the house painter George died in a hotel room in Enid, and whether he said on his deathbed or not that he was Booth, he told a woman so in El Reno, Okla. Three years previously on a sickbed he wrote on a slip of paper the words, "I am going to die before the sun goes down," and signed it "J. Wilkes Booth."

His confidante was Mrs. J. E. Harper, a guest at the house where George roomed when he took an overdose of morphine. She was sitting at his bedside, and, in a benumbing moment for her, he rose up and said: "I have killed one of the best men who ever lived, Abraham Lincoln." She thought he was delirious. A police official who knew the habits of the El Reno carpenter put it down as the imaginings of a drugged mind.

The George "confession" differed from known fact in this: Nothing was said of the flight that led south in the Maryland night. Instead, this Booth declared that, after the assassination, friends concealed him in a trunk and put him on a vessel for Europe, where he had stayed ten years.

When Mrs. Harper read in an Enid newspaper of the suicide of George three years later, she told the undertakers what the house painter had once told her, and suggested they look into it.

The Bates book implied that Mrs. Harper had known the house painter for some time, declaring he was well supplied with money, the origin of which no one knew; stating he was an eccentric who claimed to be a house painter but actually did no work at it, and describing George as a well-known figure on the streets of Guthrie and Enid.

To the Ford representative she categorically denied each and all of these statements. She had known George casually for two months, said he worked steadily as a painter, if he got funds from a secret source it was news to her, and she had no knowledge whether he was well known or not in Enid and Guthrie. Only the confession itself of George to Mrs. Harper wholly withstood close scrutiny.

The book said the house painter had bought a $3,500 cottage in

El Reno. Courthouse records showed a down payment of $350 and a mortgage of $350 on a small place which George sold within four months of buying.

The alleged deathbed confession of George and the identification of the body at the morgue developed some cloudy aspects; also, Bates had George saying, through an alleged eyewitness: "I have only to say my name is not George but John Wilkes Booth and I request that my body be sent to the morgue for identification," and the undertaker saying when Bates appeared at the mortuary: "We need no picture to identify this man in your presence. This is the same man as your tintype shows."

When Black made his probe for Ford, an ex-guest at the hotel on the night of the suicide said he climbed through a transom when he heard groans inside George's room, and sent for a doctor, but that George died without a word before the doctor could administer a hypodermic.

The undertaker said: "I was never able to see any striking resemblance between the body and the tintype. In fact, Bates asked me to do all I could to make the body look like the picture and so we combed the hair and mustache accordingly."

He and his partner had concocted a new embalming fluid. The death of the impoverished George was a heaven-sent chance to try it out. Miraculously it worked. It preserved the body for years and made possible its exhibition in circuses years after death, under the challenging banner, *One Thousand Dollars to Anyone Who Can Prove This Is Not John Wilkes Booth.*

I have been unable to trace the mummy in recent years but in 1938 it was reported as still going strong, the property of an ex-tattooed man of the Wallace-Hagenbeck circus.

Bates said in his book that a letter was left for him by the suicide but was stolen from the body in the morgue before he arrived. He also claimed he received a telegram to come to Enid to identify the remains but lost the wire. The Enid undertaker said: "Bates wired me to ask if he could see the body if he came to town. He read the story of the death in a Memphis newspaper."

Re-editing of newspaper accounts reprinted in the book were regarded as questionable. In one revision the word "almost" became "absolutely" in the sentence, "The Booth chin, mouth, upper lip and general description is *ALMOST* perfect in the corpse." A story in the Enid *Wave* describing George's handwriting was changed from "large round-letter schoolboy writing" to "round scrawly boy writing." Black found no similarity between the chirography of the note George wrote and signed for Mrs. Harper and official specimens of the Booth handwriting.

A. McCager, another Tennessean, swore his stepmother married Booth in 1872, not knowing his true identity, and that later the actor explained to her some leg sores with the petrifying statement: "I got them, Miss Lou, at the Ford theatre when I killed Abraham Lincoln." Booth, or whoever it was, told McCager, the son said, he would cut his throat if he blabbed.

Blanche Booth, an actress-niece of the assassin, said she was with a touring company in El Reno in December, 1902, when a man came to her lodgings and she slammed her door on him, thinking him some stagestruck citizen and not wishing to be bothered. He left a card, however, and later when she read it, she said, she thought she recognized the writing of her notorious uncle.

Periodically, Black would return to Dearborn and run his rushes, the house would darken, the screen light up, and Ford would sit back and gustily enjoy another episode in the serial. His interest never diminished and he sighed a little when he knew there would be no more performances.

The conclusions: Neither St. Helen nor George was John Wilkes Booth. The actor had died as the record said and was buried in Greenmount Cemetery, Baltimore.

"I think," said Black, "the pair were egomaniacs who belong only in historical fiction."

Ford turned at the door on the way out. "Tell Mr. Bates we're no longer interested."

But Mary's lamb, Booth's body, the scouring of the country for a stove just like the one in the homestead—all these were but preliminaries to the main event.

He was not quite ready for that but soon would be. It was to be the capsheaf, but its form was not clear in his mind. He had just a vague suspicion. He would shortly set out on two hundred acres a museum, a village and a whole educational system to show youth, while priming it for the future, what the past had been.

The race would be better off if children did not have to lean wholly on textbooks or what adults told them, for adults were not always as sure of their facts as they let on. If the youngsters were to know the furniture of Sheraton and the china of Wedgwood, they should see and handle it. They would know a town pump if it was there and they used it. It would be best if they went down the well to Wonderland with Alice and the rabbit who had a watch and did not merely wait and take her word for what she saw when she returned.

The next project would be his *chef d'oeuvre*. It would give the kids something he did not have himself when he was a boy—and often regretted he didn't—a fine education.

Greenfield village emerges from the yearnings for the past of a man who professed to believe largely in today—and tomorrow.

CHAPTER XIII

CURIOSITY SHOP

IN LOOKING for the original chairs and china, the shawl or tea-cozy or antimacassar of the home he grew up in, Henry Ford began to poke about antique shops. In searching for a missing object he became interested in others he remembered as a boy but which his family did not happen to own.

He would pick up some article wonderingly and exclaim, "Mother, I remember this; the Carlsons had one just like it, didn't they?"

His interest pivoted at first on the period of his youth but he kept going back—farther and farther back, buying more and more. His fate was that of most collectors—the road had no end. One thing led inevitably to another.

The excursion into the past and his relish for its products contradicted his philosophy, in a way. He was indifferent to ancestry. When he bought a blue-ribbon herd of Ayrshires from an Indianian who had spent thousands on pedigreed cattle, Ford threw away the papers attesting their blood lines. "It doesn't matter what a man's grandfather did or was," he said flatly, and tore up the biographies.

In refurnishing Wayside Inn he bought more furnishings than the tavern ever could hold. He bought whole collections by the gross, entire shops. The mortality rate of post road shoppes ran high, urban auction rooms abounded in his agents, galleries of note were apprised that Ford was in the market for such and such and to be on the lookout, and he roamed the corduroy roads himself, playing 'possum by calling himself Mr. Robinson or Mr. Henry and falling out of the sky unannounced on someone who had, he heard, some salt glaze or Blue Staffordshire.

A blue-eyed springy oldster would walk into a shop, brighten over some miscellany he saw, whisper a few words to a companion and go out. The companion would glance about off-handedly after Ford departed and suddenly ask: "Will you put a price on your entire stock?" A week later the plunder would be unloading at Dearborn. He did not know frequently what he had bought until the unpacking.

A thousand shiny new Ford automobiles pushed off; a thousand gimcracks from curiosity shops pulled in on the sidings. He seemed to have no plan in mind for it except to build the mountain higher.

Years later, after the phobia had paid off in tidy achievement, I spent some time with one of Ford's many retired lieutenants. He had not shared Ford's fire but he had marveled at it.

"There was a time it wasn't safe to pass a rusty plow," he reflected. Ford certainly had it bad then. The ex-right-hand-man spoke wistfully. "If I managed to see the plow first," he remembered, "I'd draw his attention to the other side of the road. If I didn't he'd be out of the car and up to the farm door to dicker for that damned scrap."

You know, he recollected, Ford would paint up that old heap and replace the pieces it needed and in a month it would be as good as new. It beat him, he said. What good was it when he got it done? It was simply a plow thirty years behind the times.

Charles E. Sorensen, his production wizard, got the better of Ford once. His millions could not buy everything. For years Ford was after a dubious prize that "Cast-Iron" Charlie would not give up. It was, of all things, a *Bible,* and not a rare one.

Before the United States got into World War I, Ford, already dreaming on colossal lines, stopped one morning in the center of a swampy field along the Detroit River and gestured with his two hands in a sweeping motion.

"We'll build it here," he announced.

"It" was the mastodon of all Ford works, the River Rouge plant.

Sorensen chanced to walk into a deserted Methodist Church on the property before the wreckers got to it.

On the dusty cushion of a pew was an 1851 *Bible* left by some evicted worshipper. On the cover was gilt embossed, *"To Mother from*

James," and one or the other had written with a pen two scriptural quotations on the title page. One was: "But seek ye first the Kingdom of God and His righteousness and all these things shall be added unto you." The other was misquoted: "What should it profit a man if he gained the whole world and loses his soul?"

The book was an apple of discord for years.

"You got it off company property, Charlie, didn't you?" Ford would contend.

"I was the one who found it."

"What'll you take for it?"

"Nothing."

"It's mine," Ford would reassert.

"You haven't a chance of getting it."

Ford said he kind of liked the second biblical quotation.

"You do? Me too!" his balky subordinate would say—and not soften.

The conversation was repeated in a hundred forms in a hundred places but the production man never gave in and Ford never was able to coax it from him.

"Want to sell it?"

"I've got all the money I need—and you say I can write my own ticket if I want more." Sorensen spurned the cash offer.

"That's true, Charlie, but I sure would like the book, if you ever see your way clear."

Ford would drop the subject maybe for a year until Sorensen was almost sure he had forgotten it and then he'd bring up the subject some day when they were riding somewhere.

The mountain of treasure grew Alpine—mugs and churns and footwarmers and Apostle spoons—statuettes by Rogers and silver by Paul Revere, lidded boxes and perfume vials of a faraway day before scents became *parfum* guaranteed to knock a male silly at a single inhalation—Chippendale and Hepplewhite, Hadley and Duncan Phyfe—Old World ceramics, a stuffed owl from an old-time barber shop, flails and plows and footed compotes and a gate-leg table at which Lafayette dined and wined—porcelain caddies and decanters, banjo clocks, French crocus pots and handpumps—houses and inns and forges and mills.

The granddaughter of Peter Cooper of Cooper Union tendered

her collection of silver-studded harness and eighteen carriages. Lincoln had ridden in one and another bore Theodore Roosevelt to his inaugural. William Howard Taft sent a saddle and gold-braided blanket. Occasionally Ford seemed to pick up certain articles more because they were old than collectible, but they were desirable to him and that was enough.

He bought so freely in his collecting period that much went unassorted and uncatalogued for years. If fervor led him into mistakes, he could afford them; and he was a great hand to find profit in those he made himself.

He had decided to flitch-saw his Northern Michigan timber and his veteran superintendent said it would not work, damn it.

"When I want something done my way, that's the way I want it." Ford was frigid.

"Well, of all the tomfoolishness!" The woodsman spun on his heel and stomped off to give the order that was all wrong by his experience.

I was in an office with the forthright lumberman and another executive when it had been decided many months later to change direction—after a fortune had been sunk in timber operations. Ford had won his way, of course, in pressing for experiments that did not pan out.

He had paid his men three times the prevailing wage, did the best and probably the first selective logging in Michigan. He never mistreated soil knowingly. While taking timber out he wanted to conserve. He wouldn't skim the thing, take the profit and let future generations suffer. Some experiments flopped. What he did couldn't be done and compete in the market.

"So we lost $20,000,000, eh?" he remarked as he walked into the room.

The other men were grave but Ford did not seem blue. "Well," he said, "I guess we'd better change that." He sat down and talked for a while of the soured innovations, as one who had merely dropped a penny through a crack in an old wooden walk. Yes, the company would wash it out.

He finally had to go and he got up. "We learned something, didn't we? We have to pay for an education," he paused at the door for the last understatement, "I guess it was uneconomical." He was out and down the hall. He wrote it off like that. After all there would be ways to get the money back, and if not, what he had lost was only money and he had stacks.

The period pieces mounted higher—first a few odds and ends, a tableful, a jammed room, a packed building, then several bursting warehouses. Edsel remonstrated that the hodgepodge was getting to be a fire hazard.

"We really ought to get the stuff out of here, Father," he suggested. "Let's make a museum of it."

The senior Ford said that was not exactly what he had in mind but he wasn't sure yet what disposal he would make of it. Once he was disdainful of a psychiatrist I mentioned who collected streetcar transfers, for some reason hard to understand.

"What in the world is he going to do with them?" the motor-maker snorted.

"I don't know," I said, "but what are you going to do with all your stuff?"

He said he didn't know for certain, either.

He acquired more acres of curiosa, had promises of much to come—the Uxbridge, Mass., blacksmith shop whose smithy Longfellow had made famous, the boardinghouse of Sarah Jordan in Jersey which was the terminus of the first successful demonstration of the electric light outside Edison's workshop, Wedgwood and Leedsware and Chelsea, the first mill to produce silk by power in America, a Cape Cod windmill the Pilgrims put up, a desk of John Hancock, a carding mill near his home where he went with his father with raw wool as a boy to have it made into rovings for his mother to spin into yarn on the wheel at home.

The idea of Greenfield Village—which with other units of the development was to cost him an estimated $25,000,000—shaped up slowly. He did not want a dead museum—that he was sure of. Gradually the picture took form. He would have a village which would be a cross-section of a hundred villages, grouped about a central green in the colonial pattern, but of no fixed era.

In Virginia the Rockefellers restored Williamsburg; at Dearborn Ford built a village that was a conglomeration of periods. Herbs would be planted in a likeness of a Greek garden of the thirteenth century; a limestone house would be taken apart, stone by stone, in the Cotswold hills of England and brought across the Atlantic, so that one could see how the Pilgrims lived when they set out adventurously for a new shore.

In Ford's village a visitor would see how the pioneers lived—tallow to gaslight to electricity—how their progressive sons improved on ancestral living—surrey to tandem to jalopy to wings. It would be an engineer's idea of history—a re-creation of a civilization from the objects that it used—its tools, its utensils and its ornaments.

He was suspicious of experts and he trusted largely to his own judgments. I remember standing with him when he was talking to a landscape authority about certain changes he might want. The architect suggested ways to improve the scene. Goodbys were said eventually and he drove off.

"Know the trouble with these landscape people?" Ford grimaced, as the architect's car turned into the main road. "If there are a lot of trees, they say they must cut some down to get a vista; if there are no trees, they say they've got to put in some to break up the vista." So much, he thought, for "authorities."

Thousands of words have been written of Greenfield Village. Thousands of visitors have browsed there. I do not intend to inventory its treasure. The catalogues do the job amply, but the eternal flames, honored business in the hamlet, are a story on which the guidebooks are silent and which spiced life in their beginnings.

The fancy for perpetual monuments of fire was born in the squire of Greenfield as he watched in a sobering moment, some say, the light of the Paris tomb lave the last repose of France's soldier. The inspiration may have been the less romantic fact that Ford accepted flame as a continuous living force. It endured, as he wanted memory of him and his car to endure. The flooring of his museum cost $325,000 because he demanded a wood that would last a thousand years, and the builders obliged with teak.

Herbert Hoover lighted one fire in the transplanted Logan County courthouse where Lincoln pleaded cases as a fledgling. Thomas A. Edison put match to a second in the original clapboard shop where the incandescent bulb was born, and a granddaughter of Stephen Collins Foster, beloved of balladists, lit the stove in the cottage where her illustrious forebear first drew breath.

The success of Ford in getting a light, symbolically, from the dead hand of Foster was a work of ingenuity and had overtones of drama. The original plan was to bring the closest living descendant, in direct line, to Dearborn to light the flame, but a shattering telegram arrived at the eleventh hour. Marion Foster Welch, daughter of the bard, was ill in Pittsburgh and her doctor said her presence was out of the question.

What Ford wanted, his zeal and junior generals usually got for him, and the panic was only temporary. He walked into the laboratory the day after the wired news with a new program which bore the hallmarks of phantasy.

"We'll do this," he said—and proceeded to sketch out what it was he wanted done, to the last minuscular detail.

Foster had closed his eyes, true, the year after Ford opened his, so naturally a light from the composer's own hand was not attainable. His wife was dead, too—*Jeanie of the Light Brown Hair,* a song which was to head the hit parade eighty-seven years after it was written and please the customers all the way from Smoky Joe's in Tuscaloosa to the oval room of the Ritz. Their daughter was alive but sick. Very well:

Find a couple of railroad lanterns. They were strong, and thick wire shields protected the glass. Take two, so one will be left if one is broken. They are not to be shipped, but delivered by a company driver to the Ford representative in Pittsburgh. Tell him long distance what he is to do and follow with confirmatory letter of precise instructions by the driver. The agent is to take the lanterns to the home of Mrs. Welch, describe the epochal pickle the company is in, and have the sick woman light them.

A tired courier in a spattered Lincoln delivered the two lanterns and a supply of over-sized matches to the Pittsburgh Ford agent at daybreak, and the doorbell of the Welch home rang a few hours later.

"Do you really believe you are strong enough to do this, Mrs. Welch?" the official asked solicitously, after the nurse had taken him into the sick room. He had talked by phone with her the previous evening and she had quickly agreed. She was quite strong enough to help; it was just that she was too weak for a journey to Detroit.

The agent placed the lanterns and matches on a table and smiled down a little apologetically on the willing co-star.

"I can manage it," she said. "Nurse, just prop me up, will you?" She paused for a sip from a glass beside her. The nurse put a steadying hand between her shoulders. "Now," Mrs. Welch suggested, "give me a match and hold up a lantern."

She lighted both quite easily. A different match was used on each, and when the wicks glowed evenly, what was left of the charred sticks was packed in cotton-batting in a pasteboard box.

"Well, we did it," said the patient with gayety as she looked at the two lamps shining on her dressing table. Her visitor said he didn't know the right words to thank her.

"I think I am doing very little for a father who did so much," she said. She also said she thought she knew exactly how Ford felt. "I suspect," she guessed, "they're the songs he sang at socials, in his days of wooing, at his mother's organ."

The Ford agent himself climbed on a train a few hours later with the two pieces of bizarre baggage—an open crate containing the lighted lanterns and the small box holding the unspent halves of the matches. He sat up most of the night to make sure no impious draft undid his work—and his career in Pittsburgh.

The sequel was written at the dedication when seventy descendants of the bard gathered in the rooms and on the lawn of the cottage with other guests, and Stephen Foster, who left the world a lush legacy at a basement price and never earned more than $1,500 in his best year, was formally ushered into the private Ford parthenon.

A granddaughter of the composer took one of the matches her mother used in Pittsburgh and touched it to one of the lanterns and then to the readied wood in the kitchen range.

The songs of Foster expressed the sentiments that warmed him in an idiom Ford understood. He liked and sang with enthusiasm such lyrics as *Come Where My Love Lies Dreaming* and *Old Dog Tray,* and in time, of course, the cottage had a stand-in for the original Tray.

The composer owned two dogs, Tray and Calamity, but only one achieved posthumous fame. Calamity apparently was not a go-getter, munched his bones, bayed at the moon and died unsung, never agitating a muse in his lifetime. The pride of the Foster household was a setter and long dead, naturally; and one day Ford agents came up with a gentle one of the breed who was glad to work at Greenfield and pretend he was the Pittsburgh Tray. He lived out his span happily beside Greenfield's version of the Suwanee River, despite a single challengeable flaw.

Ford found a tang in carrots many people missed, but even at the height of his master's passion, you could find a discarded ring of them around Tray's plate, where he pushed them in his resentment. Wherever a billionaire sits may be the head of the table, but it wasn't so in the setter's book. To the end he snubbed anyone who suggested he ought to eat a few carrots for the sake of politeness and security reasons, if no more.

It was in the quiet of late evening, alone, that Ford enjoyed the Foster cottage most. He could look from one window and see the home of Noah Webster in the twilight, from another that of Luther Burbank. Across the way was his own Suwanee with a side-wheeler of the same name which foundered in the floods on the night Ford died. The Suwanee of Foster rises in the South Georgia marshes and empties into the Gulf; the private Suwanee of Ford flows in a circle. Its water spills in over a water wheel from a tributary of the Detroit River, and he often steamed up his ancient bark and took village children cruising round and round in its slow eddies.

One night I found him there. Some news dispatch involving him had come over the wires in the afternoon and he said he'd be glad to hear of any later additional facts.

"Call me at the house if you hear anything tonight," he requested, and said if he wasn't there he'd probably be at the Foster cottage. He'd probably be working the Swiss music box whose small bells played *Suwanee.*

The message came over the wires but his home said he wasn't there and I drove to Greenfield and walked up the village road past a guard, who apparently had been forewarned. When I gave my name he waved me along.

"The boss is up at the Foster cottage, all right," he said.

Without knocking, I opened the door and went in. The man hunched over the organ did not hear me and did not turn around. Alone with himself, he was picking out with one finger the melody of *Old Folks at Home,* with a concentration that excluded all the motor-cars and ships at sea, the planes in the sky that bore his name, and the assembly lines everywhere making bread and butter for him and thousands of men he'd never know.

His affection for the songs of Foster got him into some early trouble. He went all out for starting the day with a song. He advocated it in interviews in musical journals. He practiced it by joining in the children's choruses in early-morning chapel. But a venture in evensong did not fare so well. When he decided to throw a dam across the Rouge on his estate many years back, he told the contractor he'd like an all-colored crew.

"Do you suppose you can do that?" he asked.

The builder said discipline was better maintained in his opinion with a mixed crew but he guessed he could arrange it, if that was what was wanted.

"Have them bring out their musical instruments," added Ford.

When the forty Negro pick-and-shovel boys arrived they brought, as ordered, a heterogeneous collection of banjos, mouth-organs, jew's-harps, even a battered violin. They also brought *Old Black Joe* and *Kentucky Home* right to his riverbank, and they constituted a fine harmonizing chorus.

Workers who did not go home at night slept in a frame farmhouse on the property. Sometimes during the day Ford would call off work on the dam and ask them to sing, and he would sprawl on the bank while out on the concrete the boys would obediently drop what they might be doing and give with Foster songs and others that Ford never had heard before.

Some evenings he would drive out from town and sit in the farmhouse to enjoy the choral work until late in the night. Occasionally he would take out a special treat of melons or steaks. The crew found it much more interesting than sinking a shovel in a river bed or shoring up a bank. They got to banking their pay with him.

But one night the contractor got a four-alarm telephone call. He had better come right away. There had been a fight. One Negro had fired an axe at another in a brawl, and it had missed the man at whom it was flung and struck a Ford engineer, one of the few white men on the job. The injury was not serious but the fracas scared Ford, who had been an eyewitness.

"Close down the job for two weeks, until someone gets a little sense," he told the contractor, reluctantly.

The honeymoon was over. Future concerts got a blanket cancellation, but he found a new outlet. He pulled the contractor off the dam. He wanted to put up feeding stations for birds and he and the dam-builder spent a good part of the day looking for locations up and down the grassy banks which would be convenient and where the birds would be sure to find them. Also, electricity was run to pans all over the estate so the water would not freeze and birds could drink from them at all seasons.

The ancient Springfield, Illinois, courthouse where Abraham Lincoln practiced law as a stripling faces on the village green, and here burns the second perpetual flame.

When Ford went to get and move it, the main door was gone, the windows cracked by winds and the stones of small boys. Time had dug scallops in the plaster, but all this could be—and was—freshenec and given almost original newness. The missing door was removed from an outhouse to which it had descended, the plaster was taken off, boxed, and shipped to Greenfield to be mixed with fresh lime for plastering the re-established rooms.

Seven months after the courthouse had been revived and opened, an actor named Miles, who closely resembled the Emancipator, paid Greenfield a visit. He had been lecturing on Lincoln throughout the country, claimed some relationship to the family and asked if there was a chance of meeting Ford.

"The resemblance to Lincoln is incredible," a wide-eyed executive informed the motormaker. He said he thought Ford might be interested in meeting the man. Ford thought so, too. The actor regaled his host with good anecdotes and it was only after an hour—a long time for Ford to let a conversation run without having to make a telephone call from which he did not return—Ford proposed that the lecturer remain as a guest in the village for a week or two.

"Make your headquarters in the courthouse, Mr. Miles," Ford invited. "You'll be able to tell our visitors many things about Mr. Lincoln they do not know, and, of course, the children will be delighted, if they're not scared to death."

The actor strolled over unobserved to the courthouse in the afternoon with a guide to show the way, arranged his belongings and wearily sank into a rocking chair in front of the hearth for a nap before going to the inn for dinner.

There in that corner is the cupboard the rail-splitter fashioned. That table is from his Springfield office. Yonder is the theatre chair in which he was sitting when the assassin Booth fired his shots. The ghosts that people such rooms might well have looked at the dozing actor and asked if they had miscounted time. Here was young Lincoln not markedly different from what he was in 1845.

The burning wood crackled. Quiet settled on the room. The sleeper's head fell slightly to one side. When the night watch thrust open the door, he stared unbelievingly at the lank figure in the rocker. He tried to speak but no words came, and in desperation he banged the door and fled down the path. The eternal fire could stay lit or go out, if he had to deal with graves reopening.

"I've seen a ghost," Joe panted breathlessly to the first person he met. "Lincoln's up in the courthouse takin' a snooze." His voice rose in shrill fright. His heart pounded and he ducked into Sam Lamiere's tintype shop for refuge and companionship and hysterically repeated the alarm that Lincoln was at large. He slumped into one of Sam's chairs and wiped his forehead.

"They can have my badge!" he said, and slapped it on the counter to prove he was not fooling.

Sam stepped out to the sidewalk and looked skeptically up the road to the courthouse, but it seemed no different or more dangerous than it normally was.

"It's your stomach," he told Joe coldly, but the watchman only stared back bleakly.

It took hours to quiet Joe and villagers for days would meet and twit him about his scare. "How's the ghost makin' out, Joe?" Even Ford gave him a small autographed book of ghost stories, apologizing for its omission of the story of Joe and the Lincoln apparition, but the watchman never quite recovered and in time quit to work for Packard where, somehow he figured, a ghost was less likely to call.

The third eternal light was from the hand of Edison. It burns low beneath the boiler in the Menlo Park laboratory where, with a world tuned to its radios, the accouchement of the first incandescent bulb was reenacted in 1929.

Edison sat on the same chair, his assistant Francis Johl on the same step-ladder, operating the mercury, and performed a second time for a new generation those final experimental steps by which man graduated from the unsure flicker of wick and tallow.

Here Edison had invented the carbon telephone transmitter. Here came into being the phonograph. Here Edison had toiled on fuses and switches, lamp sockets and what many regarded as the first practical motion picture camera. For ten years here he had applied a boundless inquisitiveness to many things then secret.

Menlo Park and most of its recovered appurtenances were moved to Greenfield from New Jersey and reconstructed, even to a hickory stump by which the building stood, and several carloads of red clay on which it rested. Ford himself found and patched the original mortar and pestle.

The Pennsylvania Railroad was an involuntary contributor of $1,400 to this realism. The Department of Agriculture charged that in shipping an acre of ground the railroad did not treat the soil chemically.

"It dumped on Michigan," argued government lawyers, with no soul for historical similitude, "the larvae of enough Japanese and Asiatic beetles to have done a great deal of havoc if they had not been arrested in time."

The railroad wept softly on its counsel's shoulder but eventually agreed to a penalty of $100 on each of fourteen counts.

Ford restored the setting of Edison's early victories with such fidelity that Edison himself had only one fault to find when he saw it again.

"Henry," the Menlo patriarch said, after an appreciative look about, "this is 99½ per cent what it used to be." His eyes made the round of the room again. "It would be perfect," he decided, "but for one thing."

Ford, depressed, asked where he had fallen down.

"It's too damned clean," Edison chuckled.

Ford had no flame to burn in perpetuity in the seventeenth century shepherd's cottage he took apart in the Cotswold Hills of Warwickshire and shipped, in numbered pieces, so the jigsaw could be put together without trouble when the cottage took out American citizenship papers, but he astonished the king's stone masons brought from England to reassemble the ancient dwelling.

The house from the Western Midlands and its encircling shrubbery were photographed in all their various arrangements, the wood and stone stowed in a ship hold and, six months later, the cottage—500 tons of it—was in new position as a Greenfield unit. To all appearances it looked as it had in its native sheep country, except for landscaping.

Ford called at the cottage to say he was wholly pleased by the craftmanship of the three British masons.

"Did you fellows get a good look at New York when you landed?" he asked them.

The spokesman said they had not had time. There was, he knew, that trouble at immigration. Admission had been granted only when Ford pledged the Department of Labor the stone masons would go home as soon as the job was finished.

"Well, you break off here," Ford said, "and go down there for a week or so. Have a holiday as our guests." He said they had done good work.

They thanked him and the four stood in front of the cottage and scrutinized it closely.

"Do you think it looks the same?" he inquired.

Well, they weren't sure. Two shook their heads. One said it wasn't green enough. The other said it certainly needed the trees and grass and bushes.

"Well, another month or two and they'll be in," consoled a third. "Then I swear you won't be able to tell the difference."

"Yes, a month or two," agreed Ford.

Before they returned from New York, six days later, Ford had thrown in his own landscapemen. Black earth was unloaded at the site, sod put in. Photographs of the original plant life were followed minutely. Trees were planted. Bushes went in. The interior took on livability with trestle table, beds, fireside settee, hutch table and a *Bible* chair with bun feet. The lights came on. The green that had been missing deepened. The stone masons walked in on a *fait accompli.*

"Now it's the same," said the astounded first.

"So 'elp me 'Arry!" exclaimed the second.

"Gor blimey!" softly muttered the third.

Ford didn't know what two-thirds of it meant but he was content with his surprise party. The Cotswold cottage, in its finished green setting, was detail for detail the same as when the masons tore it down for its 4,000-mile sea voyage. It required only one more touch. One of the masons recalled there was a Newfoundland dog—a black Newfoundland.

The motormaker would have got the original, of course, but the masons said he undoubtedly adored the king and did not like boats and probably, being on the supercilious side, would object to packing his redheart lunch and trotting down to Ford's place every morning with a metal tag to show he was a regular automobile worker. His life in the hills had been too free for that.

A substitute from Sault Ste. Marie, Mich., proved a bit of a devil. He was three weeks old when he came to be a Cotswold sentry. He slept in the hay in the barn, refused to let other village dogs approach the cottage, and grew huge enough to insist upon it.

The Newfoundland heeled only for the man who nursed him to bigness—Gus Munchow, who transformed the land about the old stone cottage into a fine English garden. When Gus was taken to a hospital, the dog pined and would not eat. Ford was notified and drove over.

The watchman at the house said the dog undoubtedly was grieving for the sick master.

"Well, pile him into the car," Ford directed. The animal was hoisted to a seat and rode in state to the hospital. He padded obediently into the elevator and up to Munchow's room. The reunion was the tonic. It was all they could do to persuade the Newfoundland not to bed down permanently and to get back in the car, after giving Gus some fine wet licks and a couple of heavy slaps that nearly put the patient back into a coma, but once back at the cottage he went promptly to his platter to make up for lost time and then to the gate to see that no coach dog had taken advantage of his absence. He had located Gus; from now on he'd take care of the place as Gus would expect him to do.

The Ford collection never ceased growing. He had the largest and smallest incandescent lamps in the world, the one a 36-pounder, the other no bigger than a kernel of wheat; a section of every cable laid across the Atlantic, a sulky which Nancy Hanks drew; an opera coach Lucky Baldwin drove; sombreros and poke bonnets, hay forks and treadmills that dogs used to power to ease the labor of plunger churns on the farmer's wife.

As spotless as a Ford engine room, Greenfield always was a beehive of housecleaning, except once when he returned from Georgia in advance of expectation. The war had been won, the company was making over for peace, tools of battle moved out and those of normal manufacture in. A woman worker in overalls ran up and slapped her gum in goodby on the underbelly of the last bomber and the hum of Willow Run subsided. The company rolled up its sleeves for the competitive race ahead and cut loose of money-losing externals with which the senior Ford had regaled himself.

Somehow in all the maelstrom of conversion no one had paid the usual heed to the village until the senior Ford walked into the square one morning and looked about with affronted eye. He was thunderstruck by a spot or two which to him gave the hamlet an air of abandonment, and if there was any idea that grandfather was inactive he disabused all hands. He let out some searing expletives of the kind that did not appear in sedate profiles of the "real" Henry Ford.

"Get over here!" he commanded. "This place is a mess."

No one fooled with an order like that. He hardly had the words out before maintenance gangs poured up the road with brushes and brooms and ladders and paint and fly-swatters to work under his vigorous vigil.

There were times you thought the village a monster flat of stage scenery put up each morning and taken down at night. No eaves trough hung by a rusted strip, no shutter swung in the wind, no faucet dripped or chair teetered on a loose leg. Children came to class in the village schools. In the church on the common people worshipped and couples wed. Men did their village chores as their prototypes did them a century or two before.

The old stage coach under his rejuvenating hand became a new one fit again for a run through Death Valley. The debilitated 999 in which he had lowered the automobile record for a mile on ice in 1904 to 39 2/5 seconds became again a dashing wonder of a racing car champing to do it over again.

Even Ford failed to get a completely animated museum. The plush rope and the glass cabinet he could not escape. Some miracle man still had to find a way to present the bygone times in shirt sleeves and on wash day instead of always in Sunday waistcoat.

One still did not know how the coach looked mud-spattered and passengers in panic after a brush with road agents. The shiny 999 of the museum still did not tell the whole story of the whipping wind, the banked snow that threw the record maker Ford just as he finished, the excitement as the three clockers agreed he had bettered the world's mark by seven seconds.

But many of the clues were there in Greenfield to how man in America, eternally dissatisfied with what he had, tried for 250 years to improve his lot, never content at any stage with what he attained and always pressing toward some new fancy of Eden he was not quite clear about.

"Ten poor men sleep in peace on one straw heap, as Saadi sings, but the immensest empire is too narrow for two kings."—W. R. Alger.

CHAPTER XIV

EDSEL

THE ONLY child of Henry Ford was not a chip off the old block, and in many ways was the antithesis of his father. He left the applause to his sire and he had no wish for a seat in the show window, which was just as well, for, while the late Edsel Bryant Ford wore the title of president of Ford Motor Company for a quarter century, his forebear never squeezed over to make the son's seat entirely comfortable. When the senior Ford handed over the royal pen he broke the nib and it never wrote as well as one had a right to expect. There never was any question who was boss or whose word was law.

The egocentric creator of the Tin Lizzie believed nothing could be finer than if he made his son into a reasonable facsimile of himself but he couldn't pull it off although some commentators had them alike as two peas. They had dissimilar characteristics and philosophies for which a difference in their generations and an unlikeness in natures were responsible.

The elder Ford was an industrial autocrat, the younger a democrat. One was gentle and liked people, made friends and held them; the other could be as hard as his forgings and distrusted friendship as a general proposition. He allowed himself few. It would have been a matter for more surprise if the motormaker had not been hardened by his climb to the mountain-top, for along the twisting path he had met a variety of gentlemen who wished him down a crevasse and would have been delighted to assist in the fall. He wanted Edsel, his son, to believe that nine times in ten he would find a wolf in the bed instead of grandma. His son did not think it was so. He wanted to make Edsel something he was not—a bellicose type.

The father was quick and impetuous and operated on hunches. The son was never precipitous. He thought things out and tried to develop decisions by logical processes. Sometimes he got the wrong answers but some of his father's hunches were weak hand-rails also. The senior Ford made unpublicized errors and some of them were blingers, except that when he made them he passed them off as lessons learned.

Edsel was a good listener; Henry listened closest to words with which he agreed. The father was an extreme extrovert and always had his eye on the center ring. He was the spectacular dot on the swaying girder 40 stories up. The son was content to pridefully watch the maneuvers and efface himself.

The reactions of Edsel Ford were those of the normal human being—those of the father dramatic and often violent. He was forever the actor.

A farmer who had business with the late William B. Mayo, chief engineer, sat down to wait when told Mayo was somewhere about the building but would be back shortly. The senior Ford walked in.

"Will I hunt up Mr. Mayo?" asked a secretary. "He's somewhere in the laboratory." Then he remembered the visitor, half screened by an open door. "Here is a gentleman," the secretary waved his hand in the direction of the caller, "who says he met you many years ago, Mr. Ford, although he doesn't think you'll remember."

"Don't tell me. See if I can remember," Ford insisted. The caller got up and moved out and shook hands. "Northville, Michigan fair, 11 years ago, wasn't it," Ford looked for confirmation. The pleased visitor nodded and said that was right. "I stole some apples from you." Ford grinned and sank into a chair.

The other man said he could not recall the theft. Ford said he had admired the prize apples so much he had pocketed three of them when no one was looking. They gossiped about the fair, mutual friends, how crops were coming.

"When you're finished, have Mr. Walker here bring you down to my office." Ford got up to go. "I want to show you something." The apple-grower said he'd be delighted. Walker said he'd see to it.

"I want to take you over to the farm," the motormaker boomed triumphantly, "and show you the orchard I grew from the seeds of those stolen apples."

Whether an orchard of the size Ford showed him could be grown from the seeds of three apples puzzled the farmer for a long time afterward. He finally told himself it couldn't be done but never accused Ford of romancing. He said Mr. Ford undoubtedly had shown him the wrong trees.

Young Ford was appreciative of things done for him and did not forget them. He went out of his way not to cause any one pain if it could be avoided. The father could be shy and unassertive—courtesy personified—and hit to the jaw five minutes later. Edsel had a temper but it was under control. The only evidence of anger was a taut neck muscle, a thinning of the lips. When crossed his father was infuriated and made no effort to conceal it. One could predict with reasonable accuracy how the son would react, but the senior Ford usually did or said exactly opposite to what one guessed he would.

The industry was not a little afraid of what he would do and some members of the family were no less apprehensive. He cast an extraordinarily long shadow. A charming in-law who always was ready to fill in society editors on coming events telephoned an editor one morning and asked if this time the paper would do her a favor. The editor said she'd be delighted.

"I thought you might get wind of this and print it. I wish you wouldn't." The distressed lady on the telephone hesitated over her wording a moment. "We'll be in the soup for sure if it gets out that we . . . gave . . . a . . . cocktail party . . . yesterday!"

The editor said yes, she knew Mr. Ford's aridity, and made a note to spike anything on that soirée that might come in from other sources and to forget who was there.

When the senior grandson was prepping for Yale, two classmates decided on a heady if no new adventure—they'd run away and ship before the mast or something. They tried to inveigle Henry Ford II into the odyssey and the idea first attracted him as the three plotted in a Hotchkiss room.

"I'd like to but I just can't," the motormaker's grandson finally made his hard decision. "Why, my grandfather would get out the militia!"

He decided he could not stomach the militia marching up a gangplank and taking him off, probably in irons, to a dungeon grandpa could cook up and probably have finished in a half hour.

Henry Ford had no interest in the popular diversions of mankind. He raced cars in his younger days but he did so because he regarded it a good way to advertise his product. When his son was growing up, Ford was busy making a million into two, two into four, four into eight, and one never could picture him in those days taking time or having time to whisper conspiratorially to a restless boy. "I know a brook that reeks of trout, Son. How about you and I being off tonight with a pup-tent and ready for them in the morning?"

He came home delightfully tired from the plant and hardly could wait to return next day and get as delightfully tired all over again watching his magic beanstalk grow. His hunting was for ways to make the car better, the price lower, the miles of thumping machines as prolific as a rabbit. He was too busy with his heroic dream to spend time on a boy's.

The background may account for the fact that when Edsel matured, he took a sportsman's interest in sports. He golfed, skied, boated, played tennis, ran the yacht to the Thames and Hudson regatta days. He and his wife knew about and could talk intelligently of the baseball pennant races, how well some favorite player was hitting, had their own riding horses on the farm, were often at the football games, and occasionally at horse races.

I recall the junior Mrs. Ford exhibiting as much excitement one afternoon as the horses pounded down the stretch as if the whole Ford fortune was riding on the result. She was very pretty and flushed and exultant, I remember, as the horse she had bet landed home by a whisker, a man in the party said, "That's your horse, isn't it, Eleanor?" She jubilantly waved a ticket.

"And I had $5 on him," she responded gleefully.

There are no pictures extant of Henry Ford and the boy Edsel putting out in a punt with a can of bait and two bamboos or beating their fists together as Ty Cobb stole home; there are plenty of them sitting with feigned exuberance in the seat of the first car as it was rolled out each anniversary, canned shots of Henry and son examining a stamping machine, regularly timed pictures of them standing by the ten-millionth Model T, the twelve-millionth, the fifteen-millionth, a jeep, a tank, a bomber, pretending an aliveness for the photographer over an engine as if it was the first they had seen and couldn't believe their eyes, but there are no pictures of Henry and Edsel Ford at unrestrained play, holding up a defeated tuna or pounding each other on the back as some Bronco Nagurski crossed the goal line.

But there were plenty of Edsel and Henry II at the World Series, of Edsel and Benson straining to see how the crews were making out as they knifed toward the finish buoys, of Edsel and sons crouched forward to see if the wrestler's shoulders in the ring overhead were both squarely pinned, pictures of Edsel and daughter, Josephine, at the horse show, of father and Billy watching Tilden rear back and take a match in straight sets.

The motormaker said books mussed up his mind but he got his idea of a world parliament from Tennyson, had one of the great collections of Dickens and quoted right and left from Ralph Waldo Emerson. Edsel waded through business publications, art journals, the slick magazines, trade papers, enjoyed *New Yorker* cartoons while his father fretted over Orphan Annie, and mixed new books judiciously with classics.

I remember a discussion of Benvenuto Cellini in which Edsel left everyone far behind. The others had read Cellini as a class-room requirement—and forgotten what they had collegiately gotten perforce. Ford's son felt strongly over the fact that he had not attended a university and one got the impression of a planned effort to make up for what he had lost. The belated opening of doors enabled him to catch up with and pass many old-tie associates whom he privately envied for things he thought they knew but which often they had long forgotten. Museum directors found him intelligently authoritative on sculpture and ancient art techniques. Starting late he wound up fresh on cultural titillations on which early starters had gone stale.

Attention embarrassed him. He rarely spoke of himself. When he did speak it was usually of the company, whereas his father talked on everything and anything, from the proper length of women's skirts and fingernails to what kind of life was probably before man after death. Shy, Edsel rented a cottage during the San Diego, Calif., fair and considered it a pleasant triumph that he managed to visit the exposition nineteen times without being recognized.

A guard would not let him into his World's Fair building

when he was waiting for a company executive to lock up for the night. Instead of identifying himself, he asked the sentinel to step over to the office with him so that he could be vouched for.

When the Duke of Windsor, as Prince of Wales, was entertained at his home, he delivered the royal Edward to a private club for luncheon but refused to enter himself. "Thanks . . . thanks, greatly," he said hastily, "but here it's father's party." He almost ran.

A Washington press photographer taking an outdoor shot of a Senate committee with which Edsel had been visiting did not know who he was and waved him out of focus. "Bud, would you mind—this is just for big shots?"

Unceremoniously he put over one $5,000,000 loan while taking a shower at Detroit's Racquet Club. In the next stall was William Nagel, city controller, and the two dealt over the dividing panel.

"Do you want to make some money?" the controller began it.

Edsel asked what his neighbor had in mind. Would Mr. Ford loan the city of Detroit five million dollars?

"Sounds a good risk," piped the voice on the other side of the slate. "Why me, though? What's the idea?" Nagel said the idea was that New York was trying to sandbag the municipality for 5½ per cent interest and he thought the rate outrageous. Edsel turned off his faucet. "So do I," he agreed. "Detroit's a better prospect than that." As they walked together back to the lockers he said to see him next day.

"How does 4 per cent strike you?" he asked when they sat down to his desk as scheduled. The controller said that rate was more like it. "You can plan on it then—I'll take it up with the boys and they'll get the money together." The deal was wrapped up in five minutes.

Edsel Ford was a personality in his own right but he was more or less overlooked and submerged because his father was a more electric and involved study. He hated pushy people, showoffs, his father's attack on Jews, brass-knuckle labor relations. He could be argued with and had an abiding sense of equity. He was for giving the public other paint than black. He was out of sympathy with his father's fight with NRA in the depression years. The government, in an economic extremity, asked co-operation; the government should have it, he argued, times being what they were.

His interest was not in engineering but in styling—in the type of car as it would affect sales and the market; his father's concern was with what made the automobile run. The trade credited the son, not the father, with the stream-lining of Lincoln and Ford models and it was only after Edsel's appearance in a major role that radio programs, progressive sales campaigns and the use of practically every form of advertising media appeared in the Ford picture.

He got his father to buy a small airplane company with which the Fords made a beginning in plane-building, and it was the younger Ford who mobilized the engineers and technicians, with Charles Sorensen, the production chief, and set them to developing a conveyor system for mass production of interchangeable-part bombers in World War II.

When Henry Ford drove up in his two-cylinder car, the one with the bicycle wheels and tiller, to take 10-year-old Edsel home from a birthday party at a neighbor's home in 1903 his son was jubilant. The hostess had made a caramel cake for the boys she had invited to celebrate the day with her son and she baked into it seven pennies and a dime. A survivor of the orgy still nurses 45 years later a slight grudge over what happened. "Wouldn't you know," he says nowadays, enviously, whenever he repeats the story, "that Edsel would get the cake with the ten-cent piece in it?"

The event is more firmly fixed in the brooding man's mind by what the senior Ford said to his uncle and his uncle said to Ford while the boys, the party ended, were getting their reefers and rubbers from an upstairs room.

"I really have this engine licked, Charlie," Ford had confided. "If you come in on the ground floor you'll make yourself some money."

Uncle Charlie said he just couldn't do it. Money wasn't too plentiful. He had just sunk his ready cash in a building lot on a nearby street and he was trying to negotiate a bank loan so he could build. He did not say, as he might have, that he was not at all enraptured by Henry's box on bike wheels which stood at the moment in front of the house looking anything but a harbinger of revolution. Henry, with Charlie's refusal, and Edsel, with his party booty, chugged away.

"I'm glad you didn't put money into Henry's silly buggy," said Charlie's wife, when the last child had gone. Charlie invested money instead in another company which blew up in his face unhappily, the same year Ford Motor Company declared a 1900 per cent dividend but what Charlie's wife said then is not a matter of record.

When Edsel was 21 he received an even prettier prize. This time the cake contained $1,000,000. On that day the senior Ford strode into a Detroit bank with his son and into the president's office.

"Bill, I have a million in gold here," he reminded the official. "This is Edsel's twenty-first birthday and I want him to have it."

Edsel, with reasonable curiosity, stumbled down to the vault just to see what that amount in gold looked like. He was accustomed to large sums but hardly that kind of money. Then he drove to the plant and recalled in later years making more errors the rest of the day than he ever did before or after.

An excusable assumption from the gift of a million and the dime in the cake would be that the younger Ford had in his wealth an unfailing luck-piece which protected him from the slings of fortune. Instead, the fates seemed often in collusion to disprove by his case any belief that grief can be bought off. He lived with frustration and humiliation a good bit of the time.

Orders he gave were countermanded and often ignored. Plans he made were vetoed. Men he fired did not stay fired, others to whom he was devoted and who were devoted to him mysteriously vanished from his side. The father appointed himself sole referee. Few wholly trusted associates of the younger man were able to dissuade the elder Ford of his certainty that friendship with Edsel had a self-serving motive. The senior Ford was a martinet made doubly difficult by the fact that no one was surer of his own omniscience.

When the British were so hard-pressed in 1940 and needed more Spitfires if they were to beat off Goring's Luftwaffe, they wanted an American supplier to make Merlin Rolls-Royce engines to power their best fighter planes.

Edsel and Sorensen went to Washington and in 12 hours committed Ford Motor Company to manufacture 9,000—3,000 engines for use in the United States and 6,000 for England.

Two days later Edsel telephoned William S. Knudsen, in Washington. "Bill," he said, "father won't do it."

"Aren't you president?"

"Yes, I am," said Edsel, slowly, "but you know how father is."

Knudsen flew to Detroit, walked in on Edsel and Sorensen. When the elder Ford came in the door he began to crackle from the start.

"You're all right, William," he said to Knudsen, "but you're in with a bad crowd down there."

Knudsen blinked at the left-handed compliment.

"You've got a Rolls-Royce job in here and I want you to get it out of here," Ford said. He offered to make all 9,000 engines under contract for the American government but he would not make any for England, a belligerent. Ford acceptance of the Rolls-Royce contract already had been announced.

Knudsen said, "There'll be a stink over this." Ford shrugged. The deal stayed off. He brushed off Edsel's agreement as if it had not been made. Besides, he couldn't see the Rolls as a production item.

To some the severe supervision was a mere toughening by which Ford was only trying to train his son for survival. Others said Ford looked upon his only son as a guinea pig. I asked a grizzled industrial warrior, always high in Ford's esteem and now retired, to describe Ford's affection for his only son, and he turned to a shelf and got down a Bible. He put his finger without comment on a text that read, "And it came to pass that God did tempt Abraham and said unto him, . . . 'Take now thine only son, Isaac, whom thou lovest, and get thee into the land of Moriah; and offer him there for a burnt offering upon one of the mountains which I will tell thee of.' "

In a plant where the overweening ambition was to be No. 1 with the senior Ford, the general plan of contesting pressure groups was to try to cut the ground from under anyone who seemed to be getting an inside track, and it is said the wrestling groups were undaunted by the fact that Edsel happened to be a Ford. Keeping on the soft side of the elder Ford, when a soft side was to be found, was what counted The junior Ford never considered himself important or gave any sign of it if he did. Occasionally one got an idea that he did not even consider the Ford company important to the point where its dissolution meant the finish of the world, but if he thought so he never said so. Periodically he was suspected of harboring the thought he might live more satisfactorily if on getting up some morning he found himself foot-loose and able to range freely and not have to head out for the Rouge and the clangorous leagues of machines, each stoically doing its stint as it had the day before and would days without cease.

He was a princeling whose part was written for him. It may have been the one he would have chosen if he ever had a choice, but choice was one thing he did not have. He was born to a genius who passed on to him a factory and a fortune regarded as the mightiest in the world.

The son was wholly conscious who built the wonder. It was his father's business, reared block by block, belt by belt. The interminable movement of cars off final assembly, the sprawling plant banding the earth, the net surplus which once struck close to a billion dollars, the shifts pouring in and out, were his father's doing, not his.

The year he was born, 1893, Edsel Ford heard the first explosion of gas that was to make virtually every man his own engineer. It came from the kitchen where his father and mother were bent over a sink tinkering with the first engine. As a youngster he rode on his mother's lap in the first car until his father built him a special seat. At 12 he would climb on a stool in the plant and lick stamps. At 19 the factory swallowed him. He was secretary at 22 and president at 26. By the time the son was 21 the father was the cherished pet of destiny; riding a star-wagon. For the son there were no ham-on-rye days, no what-are-we-going-to-do-when-the-rent-comes-round days.

When William Ford, County Cork father of Henry, tried to write Henry Ford's role for him and said he was crazy to be anything but a farmer, Henry politely told William to clear out of his way and he'd set his own course. But Edsel was unable, if he ever wished, to match such independence and break the hammerlock of a strong parent.

When Henry measured his father's acres all he could see was a mildly prosperous farm entailing a lot of hard work for a modest return. When Edsel Ford glanced out the window it was on an incomparable colossus, and he had respect both as a son and an academic observer for what he saw and for the man who had brought it to fruition.

The struggle could not come out a tie. Henry Ford wanted a son in his image, ready for battle without notice. He put indescribable obstacles in the younger Ford's road and the purpose was, it was said, to make him fight back. Edsel fought back only to a point. He would never go to the limit of an ultimatum. On his side, Henry Ford withheld from the son from first to last the full power with which in the end he invested his oldest grandson. By then, Edsel was dead and the senior Ford's stamina for warfare was running low.

Usually at a point in their differences, the son of Henry would follow the course of others surrounding his father. The attitude was: "Well, it's his plant. That time before we thought he was nutty but he was perfectly right. This new idea does not sound good, but it may be just as right." The senior Ford cashed in so many distrusted hunches that those who disputed him finally arrived at the belief that his genius had no ebb and would last as long as he did.

When the pressure on the older Ford to do what he did not want to do became annoyingly strong he had an unusual method of postponing the proposed change. He would do what he was persuaded to do but so badly that the end product would not be practicable. In other words he deliberately saw to it in some cases that an experiment fizzled, as he said it would, or so it seemed to many of those close to him.

For a dozen years a single litany, and only one, obtained. Mr. Ford would justifiably say, "The Model T is the most perfect automobile in the world" and a convinced round table would say in a certifying chant, "Ay, the most perfect car in the world is a Ford," and go out and sell another million, but in the middle Twenties the response grew less hearty and sincere and unanimous. Not without some inner boiling, the motormaker noticed that even his son, of all persons, was one whose "Ay" was lukewarm. The noon luncheon table became a stormy quarter-deck.

They wanted to get rid of his planetary transmission. They would ditch his mechanical brakes. They spoke, in flagrant mutiny, of painting the car some other color than black. Ford could not believe his ears. As they jangled there was not a passable road in the world not being traversed by his cars. What sort of revolution was this? He would be hard-shelled while pretending otherwise. A farseeing and brilliant executive found himself outside the gates for advancing the theory that this was the best the company could do in the way of a car and in putting the same idea, Henry Ford was convinced, into Edsel's mind.

Edsel wanted a Six, but when his father could be brought to admit that any engine at all could hold a candle to the Tin Lizzie's, he still would not subscribe to a Six because he said it could not be balanced. Chevrolet was winning a firm toehold with one and Plymouth had come into prominence on the performance of a Six. Ford engineers said with dangerous stoutness that of course a Six was inherently in balance.

Ford said it wasn't and he didn't want any. The tilting continued, nonetheless.

Now as to an Eight, the weaving Mr. Ford said when the pressure for change grew so it was not easy to brush aside—well, he did have an idea for an Eight and it might be the answer. He'd see.

He did? He would? Grudgingly he seemed to give in and elation was general. And it could be prettied with something besides black paint? Why not! "Very well," he said, "I'll get on with it." On the surface it rated with historic surrenders—a decision to end a model which had sold millions and filled high the company's money chests. The end of an epoch? It was nothing of the kind.

The experimental engine he turned out in 1923 was an eight-cylinder, X-type, with four sparkplugs up and four down in a position where there was very little water and dirt on the road they missed. Several were made. None of the engineers thought it was any good. Neither possibly did Mr. Ford, privately, for it never went into production. What it did was quiet critics in the ranks for a spell and gave Ford some peace while it was being put together.

Thirteen years elapsed before son Edsel won his campaign for a Six. The company had put one out in 1909. It was not until 1936 that his father gave in and built another. In getting ready for 1937 models Edsel called six leading dealers to the Rouge. Business was off—he wanted a frank opinion from them of what additions to the line would regain lost ground.

The dealers were a united front. A Six was needed on the floor beside the Eight because competitors had sold a great number of people on the virtues of a Six. The senior Ford arrived in the midst of the meeting and merely listened. He did not say anything aloud in response to the one-sided sentiment but going out he whispered his belated surrender in his son's ear.

"If the Six is what they want, give it to them!" he stooped and instructed.

He started the designing of a six-cylinder engine next day. He exhibited interest for a short time but never became enthusiastic. Derogatory remarks drifted back from the front office to where the work was advancing and were attributed to him. The Six went into production, but he never permitted it to be pushed where it might displace the Eight.

He could be meek one moment and bash a head the next. When he was coming up to his seventy-eighth birthday, a press friend asked him if he would mind setting down five or ten rules to guide young fellows going into business.

"I'm not a business man." He was unaccountably humble. "I never have been one. I've just been a very lucky man. I had what the people wanted—and Mrs. Ford."

But another year, when he listened to some sales managers grumble that the company was not putting out enough models, he finally rose and lectured them: "So far as I can see the only trouble with Ford cars is that we cannot make them fast enough." Then he walked out of a meeting that had been completely silenced.

The son fought grimly for years the objection of his father to installation of a thermostat as standard equipment and was nervous over the car's mechanical brakes. He wanted hydraulics. The motor-maker said no, and in both cases the reason was a tendency to condemn forever any device that once went wrong.

Shortly after the Lincoln Motor Car Company was acquired in 1921 the senior Ford drove into the country. The big car had a shutter in front of the radiator operated by thermostat. When the engine warmed, the thermostat opened the shutter; when it was cold, the process was reversed. The instrument broke, the shutters would not open and the engine overheated. His chauffeur stopped near a corn-field and Ford hopped a fence. He was back with a corncob.

"Wedge it open with this," he proposed.

When he got back to Dearborn someone asked him if corncobs had become standard Lincoln equipment. The quip did not sit well. He looked venomously at the humble corncob. "Thermostats are crumby" was his verdict. He despised them for years because of the single breakdown.

The younger Ford could not persuade him to accept hydraulic brakes because he was afraid the rubber hose lines would deteriorate and let out the fluid, and he was indifferent to the fact that beginning in 1924 Chrysler had apparently proved the opposite. It was not until 1938 he gave in. Another breakdown cemented his opposition.

Without his father's knowledge a few years before and in the hope of junking the old-time mechanical brakes for good, Edsel installed hydraulics on ten experimental cars, and they tested splendidly.

They were parked near the engineering building, awaiting a propitious hour, and one morning the chief engineer accosted the senior Ford and said there was something outside he wished he'd try but did not tell what it was. A driver picked a car at random from the ten.

"Drive it, will you, Mr. Ford?" the engineer pointed to the seat behind the wheel.

The motormaker wheeled off. Edsel smiled in satisfaction at an upstairs window. Here to him was the successful end of his long contest to get rid of a braking system which never had satisfied him any too well however much it pleased his father.

A few miles away, however, the elder Ford had just tried to slow the experimental car, and what happened was what he always said would. A hose broke, the fluid leaked, and the brakes would not work. He got out of the car disgustedly and walked away. The incident firmed his conviction that hydraulics were no good and the breakdown postponed their adoption by the company for several more years.

"Ten cars, and we'd pick that one," Edsel said morosely afterwards. The other nine ran for years without mishap or any difficulty with the rubber connections. Father Ford told Edsel later he would compromise, however. "I have," he announced, "an idea for an *improved* mechanical brake." The whole question of brakes was back where it started.

It always seemed a contradiction in Ford that while he would avidly pursue the new at times and urge men toward the undiscovered, he was invulnerable to some proven ideas. He got busy at once, however, on his "improvement." He wanted, he said, a solid cross shaft with operating levers to the brakes on the outer ends. Then a rod was to run directly back from the pedal to another lever on the crank shaft.

It did not work, engineers said afterwards, because a long shaft has a lot of windup in it, resulting in a mushy and unequalized brake, but the experiment was a major spectacle. The magnate got the idea that one of his head men working on it was opposed to the whole proposition and was sabotaging it. He packed the suspected one off to Europe. When the traveler returned he found his assistant on the verge of a collapse from trying to make the brake function the way Ford insisted. The new models went into production with mechanical brakes—and without the cross shaft. There were some who suspected Ford knew his formula wouldn't work and that again the whole scheme was simply another delaying action.

Henry Ford's son neutralized his father's indifference in the field of aesthetics. Appointed chairman of Detroit's art commission the younger Ford had meager knowledge of the world of art and decided to learn. Some Ford executive always was trudging back to school to hone up for an unfamiliar task at Dearborn and Edsel did not hesitate to do the same.

Henry Ford asked a staff member one day what he knew about wireless. The subordinate admitted he knew nothing but what he had read in the newspapers.

"Well, it's about time you learned," Ford said flatly. "Make up one of those wireless receiving outfits for me."

That night the subordinate enrolled in a technical school where a class was being instructed in wireless operations on the Great Lakes, and out of this grew the Ford broadcasting station WWI which was to link company properties from the coal and iron of the upper peninsula of Michigan to the far-ranging fleet and the rubber plantation on the Tapajos.

With the administration of civic art affairs before him Edsel arranged with Dr. William H. Valentiner, institute director, to organize a seminar and he and his equally interested wife attended class twice a week for grounding. They sailed then for Europe with the director and browsed in continental galleries to see if what they had learned had sharpened their critical judgment.

His gifts to the Detroit institute totaled $600,000—a Corot, the coat of arms of a Florentine family done by Donatello, a Verrocchio and a Titian, a St. John by Andre del Castagnio and several examples of various Dutch schools; two works of Fra Angelico from the gallery of the Duke of Hamilton, a marble by the fourteenth-century Nino Pisano, a small gilt bronze out of the Sarre collection in Berlin, some 27 panels done by Diego Rivera, the Mexican muralist; an iron lion's head of the Tang dynasty, Pierre Renoir's "Cup of Chocolate," first hung in Paris in 1879, a Virgin of Giovanni Battista, Flemish tapestries and Persian silk rugs, one a companion piece of the best in the celebrated Altman collection in the Metropolitan.

Police found a rope dangling from an upper window of the museum one morning, a $28,000 marble bust abandoned on the sidewalk, and the Ford-Persian rug of gold and silver pheasants gone. On a third floor landing was a painting by Frans Hals which also had been ready for lowering but had been left behind by the thief in his unaccountable haste. On the stone flagging below was a single clue—a torn chamois glove.

A few hours later the police walked in on a 29-year-old Canadian in a Detroit hotel room who was salving hands torn by the friction of descending by rope from the upper floor of the institute. The glove, the only bit of evidence, bore a cleaner's mark and the hieroglyphics led to identification through a charge account. A railroad baggage-room yielded the stolen Oriental. The gentleman said he had been hypnotized into making off with the animal rug by a millionaire who worked with a gang of a dozen, but the millionaire proved fiction and the prisoner landed in a psychopathic ward.

The police held the rug so long that the museum at length demanded its return, but when institute emissaries picked it up they found a mysterious notch missing from a corner. The clean cut seemed to indicate a knife or scissors had been used. Everyone was blandly stumped for an explanation, but no one ever since has been able to satisfy the museum's suspicion that either (1) the piece was clipped for evidence or (2) a police official involved in the capture helped himself to a swatch as a choice memento.

Hard luck jinxed many ventures of the young Ford. His first motor yacht ran afoul a ledge on its trial run off the Massachusetts coast and a storm caved in its bottom plates before it could be floated clear.

He failed in three tries in the International power-boat races on the Detroit River and finally gave it up as not his sport. Leaks, steering trouble, a bale of weeds and a cracked cylinder routed him. One boat foundered; another time he dropped in his clutch at starting time with the engine speeded up and broke a coupling on the propeller shaft.

He turned over funds to the Detroit Institute of Arts for the $30,000 purchase of a bust expertized as work of Mino da Fiesole. A year later a distracted art director who had recommended the deal came to dinner and told him on a following walk in a snow-storm, "The damned thing isn't right. . . . It's too pretty . . . it looks worse every time I look at it . . ."

"In other words you think it's a fake," suggested the junior Ford placidly.

"I'm afraid it is."

"Well, such things happen. Don't worry."

It was said at the time that if anyone had taken a walk in such a convenient storm with the senior Ford and made any such admission, he would have been found next morning head down in a snowbank; the bogus piece would have been quietly removed from its pedestal, and no one would have been told anything about it.

The chairman of the commission and the institute director made public admission that they thought they had been taken in, that Detroit museum patrons had been looking for a year on an artistic counterfeit, and they were certainly sorry about the whole matter. The exposure rocked art centers but the piece was returned to the seller and substitution made of another work the director and the younger Ford could catalog and be comfortable in its authenticity.

Edsel Ford had a $7,500,000 home on the shore of Lake St. Clair, Michigan, a lodge and several thousand acres in a nearby county, and a $3,000,000 stone "cottage" on his 75-acre island estate off the Maine coast, and the houses were crammed with treasure. He refused to make any home a museum, however, and it was enough that he and his wife liked a picture or a paneled wall. If they did it was not asked to fit classical measurements. For his art gifts he sought authoritative judgment to complement his own; for the embellishment of his home he relied on personal taste.

An electrical repairman smashed a $30,000 Rhages bowl in the home by dropping the wooden cover of a console. The Persian polychrome, which had weathered nine centuries, fell to pieces in a careless second. An exquisite Florentine bas-relief was shipped to a world's fair and the neck of the figure was cracked in the hanging.

Behind the rich and seemingly restful façades young Ford lived with some deep anxieties—extortionate letters, promised kidnapings, a demand for $10,000 signed by the Sicilian Anarchists' Association, whispers of plottings against his four children, sleep within a ring of guards, instructions to take red lights on high at lonely highway intersections for fear of lurking hoodlums in the darkness waiting for the car to make a regulation stop, a Ford house plan on an apprehended outlaw, rumors of gangsters picked up east and west and hosed on information from the company's plant police during a wave of kidnapings. Down the fairways as father and sons teed off would be a gentleman or two with bulging shoulder holsters, pretending to be members after a lost ball instead of private police on hand to make sure that no one broke up a foursome for a little business of ransom.

Edsel Ford was the victim of a $100,000 robbery in 1924 and party to a lush legend that was no less captivating for the fact that it was a riotous lie.

After bidding good-night to two dinner guests one June night the host reported to the police that he and his wife had found upon retiring that her jewel case was gone and with it such major items as one $67,000 necklace of pearls and a second string valued at $27,000. Also missing were a platinum wedding ring, a woman's guard ring and a gold clock. They had been left on a dressing table in a second-floor bathroom.

At 10:30 o'clock the host had seen the stones there. No one had been in the room to his knowledge from then until 12:30 when the family retired. The Fords and their guests had not left the ground floor in the intervening two hours. Because of a $1,000,000 blackmail letter recently received, four guards were on duty in the shrubbery surrounding the home.

The first theory was that the thief with accomplices had made his way by boat across the Detroit River, landed on the Ford rear lawn, and worked his way through the private police cordon to the house. By climbing a canopy which covered the drive, he then swung to a balcony opening on the second floor. The screen of a window within reach of the balcony was open. A modification of the *modus operandi* was that there had been no river craft but that the burglar had slipped into the grounds when the gates were opened to admit Ford or his guests.

After a diligent army of detectives had combed the grounds, found no trace of the stolen gems and came upon no evidence of trampled earth or footsteps where an interloper might have hidden, it was announced five days later, that the law was now persuaded to think it an inside job. Finger-prints on the dressing table did not correspond, however, with those of any member of the house staff or any known jewel thief.

On the old police report are the words "Do not publish" over the initials of a retired chief of detectives, but the caution was unobserved for a Detroit afternoon paper printed the story the day after the robbery. The chief acted promptly. He called all the men on the case into his office and chided them gently, saying "If I find the bastard who talked to reporters he'll be out walking in the woods."

Ford phones were tapped and listened on for weeks in the hope that whoever had taken the stones would attempt to bargain for their return. The case moved no nearer solution and on the sixth day a company with which the jewels were insured for nine-tenths of their value offered the younger Ford a settlement of $89,000. He refused the check and said he preferred to give the police more time.

A myth began to shape after the newspapers stopped printing day-to-day reports of no progress and it had the persistence and purple and illegitimacy of most Ford fictions. This one grew because many persons were willing to accept unsalted any wild story about Henry Ford. He had a penchant for doing the unexpected, did he not? Wasn't he, the rumor-mongers asked, the master of shockers?

The fable was that Henry Ford had been one of the dinner guests and had taken the jewels himself. The romancers differed in their reasons but not in their certainty that this was the answer. He had taken them (1) As a practical joke and they were forgotten in his pocket when he left the house. After the alarm when detectives were swarming all over the place, it was difficult for him to confess the prank, but he would, you'd see, when the furore died down. (2) He had taken them in protest against leaving such an unlocked fortune in jewels strewn upon a table; and (3) He had removed them to express his opposition to such luxury spending and had thrown the whole shebang into the Detroit River.

How the senior Ford could have accomplished all this in the presence of witnesses and on a summer night loaded his pockets and walked off without detection with two long ropes of pearls, a clock, a jewel case and some oddments in the pocket of his spring coat was blithely disregarded.

Only a fertile imagination supported the stories. The jewels never reappeared. All leads petered out. The case still remains open in police records. An appraiser of precious stones was under surveillance for months but there were no tangible developments, and many weeks after the robbery a governess and a gardener resigning from the Ford house staff and returning to Europe were searched upon arrival at Cherbourg and Southampton on the police theory that one or the other might have taken the pearls, cached them and used the Atlantic voyage to smuggle them out of the country. Who took the jewels, and how, remains an unsolved mystery. The attending fable was merely a sample of the opulent fiction in which the senior Ford's life abounded.

What Edsel said he meant; whether his father did, you had to wait and see. To my regret I once misjudged him when he asked about a Continental honeymoon. I put down his interest to civility only and his offer to put me on wheels as something not to be taken too seriously.

Why, he asked, did I not take a car to Europe? It cost too much, I remember saying.

"We've got a place in Paris, and I think, in Milan." He had several millions invested in his Lombardy works but it apparently was not worth remembering. He said he'd make sure what kind of a setup the company did have in Italy.

What did he mean by this? Was he talking for talk's sake? He probably would forget the conversation next day. A car in Italy and one in France? Not bad! Maybe a Lincoln, even. How would I be at those Swiss humps? It certainly would impress the bride. By the end of the week I put the whole thing out of mind as something not worth following up since it probably was only a casual remark.

A week before sailing I did go to Dearborn on an outside chance my guess was wrong but there was no way to test it. Ford was getting his mortar-board ready for a trip to the University of Michigan to receive some honorary degree—Cameron, his editor, was tubbing for the same mission. I dropped the whole thing.

Back in three months I ran into the late Frank Campsall, Ford's personal secretary, at Dearborn.

"Where in the world have you been?" he saluted.

I told him. "I've got a couple of letters in my desk for you from Mr. Ford," he said. "So long ago I've forgotten what they're about." He said he'd get them.

They were dated three months before. They were orders to the French and Italian plants to place cars at my disposal for whatever touring I wished to do in those countries and adjoining states. I believed everything Ford said after that, or nearly everything.

The mechanical maze of the Ford empire paused memorially

on the day in 1943 when the son of Henry Ford was buried, as it was to stop four years later when father followed son. An unsigned bulletin said that on May 26 Edsel Ford had died at his home after an illness of six weeks from a "condition" which developed from a former stomach malady for which he had been operated on sixteen months before. Undulant fever also was present.

The last B-24 from the Willow Run assembly line is enshrined today not far from the plant as a peace memorial to him. He died too soon.

The Boss' whims were iron law to some upperclassmen who ruled by proxy. They were his strength sometimes, his weakness at others, and often his alibi.

CHAPTER XV

THE PALACE GUARD

THE LATE Charles M. Schwab, chairman of the board of Bethlehem Steel, once asked a Ford official if he knew the difference between him and Henry Ford.

"I hire men to tell me what to do," the steel magnate said, as if the difference had been clear to him for a long time. "Your Mr. Ford hires them so he can tell THEM what to do."

First there had been one man doing it all—Ford himself puttering in a shed, at a kitchen sink, with a scorned idea. Later there were 100,000 employees in a stupendous shed and he wanted them to do as he, the one man, said. The place was his—why should he not do as he pleased with it? Was there any other man who had built such a pyramid? Every time he showed his face did not the windows of the tallest buildings fly up and people throw confetti and ticker tape and the office telephone book in homage?

The tool he bored with was so big, the kingdom he ruled so heterogeneous, his interests so catholic that errors were unavoidable, but he saw no reason to change a system of absolutism that had paid off so fruitfully. If there were better men than he they would have done what he had done—and they hadn't.

The Ford plant was no place for weaklings. It was a vast whispering gallery sown with booby-traps. Internecine rivalries carried with mounting intensity up through the intricate hierarchy to the daily luncheon-table where the favor of Ford was wooed. An employee in the anonymity of a badge and not knowing whether the man next to him was a friend or a snooper reporting to the service department whatever he saw or heard, was no less uneasy than a member of the inner cabinet wondering who had told Ford what in an effort to unseat him.

Power ran in cycles. A man was on top—tomorrow he might be ignored. If he was not cast out entirely and managed to survive the pushing, reconciling himself to the new climate, the wheel might make another half spin and he'd be back on top where he started or back on the bottom if he had been on top. It seemed to stem from a philosophy that a Ferris-wheel ride kept everyone on his toes. No one found it safe to walk with his chest too far out. Behind the next post might be a man with a pike on a hunt for egos. Even if the chest remained normal, its owner might still find himself impaled.

I saw Ford show regret only once at the loss of an executive, and he would have been classified as minor in an organizational chart. It also was the only time I ever saw him cry. The mourned man was a dead test pilot in the ruins of a plane Ford had made—the first American flying fortress, although at the time the term had not been coined. The flyer was Shearman Leroy Manning. The craft itself was a tri-motor experimental bomber which Ford did not care much about building but which was counted on to neutralize losses in his never-in-the-black airplane industry.

Work started in 1931 at the instigation of the War Department and the plane came along nicely. It had five gun mounts so arranged as to cover a plane coming in from any angle. When finished it went to Wright Field, at Dayton, Ohio, for a five weeks' testing. Some changes were recommended and it was received back into the Dearborn engineering shop so alterations could be built in. It was wheeled out in September for new trials by Manning, chief test pilot of the company.

He and Ford shared a hobby and were drawn together by it. Both were interested in watch repair. When the flyer had been in England at the same time as Ford he called on his boss.

"You forget about planes for a few days," suggested the motor-maker. "We'll look for watches."

Manning never got over talking of the shopping spree with a buyer who did not, as he did, have to examine price tags.

On the test day at Dearborn Manning did about everything with the fortress. He said a couple of nights before to Fred Black, an admiring friend, that he knew from an unofficial trial that the plane was the answer to the War Department's hopes and had more diving power and speed than any he had seen in England.

"I'll give her everything Saturday," he boasted.

Black remonstrated. "Shearman, better take care up there." Manning made light of the risks. "We'll get up ten thousand and we'll have plenty of time to get out if anything happens," he assured his companion.

He and the mechanic did as promised. They put the new plane into extreme power dives again and again and it stood up beautifully, and at length Manning brought her down and flattened out about 200 feet off the ground for the three-mile speed course. As the flyer climbed in a sharp vertical turn, he sheared a wing-tip; neither he nor his mechanic had a chance to bail out.

Ford walked into his editor's office an hour later with tears in his eyes.

"I suppose you've heard what happened to Manning?" he asked.

The editor said it was a terrible thing.

"Well," said Ford, bitterly, "we made a plane to kill people and see who we killed!" He lost all interest in the war plane.

Ford's grief at the crackup of his test pilot is recorded because sentimental attachments were exceptions. The rise and fall of company executives was usually unaccompanied by coddling or tears except those they may have let drop themselves. Distinguished heads fell. There was an insecurity which militated against a good night's sleep.

What some executives learned too late was that Ford owned the business and intended to run it his way. The only method he found to handle men who got power-conscious and tried to run it some way he did not want it run was to cut them down or off. He did not enjoy men who told him what was best for him to do. He knew what was best and he would tell them.

A number believed they were on the mountaintop for keeps, not noticing it was icy and narrow and marked "strictly private" in the largest of letters. One by one those who climbed with him or went up on his back lost their holds. It was a one-man summit. Only when Ford failed physically did he get down and surrender to his senior grandson the peak so long and vigilantly held.

A quartet of men came to exceeding power. One was a car checker, one a pattern-maker, the third a bank cashier, and the fourth an ex-seaman in the Navy. The first was James Couzens, only Ford administrator outside the family with a real stock interest. The later men in the upper slots were Charles E. Sorensen, production superintendent; Ernest G. Liebold, Ford's business secretary, and Harry Herbert Bennett, chief of the company's private police. One attribute the last three shared—a Ford wish was an edict from Sinai.

For long Sorensen was a fabled Hercules striding the factory aisles getting rhythm into production, doing amazing things with metals, building a three-mile conveyor line for bombing planes, taking a sledge in temper and cutting a roll-top desk in two. For a period a question in the trade was whether Bennett worked for Ford or Ford took orders from Bennett. To some he was just another fellow in an inevitable blue shirt and soft hat who liked athletic friends, trap doors, subterranean tunnels, secret panels and could tell Ty Cobb's batting average for 1920. To others he was a feared figure with hands stained by a thousand shady marplots. At an earlier period Liebold sat advantageously on an upper step of the throne, said who and who could not approach the dais and was charged with egging on Ford in his Jewish campaign.

The three grew in stature in the Ford organization. They represented to workers the penultimate in arrogant power. It was a power that did not run concurrently but there was not much difference in time when the triumvirate fell. Liebold's authority ebbed in the early Thirties. Sorensen's was in steady ascendancy, and in the public eye in World War II he seemed bigger than ever, but a magazine may have quarried the first stone of his sepulcher by heralding him as the wonder man of the Willow Run Bomber plant. There was only one wonder man—and it may have been that Mr. Ford, not feeling too well as it was, looked up from his reading at this point and said "Huh!"

Sorensen and Liebold left in 1944. Bennett was last to heed an injunction laid by him on many workmen. Fronting the Rouge plant is Miller Road. Here had been a collision of police and marchers which bloodied the pavement. Here on an overpass Walter Reuther, current president of the United Automobile Workers, CIO, and Richard Frankensteen, an accompanying unionist, were kneed and slugged and hurled down a long flight of steps by plant guards. Here the union by a strike brought the operations of Ford Motor to a standstill. It was customary for some foremen to say to workers they were firing, "Hit the Miller Road!" Cheek and jowl with fascinating rumor Bennett hit it in 1946.

His parents brought Charlie Sorensen to the United States from Denmark in 1885 when he was four. At 32 he slung a rope over a shoulder, shook a blond cowlick out of his eyes and pulled a Ford Model T chassis 250 feet of factory floor through tentative assembling to time the processes and assist in establishing the automobile production line technique.

Behind him marched six men stepping off industrial history with him. They walked beside the moving car-to-be and picked up parts from carefully spaced piles, and they arrived at a combination by which a chassis which had taken 14 hours to assemble previously, required only one hour and 33 minutes, a miraculous feat in those days of 1913. Thirteen years later with seven others he stamped 15,000,000 on the motor of the last Model T. Under his leadership forging gave way more and more to casting. His name was on many Ford patents.

In World War II he was trumpeted as one of the world's great production men with an empirical knowledge of metals and dramatized as sitting down in a cramped California hotel room, sweating through the night and stepping out into the morning sun with a rough layout of the world's most colossal bomber plant complete in his pocket.

Several Ford plant police came to his garage in 1944 and took away, without asking him, a company automobile in which he had just arrived home from Florida, and the act constituted, whichever you will, a notice that Sorensen was fired or that the company had accepted his quoted words from Miami that he was resigning because of ill health.

For long storied years it was touch and go between Sorensen and Bennett. Now Henry Ford had emptied his knee of one of them. The subterranean stories that followed had only the backing of second or third parties, but the conclusion was that Bennett was winner and Sorensen loser in the tussle for power. The climactic collision between what were considered an irresistible force and an immovable object proved that one had been misappraised. Some saw in it a verification of rumors reported by the magazine *Fortune* that Henry Ford, approaching eighty-one, was under the spell of Bennett and that all Ford executives who would not bend the knee to Bennett had "resigned."

Workmen were badge-numbers to Sorensen. William S. Knudsen, his one-time superior when they were building Eagle boats, soft-soaped—Sorensen drove. He was a symbol of rough, free-style, old-school competition, kicking a stool from under a man if he thought he ought to be standing and axing a desk of a supervisor he thought was swelling with self-importance. In the shop he was cold and combative; socially, he was as pleasant as the next man and his extraordinary good looks thrust him forward. When he went to Europe and Ford cabled or dropped him a post-card, the motormaker would often omit the last name and address the communication simply "Charlie, Ford Motor Company." It always got through.

Knudsen described his fellow Dane as a person as soft inside as a ripe peach but workmen favored less flattering similes. The tale was told and retold of Sorensen mistaking a sitting Detroit Edison worker for a Ford employee and kicking a box from under him, only to have the Edison man get up and knock him sprawling. When the story was printed in *Fortune* the production superintendent offered $1,000 to anyone who proved it true and no one appeared to claim the money, although it may have been because electrical repairmen do not read dollar-a-copy magazines. If the fellows out there called him slave-driver and bone-crusher that was just too bad. He had to meet production quotas, didn't he, in this dog-eat-dog business?

He learned a lot as he went along. One was not to puff a competitor's program, and that often the best way to get over to Ford a desirable experiment of a rival was to back into it derogatorily by saying General Motors or Chrysler had gone hog wild and was doing something preposterous. He learned this lesson one noon in telling of a program G. M. was trying and allowing a note of interest if not approval to creep into his voice. Suddenly a steely eye on the other side of the table stabbed him.

"Well, I see they got you, Charlie," Ford said. "They sold you, eh?"

Those at the luncheon remember how quickly the subject was changed. Sorensen had forgotten to say beforehand that G. M. was a fool, as always, for trying whatever it was.

He learned that spending Ford millions was not as easy as most people thought. "When I get it spent," he used to say, "Ford Motor Company must still have it." He learned not to play safe by saying something would cost the company more when he knew it would cost less. When another executive submitted estimates, the Ford-Sorensen combination always knew they were too damned safe and high, as they put it, and it was logical to chop them because the profit would still be there. "He thinks to be high is doing a good job," Ford grumbled to Charlie.

He found that Ford did not make good drawings. Some were miserable. Funny, that, he thought. But Ford didn't have to ram his ideas into Charlie's head. Charlie could get some of them before Ford could commit them to paper. Sometimes Ford would scribble them on a piece of an envelope, or trace them with a finger-nail in the palm of his hand, or he would figure on a shingle. They hit it off. It was the reason a $3 a day pattern-maker of 1906 was a $225,000 a year man in 1944 and that Ford kept saying "Take what you want, Charlie, if it isn't enough." Sorensen was always able to make a model of a dream.

Models were all over the place—there were miniatures of Willow Run, the Rouge, a 12-cylinder engine, always staring at you from the office next to his. He always built a model—said if you could not see a thing you couldn't simplify it, and if you could not simplify, it was a fairly good sign you could not make it. By mocking up, the sketchy idea could be seen, felt and studied, and from the model one could go on to what was wanted, figuring first how to do it and then how to do it cheapest and fastest.

Ford's order was a stroke of the royal pen.

"Take Charlie, there, and what do you have?" a man beside me said 20 years ago at a luncheon table, pointing to Sorensen. "Do you know how he feels toward Mr. Ford?" I knew, I said, only that Ford gave him big things to do.

"Sorensen"—the next-door neighbor proceeded with his lecture—"has a great outstanding value in Mr. Ford's eyes. It is this: Suppose Mr. Ford should suddenly say, 'People are crazy to go around the earth when the shortest way is through it.' Charlie would go back to the Rouge and start digging. He would muster an army and he would find ways, of course, to improve the machinery so he could bring up more and more dirt with fewer and fewer men. He'd get the thing into a rhythm." The luncheon guest took a second appraising glance at the subject of his sketch. "Of course, Mr. Ford might appear some day and say, seeing the hole, 'What are you doing, Charlie?' and Charlie would say in surprise, "Why, digging right through the earth. Don't you remember saying people were fools to go around the world when the best way was straight through the center?" Mr. Ford would say, vaguely, 'Oh, yes,' and then 'Well, I guess we've had enough of that. Better fill the hole up again.' " The gentleman next to me thought it was wise to bear in mind there were two other reactions, of course, that Ford might have. He also could say he was sure he had never said anything of the kind or he might toss in a suggestion that would enable Charlie to raise the number of scoopsful an hour from 100 to 130.

England asked for him in World War I when its food situation became desperate. It needed tractors and Ford said, "Get over there!" When C. S. tried to get British factories to make them, the low bid was $1,500 with no promise of when as to delivery.

"We will make 5,000 at Detroit at a unit cost not in excess of $700, start shipping in sixty days," he promised, and the whole order was in England within three months.

He went to Russia in the Twenties and came back with an initial order for $75,000,000 that later ran into a staggering total. Ford thought anything done for Russia would help everybody. I asked Sorensen what he thought now.

"I only know what I read in the papers," he said laconically.

He remembered best the initial contract. The first year the shipments were without fenders and radiators—Russia began by making those. The next year it was without axles.

"What I remember most"—he was looking out at his ship in the boat well, "is that every contract was met on the spot, every bill paid, no bill ever questioned."

World War II brought fresh problems. One was the press and the magazines saying pleasant but risky things about the boss of the Rouge as war gathered momentum. It was he, they said, who had the idea of casting motor blocks, crankshafts and gears in making automobiles. Some attributed to him the entire development of the conveyor system and assembly lines that had put the Ford Company in front. One story said he had become a "major and constantly growing influence in all the ramifications of the Ford company." There was one eulogistic caption in particular, "Huge Bombers Roll Out Under Ford's Master Producer."

He had built and equipped Willow Run. He was Ford's "daily

consultant." Many of the improvements in the Ford car, the processes of manufacturing and the patents developed, sprang from ideas he originated, the authors said. The President of the United States was reported calling him to Washington. King Christian of Denmark made him a Commander of Dannebrog.

The War Department asked for an organizational chart of the company and Sorensen said they didn't have anything like that. The War Department said the company could make one, couldn't it? Charlie said it couldn't because Ford was not going to fritter time away on pictures—there was too much else to do. Besides, "we don't operate that way." When Charlie got back to Dearborn Ford said he had had a telephone call, and what was the fuss in Washington? His production man told him.

"What did you tell the Secretary of War?" asked Charlie.

"I told him to see you," said Ford. "That was your department."

Generals, foreign missions, Washington officials, ordnance experts, airplane people often put themselves under his wing. After all, he had a lot of answers they were seeking. It may have been he was more accessible. Ford was off somewhere or over in Greenfield Village or indisposed and the messengers of war did not have time to waste and wanted to talk turkey in a hurry.

Slowly the senior Ford became a little more abrupt and waspish. Sorensen did not seem to be getting the old-time co-operation. Ford was slightly less attentive to what he said. Besides, it was well known that the motormaker first hunted up Bennett each morning. They went for long rides.

Some soft drink machines appeared in the plant without Sorensen being told in advance.

"Who put those in here?" he demanded.

"Mr. Bennett."

"He and I used to talk over those things," Sorensen complained. "What's getting into him?"

He said to get them out before someone began pitching empty bottles exuberantly into the machines.

Some bonus checks were reduced 25 per cent. He took it up with the Old Man.

"A lot of fellows are working damned hard," he complained. "They ought to get an increase instead of a decrease."

Ford said he didn't know anything about it. The next week the checks for the subtracted 25 per cent came through. The senior Ford passed on all bonuses. Sorensen finally walked in and said, "There doesn't seem anything for me to do, so I guess I'll go to Florida." No one said not to go.

Stories differ from there on. One was that he had no more than reached Florida than certain of his lieutenants at the Rouge were radically shifted on orders of Bennett. Word came to Sorensen and he telephoned Ford at his Georgia plantation. A secretary brought word back that Ford did not want to talk to him. It was said he persisted and that the secretary returned with a different message.

"I'm sorry, Charlie, but Mr. Ford says I'm to tell you you're through," he is purported to have said. It was said that Bennett had made the changes at the Rouge on Ford's orders.

Another story was that in Florida Sorensen wrote a letter to Georgia, after trying to reach Ford repeatedly by phone. He got no answer. After long delay Ford's secretary called and said Mr. Ford wanted to know when he was returning. "When is he going to reply to my letter?" snapped the production man.

Around midnight a second voice, this time from Detroit, said, "Tell Charlie not to drive that company car back to Detroit but deliver it to the branch in Jacksonville." There was no explanation. Sorensen got Jacksonville and they didn't know anything about taking delivery of the car. He got suspicious. He threw his bags into the car, left Miami at 5:30 in the morning and headed north. The Jacksonville branch is said to have been advised at 8 A.M. to go to Sorensen's address and pick up the car he was driving. If it missed him, it was to have the car impounded at Atlanta. Sorensen came home through the Carolinas and missed the road blocks. The day after he reached home the plant police took the car out of his garage.

I went to see Sorensen at his summer place in Algonac, Mich., after he had finished with Ford and in the course of an afternoon in his study I admired a wood boat under glass and commented on it. It was a delicately carved ship but he made it much more. He held it with the bowsprit toward me so I could get a fore-and-aft view.

"Picked it up in London several years ago. Do you like it?" He called attention to certain spars and the painstaking care that had gone into its making. Then he walked over to a better light and turned it so

I could see its details athwart. "Now look at it!" All the time he talked with enthusiasm of the rig and the detail, and as he did one caught a glimpse of the talent which probably had carried him up. The ship seemed to swell to his praise and become more than a trinket under glass—it took on a normal ship's dimensions and seemed ready to set out for Buenos Aires if put down in the Detroit River not fifty feet from the study door.

It was a paneled room of reels and rods and the skeleton of a 348-pound blue marlin on an oaken board; some dueling pistols, water colors, and walls papered with pictures of Hap Arnold and Charlie, Eisenhower and Charlie, Walter Hagen and Mickey Cochrane and Eddie Rickenbacker and Jimmy Doolittle and many other celebrities who had come at times and looked bug-eyed at the Rouge. Scattered among them were group pictures of Ford executives from 1905 to 1943, rising out of camera shyness and stiffness to aplomb.

Off an adjoining garage were other rooms reminiscent of ship's quarters with blue and white enameled plates indicating the captain's and the crew's accommodations. A few feet off the entrance to the study his yacht was at anchor. His sumptuous *Icaro,* with its radio telephone over which he used to issue orders to the Rouge when he was cruising, was a familiar craft off the Bahamas. He always had a boat from the time he paddled a raft on the Niagara River; later he was commodore of the Yachtsmen's Association of America which ran the Harmsworth races.

To many, the Ford-Sorensen separation marked the end of an era and a legend, but he looked little different from the time when it was freely said when he walked down an aisle at the Rouge it would not have been surprising if someone threw a wrench at him. A heavy casting, dropping somehow from a height, missed him by a hair. In a towering rage or a fit of exhibitionism he would smash a desk—or several. He would take a hammer and split one in two. If you did not work in the plant and know him you simply didn't believe it.

The plant lore was breath-taking. Desk-smashing was said to be a provocative way of notifying whoever came to the ruined desk that he was not to get too big for his breeches or nurse any false ideas of luxury due rank, or simply that he was through. The legends climbed the plant fences and spread and in the long ago seekers of drama driving past were a bit disappointed not to see broken chairs and desk tops raining from the windows, and could only explain it by an assumption that they had arrived too early or late for the performance.

The Rev. Dr. Samuel S. Marquis wrote on the eerie breakage in resigning in 1921 as head of the company's sociological department:

"If the work of certain clerks in the shop is not wanted, why tell them? Smash their desks. That is unusual, grotesque and very amusing. A man who ventures to wear a white collar in a shop deserves to have his life made a burden. Expensive tools of workmen are scattered over the floors. Foolish? Humiliating? Insulting? Not at all. It takes the conceit out of a man who prides himself on his work. It prevents him from getting into a cozy-corner and admiring himself." [1]

An oft-repeated story was of a recreation building that was said to have melted away over night when some employees' antics at a dance were reported to Ford. The tale is that when workers filed in the gate 24 hours later there wasn't a sign that the building ever stood where it had. A whole department was banished when he could not figure why the company had 300 people at the work the department was doing, although the work was standard office practice. It had to be done—and was—except that to get by Ford's objections the unit had to be dissolved and the same work carried on by the redistributed staff without his knowledge in a number of departments instead of one.

A collector's item involved the senior Ford, Sorensen and the late William B. Mayo, one-time chief engineer in charge of development. Mayo and Sorensen feuded, and romancers proceeded to tell with the gusto of eye-witnesses of a day when the engineer walked into his office and found his furniture had come apart under an accomplished axe. Ford reacted judicially.

"If Charlie smashed your desk, why don't you go over and break up his?" he was said to have advised. The shrug that went with the remark seemed to say the pattern of revenge was clear.

The story had no truth in it but gained credence, as did others like it, because of a prevailing belief that the recipe for retaliation was one he *might* have given *if* his chief engineer's desk had been demolished.

With Sorensen an epoch was ending.

"Any regrets?" I asked.

He waved an arm at the pictures.

"Mr. Ford gave me a look at the world and an acquaintance

[1] *Henry Ford—An Interpretation,* by Dr. S. S. Marquis, Little Brown.

with people I'd never have known if it had not been for him," he said appreciatively.

Tops in power in the later years of the Henry Ford regime was Harry Herbert Bennett, former Navy man and sometimes called, when the description was not more blasphemous, the little man in Henry Ford's cellar because that is where his office was. He was captain of the watch and he lived by one rubric—to get done what the motormaker wanted and alertly anticipate what he wanted if he could. The end justified the means. He was chief of the most potent private police command in industry though he preferred the obscurantism of director of personnel.

"If it were my business I would know how to run it," he simplified his philosophy. "Being Mr. Ford's, he knows how he wants it run and up to the hilt I try to run it his way."

Ford had Augean stables to clean and hydras to be slain, and when he wrote out the order slips Bennett made delivery for close to a quarter century or did his best, fastidiously or otherwise. His orders came to him in a usually standard form. Ford simply would say, "I think something ought to be done about that." Afterward he would remark thankfully, "Harry gets things done in a hurry," and he said it so often it came to sound like a recording. In the internecine in-fighting within the plant the director of personnel lasted longest. Until a few months before his death Ford telephoned him each morning as soon as he woke.

A magazine writer called the motormaker late in the war and asked if he could see him if he came to Dearborn, and Ford said to come along. A few hours later he and Ford, Bennett and a Detroit newspaperman were in a car heading for the bomber plant. At one point in the conversation the magazine man remarked that in his eighty rocketing years Ford had met a great number of statesmen, crowned heads, a galaxy of scientists, engineers. Would he care to say which of these he considered the greatest he had ever met?

"Him," said Ford, thumbing in the direction of the passenger at his side.

The writer looked at the pointing finger and was a little perplexed.

"Whom do you mean, Mr. Ford?"

"Harry Bennett," said the host, beaming upon his candidate.

The two writing men on the ride were not quite sure if Ford was sincere, Bennett's position as exclusive confidante being what it was at the time, or whether it was merely his way of turning aside a question in which he was uninterested.

Bennett had five homes—one a ranch-type cabin with a deer pen on an island in the middle of Michigan's Huron River, one a stronghold not far from the University of Michigan campus, a cottage on Lake St. Claire, a ranch house on the West Coast and a place of Oriental decoration on Grosse Ile, an island in the Detroit River, which he is said to have traded for his Palm Springs retreat, unseen, when a new road was cut through the island and gaping passersby disturbed his privacy. He was well roofed for a man who once said he lived two years in the basement for lack of funds to go on when his Ypsilanti, Mich., home was building.

He and Fancy embroidered whatever he did, and a venturesome life produced, of course, departures from the norm. At a touch of a push-button in his riverside castle the back wall of a shower swung open on silent hinges and enabled him to walk in safety from house to garage by a 40-foot tunnel. In his Chinese-style establishment on Grosse Ile picking up a bottle no different than a dozen others released a spring, the private bar swung open as though on a revolving stage and behind it steps descended to the boat well of his 70-foot, all-steel yacht.

These dreamy devices were by no means the phobia of a man with a nightmare over an Inner Sanctum performance. They were safeguards against any caller who came with a sub-machine gun and a score to pay. Bennett knew many people who did not wish him well.

For Ford he carried out many important missions, and what he did he did without question. Ford's opinions were his. He ruled with an iron rod, but of course if Ford had not wanted it that way he could have taken the rod out of Bennett's hand at any time and locked it away. As a matter of fact Ford delighted in the game of cops and robbers, and the service department was that.

Bennett was an intermediary when Ford decided to patch his differences with the Jewish people by a complete apology. He was the agent to the underworld when Ford became panicky over the safety of his grandchildren. He was in the foreground of the parleys which led to the signing of a union shop contract with the United Automobile

Workers. What was most significant was that while the right of collective bargaining had been supposedly established by law in 1933, the breastworks Bennett threw up still stood long after the defenses of competitors had been flattened and nine years elapsed before a National Labor Relations Board election was held in the Ford plant.

An unexplained explosion below decks ripped the seams of a ship in the harbor of Port St. Louis, African terminus of the Cadiz cable, and fire burned her quickly to the waterline in 1916. It stopped for good some salvage work and the making of chart sections for the French government off the coast of Senegal.

Two members of the crew, stripped of all they had, set out afoot for the nearest port 160 miles down the coast. The travelers lived mostly on peanuts and rice, wishing the land grew something more tasty.

Seven days later, bearded and pooped out, they dragged themselves out of the swamps at Dakar with a parlous tale of a native who had slashed the face of one and the lobe of the other's ear before they managed to toss him and his knife into a handy bog—then onto a Spanish freighter they went, standing out that night for Jersey.

If one sailor prized anonymity no one disturbed it. His name is forgotten. It was his companion who kept on going and took on might. His name was Bennett, or Sailor Reese as he was known in Navy fistic circles, and he was hired at the Ford River Rouge plant when the company was getting started on World War I contracts.

At the time only a furnace and one building were up. The air was electric with alarms. It was the nation's first experience with a war of such dimensions and whispers were plentiful of Hun agents in overalls spying on America's preparations. New employees poured in and there was no time to be choosy about pedigrees. An army of 75,000 was going to be no picnic to handle.

A worried production boss thought to forearm himself by telephoning a boxing promoter and asking him to recruit all the plug-uglies he knew—the tougher the better—and the *entrepreneur* delivered as gaudy an assortment of cauliflower ears as ever assembled in a back-street gymnasium.

One of the supervisors selected to give the motley force direction was Bennett, just done with two hardening stretches in the Navy and the jungles of West Africa. A hard-bitten giant of a steel-worker showed up at the gate and tried to muscle aside the 5-foot-5 Bennett when asked to produce his badge. Rules had been tightened and orders were to admit no person without one.

"I'd like to see anybody stop me!" The badgeless one came on, moving to brush away the puny barrier.

Quarter-deck fights against some of the best lightweights in the fleet had done well by Bennett's muscles. The belligerent got up from the cinders with a sheepish look of disbelief and all for peace.

"Maybe I better go home and get my badge." He backed off and went out the gate.

A superintendent making Eagle boats for Ford was an eyewitness. He picked Bennett to oversee the motley task force, and from this beginning the sailor won for himself over the years a pervasive power and built an espionage system of such efficiency that even after a New Deal had been declared on Miller Road, two employees talking at a desk with an intercommunication transmitter on it stopped, affrighted, when one said, "Say, are you sure that damned switch is closed?"

After ten years Ford assigned him to a basement office in the Rouge plant and this was his grandiose sentry-box. This was the plot room where service men were briefed in what Mr. Ford wanted. Here was hatched Ford strategy and here was assembled a strange garrison whose membership ran from pleasant all-American athletes to unpleasant all-American muggs. Here in time most visitors were sifted and told if they could or could not see Ford. To this room the motormaker telephoned first each morning to ask "How goes it?" Here you could learn by listening close which executive probably would walk the plank next, how far that running back dashed through tackle for Southern Cal in some year or other to beat Notre Dame, why the Yankees figured to take the world series. Here informers told what they knew.

In this room was planned the defense intended to prevent a duplication in the Ford plant of the sit-down strikes which had embarrassed competitors. Here underworld contacts were made when the nation shuddered over kidnappings and it seemed probable the names of Ford grandchildren might be in the hat and drawn at any time.

"I can replace factories but not grandchildren," the senior Ford put his foot down. "Drop everything and get busy."

Bennett was reported thereafter going from underworld hideout to hideout and acquainting shady, flint-eyed gentlemen with a message that if any harm came to the Ford children their grandfather would sell the plant and devote the rest of his days and considerable fortune to giving gangland a taste of cut-throat war on a scale it never had known before. At tough games he also could play for keeps. Now, possibly, a little trading could be done—

A quasi-official biographer, James Sweinhart, was to write later in the Detroit *News* of some of this dealing:

"As time went on, here and there over the country some one near to a gangster chieftain in one kind of trouble or other found legal aid appearing from some unexpected source to help them get all they were entitled to under the law, and this did not lessen Bennett in their esteem.

"The novel approach bore fruit. Several times well laid plans of kidnappers leaked through to Ford's men from grateful figures in the underworld in time for him to block the attempts by exposing the plans to the conspirators themselves. The conspirators greatly appreciated the fact that he did not wait until they attempted the kidnappings and were killed.

"An automobile loaded with armed men stopped for a red light near a gate of the Rouge plant on the way to stick up a pay office. Bennett called one of the men from the car over to the fence and advised him and his companions that guards with machine guns were waiting their arrival. The mobsters were thankful for the tip and called the holdup off."

He hid on a Ford boat for a month a frightened eye-witness of a murder whose testimony sent three gangsters to prison for life at hard labor.

The service department took on a picaresque flavor. To it came an erstwhile welterweight champion on parole from San Quentin after eight years for killing a woman, a big league pitcher tossed out of organized baseball for throwing a world's series, a Sicilian bad man who was rubbed out by his countrymen with two bullets in his head a few months after he and the company parted and he returned to private practice.

The police regarded as long overdue the misfortune of Chester A. LeMare, vice overlord. They had arrested him seventeen times but had not been able to make any charge stick. Trigger-men brought in their verdict, however, and quickly put it into execution. LeMare wound up a busy iniquitous life on his kitchen floor and he was unlucky in that it was the only room where there wasn't a gun under a pillow, but at the automobile plant he had a profitable fruit concession and the underworld said he ran his rum-runners and hi-jackers as a petty sideline.

A New York newspaper later charged that LeMare had been hired as Ford's personal bodyguard when an automobile mishap in which the motormaker was sideswiped into a ditch and had to be hospitalized was interpreted by the service department as gangland's answer to a refusal to pay "protection."

The plant corpsmen never were drawn up for review, so they could not be counted or recognized, but estimates of their number ran all the way from 400 to 3,000, inclusive of sweepers, straw bosses and informers generally. They were not uniformed. In the forefront were the bright-eyed athletes. It was only in time of battle that there seemed to climb out of culverts a seamier band to tear up reporters' notes, smash photographers' cameras and bash recalcitrants' heads. Reporters often wondered where they had seen men like these before and only could think of the morning police showup.

Service men spied on workers and undercover men spied on servicemen. Lunch-baskets and lockers were searched for subversive literature, subversive meaning any reading matter which spoke well of trade unionism. Informers posed as mechanics, worked in the shop and tattled on their fellows. Unionists complained of union buttons yanked off work-shirts, of men whose feet were jumped on to provoke revolt and provide excuse for firing. Negroes complained up to 1938 that it was impossible for them to get a Ford job unless they went to a limited group of important Negro preachers who had demonstrated complete agreement with Henry Ford in politics and in industrial relations, i.e., pro-Republican and anti-union.

The expanding plant became a series of spotless caves where sometimes even Mr. Ford got lost. It was so big, he once remarked disconsolately, it wasn't fun any more. It certainly got so large a hundred Fords could not personally keep a finger on all its activities.

Bennett's basement office had everything, even to discussions of art. He did a little himself and ornamented the walls of his homes with the best from his brush, although an enemy once said it was after Ford had inspected his gendarme's canvases that he said he would not give five cents for all the art in the world. Once when Clyde Beatty, animal trainer, gave the personnel director a pair of lion cubs, Bennett posed them and painted them in the basement studio before taking them home.

Someone hung on him the description "The Little Man Who Gets Things Done for Ford" and others used a diminutive "The Little Guy." One correspondent reported he held one of the ten toughest jobs in the United States but blithely failed to identify the other nine. There were thousands who used all the epithets in the lexicon of abuse in speaking of him, however—and then began with the A's again.

He raised beef cattle, delighted in saddle horses, thought *Moby Dick* the best book ever written, played a saxophone and carried a gold-plated revolver. In his office he popped away at a six-inch target so arranged that pellets would slide into a slot instead of spraying the room. Ford had one like it. Once after two warnings that smoking was not permitted in the Ford plant, Bennett shot a cigar out of an astonished caller's mouth. He liked chows and music, didn't like flowers or driving an automobile. He loved a practical joke, as did his employer, and to many his informality, heels on desk, was a relief from the stuffy decorum of some other officials.

A judge almost parted company with him over a hunting prank. Going to an upstate lodge Bennett came on an old harness shop with a decorative wooden horse in front. He bought it and loaded it into his car. The jurist, who arrived next day, had no more than reached his favorite runway when he opened fire on a first-rate buck but when he came up with it he found instead he had mortally peppered a pine horse. Bennett and his confederates had spent two hours the night before wiring antlers to the harness man's dummy and another half hour planting it strategically in the woods to make an attractive target. The judge took it badly. He got into his car and drove home.

Bullets were reported raining his direction. He said his daughter had answered his Ypsilanti door-bell and a stranger let go with two bullets intended for him. A bullet ploughed through his windshield another time but he believed he was accidentally caught in the cross-fire of rival gangs. Five men in an automobile were reported as crowding him off the road but he allegedly drew his gun and the quintet made off. In 1932 he was felled by a paving block in a demonstration before the plant in which four marchers were killed. Rescuers found Bennett under a parader. There was a slight difference between the two. Bennett was merely unconscious—the marcher was dead.

Political candidates waited to get a good word from him. His influence was broad and had long talons. He did many favors and naturally where they did the most good. An enemy leaving the plant might find his car would not start or a tire mysteriously flat—a friend might discover a wash and a grease job and occasionally a new motor. The department was eminently practical. Whomever Ford might plunk for, the service department buttered its bread on both sides and even on the edges. It made connections where connections might be profitable, and it was impossible to guess always where that would be. It was policy to know the right people.

Bennett was a realist. Two collaborators did a book about him and when they finished it submitted the copy. He was disappointed and said no one would recognize him.

"In what way, Harry?" asked one of the authors.

"Well," he responded, "you don't say I'm a son of a bitch."

He said that no one acquainted with his reputation for toughness would accept any book which did not blast him as a scoundrel. He was sincere in his criticism and refused to sanction a log-rolling script which made him out a completely lovable fellow. He handed the pages back.

"You know what they say of me," he completed the lecture. "Well, write it in the book. If you don't, no one will believe a word of it."

Newspapermen got along well with Bennett. They liked his breeziness and willingness to provide background material. One did a four-column feature calling him "This rugged, proud, impulsive bundle of dynamite." A second did a series of articles as the result of a futile search of files when Bennett fell from a horse and a newspaper found it had little biographical material.

"Drop everything," said a worried editor, "and get an obituary of him. He's being shot at. Now he spills from a horse. We may wake up some morning and find him dead or president of the Ford Motor Company. Where will we be then?"

The personnel director refused to contribute at first. He said he didn't care how many other men agreed to have their obituaries prettily composed against their day of doom.

"If I did anything like that it would be sure to happen," he parried. "Why should I put the finger on myself?" The reporter said, "Come on, Harry," but Bennett again said no in a voice once described as the bark of a chief petty officer subdued to the proprieties of the parlor.

Another approach won his co-operation several months later.

"You have said yourself, Harry, that if anything happens to Mr Ford you're probably through," the reporter argued this time. "You've had an amazing life here with him and done an extraordinary job for him. Why not let me write it in case anything does happen to Ford and things come out as you think they will? Or in case you're moved still higher?" Bennett had been made a director in 1943.

The newspaper decided the resultant story was too interesting to put in storage, published it in installments, claimed a circulation run-up of 25,000. A month later Bennett wrote a letter to Henry Ford II:

"This is my resignation as a member of the board of directors of Ford Motor Company. I appreciate your request that I continue . . . but I must be free to engage in other business." He wished the company every success under the guidance of the grandson.

Rumors promptly spread, however, that the resignation of Bennett had been solicited and that a new Ford generation had taken a fancy to John S. Bugas, quiet former charge d'affaires of the Detroit office of the Federal Bureau of Investigation, who became associated with the company during the war at Bennett's invitation.

A brush between Bennett and the newcomer was later reported which ended in the latter allegedly offering Henry Ford II his resignation. The friction was said to have originated upon Bennett's return from an extended vacation in California and a discovery that in his absence the young Ford had become so accustomed to doing business with Bennett's assistant that they continued what seemed a pleasant relationship after Bennett was back at his desk.

"I think I shall see my grandmother," the younger Ford was reported as saying when the rumored Bugas resignation was received. The senior Ford was failing fast.

With the policies and methods of several executives the late Edsel Ford was not in accord in his life-time and his sons were fully aware of their father's frustrations. He did not condone some practices but he had to live with them.

The alleged outcome of the family conference was a complete delegation of power to hire or fire and make any changes Henry Ford II saw fit. In the exercise of this broadened authority it was promised that Fair Lane would offer no obstacle. Bennett went. Bugas stayed.

Once it was Ernest G. Liebold who guarded the Ford drawbridge, who hired and fired and who basked in broad power. As business secretary to the motormaker his favor was as obsequiously curried as was Bennett's in later years. Until his authority paled in the Thirties no job was too big or foreign for his confidence and energy.

When he was dropped in a mid-war purge he was the only one who publicly repudiated an announcement that he had resigned.

"I would like you to print a correction," he telephoned a newspaper, incensed. "I did not resign or quit—I was fired."

"Do you want that said?" the editor asked.

"Certainly," Liebold replied. "It's true."

Liebold was cashier of a Detroit bank in 1909 when its president decided to launch a bank near the Ford plant in partnership with James Couzens, the Ford company's general manager.

"I have agreed Jim can have the controlling interest if I can name the cashier. I've picked you, Ernest," said Liebold's employer.

As a result, Liebold only had to step across the street when he became Ford's secretary at $200 a month two years later. At the end of another two years he was not certain the change had been a good one. He had no idea if his work had pleased and while there had been bonuses and salary increases he got none.

"You haven't had a raise in a long time, have you?" Ford remarked at the end of that time, however. "I wanted to see if you would quit." He started out of the room as if that was all he had to say but he remembered in time what he had come for. "Write yourself a check for $10,000," he said. In the three decades that Liebold was with him Ford never was to sign a personal check. That was one of the secretary's chores, and he had power of attorney for both Ford and Mrs. Ford, but in the long span of intimate relationship Liebold never called Ford anything but "Mr." Ford and Ford always addressed his secretary as "Mr." Liebold.

The motormaker had his own curious ways of "testing" employees. He walked into another office once with a sheaf of papers and gave every impression they were so important they were about to burn up in his hands. He exacted a promise that they be put away securely and not surrendered to anyone but him, and he accented the mood of intrigue by furtive glances about the room and into adjoining offices as if to make sure his maneuvers were unobserved.

A young executive sealed the papers and locked them up. Three days later an assistant secretary appeared and said Mr. Ford was asking for some documents he had entrusted to the first man a few days before.

"What papers?" the foresworn custodian pretended surprise. "Mr. Ford gave me none."

He was summoned to Liebold's office.

"Bring me the papers Mr. Ford left with you," ordered the secretary. "I can't imagine your saying you haven't them—" the tone rose to bullying pitch "—Mr. Ford tells me he turned them over to you."

The gentleman in possession of the sealed envelope reiterated that Mr. Ford had done nothing of the kind and must be confusing him with someone else. After that he got out, sure of a parting thunderclap but heard none. Ford himself sauntered in two days later and asked for the mysterious papers.

"Right here," the relieved trustee unlocked the safe and turned over the envelope.

No explanation was ever given. The assumption was that the papers had no intrinsic value and that this was a test of an untried executive's ability to do as told and keep his mouth shut, for a week later he was assigned to a mission calling for both qualities.

Virtually the first chore Liebold did for Ford was to buy him a set of false whiskers; his last was to prepare during World War II a ninety-page report on German contributions to world progress.

The motormaker was annoyed upon reaching the plant one morning.

"Get me a false beard," he ordered. "Everyone on Tireman Avenue is stopping me on the way to the plant."

He came in a few days later and disconsolately laid the disguise on the secretary's desk.

"It didn't fool anybody," he said. "I'll have to think of something else." He said he had been waylaid, just as much as if he had not worn the chic whiskers, by people who wanted jobs or favors of every sort.

Incidentally, advisers never were able to break Ford of his habit of giving strangers a lift in his car. He always was escorting into the Highland Park plant in the early days some disheveled one he had picked up, and directing that a place be found in the shop for his new found friend. If accosted while walking he would not stop at the hail of someone he did not know—he finally agreed that one man might stop him so a confederate could slug him from the back—but he was sure he could handle any single person who got into his car and proved obstreperous. Strong and wiry at sixty, he managed a mad deer on the estate that butted him and kept coming. He hung to an antler with one hand, whipped a jackknife from a pocket and while being dragged along ended the battle by cutting the animal's jugular vein.

The unworkable disguise had long gone into the discard, presumably, but a carbon of the results of Liebold's last assignment is at hand. The introduction is short: "Following is a list of some of the discoveries and achievements of the Germans. They have led the world in science, chemistry and music. How much of the advancement of the human race may be traceable to their accomplishments is a question which might be interesting to determine."

He and the secretary were discussing German peace-time achievements and after running over some of the better work, Ford figured he'd like to go deeper into the study.

"Get me up a list, will you, Mr. Liebold?"

Of course the request meant only that at the moment Ford was interested in the subject—a week later he might not be. His interest in many cases was fleeting. If a report could be delivered to him next morning, a subject might be kept alive that long, but if time was required to assemble material and a week elapsed, the researcher might find when he finally delivered his report that Ford had forgotten he ordered it.

People who read ulterior significance into Ford's admiration for Germany and insinuated that the same admiration extended to Potsdam and Berchtesgaden, missed the point. He was interested in Germany because of its efficiency, cleanliness, its manufacturing methods and its products, and because he thought Germans as a race worked harder than other people. These were virtues he believed in. They were, in his book, the most important things in life.

A distinguished visitor in World War I protested the continued employment of a superlative German-American draftsman at the plant. Ford did not answer the guest direct but turned to one of his top officials, a little grimly, and said, "Charlie, if you can find a dozen more Germans as good as the one our visitor thinks we should fire, hire them!"

Ford got his list from Liebold—from the first kindergarten of Froebel in 1837 to the first Christmas tree in America which the German Imgards of Wooster, Ohio, made of a spruce in 1847 and for which the village smith fashioned a star and the family itself cut paper decorations; from Peter Henlein discovering the watch-spring in 1500 and thus the first pocket watch, to Otto Lilienthal dying on his 2001st glider flight the year Ford drove his first automobile; from Henry Steinway turning to piano-making after losing his eleven brothers in the Napoleonic wars, to Siemens and his pneumatic tube and Atlantic cables and Behring and his diphtheria anti-toxin. They are all there in the tabulation—Einstein, the 23-year-old examiner of patents at Berne when Ford started to build cars; Gelmo, the Viennese student, writing of sulfa thirty years before its curative value was discovered; Carl Hagenbeck, setting a pattern for world zoos; Gutenberg and the printing press, Count Zeppelin taking his first airship aloft in 1900 and magically staying there twenty minutes; Zeiss and Bunsen and Roentgen and the vast rest.

Secretary Liebold in the 33 years intervening between the unconvincing false whiskers and the report on German accomplishments dipped into countless projects. He finished the erection, staffed and managed Henry Ford Hospital in the early days. He was active in the operation and sale of the Detroit, Toledo & Ironton, Ford's railroad. He bought for Ford mines, ships, power plants and forests, and he acquired thousands of acres of land. In those days of feverish acquisition it used to be said that farmers meeting on the road greeted each other with "Where are you going to sleep to-night?"

He was in charge of a company housing development, managed the Dearborn *Independent,* Ford's international weekly, and was chief manipulator behind the scenes in the efforts to run Ford for the Presidency of the United States.

Portly, arbitrary, Liebold did not fraternize with his fellow executives outside the plant, drove an automobile as if every street was deserted, could tie on an apron and cook a splendid stag dinner, fished Colorado streams for trout, hardly could drag himself past a window containing a multitude of gadgets. He was an inexhaustible worker and omnivorous reader. When he tackled a project he waded into every book on the subject that he could get his hands on. He had strong ideas in many fields and they were no less strong because a field was strange to him. He spoke aspersingly of Jews but made it a point to call on Einstein in Berlin and in a letter to Ford's editor reported happily that the relativist had expressed himself "thoroughly in accord with Mr. Ford's views." What was meant by this was not made clear.

If he had had his way no word of Ford would have been printed unless he had a chance to weigh and edit it. Reporters tried his soul. It was mutual. No newspaperman ever gave him much of a break. They did not like being pushed around and they waited for him to stub his toe.

Ford pointed a newsman's attention to several men at a drawing board in an upstairs room of the plant in the first war and to others tacking blue-prints on a wall.

"What would you say that was?" he asked.

"Could be a tank, couldn't it," the reporter asked after study.

"That's JUST what it is—a one-man tank." Ford bubbled with enthusiasm. "They'll go over Germany like a lot of ants." He wound up by giving his caller all the particulars. "Now," he said, "there's an exclusive story for you—write what you want."

The reporter's telephone rang as soon as the story appeared. Liebold exploded. He had not been consulted.

"When you can talk as one gentleman to another, call me again," the usually quiet newsman said, and hung up. A moderated call came a half hour later.

"Oh, you've been talking to Mr. Ford, Ernie, have you?" the newsman asked, a friend of Liebold's for years.

"Yes—I flew off the handle."

He was intensely active when Henry Ford Hospital was building and became a storm center as its imperious manager. Ford took over a half-built hospital and said to him, "Go ahead and finish it." He traveled the length of the land getting ideas. With a young draftsman at the plant he pushed walls of beaver board up and down the floor 20 to 30 times until they decided they finally had the best arrangement to standardize.

Liebold hired the personnel, raided Johns Hopkins for the nucleus of the professional staff, moved in. It was a closed hospital, one of the first in the Middle West, and old-line doctors bristled. The Detroit Academy of Surgeons declined to meet there in 1924 and the Wayne County Medical Society declared that Henry Ford's reputation, rather than that of the hospital, "attracted patients" and he was "practicing medicine by proxy."

The society complained of so-called machine methods, that charity work had decreased, of the uniform fee scale, the closed hospital system—and "unethical" publicity. Ford supporters attributed much of the hostility to Ford's refusal to allow the hospital to collect larger fees from wealthy patients.

"The business under the superintendency of a thoroughly trained man developed too slowly for Ford," the society protested. "He was let out and Ernest G. Liebold, Ford's secretary, became the guiding spirit. Business was not good and there was not enough zip. Ordinary equipment such as an old-time stethoscope and microtome, found in any well conducted hospital, was glorified. The public's eyes began to bulge. The great Ford had manned his hospital with supreme genius and installed marvelous and intricate equipment."

The hospital's surgeon-in-chief, who is still its celebrated surgeon-in-chief, offered the academy his resignation, said curtly that the growth of the hospital testified to the satisfaction of patients; a uniform fee scale had the same right to exist as a charity system or a scale fluctuating according to ability to pay; reported that ex-soldiers had been cared for the previous year at a cost of $125,000 to the hospital—"If alleged application of factory methods means thoroughness and completeness of history-making and physical examination by physicians and surgeons trained and experienced in the larger clinics of the United States and Europe, we plead guilty." He slid over the charge of unethical publicity. But Ford, on the subject of doctors, said later that the profession made a fetish of withholding information that belonged to the public. "What would they say," he asked scornfully, "if industry said, 'Let the public find out what we have to offer if it can?' " As for medical journals he did not think the public could understand the language in which they were written.

"I'm for telling people the latest proven method of medical treatment and of the newest discoveries in words of one syllable," he said. "News of medical progress usually reaches the public only through gossip."

Ford said he was convinced a hospital could both serve and be self-supporting, but the hospital management testified in a damage suit in 1929 that the hospital had lost $4,000,000 since being founded and ran an annual deficit made up by the Ford family.

Even the staff of the hospital winced privately over some of the ballyhoo for which they held Dearborn responsible. It was full of such meaty statements as "doors close without as much as a click, signals flash but are not heard, elevators glide up and down noiselessly and the noiseless typewriter is standard" and "a volume could be written on the X-ray department only" and how the hospital had a machine "by which the air a person breathes can be measured and analyzed and the exact amount of oxygen absorbed determined," how the beds were mounted on noiseless casters, and a tone of color had been introduced on the walls "much more pleasing than the brilliant and monotonous white in customary hospital use."

Good theatre went on daily before a personal secretary's eyes. No day was without its lesson. An early one was that Ford was mercurial.

When earnings were running fabulously high in early days Couzens suggested that Ford deposit them in his bank and let them work still further for him. Ford agreed to freeze $12,000,000 across the street.

"We're going to build a tractor plant in Dearborn," he said a few weeks later to his secretary. "It may cost as much as $7,000,000. Get ready to take care of it."

Liebold reminded him that he had agreed to let the $12,000,000 in the Couzens bank stay there. Vigorously, Ford said he had not.

"If so, Couzens put something over on me," he declared. "You get it—I need it."

The bank had to liquidate some investments fast to meet the unexpected call.

The motormaker was always bobbing up with novel ideas. Once he dug a hole in front of the factory. Couzens, returning from a business trip, found a steam shovel tearing the lawn open. He asked what was going on.

"Have you been reading the papers, Jim?" Ford asked.

The general manager nodded. Ford pushed some statements across the desk.

"I read that money is going to be tight so I got the boys to get up those figures for me"—he lowered his tone. "We've got $33,000,000 around in the banks and I'm going to pull it in and put it down in that hole until the squall blows over."

Couzens used the rest of the day convincing the head man that a corking way to insure panic would be to draw in the $33,000,000 and cache it underground, and the motormaker finally allowed himself to be persuaded. He had the hole filled in.

He also stopped some digging in the same lawn when the office building went up. A tree was growing there and work was no more than started when he appeared at a construction shanty to express concern for its safety. The tree probably couldn't be saved, the contractor remarked.

"Then move the building back," Ford ordered.

It went back five feet. New stakes were driven. He was back next day and told them to get some planking to put around the base. He remeasured the distance between the tree and the new building line.

"Better move the building back a few more feet," he figured.

When the building was up Ford decided the tree did not belong in the picture after all and he had it removed.

Liebold reminisced across a luncheon table from me only a month or so before Ford's sudden death.

"Spelled a word usually the way it sounded, read like a ten-year-old, but juggled figures like no other man," he said. He had watched day in, day out, year in, year out. "You never could tell how he was going to jump and he'd often tell you only 25 per cent sometimes of what he wanted, and expected you to fill in the rest. He was right 80 per cent of the time when everybody told him he was wrong—or whispered it behind his back."

Suspicious at times, very trusting at others. The secretary asked him once if he always got the $200 put daily under his inkwell for small change and touches. Yes, he said vaguely, he guessed he did, but he followed it up in the next breath with a correction, thinking he had registered some doubt of the integrity of those about him.

"Sure I do," he said, now with conviction. "Everyone around here is honest."

Peculiar, too, was Ford's idea of rewards for good work done. Usually it meant merely the piling of more work on some of the men who most pleased him. There had been that electrical engineer who gave him a clock done to one-inch scale, a replica of a Ford magneto. Ford had been so delighted that for a month he had crowded so much work on the engineer he hardly had time to draw breath. Did not get anything more than the work, though.

Liebold harked back to the day in 1921 when Eastern banking interests knew Ford was short of immediate cash and thought they had him boxed. They would make him a loan—at a price. They would name the treasurer of the company.

They telephoned Ford and got Liebold. Ford was across the desk.

"Let 'em come out," said Ford grimly, as the secretary held his hand over the transmitter. "I'm not going to borrow a cent from them but we'll get some experience."

The subsequent parley on the loan was said to have consisted, on Ford's side, of four noes and one goodbye.

The premiership of Liebold was nearing an end but he did not know it when he went to Europe in 1931 and chopped wood at Doorn with ex-Kaiser Wilhelm. He told of his royal host's intelligence, geniality and informalism. He had been out himself at the woodpile that very morning, he wrote an American correspondent, and reported delightedly, "I chopped the biggest pile while the Kaiser operated a buzz-saw." He was bringing home an autographed colored photograph and he thought Mr. Ford would be interested in three sentences the emperor had written across its face. One was "Nothing is more likely to lead to war than the diplomatic and military over-organization of peace"; the second, "Nothing is settled finally unless it is settled right," and lastly, "Socialism is the determination of the have-nots to take away the property of the haves."

Ford's secretary called the turn on the Second World War—but several years prematurely. By the time he was ready to take off from Cologne for London, reports which he said had been given him in the "utmost confidence" had filled him with so many qualms that he looked uneasily behind as the train pulled out to see if bombs were already falling on the *bahnhof*.

His disheartening information, he wrote, was that Russia intended to declare war on Poland the latter part of 1932; everybody intended to see that French power was crushed for good; "the 100,000 men Germany has and is allowed under the Versailles Treaty will fit very well into the Russian army as its officers"; and as soon as France moves, Italy will invade France from the south." Glumly he added, "The same old crowd is playing the same old game."

"I can realize," he informed Dearborn, "that to anyone in the United States this may sound like an idle dream, and if the many things I have observed and the voluminous stories I have been told did not point so definitely in this direction I would hesitate to write you at such length. That a war in Europe is bound to occur within two years is the opinion of many I have met."

Liebold's power began to fade about three-fourths through his tenure. In the panicky days and nights following the closing of Michigan banks by a governor's order in 1933, the secretary was an exhaustless go-between. There was an offer by the Fords to set up a new bank. Behind the scenes he represented them in discussions. If he didn't speak for them, he was at the elbow of father or son. Some said Liebold saw in the emergency a golden chance to become a power in Detroit finance if the plan of a Ford bank materialized, and that what happened later did so when he learned his dream had no chance of success.

He slept an hour and a half a night—and something cracked. He needed sleep—he needed it badly. He walked out of his office one morning at 11, disappeared and became the afternoon five-star principal in a state-wide police search.

The secretary had started for home in his car, but home meant only more telephone calls, more people on the doorstep. He went there anyway. He stopped in the drive, packed a bag, headed north. He would go to a friend's home and hole in, but the friend was out and the secretary woke up in a hotel in Traverse City, Mich., seventeen hours later, registered under an assumed name. He telephoned the company where he was, had something to eat, went to bed again.

Liebold's importance at Dearborn shrank after that. Frank Campsall, another secretary to whom Ford was attached, had offered his resignation several years before and reported he and Liebold couldn't seem to hit it off. The motormaker set up a separate office for the man who wanted to resign and increased his duties. As one's power thinned the other's expanded. Campsall died in Ford's arms at the motormaker's Georgia estate in 1946.

Counsel for Ford and the treasurer of the company walked into Liebold's office in 1944 and placed on his desk a revocation signed by Mr. and Mrs. Ford of his power of attorney. They asked for his resignation and his keys.

"Mr. Ford will have to tell me this direct," said the veteran secretary. "No one else will do."

He walked over to a coat-rack, put on his hat, left and never heard from Ford again.

In prohibition days Ford posted a plant bulletin which said, "Any man with the odor of beer, wine or other liquor on his breath will be discharged and there will be no appeal," and the ukase took the liberty of promising the same treatment to any Ford workman having intoxicants in his home or on his person.

He added to the wisdom of the times by saying that liquor was the cause of war—"it made the wine-drinking French and the beer-drinking Germans suspicious of each other"—called on the Army and Navy to enforce the Volstead Act instead of going on practice cruises and maintaining their social positions at posts miles from nowhere, promised to give up manufacturing if liquor was restored to legal status and in the same breath said that there was no more chance of rescindment than of slavery returning. He also thought there were better ways to use alcohol than to drink it.

But to his heart he hugged two enchanting pixies, once in high executive position, who seceded from the United States on the temperance issue. They were drinkers in the lost week-end mold and he their forbearing shepherd. Whatever he might say on the public rostrum or to the unfamiliar thousands out in the big plant whom he simply hired to do a job, these two were his darlings—and "sick men, really," he seemed to say; "I must look after them as they would look after me if I was sick."

The service department got word to station a car near the residence of one, a brilliant figure, and report how liquor was being run into the house. Hourly the spotters were supplied with automobiles of different colors to reduce their conspicuousness and to allay the suspicions of anyone who might look out a window and mistrust an overlong parked car.

A black job would do for an hour or two. Then a maroon or blue or green car would drive past, the watchers would follow around a corner and transfer to it; and they would then resume their watch. They were not to molest anyone; they were merely to learn who was delivering liquor, and if the occupant of the house emerged, they were to follow and see that no harm came to him.

This espionage came in time to be not without danger. The switch of cars was a transparent ruse. The householder bought an air-rifle and on nights when he was especially discomposed at sight of sentries he shot at them from the ambush of an upstairs window and some of the Ford plant protection people were periodically reported as picking BB shot out of their hides. The lazy fun of sitting in an automobile of an evening and reporting on liquor movements naturally went off the list of pleasant details when lead began to sail.

About dusk, at length, a man with a burlap bag who was first mistaken for a gardener slipped around to a back entrance and was admitted. When an hour passed and he did not emerge, the Ford police grew suspicious. Here probably was how the alcohol was being replenished. The private cops settled back to tackle the messenger on the way out. At midnight a large car shot out the drive with the householder and the "gardener" and headed for the open road.

The spotters tore after it fast, but the test was unfair. The large car could do 100 to the Ford's 70. The driver of the big car, humming along easily at lower speed, did the unexpected, however, when he looked in his rear-view mirror and saw a trailing auto hard on his bumper—he put on his brakes without warning and screeched to a quick stop. The Ford taken aback by the stratagem, swung to a parallel lane and bounded past so that in an instant the situation was reversed—the pursuer became the pursued.

Mad over this proof that the company was set upon destroying a promising evening, the owner of the big car began to chase the Ford, crawling closer and closer though the service car tried to throw him off by dimming out. The protection men had no wish to be caught. The executive probably would hand them over to the regular police on some trumped-up charge and while this could be fixed, the man they were trailing would be on his way meantime and the trail would be cold by the time they were released.

The Ford swung suddenly from the main artery to a road into a woods; the big car shot by, apparently unaware that the small one had taken the side road. Back in the orthodox position of the pursuer again, the small car backed out on the main highway and picked up some distant red tail-lights. They could only race along in the hope that they were those of the quarry.

Two miles farther, the Ford came upon the big car in front of a lunchroom. The fugitive executive sat drinking a cup of coffee and staring vacantly. He was quiet until he finished when he began to pound with his knuckles the planking in front of him.

"Do you know what I think of Henry Ford?" he addressed his limited audience of one counter man and two plant policemen. He did not wait for an answer, he peeled off a ten-minute Philippic about Mr. Ford and all his works and it continued witheringly until the local chief of police walked in and hung up his cap, as innocently as though he had accidentally dropped by for a bite and had not been notified that the runaway presumably was at this particular restaurant and his chore was to get him home without publicity or injury.

"Why, hello!" the chief said, cheerily, as if this was a happy surprise.

The executive did not answer—he curled his lip. The gendarme's appearances in his life were too opportune to be accidental. This was Mr. Ford's work. When the world was taking on a lovely cerulean, the omnipresent copper always seemed to bob up through a trapdoor and say "Hello, there," with that bogus ring of geniality in his voice.

He'd tell off interfering Mr. Ford one of these days to his face. He said so very solemnly, or the Mr. Hyde in him did, and as Mr. Hyde he meant every word of it. He would do nothing of the kind, of course, but in this mood it pleased him to talk big of rebellion as if nothing would stay him from giving Mr. Ford a good piece of his mind. Actually he knew he would go home with the chief, and as Dr. Jekyll he would frown upon any rash insubordination and the next morning he would be back at his desk nodding approvingly over some statement of Mr. Ford and gravely supplying statistics to prove that Mr. Ford was absolutely right in what he said of the horrors of immoderation.

In the end he would go home with Brooks. The Federal authorities took care of the "gardener" and the bottles he had not gotten around to deliver. A whole month would pass before the service department would get word to spot a car near the residence of the problem executive and find out who was running liquor into the house. The detail assigned to watch put on its steel vests and wondered if the air-rifle was in good working order. They started off in a green car and a maroon car relieved them. It would be a re-run of the old film.

No less in favor was a man of endearing *bonhomie* who was a master salesman and discriminating adviser who punctuated about every ten words of what he said with the initials "J.C.," meaning Jesus Christ. If he even expressed himself on the weather, he would say, "J.C., it's hot" or "J.C., I'm freezing." He drank in the grand manner and ate always as a man might who had been subsisting for months on K-rations on an isolated reef. Even as Mr. Ford's luncheon guest he had four sugars in his coffee and three desserts if he felt that way.

Ford had a theory that a man who ate right thought right, and thinking right, would naturally turn his back on liquor. He became interested in a Chicago food specialist who talked up a balanced diet as a magical cure-all. The treatment was strenuous—purgatives for about a week and after that the reconstruction. For a long time he tried to gentle his unruly wards into yielding to treatment. One resisted to the end; the "J.C." man said yes, eventually, but he was a drawn figure when he returned.

He had lost a few pounds, his skin seemed a shade healthier, but his whispered reminiscences suggested a stay in Dachau. For Ford he had nothing but words of contrition and regret that he had not undergone the wonderful experiment earlier. At first Ford thought of challenging him to a foot-race for proof or of taking him over to the village and see if he could chin himself on that maple where Ford used to do the trick himself, but on second thought he felt he better not.

"Did you a lot of good, eh?" he contented himself by saying.

"Feel like a new man," the patient declared.

Ford thought he might have achieved a miracle with this pleasing rascal but he doubted it. He parted with the revivified executive, and the latter went off with friends to whom he could speak frankly. How was the treatment? How did he honestly feel?

"J.C., it was awful," he broke down. "They fed me more castor oil than Mussolini has in Italy." He peered about as if expecting Ford to spring from behind a bush. "For a week I drank nothing but water." One knew this to be tops in torment. "If I ever get away from here—" he whispered, and then stopped dead as if he realized he had better not profane the Dearborn campus by mention of the holiday he was considering. He left for his home station and a friend was glad some time later to get a cryptic post card.

"Have changed treatments," it read. "Got three cases of McCallum's castor oil, bonded, the other day."

The cause ever just, a brilliant mentor takes a chamois and burnishes the crown, resets the jewels as they occasionally work loose.

CHAPTER XVI

THE TORCH-BEARER

IF AN American League infielder had not stolen home in a game between Detroit and Cleveland Henry Ford might have been quite different in the public eye from what he was.

The runner was on third, a weak hitter up. A newspaper editor in the press-box thought the situation might do for an inspirational essay. Yes, he decided, he would say something of the shallowness of getting to third and dying there. Three-quarter runs are not marked on the score-board. Third base is merely opportunity, not arrival. The world is full of third bases. Once home, of course, no one can take away the glory. That sort of thing—not bad, he thought, not bad at all—with elaboration.

In the midst of the soliloquy the man at third, with a good lead off the bag on a left-handed pitcher who was facing first too carelessly, broke for the plate and slid away from the catcher's tag in the customary dust, acrobatics and glitter of high-flung spikes.

The editor put copy paper in his typewriter as soon as he got to the office but in the quiet of his room the plotted piece did not come as easy as he thought it would. He wrote a paragraph or two, tore the paper from the rollers, wadded it, tossed it into the basket. Eventually he admitted himself licked and walked into a neighboring office and said: "Billy, see what you can do with this, will you? The thought seems okay to me but I can't make it sing."

Pep-talk admirers had not been so exalted since Elbert Hubbard's message to Garcia. "Don't Die on Third" was reprinted by millions and reprints are still maintained to service a scattered demand. The author was Canadian-born William John Cameron, who was to become Ford's editor, privy counsellor, vendor of alarums, tailor of silver linings and accomplished public relations adviser who always and angrily denied he was any such thing and who wrote for Ford, or steered for him, many an article assigned to the motormaker which Ford never even read—as Cameron had ghosted long before for another editor a baseball play he never saw.

With one hand he tied Ford in with the company as generalissimo of all its many feats; with the other he severed him from responsibility if hell broke loose, so that the public inclined to say that Ford was often the innocent tool of bad men who somehow had gotten on his payroll and were doing things he did not know about and would not countenance if he did know.

Fortune conducted a poll in 1937. It asked two questions:

1. Can you think of any well-known men in industry or business of whom you approve? Of whom you disapprove?

2. What corporation do you approve? Disapprove?

Ford topped the list of favored employers with 60.6 per cent of the vote. But while he could preen himself on a whopping lead and the company won enough ballots to land on top, it was significant that only 20.4 per cent expressed approval of the company as against the heavy percentage applauding its founder.

At the time the base-runner stole home in 1909 Cameron was writing a column for the Detroit *News* under the caption "Reflections" and contemporaries recall he could beat out a piece about a falling autumn leaf which would bring tears to the eyes of every woman in town. His moralizing in "Don't Die on Third," in fact, resulted in a few wet eyes in the bleachers, albeit for other causes.

"All the world is a diamond," he wrote. "You are one of the players. Perhaps you have reached first by your own efforts. You get to second on the sacrifices of parents and friends. Then," he labored, "—on someone's long fly into the business world or someone's fluke on the rules of simple morality and square dealing, you have attained third. At third you are to be reckoned with. Your opponents converge all their attention on you. From third you become a splendid success or a dismal failure. DON'T die there!"

He got to real pedaling here:

"What are you doing to win the score life is ready to mark opposite your name? Third base has no laurels on which you can rest. Are you waiting for someone to bat you in? If he misses, the miss is yours. If you place all your dependence on someone else, his failure is yours. What are you doing there—waiting for something to turn up? The Detroit base-runner would not have scored if he had waited for the next batter to hit the ball, and that run was absolutely necessary to win the game. That run was gained in unmeasurable time, but the difference between success and failure is often counted in seconds."

And then the final hard ball, letter high:

"Had the base-runner been out the night before he would have played the game according to routine, but he doesn't carouse. He does not smoke or drink. He is old fashioned enough to go to church on Sunday. A clean life means a clear head. Legs that tread the path of irregularity cannot win in 90 feet against a swift ball that travels 60. Only a trained body and an alert mind could have stolen home. Work itself is a game and has its rules and sudden openings. Study conditions! Postpone thinking of luck until you hear the umpire call 'Safe!' "

Some bawdy comment may have smoked up the clubhouse of Hughey Jennings' spike-throwing Tigers when they read of such a model in their midst. The bleachers may have had something to say of the unique theory that churchgoing had some relationship to a steal of home, but editorial writers do not have to take the witness stand and offer proof, and, anyway, the language of the editorial always was being reframed in later years.

On the radio twenty years later as Ford spokesman, Cameron, Class of '36, deleted and amended the work of Cameron, Class of '09. He did not refer to the hero's teetotalism and church attendance and one assumed Cameron may have come around to the idea that a ball player might miss Sunday-school and still get a corner of the plate sliding in. Originally he said it was the ninth inning, two out, and the run won the game. Actually it was the fourth inning and the run tied the score. It made one wonder a little if there also was literary license in the editor's representations as Ford's spokesman.

Billy Cameron went to a collegiate school, and for a short time to Toronto University, but quit at 19 and said in after years he educated himself by wide reading. Curiously, in view of his own experience, he lamented on the air "the bookish ideal which many called learning."

"To know what men had written, to read what could be read in libraries, was to be a learned man—it used to be the white-collar fashion," was the way he put it, a little witheringly and with perhaps a peek out the corner of one eye at Ford.

The point he made was that in an early misguided time "a race of heroes was being born not of books but of Experience's vital touch—the manufacturer who makes some commodity that refines daily life and its range."

But did Carlyle and Emerson make heroes of such? No, no, he said—they, like the others, stuck to prophets and poets and warrior kings, so what Carlyle and Emerson did not do, Cameron did not fail at, and he proved himself an adept carpenter. He toiled for, and believed in, a hero of giant frame and as large ideas.

He became a railroad timekeeper first. Later a letter to an editor elicited an invitation to call but not to burn his bridges behind him. Cameron burned them anyway, quit keeping time, joined the paper, stayed on. He always thought that, in justice to the ministry, the story that he once filled a Brooklyn, Mich., pulpit should be taken out of circulation. He described himself, at 19, as merely a half-baked iconoclast who drank in Robert Ingersoll and William Jennings Bryan and was caught up in the liberal ferment of the times.

To have a gun to shoot when he was shot at, Ford paid $1,000 for a small-town paper and engaged an editor who begged Cameron to come to Dearborn. The editor was E. G. Pipp, a Detroiter. He quit Ford in 1920 and Cameron took over.

Presses were hard to find when World War I ended. Pipp located a second-hand one. Parts were missing and the base was cracked. "We'll make the repairs. Go ahead and buy it," said Ford. If it couldn't be fixed, it always could be fed to the cupolas and the metal made into tractors.

Pipp found men taking down the press one morning when only the day before it had seemed almost ready for a first run. He wanted to know who ordered the dismantling.

"Mr. Ford wants the wheels polished," the men said.

If they were polished, it would be possible to tell if any were cracked. Besides, said Publisher Ford, what man would keep a machine clean that wasn't clean to start? Better late the issue than dirty the tools that brought it forth.

He asked a veteran magazine representative how to make a go of his paper. If he wanted the best magazine, he should get the best writers. Who, for instance? Wells, Shaw, Kipling, Galsworthy. He could have the very best magazine in Christendom for $30,000 an issue.

"I say 'Rats!' " Ford told his editors. "How have those fellows made their reputations? By writing for national magazines. We're going to publish a national magazine, aren't we? If you write for it you'll be famous also. Go ahead and write it."

His staff felt it wasn't quite as elementary as that, but the first issue appeared in January of 1919. No advertising was accepted. Contributors got as high as $1000 an article, although standard rate was about half of that. Some names were bought—Walpole, Sandburg, Robert Frost. The paper was dedicated to "The Neglected Truth," and a cynical columnist, wooed to Dearborn by illusion of riches and pleasantly given to hearty guzzling, called it "the best God damned paper ever published in a tractor factory."

Men who worked on the paper in those days say Ford had an idea at one time of getting it out on the assembly line principle—a long table of typewriters manned by the staff. . . . Tarsney putting in the woman-reader stuff . . . Bradner dropping in some humor . . . Martin inserting news, as the story passed from hand to hand. An editor is said to have forestalled the experiment by convincing their employer that the magazine, not the individual story, was the unit—that the paper could be assembled, not the story.

Certainly it was the only paper whose publisher ever ran down a public street after an employee to apologize for an affront and ask him to come back. Ford also was, in all likelihood, the only newspaper owner to pay $100,000 for a tunnel by which to bring paper to his presses, so his engineers in the same building, would not catch cold.

The editor involved, now a member of the University of Arizona faculty, was let out by Ford's business secretary who was also the paper's general manager. He notified the secretary he was resigning and would leave at the end of the month. Presumably for the effrontery he was told he was through right then.

The writer recounted the incident to Cameron and said he'd be on his way as soon as he cashed his company savings certificates. Cameron told Ford. By this time the ex-employee had collected the money due him and was off to get himself a tonic at a nearby soft-drink stand down the street. He was nearing it when he heard a shout behind him. A sprinting messenger was calling. Ford would like to see him. The two heard a second shout and looking about saw a hatless Ford bearing down at a gallop. He took the writer by the elbow. He'd just heard, he said, what had happened.

"The general manager will see you in his office and apologize," he promised.

He said he hoped the writer would change his mind about leaving and, anyway, he was to stay as long as he liked. The reinstated worker's phone rang a few minutes after he reached his office, warm inside and comfortable at what had occurred. Would he step into the manager's office? The apology was unwatered.

"Mr. Ford says I made a mistake in firing you. He says I am to apologize. What he tells me to do I do. Therefore, I apologize." The words clipped off as if the manager was shearing nails. The staff member stayed on and quit in a month, but he never lost his place among Ford's friends and returned often to talk with him.

Twenty-five years later he was managing editor of a large metropolitan newspaper when Ford fired the factotum who had fired him. He pulled up his typewriter and with pleasure batted out the obituary. Ford read it and smiled broadly.

"I'll bet Martin got a lot of fun out of writing that," he remarked to one of his executives. "He has been waiting 20 years for the chance."

The master of Dearborn had a theory that it was often as well to give a task to someone utterly unfamiliar with it and therefore without set brain patterns. He had an instinctive preference for the amateur. Give a fellow a job who knew all about what he had to do and he would be boxed by that knowledge and wouldn't jump a fence to try something new.

In deciding to build his engineering laboratory he wheeled on an executive who already had his fingers in three enterprises and did not know a single thing about floor layout.

"I want you to make the floor plans and fit the engineering departments and the magazine printing plant into them," he said. He offered no suggestions.

The uneasy official hunted up some other executives of more experience and also the architect.

"Don't worry—we'll show you how," said Albert Kahn, architect of most Ford buildings and always cooperative. "You can help by seeing heads of departments." Kahn itemized what he thought could be done. "Tact and diplomacy, you know! Get everyone satisfied. You know how it is—everybody will want the best light and the best position."

The executive began to breathe again. He waylaid a layout man. The building went up—a $2,000,000 trinket. Two huge sliding doors worked by motor and push-button closed and opened the north end. Railroad tracks were run in.

"I want a place where I can build a pin or a railroad locomotive," Ford had said, in planning the building. Well, there it was for him, finally—with a craneway when he wanted to work on a locomotive and arrangements for a fifty-ton crane if and when he wanted to use it. The doors opened wide enough that freight cars could be backed in and the paper tonnage unloaded for the magazine, but the place was hardly open a week when engineers complained of the cold drafts and a spokesman for them told Ford that everyone would die of pneumonia.

They were open at the moment and Ford went out in the immense main room to see for himself.

"Pretty bad," he agreed, and shivered in the drafts. "I'll see to it."

He dropped in on the layout amateur and said to get the railroad track out and keep those doors closed.

"But how are we going to get our heavy paper requirements into the place?" the upset tyro asked.

"That's your problem—you solve it!" Ford was out and off on another errand. Everybody, he said, would be down with colds under the system as it was.

The man who had been directed to seal the doors permanently walked about in a bit of a daze until someone told him to talk to a fellow at the Highland Park plant who was a genius at conveyors and who might have a solution. He could not see any way himself to get the sizable rolls of paper stock into the place unless they were passed through an open window.

"Don't worry"—the man who knew all about conveyors bubbled with assurance—"I'll be out there tomorrow and maybe I'll get an idea."

At the railroad siding an elevator was built which rose to the level of a box-car floor and descended to a tunnel and conveyor which ran under the north wall of the laboratory. By such steps the paper supply could be rolled off the car to the elevator, dropped down to the conveyor and run through the tunnel to storage in the basement. It was a six-figure job but no one caught cold—at least for that reason. The craneway stood idle for years, but on the whole Ford was delighted. The whole layout was one more proof of an amateur's invincibility.

Cameron, the editor, was literate, genial, positive. Others might have an idea his steamer-chair rested on a rising and falling deck, but he did not seem to mind the roll. He was spectacled, round-faced, unathletic and had an astonishing gift for digging up a plausible answer to almost any question. It might not be an answer according to your lights, but it sounded always like a reasonable one.

He gave Ford's page in the weekly a gusset of scholarship. He attributed to his employer a philosophy of sustained rectitude and he built up in the public mind—if extra build-up was necessary—a Henry Ford who was a minglement of most of the virtues of all who had known glory. When, as broadcaster, his voice shut off after his weekly six-minute stint, there had been such calm and righteousness and certainty in it that one wondered why all the clashing elements were not immediately drawn into brotherhood, so clearly had Ford, by proxy, switched his road lights on the only path.

It is not uncommon for a man of highly specialized knowledge to put erudition on his payroll; it is rarer for one to get an apostle so convinced of the paymaster's primacy. Ivy Lee doled out shining dimes for Rockefeller senior. Cameron bore a basket of words, like daisies, and scattered them in praise of Ford the elder. He was Ford's indefatigable Peter, and, in less fortunate moments, he seemed to be Ford's Patsy, uncomplainingly confessing the arson, himself, when the employer lit a fire too hot and retired to some shade until the heat abated.

The joy balanced the grief without question, for when the editor retired at sixty-seven, Cameron still said that other men dwindled in size when Ford entered a room and that he was strong medicine for lesser men to swallow.

Cameron liked a joke but seldom told a gusty one. He accused newsmen of nursing what he called "the downtown viewpoint." They forgot, he lectured, that the world was not made up entirely of abnormal and subnormal people who were always getting into print. In a reporter's hunt for the bizarre, he insisted, he overlooked the homebodies who never were in the newspapers, and did not want to be, and who took care of their larkspur and peonies and talked to neighbors over the back fence and were America's backbone. You had an idea at times he thought most of these people lived in the country.

He was an attentive listener, an insatiable reader. The two libraries in his home bulged with volumes in intriguing disorder, books squeezed in everywhere, jacketed, out of their wraps, some bindings worn thin, ancients and moderns, incunabula to detective fiction written by his son, a quiet devil who in his youth looked every inch a seraph. His father shuddered slightly as his distressed eye ranged lightly over such titles as *Murder's Coming* and *Grave Without Grass,* and said he wished Donald had attempted a little more serious work.

You wanted to talk to Mr. Ford, eh? Very well, see Mr. Cameron! If the latter did not think you were entitled to take up any of Ford's crowded time, you did not take it up, unless you encountered the motormaker by accident in the corridor; and then Ford was likely to lean his back against a paneled wall, slip the halter and talk at length and at random. Cameron fretted at such times, in the last office down the hall on the left, and hoped the boss was staying on the preserve and not luxuriating in offhand shockers such as the one that the average pay of an American worker would be $27 a day in 1950, or that cows would be extinct in another ten years.

When Ford went to Washington to see Presidents, the editor went along. When touring bigwigs visited Dearborn, the editor sat quietly in a corner and chipped in words at appropriate moments. What Ford said was gospel; Cameron grew strident only when anyone hinted that any word of it might be wrong or outdated or had a worn-out bearing. He was also pretty hurt when Ford announced he would give $100,000,000 to American education, and an acidulous editor said "It would be nice to have that much to spend on him." If Ford was inconsistent, to Cameron he was "gloriously inconsistent." Ford was "a wondrous seer."

"Mrs. Ford was telling me," he offered as an example, "of a day she and Ford were walking in New York in 1902, when there was only a handful of automobiles in the United States. They had turned off Fifth Avenue and Mr. Ford suddenly said to her: 'Strange thing, Callie, but back there just a moment ago I imagined I saw four lines of horseless carriages.'"

He would say that if you got Mr. Ford's words they resembled strokes of a hammer; that it was natural for Ford to see a world without cows: he had helped bring about a world without horses; that Mr. Ford took no one's advice unless it was his wife's, and only asked an employee what he thought to find how many yesmen he had.

He smiled, in the manner of a tolerant friend, at Ford's view that he could rid his orchard of bugs without spraying. Birds, the motormaker held for a long time, were the natural foe of insects and would take care of any that might plague his trees. The drawback seemed to be that the birds had lighted on so many poisoned trees that they were suspicious of what they might find on them and did not know that Ford trusted to them and not to Bordeaux mixture. The birds failed him. He turned to spray in the end.

Cameron's voice rang out in interpretation from many lecterns, from rooftop and press-box, on many witness stands, before many microphones. He often brought splendor to the commonplace, discernment to hokum, a strong solvent to any spots which might appear in the Ford philosophy or be imputed to it. But he always insisted staunchly that the company had no public relations counsel since, if a company had honest management and purpose and the determination to give the best value, the public would be able to distinguish between it and a company more eager to sell than to serve.

"The best public relations man any business could have," he proclaimed, spurning the label for himself and getting in a lick for his employer, "is the head of a business who is determined that equitable principles shall prevail."

Actually, one got little at times of Ford's meaning when he was talking in disengaged fragments. Cameron would putty up the holes and gild the rough sentence. An able friend analyzed these gaps. Ford would make a basic statement. Let us call that A. Then he instinctively sensed what your probable response would be. This was statement B. To that response, in normal exchange, he would have said C and you D, and he would then make statement E. Knowing the three steps by which E would be reached, Ford would skip B, C and D and go to E himself, bewildering a listener by the leap. Ford now would be answering something the listener meant to ask him only after a couple of intervening questions he was not given chance to ask. These were statements B and D, which Ford struck out. What you had in your hands at the finish was a cable in skeleton.

Three miles separate Dearborn and the Rouge plant. At the one, they waltzed ceremoniously to dulcimer and vibraphone; at the other, they danced to an elaborate system of espionage—before Ford's grandsons took over. At Dearborn, Cameron played lulling and lofty tunes in Ford's honor; at the Rouge, Bennett played a rougher hurdy-gurdy, harsher melodies and implanted fear in workers. At Dearborn, Ford had his cake; at the Rouge he ate it, refuting the crusted adage that one could not do both at once.

Cameron assailed totalitarianism and bespoke an economy "where every man shall sit under his own fig-tree, none daring to make him afraid." The most obscure person in America, he was proud to say, might criticize public policy without fear of spies or secret police. The totalitarian state "measures its strength by the depth of its people's docility, dictating what they shall believe, what they shall read, hear or speak."

At the Rouge, Bennett planted agents at union meetings, wrote down the names of the "disloyal," and saw to it that the boys in the plant did not sit under any fig-tree proclaiming their freedom, or get any silly notions from such bosh as the Wagner Act. The totalitarianism within the walls was close riveted.

The editor looked over minutely, toned down, brushed up and hunted error in thousands of manuscripts in which Ford was directly quoted, on the understanding they would be submitted for check in advance of publication. Naturally, thousands of stories about Ford appeared without this sluicing, but untold copy went to Cameron for okay.

The editor was three persons. One-third of him never left the conviviality of the newspaper city room. One-third was in the pulpit. The last third sat at a walnut desk in the engineering laboratory sculpting his Pygmalion, but he never seemed completely pleased for long with any one of the three roles. When the displeasure boiled over he disappeared, an incurable rebel against the machine-like schedule about him.

That he reached the big-income brackets was not enough. He would tire of saying "What Mr. Ford means—" or of trying to mix his own three personalities into a satisfied whole. Failing, he would stack his papers neatly on the desk and vanish, and all information available was that he was not there, which you could see for yourself, of course.

A triple personality paste-up made for a mean problem, for you would be talking to the old newspaperman and suddenly sense he had gone, and the pulpiteer had taken his place; and then as quickly he would switch and be the mirror of Ford. It was troublesome keeping track of when he was Jehovah, Jehovah's Witness or just a fellow off the police beat such as one might meet in front of any newspaper cashier's cage trying to wheedle a little advance money. He livened up perceptibly when the press crowded his office. They were a link with his salad days.

Whatever it was made Ford forgiving of a subordinate who stuck out a tongue at the general regimentation, you would walk in one morning into the end room which had been empty, perhaps, for a spell, and at his typewriter and peering blandly over his glasses would be the editor polishing off a sermonette full of good solid things such as "Mr. Ford regards money as of no account, its function being merely to move goods from man to man as a postage stamp carries a letter" or "Mr. Ford absolutely rejects the theory that wages must be kept down or, if they rise, must be recaptured by higher prices."

If Cameron was not stretching it, his was an unparalleled independence. He said he never was told what to say over the radio before he said it, and never was criticized by Ford after a broadcast for what he did say. As editor of the *Independent* he professed an equal freedom.

Opposing counsel in a $1,000,000 suit filed against Ford by Aaron Sapiro, organizer of farm cooperatives, tried to show Ford's acquaintance with the articles containing the claimed libel. Cameron could not remember any discussion of the paper's policies with Ford, except in the "most general way," and said he could not recall any discussion unless it was "when we differed from him and gave him our reasons." He was asked for a little illustration.

"Well, Mr. Ford is against war, of course, but the paper stands for preparedness," he said. "He permits us to do so," he hurried to say, "although he would like to see war abolished."

Secondly, while Ford looked on the Russian people with leniency, the paper was opposed to Bolshevism, Cameron said.

"Mr. Ford favors the Soviet then?" Sapiro's counsel saw an opening.

"Oh, no," Cameron corrected, "but he does not feel as strongly on the matter as we do."

The editor asked the court to believe that on two major policies such as these Ford paid his editor to say things in his columns with which he strongly disagreed.

"Did you ever seek to learn his position toward the attitude of the Dearborn *Independent* on public questions?"

"Well, the attitude of the *Independent* was taken beforehand," the editor insisted.

None of the matter pertaining to material handled by the editorial department went to Ford. The manufacturer would drop into the magazine's office, the witness said, sometimes not once a week, sometimes once a day. What did they talk about ordinarily? Oh, something that had appeared in the daily press, possibly something about Ford's interest in farming. He assured the court he did not talk over with Ford the attitude of the publisher on public questions. He simply used such visits to "get his thought, his philosophy."

"We are to understand then"—the lawyer grew ironical—"that you have no recollection of time, occasion or person with whom you first discussed publication of any articles dealing with certain Jews?"

Cameron said he had tried to discuss things with Ford but he just would not talk about them. In his presence Ford never had even read the *Independent*. The editor said he tried to get him to, but he could not recall he ever succeeded.

"He must have read it some place else, if at all," he suggested, dolefully and a little unhelpfully.

When an inimical lawyer pinned him down and an embarrassing question had to be answered Cameron never involved Ford. No lawyer ever quite succeeded in getting from him a damning admission. The editor was never fooled as to what effect a "yes" or "no" at the wrong spot might have on the fortunes of the case.

Across his desk he would peer owlishly at you and say:

"Mr. Ford still believes it is early morning in America and there are fifty opportunities for every one when he was young.

"Mr. Ford says if you start a thing, you ought to finish it. It is always too soon to quit. The thrill and interest of making the first car evaporated one day. Mr. Ford said he had gone far enough to see how he could build the second car. The glowing new vision got in his way.

"Some untaught wisdom," the editor would philosophize, "must have forced him on, and soon he was learning more and more about his second car by going on with his first."

Had Ford yielded, the editor was sure he might never have finished that second car.

"Mr. Ford says that with many people the line from the eye or ear runs straight to the mouth or pen, with no interval for digestion or judgment. With others it goes back to the brain where the harvest of eye or ear is analyzed and weighed and only then, if then, does the line proceed to the organs of speech and writing.

"In Mr. Ford's opinion many men do not know that yesterday is past and still make up their minds with last year's ideas."

The Journal of Neglected Truth sank without trace the last day of 1927 except for an oily slick of a bias it had spread. It developed no Shaws or Galsworthys. It did not become the best magazine in the world. It published at a loss of $400,000 a year. It caused cleavage by a series of articles that maddened the Jewish people and resulted in an unparalleled recantation.

"Let's have no more of it," he said, querulously, in signing the execution warrant. "The paper keeps us in hot water."

The garroting of its editor was demanded—and denied. Cameron began a new life after a seven-year pause. He became Ford's radio proxy. For 54 minutes each Sunday the company brought to the American public the finest of the world's music and concertists; for the other six the editor dealt with plaguing contemporary problems, and was a passionate witness for the Ford way of life.

What Cameron said will be discussed more fully in the next chapter because what he said, presumably, was a reflection of Ford's own thought.

Laissez-faire states its case against government interference, finance management, unions, and Napoleons and holy mountains not its own.

CHAPTER XVII

HENRY FORD BY TRANSCRIPTION

SANDWICHED BETWEEN Melchior and Tibbett, Beecham and Ormandy, Sibelius and Beethoven, Henry Ford stepped to a radio microphone and expressed by proxy his views of industry, the national political scene and the situation abroad from 1934 to 1942.

In the person of his editor, he delivered over a span of 285 nights in 300,000 words a series of carefully tooled essays in which William J. Cameron did a selling job which pretended to be nothing of the kind. At 9 o'clock Sunday evening there would be a tap at the family door and there would be Mr. Ford's understudy with sample case and divining rod and for six minutes he would lay out his merchandise on the wireless cabinet.

The sales talks were unique. He had, he said, no theories to propagate, no selling arguments to offer, no political axe to grind. For a moment in such case there was doubt in a listener's mind as to why he was at the door-bell in the first place. What he was going to tell, he said, was "merely a modest contribution to straight thinking and common sense." He would supply facts which had been suppressed and complete facts which had only been partially stated. Naturally, he said, anyone would try to put an oar on the right side that the boat might make headway. The confusion was not lessened, however, by another statement that as a matter of fact Cameron would not lift a finger to change anyone's opinions—"opinions change themselves." If this was true, it left the reason for the discourses doubly cloudy.

These preliminaries finished, Ford's Warwick set upon many fallacies of the times, flogged the Roosevelt administration and its works, and gave industrial management's answer to a number of allegations—some baseless, others better founded—being popularly raised against the free enterprise system. For six minutes the understudy talked; for the other 54 Henry Ford brought to the American public the finest music and voices procurable. There were no laughs, no clowns, no indigestible zippididodah.

Cameron spoke with the easy assumption of one sure of his ground. The people, he would say, do not believe . . . are convinced . . . have been persuaded . . . do not want . . . finally realize . . . are thinking more and more. He put mass opinion on a microscopic slide and had a good look at it, although he was to admit in a later essay that public opinion was "dust that whirled in the wind" and that what mattered was conviction, "the granite stratum laid down by generations." His radio reign began when the country was taking its first creeping steps out of the depression, extended through the New Deal period, and for five months after Pearl Harbor, and the times were such as to provide abundant clay-pigeons for his fowling piece.

But Cameron was no neutral observer: he was the alter ego of Henry Ford. How much of a high-fidelity recording he was, is hard to say; but assuming that he harvested faithfully, what he said merits study, for no man was closer day by day to the motormaker or knew, as well as anyone could, the Ford genius and fallibility and artlessness. It was never easy to tell where Cameron turned from the flesh and blood Ford to put in a few licks on the Ford statue.

The feuilletons were tranquil at times, fighting words at others, always in extollation of Ford, always proud of Ford's experiments. When the editor spoke of fundamentals, he naturally meant the fundamentals Ford subscribed to. When he spoke in praise of novelty it was of Ford novelties, not Washington's. He was a querulous inspector of government innovation.

Cameron could enjoy the novelties and showmanship of Ford, but similar qualities in Franklin Delano Roosevelt he found hard to take. He could be ecstatic over Ford building a car to take the place of the horse and buggy—that was progress—as he could be scornful of Roosevelt breaking with something old—that was a flouting of a fundamental.

His talks did not pretend to be spot news. When unionists were kneed in the stomachs and kicked from the overpass of the Rouge plant in 1937, Cameron made no radio report of the incident. His next talk was on the small town and a week later it was on "the factual foundation of faith in the ever-dawning future." When Roosevelt was elected over Landon and Ford opposition in 1936, it was not until the middle of the next January that the editor got around to felicitation and a statement that "it is not abandonment of principle to say that most of us will agree that, on the whole, the re-election of President Roosevelt left a fine feeling throughout the country."

It was a polite interlude in a campaign of Ford criticism of the incumbent and his administration until death came at Warm Springs.

As early as 1934 and 1935 the editor was saying on the Ford Sunday Evening Hour:

"We have had no Napoleons in this country and we need none.

"Spectacular thunderclap characters leave no lasting mark.

"The public as a whole or in good part has not been deceived by would-be guides who are themselves misled.

"This is a day of names and reputations and sharp-ascending peaklike individualities, each presented as the one holy mountain where we ought to bow in national worship. America never has descended to that kind of idolatry, or if for a brief moment she has, it has been a rueful experience.

"The virtue most prized in public men is not a superficial brilliance but strong balance and good character.

"Our great national dream of a better life for every family is not a political phantasmagoria born lately of these distrait times, but a pillar of cloud by day and fire by night that our people have followed from the beginning.

"It is on the side of our good will we are vulnerable. The enemies of the American idea ask, 'Wouldn't you like to see poverty abolished?' Who would not? They ask, 'Wouldn't you like to see old age comfortable and secure, employment general and continuous?' Yes, and the whole kitchen side of living so strongly settled in scientific social righteousness we shall all be free to go on and conquer the higher regions of life. But to attain these things by going outside our ideal and standard we think is impossible. Ideas of social improvement are not late repentances of this nation—they are the spirit of American progress from the beginning."

The changes that count in the life of a people, Ford's proxy preached, are mostly those that occur in silence, not the noise and pageantry of surface movements—"Law never does anything constructive. We have had enough of legislators promising to do things that laws cannot do."

Ford emerged from a White House conference with President Herbert Hoover when the crash of the stock market in 1929 was spreading fright and returned to Detroit to raise his minimum wage from a $6 to $7 day as his answer to doubters. He thought to stay panic and bolster confidence, but he found himself the general of a quaking army bolting fast for the exits. It cost him $15,000,000 before he was forced to rescind the "prosperity" dollar in 1931 and began to hire in common labor at 50 cents an hour.

The full platter of relief Cameron brought to the radio audience was heaped with such morsels as "People are convinced that those who trade their liberty for bread are invariably cheated of both" and "Society comprised entirely or in part of dependents has little on which to depend" and "Unless we help ourselves there is little hope of helping others" and "We can help society first by not being a burden if we can avoid it and by contributing to the common stock at least as much as we take," and "When you see a nation successfully caring for dependents you know it can do this because it has enough people who are independent."

"If you would lift another," he sermonized, "you must have a foothold yourself. There is no one to look after our people but themselves, and what is more there never has been. The self-sufficient, self-reliant recovery effort of a community is stopped the day its government says, 'Let US save your troubles for you.' "

Cameron preached the answer of those who had to those who didn't, and it was:

"If you want food you must plant it. If you want a house you must build it. If you want an education you must toil for it, and if one can do this all can do it. The Road to the Delectable Mountains is not finished; it has been built only to where we stand by men who wrought before us. Pull your weight in the boat. Many a man wants to be a passenger but pulling his weight blisters his hands."

New Deal reversals in the Supreme Court brought pleasure to Dearborn and Cameron rejoiced at the discomfiture of "busy young men who have been making picture puzzles of the American way of living and gaily piecing new paper worlds together out of the fragments of ancient fallacies." He celebrated the melting and fading at the first touch of reality of a "perfect welter of gorgeously incompetent plans" and thought some of the things accounted important in the depression hardly would attain the dignity of brief footnotes in history.

He had Roosevelt being unseated by a plucky awakened people in 1936 but, politics-wise, coppered the bet in the waning days of the Landon campaign by urging the probable losers to take solace from the fact that a minority was not a group of discredited citizens and that right principle did not fail merely because it lost in the voting.

"In fact," as he put it, "a minority is one-half the mold into which the majority must pour its metal if its work is to have strength and symmetry."

After the landslide he scrambled to his feet to note that "the largest and most vociferous group to claim credit for having re-elected the President falls short about 23 millions of including all the citizens who voted for him. Many who did not approve the President's methods were wholly unwilling to replace him."

Government interference with business was a constant thorn. Ford's interpreter was often to dwell on the subject:

"The best recovery up to tonight (1938) has been made by those governments which had least to do with it. Government can vastly upset and injure the economic process but has no equal power to build and help. Many if not most of the things attempted by government should be done; the point is that with the best will in the world government cannot do them."

The situation as he saw it was the result of fallacies nursed for forty years—the demand on government for something entirely beyond its sphere. Federal administrators had contracted from the people the habit of trying to be something they were not and could not be. At odds with many of the New Deal experiments, he did not think the Lord would let His children play with matches if He did not know the structure of the universe was fireproof.

Unemployment insurance was to Ford's Six-Minuteman "one of the surest ways of insuring that there shall always be unemployment."

"It taxes an unemployed man's job," said he, "in order to relieve society of the necessity of finding the real cause of the difficulty. It uses doors and windows of the house for fuel and soon you will have neither home nor fire."

On the other hand he took umbrage with those who derided shovel-leaners and leaf-rakers and reported most of the men he knew on WPA to be capable of more important things and preferring employment. "American business also has its shovels," he conceded, "on which at times it is tempted to lean." He said "tempted," however, and not "did."

The NRA, of course, was a move to turn industry over to labor unions, and he remarked of the office of Gen. Hugh Johnson: "Henry Ford said, 'I'll make a buggy that will go without a horse and make it so cheap that those who can't afford a horse and buggy can afford this.' There was no NRA to say to him: 'Here, you can't buy any machinery to start a shop unless Washington says so—there's too much machinery now.' We had to wait 40 years for that brilliant idea to dawn upon the world."

He disputed the theory that wealth could be shared by taking it away from the person who had it and giving it to the person who didn't, and spread-the-work plans failed in his mind because for a time a few men got a little, none got enough, and in the end no one got anything, there being nothing to share.

"One hundred men earning $5 a day," he calculated, "have more recovery power than 500 getting $1 a day. The $5 men will buy goods that will make jobs for others; the $1 men will not be able to patronize any industry and thus will cause a decline in such industries as exist."

He regarded most Washington-bred "schemes" and "theories" as false because "they gauge all future time by present conditions." As for the dole, it was never expected to lift anyone out of the dole class.

Occasional sophist, at other times the cold dealer in previously suppressed facts, Cameron expressed the Ford point of view and supplied it in a big economy size package drenched in the Chanel of such phrases as "American principles need not that we save them; standing close to them they save us" or "To hear some people complain there are no more frontiers one would believe that frontiers were frosted cake and candy" and "Our national weakness for publicity permits every popgun to masquerade as a trump of doom."

He was fond, too, of such rhetorical lace as "Industry does not support industry; people support industry"; "We do not become enterprising because we are free; we become free because we are enterprising"; "Liberalizing to conserve; conserving to liberalize—that is the genius of the American people," and "Civilization is not produced by the machine; the machine is produced by civilization."

His seven-league boots carried him across a vast deal of plain. The weekly mailbag was full. Was the assembly line a man-killer? Had 2 per cent of the people gobbled up 80 to 90 per cent of the national wealth? How much would each Ford employee get if the company profits of 33 years were divided among them? Was industry scrapping men of 40? Did machinery diminish employment? How much did each purchaser contribute to Ford profit? Could the depression have been prevented if profit had been spent when earned instead of being banked in surplus?

Was it sound to absorb wage increases by price increases? Were storehouses jammed with surplus? Would there be revolution in the United States? Where did profits go? One by one he tackled them.

Was a domestic flare-up in the offing?

"It is an ear-catching theme. All the dissidents put together do not make a small handful. They represent no community of opinion. The American people have not authorized any group to do their thinking for them; they have not handed over either themselves or their affairs to any temporary occupants of public office, nor to those who sensationally and with momentary luck assault the popular ear. Any individual who claims to have behind him sufficient support to coerce the American people is simply deluded. The mistake of revolutionaries is to assume that America has no internal shaping principle and is a lump of putty to be molded into this or that by any hand that can grasp it. Cease confusing the fads of the moment with the trend of the times."

What would be the result of "soaking the rich"?

"Share the wealth plans usually begin with the false assumption that wealth is money. Money is to wealth what bookkeeping is to a flour mill—you may confiscate and distribute the books and bills and bank balance of the mill and yet have no flour. Money, being merely part of the bookkeeping system of society, is or ought to be the sign of wealth, but it is not and never can be wealth itself. It is further assumed that wealth can be shared by taking it away and giving it away. There is a catch here, also, for wealth is never wealth in the taking but in the using and making, and to think of sharing as taking is only a half truth."

Up to the present, the most effective mechanism that experience has devised to share the wealth is industry, the editor declared. It is a market where people bring what they have to get what they need. It is a trading center where materials, labor, skill and science are changed into commodities useful to life. The farmer brings his produce to get industrial products in return. All men bring their services. Everyone shares in the making to share in the taking. He brings goods or work, which is real wealth; he receives dollars which give him a claim on the equivalent of the wealth he has contributed. Industry can really share the wealth because its first concern is to create wealth. There is no other way! The sharing process needs constant improvement, but certainly it does not need introduction. It is already here, and operating. That was Cameron's impression.

As to surplus, two-thirds of Henry Ford's was represented by buildings, machinery, and materials. If all income stopped and normal expenditures continued, its available working cash capital would suffice to operate the business for about two and a half months. In 1929 American families and individuals had saved 15 billion dollars; corporate savings for that year were two billions. Did it injure the country that American families had a nest-egg of 15 billion? Should it have been taken away from them? That was the argument, the editor said, against corporate savings which were gathered to be used. Had enjoyment been their purpose, they would not have been saved. As it was, had business and family savings not existed, things would have been seriously worse. Had they been larger, conditions would not have been nearly so bad. "Those who in pathetic ignorance would like to see the big one soaked may not know it yet but they will be next in line."

How much did each Ford car owner contribute to Ford profit?

"Congressional debates assume that profits, like the gold of some eastern potentate, are hoarded in caves. Instead, profit is at work being used up as previously the so-called profits of 33 years were used. Some 94 per cent of the money reaching Ford went out again as money and much of the remaining 6 per cent went into improvements and economies for the public benefit."

Critics of the profit motive missed the point, Cameron contended.

"The major profit is in the article produced, and in legitimate exchange the user's profit is always greater than the maker's. The profit of a loaf of bread isn't in the pennies received by the baker but in the nourishment of the family that uses it. The real profit-maker is the public."

For those who jeered that a lot of profit was sticking to Ford's fingers whatever he might say of sharing, and who wanted in black and white what each employee would have received if the profits of $844,000,000 had been divided among the workers, Cameron had three answers.

First, Ford could not level his business every Saturday night and start from scratch Monday morning. If he had done this, the little shop would have stayed little since there would have been no money for experiment, equipment, growth. Its methods would have remained crude—the original 75 men would not have swollen to 125,000. "Profits support a business as wages support a family." If they had not been fed back into the business there would have been no business.

Second, the profits conserved and invested produced in wages four times as much as the profits amounted to—25,000,000 cars, 125,000 jobs, 200,000 other jobs in related industries, $600,000,000 in government taxes. Company profits were embedded in land, buildings, furnaces, machines—hundreds of millions had been used up and had disappeared. Ford had taken less out of his business in 33 prosperous years than was taken out of some concerns in two depression years.

Third, the answer was a wage increase for each employee of less than six cents a working hour if all dividends paid in the life of the company were added to wages. He broke it down farther and estimated that each purchaser of a Ford car added to Ford profit 66 cents a year over the same 33-year period.

Cameron challenged as mischievous the story that 2 per cent of the people owned 80 to 90 per cent of the nation's wealth and said that even if it was true the real difficulty was that there was not enough wealth to permit every American family the cherished standard of living.

"Reduce all the wealth to an exact equality," he suggested, "and even then our supply does not balance our economic requirements. It is a bitter pill to our national pride but a tonic if we will receive it.

Our immediate pressing job is to create more and produce more and render it easily accessible."

Statisticians announced employment was not increasing as fast as production. The editor called it the same old error—measuring the entire employment situation against one-sixth of the nation's work. Industrial employment HAD kept pace with production, he said; the jobless belonged mostly to other groups that performed five-sixths of the nation's work. He took government officials to task for demanding that industry employ at once an estimated 11,000,000 persons out of work in the United States.

"Any group that normally employs less than 9,000,000, of whom probably 7,000,000 are now at work (1936), cannot possibly be said to have 11,000,000 of its people out of work. Industry never had 11,000,000 people." Cameron was dryly sarcastic. "Second, any group whose highest peak of business was never sufficient to employ more than 9,000,000 persons cannot, even at government command, arbitrarily increase that number to 20,000,000. There never has been that much purely industrial work to be done."

Industry alone, Cameron said for Ford, had led in starting the wheels of employment. The impression was erroneous, he said, that in spending money to help the country the largest spender was government. The government total was about ten billions. American business besides spending all its income, took 27 billions from its savings of former years and spent that, too. Moreover it was not a loan—no one could be taxed to pay THAT money back.

He deplored the practice of robbing Peter to pay Paul—of giving a wage increase with one hand and taking it away with the other by raising the price of the product. "We cannot win security for one class at the cost of insecurity to another nor build prosperity for one on the poverty of another."

"If Paul needs more," said Cameron, "he ought to get more and our job is to produce it. As a producer of necessities the worker wants the highest wage he can get; as a consumer he wants to buy those necessities at the lowest possible price. The two demands always have been in head-on collision and yet the firm outright answer is that both are right. No one's health can be improved by injuring another's health. Wages ought to be higher—prices ought to be lower."

Enlightened industrial management, he said, was first to see these apparently conflicting forces were friends and what the transforming secret was. The surest way was through lower prices. It was something no one dared to believe before Ford proved it could be done, said the motormaker's editor.

"It is a practical accomplishment," Cameron declared, "wherever enlightened management has a free hand. Economic life cries out for its still wider application."

Wage increases could be given in only four ways, and three of these were unsound—goodness of heart or compulsion of conscience out of a surplus gathered by neglecting to pay when the employer should have paid; boosting the price of the product, thus reducing sales and employment; cheapening the product, a system under which customers vanished and the business after them, and the fourth by training men to be worth more, putting into their hands the means to earn more.

"The persistence of high prices and low wages is due to bad management even more than to bad intentions," Cameron declared.

He saw only three roads open. The country could have division by communism—or subtraction by taxation, "both methods by which everything grows less." Increase could come only by multiplication—the greater production of the needful things of life.

"When we acknowledge and are ashamed of our country's semi-poverty—not poverty compared with other countries but poverty as compared with the possibilities of America—then we shall take our problem by the right handle," he suggested.

The first job was to supply the undersupplied—bring the capacity to produce up to the capacity to consume. The first step was to greatly lower costs and prices. It would insure, he preached, continuous employment and by increasing purchasing power business would save its own soul.

"The manufacturer needs no mastery of economic theory; he needs no insight into the mystery of finance, he needs consult with no one but himself to do this," Cameron said. "He need only hitch his job to this idea to make goods easily available to the entire range of people who need and could use them. It is a business motive superior to the profit motive, more dynamic yet not antagonistic to it, for the man thus motivated will have profits to spare and all the business he can do."

To those who said that there was too much production as it was, and that warehouses bulged with goods and no way to distribute them, Cameron said the statement was not true, for one thing, and if it was so it simply indicated that the hypothetical goods in the imaginary warehouses had been manufactured under conditions of cost and charges and profit that made it hard for people to buy them.

By insisting on efficiency and low costs, production men were doing more to solve the social problem, in his opinion, than the entire pack of theorists. On the other hand, business could produce goods or dividends, he thought, but hardly both since genuine material betterment could not be bought and had to be built—"its expression is not money but goods that people can use. Men who talk of the country's dying economy have never touched the tips of their lily fingers to machinery."

Cameron claimed many big corporations prayed for the success of misguided souls who had hopes of curbing competition. When competition of merit was artificially removed by financial mergers or gentlemen's agreements, it was Ford's opinion that product deteriorated, customer costs rose, progress of invention and service ceased.

In earlier years when the motormaker used to drop into a private club in Detroit occasionally he joined a group which was discussing some business before going in to lunch. A member speaking of a deal on the tapis used the expression "gentlemen's agreement." Up to then Ford had only listened.

"I never made one," he tossed in, ironically. "In any gentlemen's agreement I think the gentleman usually gets stuck!"

Cameron paddled an international huddle at Oxford which announced it would rescue men from "the bondage of the machine." Why, he asked, did bookmen find the machine repugnant?

"None likes its results more," he reflected. "The machine made their conference possible—by land and air and water. Did it not transport them to where they are? It prints their books. It is the instrument of much of their science and gives refinements to their colleges and homes."

What he called the neurotic attitude of hostility to the so-called Old Order and "the recoil from the machine of the so-called intelligentsia" seemed to the Ford editor a group delusion fostering itself within itself, writing books about itself for itself to read, lecturing to itself but drawing its bread from the system it "pretends to despise."

"It is a clean-cut pathological case," said Cameron, his mind lyrically reverting to his world of turret lathes and presses and crimson furnaces. "Its recoil from masculine competition is effeminate; its fear of the size and power of machinery is infantile. This is pernicious anemia of the intellect. Not even a subversive force wants them around. Persons of this type were first to be shot down by the Bolshevists after serving as stooges for the revolution."

Where did the bonds of the machine impinge unfavorably on life? There was plenty of bondage in work before the machine came—people were bound to their work 12 to 16 hours a day . . . hands were the principal tools . . . no freedom from heavy physical burdens . . . no home freedom for woman or child.

"Then the machine appeared," Cameron rhapsodized, "and freed seven hours a day from bondage. The labor of one machine now supports a family. Man's rise in intelligence can be charted by this machine civilization."

He thought the term "machine-made civilization" an error and also considered it a mistake to call the machine age "complex." How could it be complex, he argued, when harnessing a team of horses forty years ago was compared with the simplicity of an electric starter, with lighting a lamp by pressing a button, of heating a house, preparing a meal, taking a bath? Hand-tied knots were good but buckles were better; buttons were simpler than buckles and zippers were best of all, the thesis ran.

Actually what the world had was a "civilization-made" machine. The more man mastered his environment, the better he made machines to ease his toil and improve the quality of his work. They did not make him nor did they rule him; he made and ruled them. Life was noisier, not more complex. "It is more filled because we are crowded together and do more."

Progress always absorbed more workers than it rejected. No useful industry was ever superseded or destroyed by mechanization. The typewriter opened new professions to tens of thousands. It did not even disturb the pen and pencil trade, as witness the new business in fountain pens and patent pencils. Electricity did not efface gas. Many present great industries did not even pass through the handicraft stage—they began with machinery and added a service that never existed before. "Who built the automobile before the machine age? No hand-worker could make a modern automobile."

The machine displaces men? Faugh! Taking industry as a whole and the same output of cars, where 74 men were required in 1929 there were 98 in 1936 since the new cars required more fitting, more finishing, more time and better work, according to Ford's pinch-hitter.

"The fact is established by a study of the entire national employment situation for the past 40 years that jobs have multiplied faster than people during the machine age. Employment has increased more rapidly than the population. While population was increasing 118 per cent, the number of employed persons in the population increased 191 per cent—and the earlier lower figure included a great deal of child labor from which the latter larger figure is free. In 1870 it required 324 persons in every 1,000 of the population to produce what consumers demanded; in 1930, with the machine predominant, it required 400 persons of every thousand.

The speed-up, said Cameron, was an abuse of the assembly line and he alleged only short-sighted management used it to force production. It deprived the job of care and skill and always turned out inferior goods, he asserted, and to say an employer intelligent enough to train a permanent working force and build a quality product would call THAT good management was like saying a railway company would inaugurate a 90-mile-an-hour passenger schedule with 60-mile-an-hour locomotives.

If employers were in collusion to make men of 40 obsolete, the editor said Ford had not joined the plot. In 1937, the year of his report, the percentage of Ford employees from 40 to 65 was reported higher than it had ever been for the nation as a whole—43½ per cent of total employees against an all-time national high in the age group of 35 per cent.

Cameron felt the answer was in the greater concentration of this group in industrial centers and the new promise of older people able to work. "More men live longer than formerly and our older men are younger than they used to be. Under old strains any one fifty years old was pretty well used up. Putting the burden on machines and lifting it off man, cutting the work day a third and the work week by 44 per cent, and by doubling and trebling wages, modern industry has helped to preserve the prime of average working life to fifty and beyond."

At the time of the radio talk 19,000 men were in the Ford shops who had worked there 13 to 30 years. Of these, 5,600 had worked for Ford twenty or more years.

Free enterprise was to Cameron the spinal cord of every period of progress. Democracy under the system had done more for Americans than had been done for any other people anywhere in the world at any period of history. Capitalism rose because it was a good and liberating force over the system prevailing before it. No next step could be taken which curtailed any of the liberties won under it. They would have to be enlarged.

What plain man under feudalism, he asked, was free to earn or own, use or dispose of what he earned? Under capitalism a man's earnings were established in his own control to be disposed of as he would. The men of business were no less praiseworthy than their philosophy.

"All our major economic and social advances either originated with practical business men," the editor vaunted, "or became general law and practice because business thoroughly tested them and found them workable."

The business man, he owned, had not always been sinless. Twice he had allowed his mind to be diverted from his proper business, the editor confessed—the "boom" of the late 20's had taken the minds of some men off their real function and men who were competent to make goods for use suddenly felt competent to make money by speculation. The price of goods went up and quality of goods down because the speculative obsession deprived so large a segment of business of the attention of its managers. After that, Cameron declared, came the experience with attempted political control in which the business man first became afraid of what government would do TO him and then fawned in hope of what government could do FOR him.

Of labor leaders, Cameron said the title was misplaced when given to "anyone whose influence is toward idleness. Production leaders, discovering methods to economize on costs and so reduce prices, and by reducing prices widen markets, and by widening markets increase wages and expand, and by expanding employment contribute to its continuity by multiplying opportunities for work . . . have alone led labor to rise."

Lost days from strikes from 1933 to 1937 totaled 93,000,000, he found.

"Not all this stoppage was approved by labor advisors," he conceded; "some of it was spontaneous combustion of irresponsible elements.

"Undoubtedly there were instances where wages and working conditions had fallen below fair industrial practice, and a protest by striking back was at least understandable. The good ship *Industry* had barnacles, too, unfortunately, even if the circulatory volume of vitamins is growing fuller and richer.

"But no one seriously contends that in the most enlightened country industrially, general conditions ever have justified a setback of 93 million wasted days."

He developed at length the argument Ford long sustained, and a long line of debaters before him, that industry had brought to the fore two conflicting economic schools.

Capitalist economy, which Ford opposed, consisted of those, the editor said, who believed industry's primary purpose was to produce dividends and was inclined to slow down on improvements and call a moratorium on progress.

"The short-sighted money mind," the interpreter preached, "is wedded to the old idea that the principal thing business makes is money. It wants to see at how high a level it can stabilize prices, to see production methods grow obsolete and remain so for a longer time, and to make up resulting costs by high prices. It would do this by putting industry under political control."

Management economy, which Ford supported, believed that today's changes were rapid and was eager to surge ahead.

"Revolutionary discoveries," the radio analyst expounded, "are so numerous that to keep productive management up to the minute requires spending of large sums which usually give the public higher values at lower cost."

I am one of many who think that when Henry Ford fussed with his first engine he did not think in terms of making money or of getting rich but of mastering the principle of a gasoline engine, and that at no time did he change much as he went along. He wanted to build many factories, build many cars, perhaps reach the ultimate in motor transportation, and provide work for many people.

In 1944 I was close to him at Willow Run as a bomber was landing after a test run. He was standing with an Australian production expediter and he said something he had been saying all his life.

"Biggest place I ever saw, Mr. Ford," the man with him was remarking, allowing his eyes to sweep over the vast war layout. "And what a money-maker that tremendous place the Rouge must be in peace times."

Ford turned quietly to his guest. "You know," he said, "I don't build automobiles to make money."

Near me was one of his grandsons.

"That's a fine thing to say," the young man remarked to a companion, a bit ironically and in a low voice. The wind carried what he said and the grandfather stepped spryly over. He poked a playful finger in the young man's ribs.

"Just two generations from shirt sleeves to shirt sleeves," he lectured, reprovingly, and rejoined the man to whom he had been talking.

As war neared, Henry Ford was unchanged in one respect. He had a hate of it as abiding as when he sailed on the fruitless voyage of his peace ship, but four years before Hitler struck out into Poland the motormaker was examining the omens and coming to the conclusion that new bloodshed was in the making.

His Cameron, on the air, asked for close inspection of any conflagration that others might start and urged that defense stay defense—it was not to be stretched to such dimensions as to suggest aggression. "We want no irritated official or outplayed diplomat plunging us into international difficulties because HIS imperious attitude is checkmated or HIS pride humbled."

In 1935 he was finding small hope of rescue in the three prevailing currents of pacificism.

"The pacifism of horror makes a low appeal and that of idealistic co-operation is largely in eclipse for want of ideal co-operators," he reported to his radio followers. "The pacificism of internationalism is an extension of the crude social philosophy which sets out to destroy family loyalty and solidarity, and carried a step farther becomes the dispersal of loyalty to one's country and people."

In June of 1939 he was warning that while the United States would win any war it entered, the cardinal question was whether Americans would still be a free people after the victory. In war the nation would be subject to a virtual dictatorship—"and once that occurs the recovery of our liberties will be no simple matter."

"The ultimate danger is that in winning the war we may lose the Republic," he preached; "the danger is that those who desire that may try to maneuver a war as a means to it."

When war came to Europe, Cameron reiterated that the primary question for America was not whether we would get into it but whether we let the war get into us. Negative conceptions of peace as merely a state of unexploded bombs would have to make way for something more positive. "War is mental before it is military—and our danger point is there." He attributed the holocaust to those who had failed in their economic tasks. In the dictatorships a labor shortage only meant that with more hands than ever before and all hands regimented, every hand was producing less. "Two men on a job, but so ill rewarded, so beaten down, they cannot do ONE man's work."

Always there were learned economic men, he recalled, to explain by economic cause stealing as practiced by nations. Need any nation in this age fight for land sufficient to raise its living? Not if it would learn to USE the land it had. Need any nation make war to extend its markets? When a war-maker alleged markets to be his aim, he virtually declared he would not pay a fair labor wage and would not build an economy that would make his people their own best market. War in its inception, thought Cameron, was a short-cut a brigand chose to evade the discipline of economics.

"Consuming his people's strength in making armaments," he expatiated, "he leads them to manipulate armament in the fool's hope they may win by war the fruits that only work can yield. The fallacy that plunder enriches the thief is a statecraft begun with 'noble knights' who robbed caravans on the road."

What the world was seeing was not history but an interruption of history—a bull in a china shop was a distracting and stubborn fact but he was not history. "He is not symbolic of a time when bulls shall be general managers of china shops." Nor was the war prophetic of a militarized future where family firesides would be bombproof holes in the ground. The meaning was that evils we had let live and grow without effective protest, had simply given effect to the law by which one evil bred another to be its nemesis.

"This is not history but time out from history to pay the penalty of our fault," Cameron described it. "There was a point where we stopped making history and began to make disorder. We had neither the courage nor decency to put away by civilized means the disorder that accumulated."

In the background the Ford company, in the defense emergency, built a Navy barracks to train men for the mechanical maintenance of the country's battle fleets—an institution completed in 40 days out of Ford's own money and geared to train 4,500 ratings a year. At the Rouge sprang up the first section of a $21,000,000 airplane-engine plant inside a shelter box of 900,000 square feet heated by charcoal braziers to form a sheath for steelworkers and cement crews and bricklayers working through the dead of winter. In preparation was an $11,000,000 airplane parts assembly plant. Up also was the world's largest magnesium alloy foundry at a cost of $800,000, widening one of aviation's bottlenecks. A thousand Army staff cars had been delivered, 1,500 blitz buggies. Forehandedness, said Cameron to critics who complained of delays, had in fact saved months of time.

Pearl Harbor was only two months away when Cameron preached on the economic disaster in aggression. Defense might mean the revival of all that was best in people—aggression took more years out of a nation's life.

"Today's aggressor nations had ten years to prepare their attack," he suggested. "They were ten wasteful and impoverishing years. The production necessary to start war never is so efficient as the production necessary to repel war. Forced upon the defensive a nation's motive is so urgent, its objective so clear, it will do the work of ten years in two. Plans to attack our neighbors cannot marshal our energy and intelligence so commandingly as defense of our homeland."

The Nip came down in Hawaii on a surprised Pacific fleet and Cameron appraised the fissures in war materials at home. He doubted a little that the country had been as rich as its people boasted.

"Our 7 per cent of the world population owned 40 per cent of the world wealth," he itemized the resources. "An hour of American labor brought 2½ times as much food as the same labor would buy in Britain, 7½ times as much as in Russia. Wages had gone up 40 per cent, the work day shortened 30 to 40 per cent in a lifetime. With $131 million in life insurance policies in force, $45 million in savings bank accounts, 14 million house owners, we live longer and in better health than most people on earth.

"But you can smudge the whole picture with a toothbrush by telling what we have not, that we ought to have more mechanics, shop training facilities, houses, ships, railway cars. A year ago we would have laughed at the idea of gasoline rationing. What with collecting scrap, curtailing vital manufactures and threats of further restrictions, there is present every symptom of lack."

How strange, he observed, the last 25 years had been called a time of peace. What a strange illusion to identify war solely with guns! People will almost complacently go through "a terrible and obscene war of mental and spiritual forces and imagine it is peace, who will give every evidence of being profoundly disturbed the moment a shot is fired." The beginning of war on the Continent in 1939, he said, was not merely slipping from a state of peace into a state of war but only from the mental and spiritual stage into its munitions stage.

He still had time to refer two weeks after Pearl Harbor to the "fantastic economic proposals that went about America like wild-fire only five years ago," upsetting those who had no anchorage in principle.

"Is it fancy or do we hear a sigh of relief," he asked, "that now we can suspend the hard vocation of peace and indulge in the much easier work of war? Oh, fighting a war is so much easier than building or restoring an economy that its appeal is subtle! It is always easier to make munitions than to create and supply markets."

Later three pressing questions were to engage his attention. Why was conversion of automobile factories to war not more rapid? What did the oft-repeated motto of the British mean, "Business as usual?" Why were buyers suspicious of certain American goods compelled to turn to substitute materials?

It took 14 months to design and tool for a new automobile, but somehow the industry was expected to produce a tank in a trice as a conductor provided a transfer. An impatient public clamored for speed without any good idea of how it could be achieved or whether it was being achieved.

Cameron got his answer into one-syllable words. A shop or mill produced a staple like flour, textiles or wool—something the government could use "as is." Simply the customers, not the nature of the work, was changed. These were not conversion problems.

The government did not want automobiles but the use of the automobile factory itself to make jeeps and tanks and planes. If a typewriter factory had to stop making typewriters and make refrigerators, you would not expect the changeover in a day, would you? The imposing mass of automotive machinery appeared capable of making anything, but was it?

"Much of it," said Cameron, "is specially designed and most of it specially tooled to take hold of, move, treat and shape pieces of metal exclusively for the motor car."

The car used thin steel sheets; the tank used armor plate. Automobile panels would not serve as airplane wings. Dies made to form automobile parts would not do to form parts for military weapons. Either send a job that fits the tools or change the tools to fit the job—that was the problem behind conversion.

For Ford Motor Company, as the editor described it, war work meant almost complete retooling—a 90 per cent new machinery installation for airplane engines, 85 per cent for planes, 50 per cent for tanks. "To make complicated war weapons the total necessary change in equipment is about 75 per cent—and the materials must be obtained by government allotment.

"To accommodate government work assigned to us, buildings have been erected that have actually doubled the size of the Ford Motor plant in this area. There has been no delay. Uninformed critics say the motor industry delayed conversion by clinging to its own work too long. The fact is that for several causes motor cars manufactured in recent months have cost more to make than they can be sold for. There is every reason to hasten conversion."

Substitute materials were not makeshift materials. Industry always had relied on alternate materials but never on inferior ones to protect the continuous flow of its peace work.

"Industry does not depend on any single material or any single source of supply," he explained, "but always has alternates not only in reserve but in partial use. That military needs require a wider resort to these is no reason to assume they are inferior." Ah, but if they are so good why doesn't the Government use them and not upset industry? "Because," the editor reasoned, "the defense program is a race against time. It uses the materials the majority of machines are meant to handle. Of course the government would have used our present alternate materials had this emergency occurred several years ago when these alternates were standard, for industry then would have been tooled up for them."

This then was Henry Ford in the depression and recovery days, in the time when Hitler readied his Stukas and the Japs advanced on Hickam Field—if the Cameron carbon paper was good. It was at least Ford as he appeared through his editor's glasses.

He plugs a monastic diet and serves a carrot in lieu of ambrosia, but fills up on wheatcakes on the eve of a major operation.

CHAPTER XVIII

PLAT DU JOUR

THE PALACE guard at Dearborn bore no load with less zeal than Henry Ford's dietary fancies.

Carrots were chosen the secret of longevity and he frowned on those who would not go at them as if they were duck from the ranges of Voisin. Soybeans took the place of carrots or were added; he was on and off oranges; he said milk was not fit for anyone over eight and he did not pasteurize the yield of his own herds. Orange juice promoted arthritis, in his opinion, and it went off the menu. He set experimenters to work on African grapes as a possible cure for cancer. A treatise of a Chicagoan on how to eat for health had an inning.

He would go in jumps. He'd discover sarsaparilla and drink it madly for a month. He'd be on butter and off butter. A food would be popular for a spell and then he might exile it permanently, having learned it wasn't for him. He went from one extreme to another. This unbalanced diet, if rules meant anything, should have done him more harm than good, but for four-score years he seemed indestructible.

Once people knew he was interested in diets, thousands sent him tips. In early days he sold himself on some of the gratuitous theories without any more guarantee of their merit than some correspondent's exuberant adjectives. Much time elapsed before he would permit his hospital to screen communications of this type and run cultures.

The staff assisted other men in the industry occasionally to sift mail of this character. A Chicago letter-writer laid a novel scheme before Charles F. Kettering, world-known automotive researcher. He could corner, he promised, packing-house bonemeal. He proposed to capsule it as a cure for pyorrhea and he wanted financing. He even tabled the tonnage of bonemeal available to him, how many capsules to a ton he could get, how much profit could be made at a stipulated price.

Kettering turned it down, said he had reached an age when he was less interested in making more money than in disbursing what he had, but after he had dismissed the business proposal, he continued to wonder if bonemeal would cure pyorrhea. His correspondent had been more interested in profits than in the efficacy of the alleged remedy.

The scientist telephoned a Ford Hospital friend and asked if bonemeal was being used in the treatment of pyorrhea. No? "Well, could it be?" Never heard of it, the man on the other end said. "If you're interested, Ket, we can look into it."

"Will you?" asked the inquisitive Kettering. "I'd be very grateful."

"No trouble."

He got his report a few days later. Bonemeal had no curative effect on pyorrhea.

Ford's eating was simple, monastic and slightly bizarre, and he found in the writings of Luigi Cornaro, the Venetian, who had lived to ninety-eight by abstinence and a nod from his Maker, a good fellow to model after. During his days at the knees of the fifteenth-century Latin, a good trencherman only had to mention to Ford a superior dinner that had pleased him—guinea hen, caviar *au blinis,* strawberries Romanoff and a good wine, we'll say—and he would unhinge his hands behind his head, get up from his chair and take a book from a stack on his desk.

"Read this." He would hand out Cornaro's discourses on what stuffing did to the human stomach. "It will make you live longer."

The Venetian, overcoming infirmities at forty, wrote at ninety-five his final word on piggishness at the dinner table and its racking results. Ford bought 500 copies of an American reprint and used them to rebut anyone who expressed a preference for a well-sauced life over one based on exact caloric content.

He reached into a pocket one morning and got out a folded paper on which a few words had been scribbled.

"Read it aloud," he invited, tilting back and lifting his feet comfortably to the edge of a desk.

It was an unattributed quotation. "Physicians by debauch were made; excess began and sloth sustained the trade." He asked, smiling broadly, if I knew who wrote it and I said I never heard the words before.

"Dryden," he revealed. "What do you say it means?"

"You're going to tell me it means we dig our graves with our teeth." I beat him to the cliché. He put the paper back.

"Hits it right on the head, doesn't he?" he suggested and presumably expected no answer, for he went on, "That book of Cornaro will put fifty more years on your life if you do as he says."

Gourmandizing is suicide. The secret of health is in eating the right foods. The secret of disease is in food deficiency. Take care of the body like a car. This was Ford's preachment.

When it was he decided to start for Bimini to find the curative waters is hard to say but it was long ago. Somewhere along the line he made up his mind, he once said, that if a salmon could live to a hundred years, so could he. He would put off senescence and pathological change. The psalmist said three score and ten—well, he'd do better.

His phobias in foods were not an irritant so much in themselves as in the air of infallibility in his recommendations. "I reproach him not so much for hiding the ace of trumps up his sleeve," a Frenchman said of England's Gladstone, "but for pretending that God put it there." It would have been interesting to see if Ford could have chinned himself so nimbly on trees about his estate or run as fast as long as he did if he had spent more time tending his own furnaces or doing himself what was to be done on his closely clocked assembly line.

The annoyance lay in his firm confidence that the world would be better off if it ate as he did and in the fact that his was the easy abstinence of a man never tempted. Actually he ate when, how and what he pleased, but because he took no especial delight in the art of cookery and was insensitive to Sybaritic viands he made a virtue of his indifference and a vice of epicureanism. If all his foods had come powdered and in pellets, rightly measured as to vitamins, it is probable he would have felt no deep loss.

His predilections in diets did not always square with those of his hospital, and his sporadic efforts to impose his views led to situations which could be saved only by a defense in depth. It never was best policy to argue these points too strongly—it might only firm him. To put him off as long as possible in the hope he might get a run on something else and forget the original undertaking became accepted strategy.

He anticipated by years the present professional unanimity on the values of early ambulation by getting out of bed a few hours after a major operation in 1932 and going home long before the physicians thought it safe for him. He shocked the doctors when he was going into the hospital. They went to Fair Lane to check and make ready and were met at the door by a jovial and hungry patient.

"I've got some fine new buckwheat flour," he greeted them. He said they were to come out in the kitchen and he'd personally whip up a batch of pancakes for all of them.

"But Mr. Ford, the operation—"

"Come on," he urged, shaking off their protests, and led the way. "They'll be wonderful for all of us."

So in no time their billionaire chef was at the range and produced a bumper breakfast for guests who didn't know what else to do but fill up. He joined them and had a fine helping of cakes for himself. Seven hours later he was on the operating table. The next day he got out of bed, and in half the time usually prescribed for convalescence he walked out and went home although in performing an appendectomy the surgeons also found a femoral hernia.

In a report of a study of ninety operations for femoral hernia published six years later, the operating surgeons still had not forgotten the ways of their problem patient. They said a little stiffly for the exclusive reading of their colleagues that "Patient H.F., 68," would not remain in bed—walking into the bathroom each day, including the first post-operative day, although they admitted that convalescence was uneventful. They also confessed that despite the patient's unusual deportment "it is now six years since the operation and there has been no recurrence of the hernia in spite of the fact that Poupart's ligament was partially severed." The report said nothing of the invigorating syrup-splashed buckwheat cakes.

Carrots were the *plat du jour* for months, and it was not unusual for Ford to come into an office in the early morning, unroll a handkerchief and expose before a subordinate's affrighted eyes a couple of carrots which he had brought over from his own bins.

"Want to join me?" he would say, hospitably.

He would give the executive one carrot, take the other for himself, and the two would munch on them, the employer with evident relish and the employee with what enthusiasm he could feign as they talked over the business which had brought Ford into the office.

H. William Klare, a hotel manager and an old China hand at wangling publicity, and some caterers arranged a twelve-course, all-carrot dinner for a small group to toast Ford and his fad of the moment, and they invited a number of doctors, several citizens of his liking, and, by merest chance, representatives of the entire metropolitan press.

The climax was disruptive, for up to the final talk of a forthright dietician, one was amazed by the succession of dishes made with carrots as a base, and the affair coursed along brightly, conversation was lively, and the party was a neat nosegay for Ford's latest love in nutriment.

The room was blacked out in the beginning and after a proper stage wait a baby spot picked out a gowned figure in a black and orange domino who stood at the left of Mr. Ford's chair at the head of the table and said, substantially:

"I am King Carrota! I am full of vitamins, full of iron, full of iodine, full of bottled sunshine. I have no enemy but a bad cook. I am a friend of flappers and the bald-headed, the spindly baby and three-chinned monsters, but who shall mix me with canned peas shall be consigned to outer darkness."

It set off, on the right note, a rare dinner of carrots l'orange, carrot soup Crécy mirliton, pickled carrots Greek style, carrots hors d'oeuvre, mousse of carrots, carrot loaf ravigote, carrots au gratin, carrot marmalade, carrot salad Henri Ford, carrot ice cream, carrot tarte, and the whole swigged down with a magnum of carrot juice. I remember the guest of honor saying over the stiff demi-tasse that the feast was Lucullan or something that meant as much.

No one planned the unhappy denouement. The evening motif naturally was that carrots were fruit of Olympus but the mousy dietitian began to say near the finish that he thought it would be unfortunate if the public drew wrong conclusions from the dinner and yielded to a general carrot saturnalia.

"I remember"—he rose to make certain there was no misunderstanding of his scientific objection—"I remember a New York orpnanage with which I was once associated overfed its children with carrots a few years back. The vegetable was plentiful and cheap but some of the children later turned yellow."

The startled diners looked furtively at their neighbors to see if they had begun to yellow. "You see," the dietitian was saying, "there is a lot of pigmentation in carrots—more than in most vegetables."

The alarmist seemingly thought he should sit down on a more cheerful note.

"The discoloration," he soothed, "actually is not harmful, but I do know the children—*did—turn—yellow*." He put the last three words in italics.

Everyone present, if not Mr. Ford, peeked at himself in the mirrors in the hotel lobby on the way out and checked again as soon as he got home, but Ford was unmoved. Carrots remained a favorite at Dearborn.

In common with most men Ford had great confidence in his own distinctions between good and bad. He didn't drink—therefore liquor was bad for those who did. He did not smoke—accordingly, tobacco was a vice and waste of time. He was spry and well and considered it was so because he lived right. The other fellow could be the same by doing as he did.

He hinted at times it had something to do with his mother and the way she brought him up. He remembered her saying, "If you eat too much you'll get a stomach ache," and he used to add on his own: "Every mistake carries with it an ache of some sort," but he was twelve when his mother died and in view of the universal litter of busted and forgotten maternal concepts, it is more likely that what he did in experimentation he did on his own and rationalized it by whatever supporting data were handy, real or imaginative.

I remember a sudden interest in the painter Titian when Edsel gave the Venetian's "Judith with the Head of Holofernes" to an art institute. The senior Ford's interest was not in Cornaro's work but in how long he lived; in Titian's case he was not attracted by Titian the painter but by Titian the nonagenarian.

"That man got up to ninety-nine," he said admiringly, "and then it took a plague to knock him out."

A reporter asked if Titian was fond of carrots.

"I don't know but I'm going to find out," Ford said promptly and crooked a finger at a secretary in the next office. A project in Titian research got under way. Around the corner a draftsman was working on the automobile of the future; close at hand two executives gave themselves over for a week to a more urgent project: what had Titian Vecellio eaten or not eaten that served him so well? Ford got an eight-page report on it before he was through.

Ford was telling a newsman he never overate and often went hungry but he failed to mention his appearance at the desk of an engineer shortly before noon one day, ready to cast out temporarily all his diet principles.

"Let's you and I go over to the dining room before the others get there today," he invited in a plotter's tone. "I feel like getting drunk—food drunk! Let's go early—now—and eat everything in sight."

The engineer said that suited him. Ford, who usually nibbled, gorged. So did his surprised confederate. The dishes were cleared away before the regular shift of officials barged in. Then Ford and the engineer had a bite or two more for appearance's sake. When the bumper meal was finished, Ford drew his engineer aside. "Now let's get away—I want to show you something." They strolled over to another office and to a shelf containing a dozen unlabeled boxes. Ford took one down.

"I'd like you to try this," he said.

The engineer examined the pasteboard cylinder. He took off the lid and was no wiser. He asked what it was.

"Well, it's a new laxative." Ford said it was good—he was trying it.

The engineer, who had thought himself a preferred banquet guest, suddenly was depressed—he was really a guinea pig.

It was a newspaperman, veteran Kenneth F. McCormick, who disagreed with Ford on his theory of undereating and going hungry. It was his opinion, he informed Ford, that no such arbitrary practice would do. Take his wife, he said. She had not been feeling well. He was positive if she ate more she'd feel better. She never did eat a great deal and what appetite she had, he reported, had practically deserted her several weeks back.

Ford asked a number of questions. The newsman forgot all about the conversation until he reached home and a distraught spouse said now what had he been doing. She had had a telephone call. It had been from Dearborn. It was a personal message from Mr. Ford whom she had never met personally. He wanted to know if she could go to Henry Ford Hospital for a checkup and a diagnosis as to what was causing the lack of appetite reported to him. Mrs. McCormick wanted to know if Mr. McCormick could not keep anything to himself.

"Heh, wait a minute until I put in a call," her husband finally injected. He got Dearborn. "Say, what is all this about my wife going to Ford Hospital? . . ." "Oh," he said. "Oh," he said again. "He did? Well, that's very kind. Well, thank him, will you, and I'll thank him when I see him" . . . "Wednesday? Well, I'll try to get her there."

The lady went to the hospital. Her appetite surged back. In a month the grocery bill had soared. The newspaperman said he wished he had known enough to keep his big mouth shut and let Mr. Ford's remark about occasional fasting stand unchallenged.

The motormaker fancied his fleetness as a runner even in his eighties. If he had a guest, younger or older than himself, he invariably challenged him to a foot-race. Few managed to outstrip him, although some of his younger opponents—a mere supposition and possibly a canard—were suspected of working under a strong pull and not giving their best.

Ford would be sauntering over to the Scotch settlement house in Greenfield where he schooled as a boy, and on the way, as a warm-up, he would vault stone fences or leap for the lower limb of a tree and chin himself. He simply felt like a nip-up; it made no difference whether he was alone or was walking with someone. He pulled himself up four or five times and let himself down and would drop to the ground unwinded.

A guest barely had recovered from the shock when Ford would say: "I'll run you over to the school!" and be off. Many a visitor broke his heart trying to keep up with Greenfield's star letter-man.

In an athletic burst on his yacht the *Sialia,* he would defy a fellow passenger and charge around the deck.

"Now on one foot!" he might shout at the end of a lap, and the second time round would be a strenuous series of hops.

He flung a challenge at William S. Knudsen, once president of General Motors, and his own secretary, Liebold, and bolted down the Union train-shed in Washington for his private car with the other two tailing. Liebold was a short, chubby, unathletic man, but this time he was possessed and passed the flying Ford at the wire. For some weeks afterwards the secretary decided the victory was impolitic. Ford, in his humiliation, avoided Liebold as if he had some contagious disease. The next race between them Ford won. In his defeat he merely was in a slump or overtrained or had too many baggage trucks to sidestep.

Drew Pearson broadcast a report in 1944 that friends of Ford were worrying over his physical condition and that the government might move to take over and operate his war plant. The tycoon of Fair Lane did not have anything wrong with his lungs, although his health was causing concern, and from his summer lodge in Northern Michigan he challenged the columnist to a race.

"I can lick him at anything he says," Ford declared, or his publicity people took it on themselves to say for him. "Never felt better in my life. I do not know how young or old this Pearson is but bring him on!" His personal physician, a natural second, remarked that Mr. Pearson was probably in for it and the furore was so loud that the commentator, who had been only half wrong, recanted and said he was sure no one need worry over Ford's energy and way of doing things. He declined a test on the Dearborn straightaway.

Only the superintendent of his garage ran Ford into the ground with what seemed a reckless regularity. They were old friends and it was said that in their younger days he had beaten Ford so badly that the memory of it long nettled the Fair Lane sprinter.

The two were about the same weight, but the superintendent was shorter and stockier and older by ten years. They would run on the concrete from one end of the long Highland Park garage to the other. Ford bided his time. There surely would come a time when the superintendent would lose all that bounce, but he turned sixty and then seventy with no lessening of speed or it may have been he did lose some but maintained the differential between himself and his employer. Ford's record was still a shut-out.

One day when Ford was seventy-five and they were about to go to it, some of the top brass got the garage superintendent aside and said that, damn it to hell, Joe, wouldn't it be nice after all these years to let the boss win once—just a gesture? He would not connive.

"He'll never beat me," he blared back at the circle of fixers, "so long as I've a breath in my body." Mr. Ford came in second.

Nothing could stop the motormaker's running until in sprinting from his car to a plant door at seventy-nine he fell on his face in the cinders. After that he walked. No doctor could stop him. It required the spill to convince him he was not as durable as he had been once.

One nonagenarian nonplussed the Dearborn roundtable for a time. He was the late William Henry Jackson, who came to see Ford when the British were on the beaches at Dunkirk. He was in his middle nineties, had fought at Gettysburg, photographed the construction of the Union Pacific Railroad and was regarded as dean of American photographers. Ford was twenty years younger. He was absorbed in the account of Jackson's experiences but his eyes had time to take in his guest's heaped plate and wonder at it.

The visitor was obviously ravenous and when he made his first selection he chose a rare steak and said he would have all the side dishes. For dessert the waiter suggested hot apple pie—"Very good today, Sir."

Jackson waved him to bring it on. Perhaps strawberry ice cream on top of it? "Capital idea!" The shuddering host's theory of moderation was falling to bits beside him.

"If you don't mind my asking, how do you do it, Mr. Jackson?" he finally asked. "Your appetite, I mean."

The ninety-six-year-old guest thought it could be due to living out of doors as much as he did and not worrying over things he could do nothing about. "I think," he said, "both those things have something to do with my pleasure in good food."

Ford probed for a better clue.

"Ever drink?" Jackson, after all, might be a brother teetotaler and this would answer the riddle.

"Sherry and some of the modern whiskies I find stimulating, Mr. Ford, and I'm not amiss to a cocktail," said Jackson, cheerily, with the easy air of a good liver and one who never had stinted himself. He said he would be honored if Ford would accept a gift from his private stock. The abstemious host said his guest was most kind but as for himself he did not drink.

"How about exercise? Get plenty of sleep?" Ford coupled the two questions in his haste to learn what made his guest tick so well.

Jackson confessed he was afraid he did not get much exercise. He was a patron of taxicabs, and most of his friends, one gathered, kept dissolute hours. He made a little gesture with his hands which seemed to say his friends were a deplorable and unredeemable lot. He returned to his pastry and Ford stared blankly out the cottage window. A magazine writer coming up the walk with a cigarette in his mouth gave him sudden new hope. He whipped back to his guest as if he had hit upon an answer too simple to be true.

"I forgot to ask, Mr. Jackson, if you smoked," he purred.

The nonagenarian looked up from his hot pie à la mode long enough to say that smoking was one indulgence of which he was free and innocent. Vindication had arrived at last. Ford put his hand triumphantly on the older man's shoulder.

"That's it! That is it! I knew it!" Ford was exultant. He finally had found the basic reason for the longevity—his guest did not smoke. Jackson raised the last forkful of rich flaky crust. "Because you don't smoke you have stamina," Ford remarked and Jackson bowed in presumable assent. He said, though, he would like a second small piece of that very good pie.

The motormaker never had a spare pound of flesh on him. Sixty, seventy, eighty—there was buoyancy to his stride, spring in his knees. His juniors gave up hope of matching him in vitality even by measuring out their quotas of carrots and soybeans and oranges or whatever seemed the reigning favorite.

A Savannah doctor at Ford's Georgia estate had evidence of physical prowess at a time when most men had a wary eye out for sclerosis. The doctor had suggested that such prodigality in the use of energy would take a toll if Ford, then 72, did not slow up.

"Got that thing-a-ma-jig with you for taking blood pressure?" asked the host. The count taken, he rolled his sleeve down and started for a steep staircase. He took the flight two steps at a time, ran down again, made a face at the disapproving doctor, repeated the ascent and flew down once more at unabated speed. He jogged over and rolled up his sleeve again.

"Now try it," he invited. There was very small difference in the readings.

"I still don't like it," said the unconvinced doctor.

The soybean era dawned and the oldest food crop of the Orient appeared at meals, on his farms, in his executives' fields, in enamel to paint the car, in knobs to shift the gears, horn buttons, accelerator pedals, experimental door panels. He had a suit made of soybean wool, and a matching tie. He predicted in the early thirties that soybeans in the cornbelt would eventually surpass corn and in 1944 corn states doubled their soy yield. A small patch behind the Ford laboratory attained prodigious stature. In two years he spent $1,250,000 on it. He engaged an ex-curator of the Royal Botanic Society in London to experiment on his English farmland, and grew nearly fifty varieties of soybean originating in North America, Canada, Manchuria and Japan.

He distributed among newspapermen loaves of bread which contained about 28 per cent soybean meal. You could leave a slice on a window nine days and it would be as fresh at the end of that time as the day it was baked.

The soybean brought him one setback. The barn his father built the year his first son was born and where Henry later began the revival of old-fashioned dances was dismantled and reassembled to house soybean processing machinery at the Chicago Century of Progress exposition. It accidentally burned. It was a barn no different than anyone else's but none was more streamlined or better groomed. It enjoyed the care of a suite at the Savoy and was always a landmark in Ford's life which he extolled probably more in later years than when he played in its mow and went reluctantly out to work in the fields about it. The barn stood for something pleasant to him, although he chafed at any glorification of the motorless rustic life he knew as a boy.

Only one-third of the barn was destroyed, and it was rebuilt with dispatch within a week. Fellow exhibitors, pretending to scent a plot, called at the Ford space to ask, "Aren't you getting enough publicity here as it is without burning your barn down?"

His cooks served an all-soybean dinner at the exposition. There had been only twelve courses of carrots five years before; soybean dishes came to sixteen. We had tomato juice seasoned with soybean sauce, salted soybeans, celery stuffed with soybean cheese, purée of soybean, soybean crackers, cakes, cookies and candy, soybean croquettes with tomato sauce, buttered green soybeans, pineapple ring with soybean cheese and dressing, soybean bread with soybean butter, apple pie with soybean crust, cocoa with soybean milk and soybean coffee. The building itself was covered with paint containing soybean oil as the only drying oil. Ford had begun to paint his cars with enamel having 35 per cent of the oil of soybeans.

A radio announcer walked amongst the guests at the soybean dinner with a portable microphone. He would hold the hand mike in front of you and say: "Ah, I see you are having a pineapple ring with soybean cheese—do you like it?" Some guests took it in their stride. Before others could swallow or recover from mike-fright enough to say "Splendid!" or uncooperatively that the whole thing was poisonous, the announcer would have passed on to ask a neighbor if he, also, didn't think the croquettes peachy.

It was by accident I found that Ford was a crusader who occasionally dismounted, allowed Rosinante to graze, had his armor patched and even consorted a little with the devils he was battling. I walked into an obscure restaurant in Dearborn and found him with two pieces of pie in front of him. At least, nothing but crumbs were left of one and he was well into the second.

"I feel hungry for some reason," he said blandly. "Can't understand how it happened."

After he left the proprietor said it was not unusual for Ford to drop in for an occasional snack. Those about him thought the backsliding due to an imbalance in what he did eat—sometimes it just did not provide the needed head of steam for the daily whirligig.

His private office and desk might as well have been assigned to someone else for few ever saw him there. Even when Edsel arrived, they'd go upstairs and discuss over a drawing-table what it was they had to talk about. Ford always said he did it because he could get out of another fellow's office faster than he could get another man out of his. On the desk might be a stack of wax dolls or a pair of old skates but behind it was no one jousting with interoffice phones and buttons and posing as a cyclone off leash. Blue Monday was blue to Ford only because he loafed Sunday—he said it took all Monday to rest up after doing nothing.

The crew of his yacht was a little sorry for the owner. They were fine trenchermen but if Ford got real pleasure from a particular food he seemed to grow suspicious. They told him he was missing a good deal. It was in Florida waters he first met scallops and he liked them so well he was a little skeptical of them.

Coming up to meal time, it was not unusual for him to appear in the galley to see what was cooking. Once he caught the fragrant odor of hash.

"Jiggs, eh?" he brightened, associating the smell with his pet comic-strip character.

Often he was unable aboard ship to stick it out until the regular hour and would beg a snack to eat in the galley before dinner. There seemed to be a tacit understanding between Ford and his crew, in such cases, that these clandestine lunches were not to be gossiped about. The hash was so tasty he ate a plateful and it spoiled his appetite. He only picked at his regular evening meal. His wife was solicitous.

"Aren't you feeling all right?" she asked, looking at the plate that was scarcely touched.

He said it was odd but he didn't feel hungry. Feeling fine, though, he said, reassuringly. The waiter, expressionless, took the plate away.

A dish was served with which he was unacquainted. He drifted back to the galley and asked if there was a little portion left over. They found some for him. He did not want to eat it. He sent a sample back for analysis to his dietitians in Detroit. It was almost as if he thought anything so tasty must have something wrong with it and wasn't for him.

Yet the food at his inns was excellent and the sailors on his *Sialia* considered themselves the best uniformed, best fed and best paid in private service. A strict budget might be imposed by other owners, but on Ford's yacht no limit was set. The crew ate as much as it wanted as often as it wanted of whatever it wanted.

He broke the heart of a man who had been beaten for sheriff by a politician Ford did not like. He sympathetically gave the defeated candidate a restaurant concession in one of his plants and when the grateful politico heard one day Ford was coming to lunch, he had his cook make a special cake and roast two turkeys. The table was dressed in suggestion of Thanksgiving.

'I'll have some crackers and milk, I guess," said Ford as he sat down, dismissing the rich testimonial with a cold stare.

He was asked at eighty for his rules of living and recalled a man who had started a chicken farm, failed at it and wrote a book on how to raise chickens. The story did not fit. Ford had done pretty well with the prohibitions he laid on himself, eating what he thought good for him and not too much of that, keeping flexible, never crowding his stomach. Those who sold health nostra by jingle would have starved if their dosages had no other market.

Lover of knockabout, Ford lined up with the practical jokers. At times the fun was puckish, more often corny and unbuttoned.

CHAPTER XIX

THE JESTER

IT WAS NOT LONG before Henry Ford died and when he had been around the plant only at irregular intervals that he walked into the enormous drafting room. Men bowed over drawing boards as far as he could see. The setup was new to him and he asked what this department was—what were all these fellows doing?

"Why, Mr. Ford," the cicerone beamed, "they are building your 1948 car." The man who put his first horseless carriage together by hand looked as if he could not believe it.

"What? With pencils!" he asked, dryly. He waggled his head over the phenomenon.

The astonishment was bogus, naturally. He had seen drafting rooms before even if they had been only quarter the size of the one he was in, and he was used to magnitude. He was simply having fun and his fun came in all sorts of canisters.

Some of it was sly and puckish, some strictly hotfoot and B-picture, but however light the jest, laughter convulsed the nation's copy desks. They worked by one logical rule in his case. A canon of the trade for years was that what Henry Ford said or did, wise or corny, interested more readers than any pearl of poorer men.

The late Calvin Coolidge gave him a sap bucket and Brooklyn a trolley car of 1868. Bellboys of Boston voted him their favorite tipper and chauffeurs of Ecuador made him a member of their union. He acquired a dray which hauled part of the stone for Brooklyn Bridge, a revolving rake a century old from Rhode Island, the second oldest backsmith shop extant, and New Zealand schoolboys proclaimed him one of the three greatest men of Christendom. A nation smiled. A world read of it with interest. All were good for Page One.

His cross was that his lightest sally had a way of shinnying up a telegraph pole and being off at once on the news wires to be served with the next morning's grapefruit. Bubbles swelled to balloons. A little quip grew into the gag of the week. What he might say as a mere pleasantry became eventful through no fault of his. Joe Doakes could have his joke and the world not suffer a tremblor, but not Ford.

The squire of Dearborn drew fun at many wells. Few who worked so hard played so hard. He whittled toys of cedar shingles for children, peeled off jigs on a Stradivarius, dancing the while as he played them. He tried to ride a square-wheeled bicycle on the stage of the New York Winter Garden when the curtain had rung down and the audience was filing out. When pressed to choose the greatest man he ever met he named his own police chief, and one fellow he remembered was the straggler who called him a liar at the Canadian locks and found out better and ran alongside the yacht shouting in apology, "I did not know you without your shoes, Mr. Ford."

A lawyer on Ford's private railroad car woke early and after trying to go back to sleep decided to get up and check some papers. The party was returning from Washington to Detroit after a showing before the Interstate Commerce Commission. Before settling to work the lawyer stepped out on the rear platform. The train had slowed and on the roadbed between the tracks sixty-year-old Ford, who had shucked his coat, was running spryly, knees high, head back, breathing easily. He quickened his stride when he saw he had an audience and swung to the lower step of the vestibule.

"Just having a little fun for myself." He put on his coat. "Thought I'd work up an appetite for breakfast."

The attorney was inured to shock. The motormaker had extended his hand across the dinner table the night before and borrowed his pre-Waltham watch, a willed timepiece from a grandfather. Ford asked the porter to set up a side table, produced miniature tools from a side pocket and proceeded to disassemble the heirloom to the smothered anguish of the owner. Satisfied a half hour later with what he had learned he put together the pieces to the relief of the shuddering lawyer.

"A very fine watch." He was unaware of the consternation he had caused. "I fixed one as a boy but I haven't seen one like it since."

The two other men at the table watched the performance indifferently. They had seen the show before a hundred times. Ford always was taking watches apart down to the last wheel. Usually they ran much better after his tinkering, but not always.

A reporter who knew him intimately got under his skin for some years by insisting that after Ford took his watch to fix, it never ran again.

"Ruined it," he would say, accusingly.

Ford always looked on the newsman with lowered eyelid and thought he was being ribbed but never was quite sure. He tried for years to get his hands on the watch again. "Bring it out if there's anything wrong with it," he would urge. The newsman always maintained he had thrown it away in disgust—it was no longer any use to anybody. Ford was rather glad when the fellow took a job on a West Coast paper.

He bought the London jewelry store of Sir John Bennett, with its Gog and Megog, and shipped it home to house his collection, and when he was restless the sedative was in an elaborate shop over his garage tinkering with his array of timepieces. He thought at one time he would make watches by mass production to sell at 40 cents, just as he considered the idea of violin-making on a huge scale. There was no reason he could see why Dearborn could not become the American Cremona and turn out fiddles of quality as the old Italian craftsmen once had. He never got around to either. He had too many other things to do.

He and Mrs. Ford week-ended at the Cliveden home of the Astors in 1928 with England's king and queen. As he made his way to his quarters an hour after arrival he met a member of the house staff in an upper hall and the man stopped for a word.

"I took the liberty, sir," he said, "of laying out your apparatus."

Ford nodded blankly, uncertain of what was meant by "apparatus" but judging it a colloquialism for baggage. He was enlightened and amused when he opened the door of his suite.

A man of restless hands, he fancied functional things in miniature, and always on a long journey he packed a kit of small tools. When his son was in knickerbockers Ford made toys for him with a jackknife; when his son's sons came along, and a granddaughter, he built them a junior-size thresher, a sulky and midget motor, and I remember the thresher was called the "He-Be-Jody," a contraction of the first names of the first three children, Henry, Benson and Josephine.

When he walked into his Astor apartment he found the rosewood box in which he kept his tools had been unpacked and on a dressing table in a neat row were all 52 pieces—pliers, wrench, vise, tweezers, so on. The houseman who had taken care of the luggage had taken for granted that Mr. Ford, to keep his hand in, might wish to put an automobile together in the drawing room after dinner.

He visited Edward T. Stotesbury, Morgan partner, at White Marsh, cushioned for sumptuous living with 145 rooms, fourteen elevators, 45 baths and gardens reminiscent of Versailles, he reported. Beside it the Ford home was a lean-to the other side of the tracks. Mr. Ford's weekend ended with a shirt-sleeve session with Philadelphia newsmen who wanted to know what kind of a time he had.

"The Stotesburys are charming," he reflected. "Yes," he said, "delightful people." He re-added the pleasures of his stay and seemed to think he had understated his good time. "It's a great experience," he said, "to see how the rich live." It was good as amended for a front-page box. He had an eye on that box or feature head always.

Kenmore, Virginia home to which Betty Washington returned to find her illustrious brother George in her best bed, his boots still caked with Yorktown mud, preens itself on a grandfather clock, and on a visit an attendant called Mr. Ford's attention to it and told him it was 200 years old.

"Keeps excellent time, too, sir," the custodian was properly proud.

"How good? Guess I'll see," Ford took out his own watch and studied. He looked up after a short pause. He had the expression of a man who had caught another in grave error. "It's slow," he announced.

"Slow?" The keeper of Kenmore stared at the clock trustingly and at Ford in disbelief.

"A full second," Ford estimated.

A fleet correspondent sprinted for the telegraph office and the world was soon told that Ford had found a second's flaw in the clock by which the Washingtons once rose and retired.

He was not the best of sailors and even in a calm was fitful in the constrictions of deck space. When his yacht was locking through a canal he'd hurriedly vault a rail and welcome the chance to feel the boundless firm ground under him. He would make the ascent or descent of the locks afoot and let his guests ride the ship if that's the way they wanted it.

He went over the side of the *Sialia* when the yacht nosed into the Cornwall locks below Montreal one cruise, and when he got to the bottom level he found his radio operator was already there and was spread out comfortably on the stones, shoes and stockings off and trailing his feet in the water. Ford lowered himself to the shelving, off came his shoes, and his bare toes joined the radio operator's in the eddies.

By the time the *Sialia* reached the second basin, a loiterer beside the bathing pair was gazing admiringly at the descending boat. The operator wore the braid of his rank but Mr. Ford was only another foot-washer to anyone who could not read the black bands on his sleeves denoting owner status. The wayfarer turned and remarked on the yacht.

"Nice boat, eh?" he said.

"Yes it is." Ford glanced up and nodded.

"Whose is it?"

Ford said, "I guess it belongs to me."

"What a liar you are," boomed the stranger, unexpectedly, and moved off. No barefoot lounger could fool him. He strolled over to the lock-tender and engaged him in conversation. It was apparently still about the *Sialia* and seemingly he got confirmation, for as the ship set out for the Upper St. Lawrence and Mr. Ford reappeared on deck fully shod again, the stranger was shouting apologies.

"Ahoy, Mr. Ford!" He was waving now. "I didn't know you without your shoes, Mr. Ford," he was yelling contritely, running along beside the moving boat to make sure he was understood.

The motormaker had a similar experience in Northern Michigan when he and some mechanics were doing a test run through heavy sand with a new model and camped on the edge of a wood at the end of the day. They set out to forage for food and found a bereft native in a nearby barn who had some eggs to sell but whose angry concern at the moment was a decrepit Ford car on which he was working blasphemously. The medication did not seem to improve the engine's cough. He had bought it only a few hours before and when he got it home couldn't start it again.

Ford and his overalled crew found what was wrong without too much trouble. The pleased owner listened to the regular purr of the motor and asked what he owed. Ford said nothing, but the backwoodsman laid down a dollar and a half. He insisted it was worth that to him anyway. "You gave me some tools and parts," he reminded.

Ford pushed the money back and said he really had all the money he needed. That did it. The farmer snorted.

"Don't tell me that," he said, pleasantly enough but undeceived by what seemed a sheer boast. "You can't have all the money you need—and still drive a Ford car."

The debate might have gone on with no settlement, so Ford pocketed the money. The native got a check for it a couple of weeks later. It was signed "Henry Ford" and with it was a brief scribble, "I do have all the money I want and I do drive a Ford car. What's the matter with that?"

Ford's own low inventory of yarns caused him a bit of embarrassment at one time and he took steps to build a stockpile much as he would if he had found his bins bare of some particular car part.

"Say, Bill," asked one of his able supernumeraries after quiet study of an old friend who was calling one morning, "have you heard anything lately in the way of funny stories, fast or otherwise?" The executive leaned back hopefully.

The caller thought for a full minute and then confessed he knew nothing lethal at the moment, and just why, anyhow, was he being invited to be funny at this hour of the morning?

"Mr. Ford," the secretary said, "is back from camp. In the evenings he and Harding, Edison, Burroughs and Firestone sat about the fire and told stories."

The visitor said he would be happy to hear a couple if they were any good.

"That's hardly the point," the official said patiently. "Mr. Ford ran out of what he had."

Now, he said, he was collecting some stories for the boss—he was again the man of action carrying out probably a voluntary assignment as if it were unsurprising routine—so that when Ford went to camp next season he could earn his seat beside the blazing brushwood.

No report was issued on the research, but since the official was accomplished there is little doubt that when Ford left for the woods again he carried a full sample case of the best gags obtainable, and that some bit of primeval forest rang with appreciative laughter.

The venerable Thomas Edison, earthy patriarch of the electrical field, was reported on his way to lunch with Mr. Ford for the first time, and two young Dearborn executives worked themselves into a fine froth over the meeting of giants. Such a communion of minds, they reasoned, held storybook promise. They ate regularly at a little white cottage where the colossi would eat, and the two hardly slept in anticipation of shiny dialogue.

They were a half hour earlier than usual for lunch on the starred day so that no one would usurp their seats, only a dozen feet from the open alcove where the renowned always lunched. They fell into a hush when the cottage door opened and the wizard from Menlo Park, his host and a few others sat down at the round table.

The waiter took the order. A man spoke. It was the inventor, who had a penchant for a lusty tale.

"Henry," the voice said, "have you heard this one?"

The tale ran to a heated climax. Mr. Edison chuckled. Mr. Ford chuckled. The other men said that was a good one.

"And this one—" the guest was off on another yarn of the same category. The young executives looked at each other bleakly, took a last swallow of coffee and left. The day had simply turned out badly for pearl-fishers.

No one ever was quite sure if Ford was playful or slyly malicious in a surprise he reserved for some visitors. It was noticeable that he usually chose for his prank a chesty guest with whom he was a little bored. The dulcimer and the vibraphone would combine in a languishing tune as Ford and the visiting bigwig stood talking on the edge of the waxed engineering floor and Ford suddenly would cock an ear, appear to identify the tune as one of his favorites, and look innocently enough at the man beside him.

"This is one of my favorite waltzes," he would say. "Let's try it!"

Before the palsied visitor had time to collect his wits or realize what his host had in mind, he would find an arm about his middle, a hand pressed lightly into the small of his back, and he and Ford revolving on the floor. Only one who had developed a high stoicism ever returned to the sidelines unaged by such an experience, particularly since the host himself usually wound up unruffled and saying courteously, "That went fine, didn't it? You dance well!" or letting the dance pass without a word if the visitor had proven unwieldy. The average guest was tongue-tied either way at this point and trying to believe that the whole thing never happened. He would forget to tell his directors when he installed himself again at the head of the table where he was kingpin.

With all his eye for publicity, there were many times when Ford did not want to be bothered. A young reporter hustled up to him and a companion in a Cincinnati train shed after Ford had examined the engine of his train, climbed into the cab for a few words with the engineer and lowered himself to the platform to go back to his private car.

"They say Henry Ford is on this train," the young man hailed them. Apparently the light of the shed was too poor for the reporter to recognize his man right there in front of him. "Did either of you happen to see him?" he panted.

Both shook their heads and said they were afraid they could be of no help. Ford did volunteer that he had seen an old, thin, gray-haired fellow getting up in the locomotive cab a few minutes before.

"Could be him," the newsman nodded over the description. "In the engine cab, eh? Queer cookie, this Ford!" He said thanks as he hurried to the front of the train.

"Must be," Ford nodded and resumed the walk back to his coach.

Ford served his apprenticeship in comedy in machine shops and boiler rooms and his humor often had a left-handed screwdriver color—blowing sulphur fumes with an improvised bellows through a knot-hole into a closed room where two cronies were working, making off with a bicycle the dynamo-tender had borrowed to teach the corner milliner to ride, threading a cigar with horse-hair as a surprise for his Highland Park engineer, spiking a sloven's shoes to the floor of the Edison Illuminating Co. to teach him a lesson in order. Disorder to Ford was a cardinal sin. The worker was forever leaving shoes and clothes and tools scattered about, dropping them wherever he was at quitting time.

He was an addict of the practical joke and if he could not think of one that pleased him he made an assignment of it. On a trip to his timber stand in Michigan's upper peninsula he conceived a watch-smashing trick that was rewarding, and he was sitting on the edge of the bed the night before the return to Dearborn when it occurred to him the journey would be incomplete without some fun at the expense of Charlie Sorensen, his lieutenant at the Rouge, who was on the trip with him.

He asked the switchboard to connect him with his secretary's room. Could he come in a minute? It seemed that Mr. Ford had decided that a practical joke had to be played on his production boss but his own fertility had failed him. The party would start home at 8 A.M. It was now 1 A.M.

"You think one up—a good one," Ford instructed. He got under the covers and snapped off the light. "G'night," he said.

A clapping of imperial hands at 1 A.M.—let's have a practical joke and it must be good. A good Ford executive had need of diversified talents.

Before going north to inspect the timber holdings Ford suggested a shopping expedition to his secretary. He wished, he said, to play a prank on Frank Klingensmith, his purchasing agent, and for it he needed a watch that looked as much as possible like the prospective victim's.

"You know that watch of his," Ford remarked. "A Howard, isn't it? Get a cheap one like it."

A couple of screws in the balance wheel were loosened so the counterfeit would lose time, and a third man, Sorensen, was taken into the conspiracy. The doctored watch was substituted for the genuine aboard the Ford yacht when Klingensmith hung his vest on a cabin door and went to wash at midnight. When the passengers got up next morning they were berthed at Escanaba.

"Be at the hotel promptly at noon," Ford issued instructions to the group on the wharf before it scattered. "We'll talk over plans then. Better see if your watches are right."

All watches but Klingensmith's pointed to 10 o'clock. His, unbelievably, insisted it was 6 A.M. It had been a miracle of precision and he put it to his ear to see if it had run down. But it was going.

"Never did that before." He stared at it. Sorensen reached over. "Well," he said, "a watch that won't keep time isn't worth saving." He lifted an arm and aimed for a nearby stone wall. The watch dissolved against it.

Its owner went white and moaned audibly as he got to his knees and fumbled in the ruins in what seemed a vain hope that the damage was not irremediable.

"You shouldn't have done it, Charlie," remonstrated Mr. Ford.

Sorensen had a moment of contrition.

"It was a fool thing for me to do, Kling," he said to the man pawing the ground for the dispersed fragments but got only a stabbing glance. Silently, Klingensmith went on with his salvaging. The party walked off the dock, leaving him picking over weeds and gravel and putting what pieces he could find in a handkerchief. He joined the rest of the party for lunch but sat sullenly through it, accepting mock sympathy with a grunt, scowling at Sorensen. He had not quite recovered a week later when in going through a suit at his home he found his watch unscarred in a pair of trousers where Ford had asked Mrs. Klingensmith to put it.

Mrs. Ford wanted pie tins in an early day. She asked him to bring home some. He forgot and she reminded him. It slipped his mind and she persisted. The business went along in this fruitless fashion for weeks, she recalling her need periodically, he steeped in making cars and not remembering. And then one day it struck him that Mrs. Ford had been asking him to drop in some place and get some pie tins for her. He landed home with the pleased air of a man who always could be trusted to do any errand a wife wanted done.

"Got your tins," he announced as he came into the kitchen.

He took her over to a back window and pointed to a carful. He had bought out a dealer's entire stock. His wife did not attempt to count them and may not have been too pleased by the windfall, he said, but he made sure no Ford unto the third generation would ever want for a baking pan.

To some of his jocosities Ford gave a care which seemed out of proportion to the jape itself. A friend put a package on a chair in his office one mid-afternoon. He had no more set it down than the bundle gave off twittering evidence of life inside and Ford asked what he had there.

It was a canary. He unwrapped the cage. It was a song-bird for his wife. Surely Ford remembered, or did he? It was their twenty-fifth wedding anniversary. Ed, the visitor, remembered one thing very clearly that happened at the ceremony.

He had gone to Henry during the evening and complained nervously that the boys had promised him and Ethel an old-time chivari and neither he nor his bride was looking forward to it with any relish. If he could sneak off—if they only could get away somehow. Henry had said, "Come on out here," and had taken him by the arm to the kitchen and closed the door.

"What you do," he said, "is take my car and you can get away from them." The bride and groom escaped and it being a day when horses far outnumbered horseless carriages, Henry and Mrs. Ford and Edsel went home on a streetcar.

Ford said Ethel certainly would be pleased with the canary. They closed the subject and got on the purpose of the present visit. Then Ford switched to another new subject. "Say, we've got some new tweeds over in the tailor shop," he remarked. "Why don't you go on over before you leave and be measured for an anniversary suit so long as Ethel is getting the canary?" He said he would like to give Ed a suit in remembrance of the day.

For years Ford patronized a tailor in a nearby university town and finally allotted him space for a sub-station in the engineering laboratory. When the tailor himself could not be at Dearborn an assistant took care of Ford's mending, cleaning and general sartorial needs.

Thereafter the grandee of Dearborn passed out suits to friends as John D. Rockefeller gave away dimes. It was not at all extraordinary for him to interrupt a conversation with an executive, a newspaper man or a visitor he knew well and ask him if he could use a new suit of clothes. "Just got a fine new shipment of herring-bone," he'd say. In an expansive moment he might even walk one over to Greenfield Village and have the cobbler measure one for a pair of shoes.

His friend away to the tailor shop, Ford lost no time. He removed the canary from its cage and tucked it gently in his pocket. He and a secretary rode off on their bicycles, but when Ed came back from the tailor Ford was at his desk and Ed's package was wrapped as it had been originally.

"A little present I thought you'd like," Ed said when he got home, putting the bundle on the library table.

His wife seemed a little puzzled when she tore off a piece of paper and peeked in.

"Why this is nice, Ed," she said, however, in a quick return to appropriate anniversary enthusiasm, "but how did you happen to think of it?"

She swept off the last bit of wrapping. Ed was stunned and mystified. It wasn't the way he had planned it. This wasn't what he had bought. On the cross-bar where the canary had sung was an angry field sparrow bewildered by recent events. He had been minding his own business in the woods on the Ford farm when Mr. Ford himself descended on a bicycle, let loose a canary and snared him in what was a palpable kidnapping. The canary had flown off and Ford had stuffed him into this coop. He was unimpressed by the joke, wedding anniversary or not. He felt he certainly had a case for J. Edgar Hoover.

It was fun for Ford to get Jep Bisbee's auto into the barn—fun of another kind. A rural fiddler of Michigan was the beneficiary of some carpentry by probably the most expensive and celebrated crew of workers ever to swing a hammer at a nail head.

The motormaker liked the Michigan farmer's home-made violin so well he gave him $100 and a car for it and was never near the Bisbee home that he did not drop in. He took Edison and Harvey Firestone, rubber magnate, with him on one visit and was pained to see the automobile standing out in bad weather when it seemed easy enough to run it into the barn.

Why didn't Bisbee put it under cover? The farmer-fiddler pointed to an interfering brace across the opening of the barn about a foot off the ground. It was a hurdle too high for an automobile even if the horses and pigs could leap it all right.

"I'll tell you what to do, Jep—build a ramp." Ford thought that with an incline the car could make it. Bisbee said he'd do it—surely would. Ford said Jep was getting along in years and better go easy.

"You get the planks and the rest of the stuff and we fellows will build it," he proposed as an alternative.

The impromptu construction firm of Ford, Edison and Firestone built the ramp in a half hour and stood aside satisfied with themselves as Bisbee drove the car under its first roof.

When Ford went to concert or theatre he might be wholly disinterested and only obliging, so he developed a habit of sitting without seeing or hearing and wrestling inwardly with a shop problem or some interest more engaging than what Sir Thomas Beecham was doing at the podium or what Lunt was saying to Fontanne about the brat come home from Canada.

Miss Helen Hayes was one of his favorites, however, but when he walked backstage with Mrs. Ford to say an appreciative word after *Victoria Regina,* Miss Hayes had not finished dressing and could only receive Mrs. Ford and anyway Mr. Ford was enamored, the stage crew remembered, of the business of striking the set and getting the flats into vans for the jump to Cleveland.

A performer who captivated him appeared in *Hellzapoppin'*. During the New York World's Fair the Olson and Johnson revue was playing the Winter Garden and had a trick cyclist, Walter Nilsson, in the cast. Ford caught a matinee and was entranced by the low wheels and high wheels and square wheels and other mechanical contrivances.

He wandered in again and again. He wanted to see the machines close up and the management agreed not to embarrass him by clowning or to capitalize the visit by publicity if he wanted to come back of the curtain. He caused the performers more uneasiness, in fact, than they did him.

The Ford interest was news to Nilsson. He was getting out of make-up when a woman's voice at the door said, "Walt, Henry Ford is asking to see you."

"Going to understudy you," the young lady guessed pertly. "Going to take your place on the road."

Ford told the bicyclist he was interested in his machines and would he mind if he looked at them up close. The freak miscellany stood in racks against the rear wall of the showhouse—unicycles of varying heights, a machine known to its owner as a Swedish egg-beater and consisting of a single three-inch steel sprocket with a chain connecting vertically with a larger sprocket with pedals three feet above it, the whole surmounted by a motorcycle saddle; a single 28-inch wooden disk with pedals on each side, a bicycle with square wheels.

"Now that's the one for me." Ford bent over to inspect the last freak closer. Enthusiasm engulfed him. He asked how it would be if he rode it around the stage as Nilsson did in the show. Unicycles he had ridden, but a square-wheeled bike was a new experience.

The management had no wish to see Mr. Ford break his neck in the *purlieus* of the Shuberts, but neither did it want to spoil his fun if he thought he could get any by riding a lap on the trick bike. It required considerable verbal maneuvering to dissuade the seventy-year-old guest. He merely sat in the saddle and was photographed. Some night, he hinted darkly, he would come in a skylight when the timid cast and the Shuberts were in bed and get in that ride, but he never did. He was quite sure he could have ridden it.

"Bring it out to Detroit when you play there," he persisted to Nilsson. "You and your wife come to see me."

"How does anyone get to you?" The bicyclist had an idea that crashing the gate was hardly that simple. "You telephone Campsall [a Ford secretary] and I'll be waiting out in front," said Ford. "Now be sure to come."

Nilsson wasn't in the road show that played the motor city but Ford made sure of it—he telephoned the theater personally to check.

When a niece graduated at eighteen and in valedictorian wisdom pasted big business for failure to pull the country out of the depression, those about Ford in the commencement audience looked to see how he took it, but no one applauded more heartily and when the exercises were ended he was first at the stage to tell his young niece lavishly that hers was "the best address I ever heard."

The overlord of Dearborn was more surprising than ever surprised. He seemed insulated against shock. When Bandmaster Fred Waring's son was a few weeks old, Waring was under contract for a series of programs for the motor company. Answering his buzzer one day, there stood his boss on an unannounced call.

The Warings moved about panic-stricken to straighten up the place a little but made the mistake of handing the un-housebroken Waring to Ford to tend. The usual catastrophe occurred and Ford found himself the *chalet de nécessité*. The Warings could only groan and make fluttering movements with their hands.

"Don't worry." Ford was quite soothing. "Edsel used to act this way as a baby—though of course I never did myself," he said, and saved the situation completely with laughter.

Long before the King of England abdicated, before he had come even to the throne and was a house guest of the Edsel Fords, there was another story current in the same classification, possibly apocryphal.

The children were packed off to bed on the strength of a promise that just possibly between dances the royal guest might come to see them if they behaved and made no disturbance. His Royal Highness himself expressed a wish to visit the grandchildren of Henry Ford and was taken upstairs, but behind the door was tumult and sustained laughter. The knob was turned and there was a strained quiet. Prince Charming had arrived and two pairs of earnest eyes riveted on him. The stillness was short lived, however. Merriment broke out anew.

"What is this all about?" asked their father. One pointed to the other. "He was so excited he threw up," he announced. The Fords were a trifle uncomfortable but their visitor was not.

"Quite a few people do," His Royal Highness said gravely to the youngster accused.

But a grandchild shook Henry Ford's poise. A joke backfired. They were dining alone at a golf club and he took the child's unfinished ice cream when he was not looking and hid it behind a bowl of flowers. It was not a happy maneuver. The dessert gone when he turned back to his plate, the child let out a whoop which drew the attention of the entire dining room. Ford sheepishly put one hand over the open mouth and with the other retrieved the dish he had taken and put it back where it decidedly belonged.

Fenders shredded, panels initialed in the freshman manner and the score of the last football game painted on the radiator, two youngsters on a Pennsylvania road were trying to coax a wreck of a Model T into action. Riding past, the dean of a university Ford was about to visit called his attention to the stalled car with hieroglyphics on the body, and the reaction of the guest of honor was totally unexpected. He lowered the car window.

"Get a horse!" he craned out and saluted the cranking boys. One of them looked up and put a finger to his nose and took it down quickly when he saw it was the dean's automobile.

Ford's second reaction was wholly inexplicable. It might have been that he regretted the impulse and the seedy catcall. He asked the driver to stop. He fished in a pocket and got out a shabby note book which was a hodgepodge of scrawled "musts" intelligible only to him. A new line to nudge his memory went into it.

The owner of the defunct roadster received an unbelievable letter ten days later. It was from the college town's Ford agency and said if the owner of the jalopy, Pennsylvania license No. So-and-So, would present himself, the agency would be glad to take in his car in even trade for a new model. No explanation was given. Ford simply had taken the number on the plates, had it checked for ownership, issued orders. It seemed merely another impulse of an unpredictable man.

No one more than the man under the spray of lilies about whom it was told would have appreciated more a story current after the body of Ford was borne from church into packed streets a few months ago. It was credited to one of the bearers. He had heard, it was said, light tapping inside the flowered casket as the procession moved from nave to door and had thought, listening carefully, he heard Mr. Ford's voice.

"Put this thing on wheels and lay off six men," the familiar voice was saying in its old demanding way.

If Ford heard it he liked it—a Ford joke at the very end. He also would have recognized in it a tale spun twenty years before to burlesque his concern for wasted manpower.

Hist! He's German born really, his name Kort; he is plotting to restore the Russian throne; he will give a car free to any girl who doesn't bob her hair.

CHAPTER XX

MYTHS

RUMORS YOWLED nightly under Henry Ford's window. Myths overflowed the filing cabinets. Some he inspired himself for deviltry or for no other purpose than to win a stickful of type well positioned in the day's news. Others had stems in the pretended ability of persons remote from the scene who could tell, with extraordinary aplomb, exactly what he was going to do in advance of when he knew himself. They usually were as wrong as they were prolific.

Henry Ford, a German, really came from Poland and was known there as "the master with the golden hands" . . . he had taken a palatial villa on the Mediterranean littoral which once housed Victoria, and was plotting with royalists to restore the throne of Russia . . . he would sell sixty-five cars on his sixty-fifth birthday for a dollar apiece . . . a star in the night sky was not a new celestial debutante at all but a memorial light to Thomas A. Edison that Ford had hoisted in the inventor's honor.

He had built a Maginot line of subterranean caves in which he proposed to fight unionization and had so wired the plant that no one could come or go if he switched on the current. The sprinkler system was ready to spray tear gas on any interloper.

He wore a red tie when he was mad and going into battle . . . he would give cars free to all mothers of twins . . . he was taking instructions from a Catholic prelate . . . he would pay a million dollars for a tip on how to reduce the price of his car a dime. He intended to give away 15 per cent of his fortune to lower his tax load, and swindlers, for a price, offered to get your name on the preferred list of beneficiaries. He was dickering for Plymouth Rock.

None of these reports was any more true than a rumor of the early thirties that Henry and Edsel Ford were most angry at Señor Diego Rivera, Mexican muralist, and his conception of the dynamic capital of the automobile industry on the respectable walls of the Detroit Art Institute. It was rumored that Ford would sue, at the very least, and would ask that some allegedly sacrilegious symbolism be painted over.

If what occurred in Detroit did not infuriate the Fords and bring the painter to proper penalty against a wall, it was said they certainly would never pardon a panel which the Señor had done for a museum in his homeland and which was said to show the senior Ford and Rockefeller starving on gold and "depicting your father," a complainant said in a direct appeal to Edsel Ford, "as a leering wine-bibbing stockbroker with one hand fondling ticket tape and the other with a glass of champagne pledging the health of a young woman not his wife." This was the crowning aspersion and the Fords should go over and flog the fellow.

Actually the *cause célèbre* Rivera was a sample of slick press-agentry by which those of artistic perception and those who had none were incited to whale one another, and they did so more or less magnificently. In a month of controversy 78,000 persons wedged into the museum and listened delighted to the cries of the embattled, an attendance unequalled in the whole previous two years.

The moment was ripe for Rivera. Times were hard. U. S. savings were gone or frozen. The new poor peddled apples, upper office windows were diving boards and everyone nursed some wounds, smelled of arnica. The worst of the whirlwind had passed but the nation was still clinging to the nearest lamppost and reaching for a steadier foothold. Into the shambles barged the heretical señor and a charming wife trigged in uncut amber.

What happened in the next ten months to Mr. Rivera's two separate contracts for frescoes, one with Edsel Ford and the other with John D. Rockefeller, Jr., seemed to prove a Ford possibly had in *savoir faire* what a Rockefeller lacked. There was some dissimilarity in the provocations but it still was hard to figure which had greater aggravation at the señor's hands—oil or motors.

For Rockefeller the Mexican muralist painted a picture of Lenin; for the Detroit Art Institute, with the junior Ford footing the bill, the señor prepared some panels in which a gasping critic thought he saw a resemblance to Christ in a fat ugly child in a halo, and those who sided with and against the Señor locked in a battle royal that was welcome entertainment for many people at a time when they needed it most.

At the height of the charges and counter-charges and assertions that the senior Ford was boiling I asked him in a break in the thunder if he had seen Rivera or the murals and he said "Who?" and "What murals?"

I do remember he was pretty much excited, however, over a situation involving Orphan Annie. He loved Tarzan and Jiggs and Annie; to his son he left Fra Lippo Lippi and Corot. He read aloud in a rich Irish brogue—and Jiggs came to life as he did it. He sweated out Annie's grief—and the staff had to bone to keep up with him.

There was nothing elective about Annie. It was either cram or be flunked. Ford would quit a hot discussion at the luncheon table of a new $1,000,000 blast furnace to take a poll of what his executives thought of the latest test of her peerless character. One executive tried to bluff his way through a debate after he had been out of town several days and had taken a vacation from comic strips. Ford was not deceived.

"I'm afraid you haven't seen the morning paper," he said, coldly, and turned to another executive who had a theory about poor Annie that made more sense. Associates said Mr. Ford never mentioned the Rivera murals and that if he did see them probably considered them cartoons several degrees inferior to Mr. Donald Gray's comic-strip.

The señor was busy on his planking quietly stirring up the unsuspected hell when the junior Ford telephoned Fred L. Black, their advertising manager, to drop into his office if he was not busy at the moment.

Popular interest in the Detroit Art Institute was nil. The city fathers could see no votes in the relatively empty halls—besides, the country was in a major depression and the relief load recorded a new high daily. The budget for art was butchered. The museum was considered by some people as a toy of the residents of Grosse Pointe and

Bloomfield Hills, fashionable suburban colonies. If they want it let them pay for it. The silk-stocking camps, times being what they were, said the institute was Mr. Ford's baby, as chairman of the City Art Commission, and why shouldn't he foot the bill? Ford, who had originally put up $30,000, now found his personal outlay at the institute over $100,000. He was paying the salaries of the director, curator and others; soon it would be the charwomen and janitors. The younger Ford thought the institute a community venture.

"That's about the situation, Fred." He said he wanted Black to see what could be worked out to encourage public participation.

The patronage of the institute consisted largely of ladies knocking about on gold-headed staves. Activities were limited to slimly attended meetings in an auditorium where by removing a few rows of seats there would have been room for basketball practice without disturbing any one. The staff prepared and read papers that were correct but hardly popular. Seldom was anyone in the place who lived in the backwash, and this hardly met Ford's ideas of a useful art museum. He wanted to get people into the place who did not point at canvases with a stick or lorgnette, knew scarcely one word of *atelier* jabber and yet might like pictures.

The immediate outcome was a People's Museum Association of dollar members, then a lecture course of broader popular appeal. Rivera continued to balance his 300 pounds on his overhead runway and splash the garden court with color. Attendance picked up a bit but more was needed—and then one day a panel demonstrating the process of vaccination horrified an observer. He was an Episcopal curate and he wrote sharply of his dismay.

"This," he stormed, "is a caricature of the Holy Family."

While recognizing the technical excellence, the Rev. Dr. Higgins objected to the spirit of Detroit as the murals portrayed it and thought that some of the work was as out of place as a jazz band in a cathedral, as he put it.

"My chief objection is a panel of a fat ugly child being vaccinated by a doctor and nurse," the clergyman wrote. "The animals in the foreground and the halo about the head of the child suggest the Holy Family."

Was this deliberate or a coincidence? Rivera said he always painted a child's hair as if it wore a halo. Dr. Higgins had no doubt in his mind what was intended.

"What," asked George F. Pierrot, a collaborator of Black, who also had a talent for publicity, "are we waiting for?"

"What, indeed?" nodded his confederate.

It was no time to be delicate and hide scandal. Clergymen and educators, critics and press were invited to the institute to see for themselves if Higgins was right and Rivera presumptuous. It was a lovely belligerent meeting. It would have made a fine Western. Sides were taken. The museum crackled with new electric air. Roads to the building were black. Even the staff, and in time the augmented guards, divided and suspected one another's critical honesty and political philosophies. Attendance was 1200 before the clouds blew up; 16,000 packed the sedate halls the week after.

"Frescoed biliousness! . . . No greater one has come since Michelangelo did the Sistine . . . Our city should have been dutifully alive before a foreign propagandist mutilated the tax-paid walls. . . . Long after critics die who now seem staggered in the face of great art, people will come from all over the earth to see them. . . . Shall Detroit belong to Detroiters, the legitimate heirs and respecters of our city's sane ideals, or surrender to a hired stranger from without its gates?—"

The press described the vaccination panel for the few who were not racing to the institute to see for themselves. A child was supported by a uniformed woman in a nurse's cap which some said was a nimbus. At the right was a doctor administering vaccine. Above were three scientists engaged in research—"the three wise men." At the bottom some animals—these, said Rivera, represented the source of vaccine; these, said the other side, represented the stable in Nazareth.

Dr. G. H. Derry, president of a Catholic college, jumped in:

"Wake, Detroit!" he exhorted. "The institute is attempting to sell out the best walls of the museum to an outside halfbreed Mexican Bolshevist.

"Watch out, Ford! On the walls of the Public Education Building in Mexico City Rivera has told the world what he thinks of your father Henry. In a setting of wine and women he has pictured for posterity your father as a leering stockbroker.

"Make no mistake, Mr. Ford, the Communist adores the machines if he, not you, owns them. It is not too late to turn back, Mr. Ford! Rivera means here, as in Mexico, to influence the workers to the determination that the way out is by the clenched fist that dynamites Ford and his machines."

When the city voted to accept Mr. Ford's gift of the $28,000 murals, Higgins, the original complainant, said in the press he could not understand such blindness. "Rivera," he said bitterly, "makes Edsel Ford appear an enemy of capitalist society," but the Fords seemed interested less than any one else.

A jeering editor said that the muralist must be a very dangerous fellow since what he had done showed sympathy for the people who did the heavy work of the world.

"Have we got something?" Pierrot enthused.

"Maybe I had better see Mr. Ford," said Black, slightly uneasy at the forked lightning.

"Seems you have a wildcat by the tail," said Edsel, not at all ill-naturedly. "Do you think it's getting out of hand?"

Black didn't think so.

To those who said his faces lacked spiritual content, Señor Rivera was curt: "Steel and stone are cold. Every day I see cars and people. I put into my pictures only what I see."

To the critical clergy he said, aciduously: "Now we have the curious spectacle of two religious organizations of European origin—one of which openly avows allegiance to a foreign potentate while the other has deep roots in alien soil—stirring up the people against what they call un-American invention."

And what was the un-American invention? Nothing but a pictorial representation, said the Señor, of the basis on which Detroit existed and the source of its worth, painted by a direct descendant of an aboriginal American stock.

When one or another abusive one seemed to be silent and catching a fresh breath, it always seemed that Black or his partner would sidle up soft-footedly and whisper, "You're not going to let him get away with that, are you? Take a poke at him."

They got a bit of added help from the belated discovery of a marble disc in the controversial panels, and those expert in symbolism said it was religion pressing on the people.

The drums ceased pounding in time and Rivera left Detroit to astonish Mr. Rockefeller by producing his picture of Lenin in the precincts of the Fifth Avenue Center. No one apparently had thought to say what was wanted or to ask what he intended to paint under the innocent enough over-all title, "Man at the Cross-Roads."

The Fords shut their mouths during the bushwhacking at Detroit. The senior Ford said nothing, although Orphan Annie was having her ups and downs. His son spoke only twice. In the heat of the affray he was pressed for comment on the frescoes and was asked if he thought they interpreted Detroit industry faithfully.

"They are Mr. Rivera's interpretation," he responded crisply.

For a half hour he listened to a councilman condemn the panels as an offensive travesty. Then the son of a very adamant father said stoutly it would be as out of place for him to ask Rivera to change his paintings at the request of any religious or political group as it would be for the Commission to remove the many crucifixes, religious paintings and church relics from the institute if it was found they gave offense to Jews, orthodox Christians "or the thousands who have no interest in any church." He sat down and was voted a budget increase.

With Rivera exciting New York, calm deepened in Detroit. It was deeper at Dearborn. I tried to get the senior Ford to express an opinion but Orphan Annie was in another pocket fighting for the right.

"I think I'll write him," Mr. Ford said.

"Rivera?"

Ford looked as if he never heard of the upsetting Señor.

"To the fellow who draws Annie." He said the trouble artist Donald Gray had gotten her into worried him.

Rumors snapped persistently at Ford's heels. Some were small, some elaborate; most were egregious lies which the company never bothered to affirm or deny and never brought to Ford's attention.

He was not going to buy the French navy, no.

He was not trying to raise the American birth-rate by offering a Ford car free to any woman bearing eleven children or more, no.

The rumors of how he proposed to wage war against unionization had dime novel overtones. He had built under the River Rouge plant, it was said, an endless catacomb in which a Ford army could hold out for months in the coming struggle with the iniquitous forces of the UAW-CIO.

"Through these tunnels of steel and concrete," the magazine *Friday* told the public, "it would be possible to march units of strikebreakers to invade any given position. Supplies could be carried through to scabs. Caches of arms could be concealed along the tunnels. It could actually become a fortified line over night."

"Could be," "would be possible," "could actually become"—nothing more definite. The story was a safe piece of distortion but as much buncombe as Ford said history was. The underground tubes "could" have been used for such a warlike purpose but were not designed for it. If there was any secrecy about the subterranean network, the company had a strange way of preserving it. The mayor of Detroit, other officials and press representatives were driven through it in automobiles years before the passageways were seized upon by thrill-mongers.

No shots or ambuscades were ever reported in the tubes. When the company negotiated with the labor union and signed a more liberal contract than the union had been able to win from any other company in the industry, it did so around an orderly conference table and not in any underground cavern. No proof of tear gas in any sprinkler system was ever offered.

Three farmers walked into an East Poland newspaper shop one late afternoon and assured the editor that Henry Ford came of a German family named Kort. They were Gustave, 80; Robert, 75, and Julian, 73, and the American magnate, they said, was their baby brother, bless his heart and gifted hands.

The editor seemed to require no more than this oral proof for he patted Poland on the back in the next edition as the scene of Ford's beginning and added his name to those of such distinguished sons as Pilsudski, Paderewski and Kosciuszko, putting the tale on the cables.

The story was that Henry, beloved brother of the editor's three strays, was one of ten Kort children who had moved to a town near the Russian frontier from a small place in the Reich. He had become an apprentice and then a full-fledged mechanic, and demonstrated such skill that someone with a gift for musical sobriquet dubbed him *mistrz o zlotych rękach,* or master with the golden hands. From puttering about machines Henry Kort turned to invention and the first thing one knew he had produced a piece of machinery which magically carried a half-ton load from Mantchulme to Volowitz, a good ten kilometers, on only four pounds of gasoline.

"We were stuck for a name for it at first," Gustave admitted.

"But the people," Julian remembered vaguely, "finally called it—What was it, Robert?"

"The iron falcon," prompted Robert.

Yes, indeed, that was it—the iron falcon—all three recalled and nodded in agreement.

Good people predicted Henry was bound for great things if he would shake off the mud of the town and the brothers said, without being too explicit as to dates, that the daring Henry eventually did just that, sold out his fields, and set off for distant America where the sequel was of course known to everyone.

Gustave, Robert and Julian, having gulled the editor, went back to their farm at Konstanttinova. American newspapers telephoned Dearborn for confirmation of the story, a peculiar contradiction of proven fact, and Ford's editor was busy for days saying blandly, "Never heard of the gentlemen" or more desperately, "It sounds very corny to me."

Ford had backed his advertising department on the ropes in 1932 when he unexpectedly stated it was not true that he made his first car in 1893, a year date used regularly over a long period in official biographies and general publicity.

The little rebuilt brick shed in which the first Ford car was made was to be reproduced at the Chicago Century of Progress and the automobile itself was to be the centerpiece of the display. His advertising men were preparing suitable material and some of it was read to him.

"That's wrong," he said when the 1893 date was mentioned.

The challenge threw everybody. For years it had appeared and never been doubted.

"I made my first car in 1896," he corrected. "I made my first engine in 1893."

A brilliant star in the summer sky which was first appraised as a newcomer to the evening constellation and then called fake and attributed to Ford hit the front pages in 1935, not long after an interesting fiction from Florida that he was about to root up an old Seminole Village in the Everglades and ship it, stone ovens, marshy ground and all, to Greenfield.

Brooding over a flood of mail the Detroit Chamber of Commerce denied that any heavenly body was in production or even on the drawing board, that so far as it knew the star was legitimate, but inquiring letters continued to stream in from the countryside, even to one from a Louisiana dynamo who saw commercial possibilities in the "star" and wanted to know by return mail if it was on the market and available in quantity.

A room in Washington stilled one morning when Mrs. Ford got up to speak and an audience of women hunched forward slightly in their chairs. Interest was sharpened by what seemed a current grass roots boom for Henry Ford for the Presidency of the United States and the speaker about to address the national officers of the Girls' Protective League was a likely first lady. All sorts of rumors were current in 1923 as to whether her husband would choose to run.

Mrs. Ford moved quickly and frankly to clarify her position in the general political speculation. She said in view of the confusion of rumors it would please her if at least a hundred women in the country—those before her—knew the truth.

"Mr. Ford," she said, "may believe he would make a good President but I don't and I have told him so. I don't think he will be nominated and I do not believe he will run."

As a political prognosticator Mrs. Ford put herself among the better prophets for Ford later announced he was not a candidate but was for Calvin Coolidge.

"Moreover," she smiled in conclusion as if she remembered exactly the moment when she put her foot down, "I have told my husband that if he comes to Washington he comes without me."

The audience smiled with her.

"Now, may I go from here and drop politics?" she suggested and turned to the subject of what to do for troubled youngsters of her own sex who might need help. She had quieted the whisperers and especially a fluttery lady who absurdly before the meeting had called her "Madame President."

The whispering grew with his dollars. He was seeking a $60,000,000 rail outlet to the Atlantic Seaboard . . . he was negotiating for the imperial jewels of China . . . he intended to make automobiles of cotton, stamping them out as a baker might cut doughnuts.

He had offered to assume the whole German loan of $110,000,000 under the Dawes plan . . . he was considering a polar flight, and also might become the grand pasha of the Anti-Saloon League forces . . .

he planned to become the greatest ship operator of his day by purchasing 400 vessels from the United States Shipping Board.

Edsel arrived at the engineering laboratory at 6:30 A.M., and his father only a few minutes later, the morning a wire service carried a bulletin out of Buffalo which quoted a shipping commissioner on the 400-boat deal. The son wanted to know what brought me at that hour.

I asked what he knew about the ship deal.

"Father hasn't said anything to me." Edsel seemed puzzled. "All I know is that 400 is an awful lot of ships."

The arriving senior Ford said he wasn't going to be the greatest shipowner in the world. He also said that 200 had been the figure mentioned but 400 was all right. Four hundred would cost less to cut up on the average.

"Cut up?"

"Buying them for scrap," Ford said.

An uncommon report was that girls who did not bob their hair would get cars with Mr. Ford's compliments. Go to the salesrooms, present acceptable proof and receive an automobile for nothing—it was going to be made easy. A misinformed young woman in New Mexico picked up a fancier version.

"I take the liberty of writing you," she said, "in regard to your ad in the paper about giving cars to the few girls who have not bobbed their hair and do not wear knickers. I am one who has long hair," she palpitated, "and can truly say I never sat in—or on—a pair of knickers in my life."

A male correspondent, a Joseph Greese of Texas, had another rendering which set up still more exacting terms. The car was free, he heard, to any woman who had twins in addition to an unclipped head. The Lone Star husband buttered the entry of his wife by reporting that she fulfilled both terms and the children had been named "Henry" and "Edsel." Mrs. Greese promised never to shorten her hair if she could have a runabout.

While not more than a handful of these fictions reached Ford's ears, he was interested in a protest of a Mississippi male over the seeming favoritism shown women in the reputed contest, if contest is the word. He said, special delivery and notarized, that he had a full beard. If Mr. Ford did not think he had a tough time raising it, he should try it himself. He said it took a great deal of stamina.

"If you are giving automobiles to unbobbed girls, I think my beard deserves consideration," the Mississippian pleaded, "for I certainly have been ridiculed more than any girl who has let her hair grow." He had been called a Bolshevik. He had been taunted as an anarchist.

"I forgot to tell you, Mr. Ford," he concluded, "about the time I am having with my wife." It seems that his wife had not bobbed her hair but had threatened to if he did not shave. It put him in a pickle. "And she pulls my whiskers," he sobbed in ending, "and you know that is no fun at all."

A Georgia miss by the name of Ford understood only ladies of that name could qualify and two in Arkansas considered their entry particularly challenging because neither wore spit curls or bangs.

The rumor mail bore unfamiliar postmarks—towns the size of the motormaker's own before country clubs and model homes and skyways and ramps flowered as he spread. They came from Mountaincrest, Ark.; Darling, Miss.; Farmers' Branch, Texas; Forrestville, Ky., and the like and they were signed by sincere, well-intentioned people who apparently were hospitable to rumor and put out the guest china whenever a vagabond tale knocked at the door. Credulity dwelt as much in the city, however, as in the hayloft.

Ford would launch a chain of 400 radio stations for business and political purposes . . . he was going to Palestine personally to drum up business . . . he would buy the Chicago, Peoria & St. Louis Railroad, abandon Dearborn as a home and take over the estate of Brewer Jacob Ruppert at Rhinecliffe on the Hudson . . . he would buy an interest in the Philadelphia Athletics.

An automobile could be had free if you found a mysterious hard-to-get number in a package of Camels and also by forming the word Ford from serial letters on American coins. We heard this many years ago but after accumulating Fs and Ds and coming on no Os and Rs put it down as a trick and spent the F-D money on some forgotten vice.

He would replace without charge any flivver that had been on the road more than ten years. He was bringing out a horn which sounded like a human voice. Ford was barely in his grave beside his forebears before a rumor spread that a man could get a new Ford car in trade for a 1943 copper penny. (Only steel-zinc pennies were minted in 1943.)

Little of the drifting jetsam was true, but the report he would pay

$100 for any flivver joke that made him laugh brought him thousands. He thought well of one he made up himself and told the late Woodrow Wilson. The President repaid him by repeating a jingle about the car but Ford was not amused and never would repeat it.

His own joke involved a man who saw another digging an enormous grave—one big enough to hold an automobile—and asked the shoveler why he was making it so big. It was for a man who had died, the digger said, and wanted his Ford buried with him.

"He said the Ford always got him out of every hole he got into," he explained, "and he thought he could count on it to get him out of this one."

Ford would paper the sky with flivver planes . . . M-G-M would do a romanticized life of him with Spencer Tracy as the automobile-maker . . . he had bought two whaling ships for no given reason . . . on the strength of a visit of a New York banker it was whispered Ford would join the directorate of his institution, and the asking price of the stock advanced $35 in five days . . . Europe reported that Ford would join with Chrysler in a life-and-death struggle with General Motors. It was news to Detroit.

"What's that?" asked Economist Roger W. Babson, pointing to a mound of putty-like substance in the laboratory.

"Glue, cotton and formaldehyde," Ford identified the elements.

What was he going to do with it? Make automobiles? Copy desks headed it: "Cotton Car Next; Steel Car on Junk Pile" with a jauntiness which suggested the car of cotton would be in showrooms as soon as the next edition reached the streets.

I was tipped one day that Ford was in the market for a railroad whose depressed securities were far from high grade.

"Where did you get the report?" the Ford office asked.

"The vice-president of a bank."

"Who?"

I named him.

"About that deal," said the spokesman after inquiry, "Mr. Ford had made no overtures for that road and has no intention of buying it."

The company assigned some of its own investigators. They learned that the bank official was personally long of the stock of the consumptive road and the fable he was peddling was designed to create an improved market for his holdings.

The same motive was behind another rumor involving a Pittsburgh company. With Ford taking part, very hush-hush conferences were reported and the guess was that the company would soon pass to his ownership. However, a few contradictions developed. He had not been in Pittsburgh for a year and a half. Neither he nor any agent had called on the company named. No offer had been made or was being considered. It was true there was such a glass company—and that was about all except that on the strength of the gossip the stock of the glass company thrust upward sharply and it was assumed that insiders got out on the bulge.

The Chicago Bureau of the Associated Press asked Detroit one midnight to see if anything had happened to Ford. St. Paul was asking confirmation of a report of his death which had reached it in curious fashion.

Ford's editor said the motormaker was well so far as he knew. He was presumably en route to his properties in Northern Michigan.

"I'll call if I get anything different," he said, and asked the reporter to telephone him if the newspaper got any more information.

Ford was asleep in his berth while the night air crackled with alarums, but he was interested when he heard of it. It was not the first or last time he was reported dead, but it was the only time he bothered to order a tracer. He wanted to know who made up such tales and put wheels under them. The answer was this:

An operator in a railroad tower in Wisconsin had noticed Ford's private car on a passing train and mentioned the fact to a friend over the wire, merely remarking that Ford had just passed. A third man at an open circuit happened to pick up the conversation but misread the message. He thought the first telegrapher had said: "Henry Ford has just passed—on." He told a friend of his at another key. The message took wings.

A St. Paul newspaper operator, also at an open circuit, suddenly heard two unidentified operators gossiping.

One was saying: "Joe, did you hear Henry Ford died?"

The other said: "What do you know!"

The first said: "Just picked up a flash. It only said he passed on, nothing more."

St. Paul's demand on Chicago and Detroit for a quick check followed.

Gentle and hard, direct and devious, it was impossible to guess what Ford would do but the surest bet was it would be the unexpected.

CHAPTER XXI

MERCURIAL MAGNATE

MINOR PROOF of major facets of Ford's character lay all about. Ford, the kindly Samaritan, walked arm in arm with Ford, the demanding; Ford, the devious and capricious, rode tandem with Ford, the straightforward and simple. He moved easily from mood to mood.

A saying in Dearborn used to be that if the first three birds he saw of a morning were black, all birds would be black that day, but this implied consistency and any soothsayer asked for trouble who tried to say how Ford would act in any given set of circumstances.

Few flat statements about him stand up. The minute one describes him as gentle and humble a hundred incidents negate it. An unqualified statement that he was harsh and overbearing can be disproved by a hundred to the contrary. He was actually the customary mixture of man's good and reprehensible characteristics. They were simply more noticeable in him because of who he was.

Some of his convictions were iron—so were some of his whims. He was fiercely unwilling to give up the Model T—to admit the world had come to want some color other than black and more to an automobile than utility. He could not rest on his oars and keep business volume, he was told, unless the government allowed the customer no choice of his own, as in a totalitarian state, or he, in free enterprise, could somehow destroy all competition. A few of his bolder executives said so; the meeker ones waited to see how the "old man" would jump and jumped with him. The senior Ford was usually immarbled by opposition.

The story is that while he was in Europe two executives who had lined up for change turned out an experimental car of comely curves and markedly dissimilar to the veteran Model T. They guided him to where it was when he arrived back and stood aside to await the verdict.

"Well, what do you think, Mr. Ford?" he was asked as they looked admiringly on their own handiwork.

The senior Ford reached for a work-bench.

"This!" he said—a wrench crashed through the windshield.

He could be equally obstinate in small things. He persistently did the untried—yet often resisted it. When old-time telephone instruments were being replaced by cradle sets months elapsed before he would permit the substitution of one of them for one of his own. The japanning was gone and the old piece was an eyesore. An installation crew rushed to replace it.

"No, you don't," Ford vetoed promptly. He said he was able to understand people perfectly and they seemed to hear him all right over the dilapidated equipment. He would wait, as some people did on new cars, until the bugs were found and squashed.

An interesting phenomenon was that Ford seldom fired anybody personally unless very mad and no one but an inexperienced executive ever attributed an order to him, and he never did it a second time. Under the system men discharged on his instructions wandered about for years blaming the men who carried out the orders and quite sure if Mr. Ford had known, he would have stepped in and stopped it. This left him in a position to say he knew nothing of the ousting of an employee, if that is what he wanted, or to escape onus if an order he gave did not turn out well.

He also had a common tendency to believe the most preposterous story of a man he knew to be a liar if what was said coincided with what he thought.

When his son had an unpleasant job to do he did it himself. It was necessary to choose between two veteran members of the teaching force of a school and let one go. The junior Ford was chairman of the trustees. The problem was threshed out and it was decided to release the man oldest in service. No one looked forward with anything but regret to telling the instructor selected that he was out.

"Mr. Ford," said a trustee, "can I relieve you of that job? Would you care to have me break the news to him?"

"No, no," said the younger Ford, quickly. "I guess it's one of my duties as chairman." He added slowly, "I always do my dirty work."

A construction man laying out a tail race at a Ford mill learned in peculiar fashion that no order was to be ascribed to the head man. A winding channel was adapted for the work. Ford said he did not want it straightened—it would look too artificial—so the natural course was followed and the bottom and banks were floored and faced with close-set stone. Some earth became loosened from the roots of a tree on one bank and fell away, and the contractor, after replacing it, also used stone about the base of the trunk. The job scarcely had been finished when two emissaries arrived from the Rouge, apparently to see how the work was going.

"Who told you to fix the stream that way?" one of the visitors wanted to know.

"Mr. Ford."

"I suppose he also told you to lay those stones around the tree?"

"No," the contractor took off his cap and scratched his head, "that's my own idea. I think it's going to work all right, too."

A telephone call from a farm some ten miles away a week later said Henry Ford was there and wanted to see him. Ford was in a dudgeon.

"Never, never tell anyone I ever gave you an order!" he stormed, gravel in his tone. "Understand?"

The contractor said he got the idea.

"That's all!" The blue Ford eyes snapped—the blue eyes that the editor Brisbane had admired because he said that any man who ever amounted to anything in history—Lincoln, Napoleon, Washington, Jefferson, Edison—had them.

The man who built the race lived uneasily with his puzzle but when Ford reappeared two weeks later the incident appeared forgotten. They drove over the property and stopped on a knoll. Ford said he wanted a cupola built on that barn.

"Mr. Ford, you'll have it," the employee promised with alacrity. He asked a few questions but suddenly sensed he was talking to himself. Ford's memory had rolled back 14 days.

"No, never mind." The motormaker cancelled the instructions. "I'll have someone else give you the order," he said. His man was still on the probationary list for the lapse of two weeks previous.

His deviousness was stunning at times. Messmore Kendall, lawyer, angler and explorer who lives in Washington's headquarters at Dobbs Ferry and financed Somerset Maugham's first play, is authority for one story of Ford's circuitousness.[1]

Before the closed car became commonplace, Kendall imported a Rolls-Royce with a patented top which could be raised or lowered by a crank. He decided upon a friend's advice to see if he could interest the Detroit manufacturer. After lunch with father and son he accompanied them to where the car was parked and offered to demonstrate the foreign equipment.

"Mr. Ford brusqely declined," writes Kendall, "and changed the subject to a collection of American glass. He asked if I would examine it and tell him what I thought it was worth.

"Jules Glaenzer (the friend who accompanied Kendall) and I did as bid. I soon became absorbed in the collection and Jules finally sauntered over to a window. Suddenly he cried, 'Messmore, come here!'

"I joined him. He pointed to our car just leaving the parking space with Mr. Ford alone at the wheel. We watched him drive a few blocks to an open space, stop, and make his own demonstration of the top's operation. He lowered it and closed it a half-dozen times, got back in the car, and returned it to its identical parking spot."

At the end of an hour Kendall, Glaenzer and Edsel reported back to the senior Ford. The hopes of the first two were now high. Undoubtedly after what they had seen, Ford was definitely interested in the equipment of the Rolls, or so they thought. Kendall told what he thought the glass was worth.

"Much too high," Ford shook his head.

"What's the asking price?"

"About half that."

Kendall said he was really no expert but that he considered the figure he had arrived at was fair. Ford rose. The interview was apparently over. The visitors waited for a word about the accessory on the Rolls. Kendall decided to chance a question. Pretending no knowledge of Mr. Ford's own overseen experiment, he asked if he would be allowed to demonstrate the auto top.

"No," said Ford definitely, "I'm not interested in seeing whether it works or not. Good afternoon."

[1] *Never Let Weather Interfere,* by Messmore Kendall, Farrar, Straus & Co.

When Ford sued the *Chicago Tribune* at the end of World War I for calling him an anarchist and ignorant idealist, insiders were convinced that he lost nothing by some able maneuvering behind the scenes.

Paralleling for part of its course the main street of Mt. Clemens, Mich., scene of the trial, is the Clinton River, a few yards from the rear entrance to the courthouse. When certain long printed matter was being read into the trial record on hot days, counsel, newspapermen and others cooled themselves on the bank of the stream. Ford himself and a member of his staff took walks, too. He carried a tape measure.

He made a practice of standing on bridges and lowering one end of the tape until it just about touched the surface of the water. Sometimes it was done from one span, sometimes from another. It was quite provocative. Word of all this traveled to town and elaborate rumors circulated. Henry Ford was taking measurements for some building he had in mind for Mt. Clemens. He was considering a dam and a hydro plant. Possibly there would be a branch factory—not a big plant, of course, but one that would be a welcome addition to the town's limited industry—certainly work for townspeople.

The more hardy approached him. They were roundabout, naturally. Ford seemed glad to expatiate on water-power and the nice facilities present in Mt. Clemens. He did not say anything definite and they did not ask directly. He naturally would not speak out until the dotted line was signed, but they spread the word knowingly that there was more than pedestrianism in the walks up and down the Clinton. Ford simply said that water-power was a fine thing, but if word of all this did not reach the ears of the jury, it had to be stone deaf, and it wasn't that.

After the verdict I remember several newsmen cornered a Ford engineer and asked straight out if Ford purposed any development in Mt. Clemens. He seemed surprised. Was Ford going to put up a power plant? Not that he knew of.

"The countryside is too flat," he said. "If the waters were impounded, good farmland would be flooded." The engineer was sure Ford had something else in mind. The reporters suspected that was true.

There was nothing devious about him when he bought some

coal properties in West Virginia. They had hardly passed into his hands when he heard that the men had to kneel at work in certain low galleries.

"I'd like some overalls," he told the former owners.

They tried to talk him out of his obvious purpose. Even when he climbed into work clothes, a veteran miner guiding him up to the entrance did not think Ford was serious. He said they'd have to go on their hands and knees part of the trip, and his glance said he did not think the new owner was going to like it.

"If you can I can," Ford said, and later as the roof lowered and his guide said, "This is it, Mr. Ford—down on all fours," the motor-maker sat down on the floor of the mine and used his knuckles as ratchets to drag himself along on the seat of his pants. He learned a lot from the grueling journey. He learned more by having miners come to Dearborn and tell him what was wrong.

Reform in his coal properties was in motion within a week. He cut cross lots to see that working and home conditions were improved. He issued orders and waited a month. Then he went to West Virginia, got into his blitz suit again, summoned up the same guide.

"Let's go down again," he suggested, "and see how much we have to slide on our tails this time."

Pay of his miners at one time was 59 per cent higher than the prevailing scale in the field and he claimed to be producing coal at a cost of only 8 per cent more than competitors in nearby areas. The daily wage average was $7 a day for eight hours when wages in the neighborhood for nine were $3.50 to $4.50.

Over a job well done Ford rarely expressed satisfaction. That was what he paid for. If he got it he saw no reason to pin a decoration on the man who did it. Usually he dissolved conceit by conveying an impression that the deed was a mite shy of what he hoped for. He was a perfectionist himself—he wanted others to be. The usual reward for a job well done was simply more work to do.

Executives learned another lesson rapidly. If the head man suggested he wanted a particular thing it was wise to move fast. If the assignee spent too much time getting information on how to do what was given him, he was likely to find that Ford had become impatient over the wait, put a second man at the task, and the job was finished or well along when the first man, beautifully primed, was ready to start.

Subordinates also knew that while a mistake he committed himself could always be excused by some lesson he claimed he had learned, he could get awfully mad about something he agreed to which did not work out well. He gave the impression at such times that he had been roped into something against his own better judgment.

He came up with one criticism—nine years late. The excellent institution which became Henry Ford Hospital had its inception in the minds of a group of wealthy Michigan men who saw a need of a general hospital in Detroit early in the century. It was to be built by popular subscription. After some money had been raised the drive for funds stalled and the project languished. A newspaper publisher thought to spur Ford as chairman of the finance committee and printed the names of the committee in his paper in blackface type. Mrs. Ford remarked on the article at dinner.

"I see you're a financial failure," she said.

"What? What's that?" her husband put down his fork.

She read the story to him. It said the city or state probably would take over the hospital because of the inability of its private promoters to raise the necessary funds, and printed prominently was the name of Henry Ford as finance chairman.

He said, "They're trying to make me look silly. I'll show them!"

He would do it, he said, by giving subscribers their money back and building the place himself. The report was groundless that Henry Ford Hospital was its founder's protest against an excessive bill tendered him after an illness of a member of his family. He paid $4,000,000 for the work already done and to reimburse donors and assigned his secretary, Ernest G. Liebold, to complete the undertaking.

Liebold visited top-ranking institutions through the country to get ideas. He recruited a staff. He assembled records for a corner-stone. Then he had to go out of town. He was feeling pretty good over the progress. This was the moment Ford chose for a ceremony.

"Like to put down a corner-stone?" he invited Dr. S. S. Marquis. "Let's go up and lay the one at the hospital."

The head of his sociological department asked if it should not wait until the secretary's return since he had done so much work on it and might like to be present but there was no challenging a Ford impulse. He felt that morning like putting down a corner-stone. It was mortared into place without the usual tidbits that are the inescapable stuffing of corner-stones. Ford either forgot them, did not know the proper records had been made ready, or considered the tradition nonsense. He may have thought it unlikely that the world of the future would ever spend a single moment exploring moldy documents and faded pictures cached in such building blocks. It would have much more to do if it was going to get itself straightened out.

Liebold came home to a *fait accompli* and stoically filed the historical miscellany under "H-Hospital." Ford did not mention that the corner-stone had been laid; the secretary learned it for himself from other sources. The motormaker did find fault with the hospital ornamentation.

Nine years later the secretary was instructed to meet him in front of the main building one morning and Ford was there when he arrived, glowering at some inset bands of terra cotta in the face of the building as outside trim between two lower floors to break the solid appearance of the wall. He pointed a crotchety finger.

"Did you ever see anything that ever looked as rotten as that dung-brindle tile?" He stormed grimly. "What did you ever put that in for?" He said he wanted it out the next day.

Occasionally such orders were held in abeyance on a chance that a mood would pass and Ford might forget. It was probable some third person whose judgment was in temporary favor had criticized the tile and that actually Ford had no strong feeling about it. Liebold decided not to tear it down and to await developments. The guess was good.

"Mr. Ford says to never mind that tile at the hospital," the Fair Lane chauffeur telephoned next morning. "He says he will tend to it."

He took care of it by doing nothing. The tiling is still in its original place. It never became a *cause célèbre* aesthetically. The chances are he never gave it another thought.

Ford had a softness easily stirred—a temper easily lit. Both could be set off by the smallest of events. Bark scraped off his favorite bittersweet along the four-block iron fence of the hospital angered him. Five hundred men in line at the employment gate of the plant in a depression year resulted in an order to hire them, along with a thousand others the 500 telephoned as soon as they got the good news. A heavy storm backed water into his Highland Park basement—and he soured on all basements—threatened never to visit Henry Ford Hospital if it had one. He finally agreed that underground space for service passageways, piping and other facilities might be necessary.

He put on doublet and plume once and played the gallant in pretty fashion. The 14-year-old daughter of an executive became unaccountably ill and lost fifty pounds. Weeks passed before the cause—a fall that resulted in a glandular upset—was discovered.

Unpasteurized milk was prescribed. He iced and delivered it each morning from his own herd. Tomato juice was recommended. Cases arrived from Ford. He was on the phone solicitously. One Friday morning he appeared at her home on his bicycle. Was she strong enough to attend an old fashioned dancing party he was giving the same evening? She didn't think so. Her parents would come for a while but would leave early since they did not wish her to be alone.

"I tell you what," the motormaker urged. "You come for a little while and sit with me. Perhaps we can have one dance if you feel up to it." He said he was sure she would be better for seeing people and listening to music.

The patient brightened perceptibly at the idea and her parents consented. The importunate caller left. A service man rang the doorbell an hour later. In his hand was a single yellow rose—"for the little miss to wear tonight." The squire of Fair Lane had gone straight to his gardens for a flower to give a discouraged young lady a little extra buoyancy.

Mild panic spread, however, when Ford complained even lightly. A fretful word became ominous as it passed down the line. Attractive rock gardens ornament one countryside because his car bumped into a boulder.

Roadways leading to some of his mills and village factories were faced with stone. It was not his idea. Field stone abounded and some of his managers thought it would protect the lawns. The trim served until he backed his car into an enormous rock and jumped out to look for damage and cause.

"Is it necessary to have these stones set out here?" he asked ironically.

"We thought they would keep cars off the grass, Mr. Ford."

He said to get them out of there. He may not have intended his order to be accepted as sweepingly as it was, but the underground worked fast in such cases. In no time those managing his properties within a radius of some 40 miles were apprised by cronies that the motormaker was against drives lined with stones and if yours is, Charlie, you had better get them the hell out of there before he sees them. Within forty-eight hours they were cleared. A lot of fellows had the rock carted home, not sure what to do with it but hurrying to get it out of sight, and made pretty use of it in their gardens.

He pursued a sentimental course in buying farms and farmhouses that was said to haunt his heirs when the company began to divest itself of some non-profitable experiments—soybean enterprises, rural hydro plants, at one place almost an entire village.

Some farmers who sold their houses and lands to him might object to outright sale. A man might say, "Yes, I'd like to sell, Mr. Ford, but this is my home—my parents' home. It's more than wood and stone, you see? I don't want to part with it. Maybe we can work out some kind of a deal whereby—"

"Sure thing," Ford would agree; "I know just how you feel." He could understand a man's soft spot for his ancestral home. Had it not been a labor of love to restore his own?

So he would ask how some sort of arrangement like this would do: The farmer could live in the house until he found another place—or even continue out his days there. Then the place would pass to Ford.

Sometimes a clause to this effect was written into the terms of sale. Often it was just an oral agreement. Ford would say it was all right with him. The farmer said Ford could have the place under those conditions. There seemed quite a few of these gentlemen's agreements when the company got ready to put some of the properties on the market.

He never followed routine or did the same thing twice. If he was out of his office his secretary seldom knew where he was no matter how much he was suspected of knowing. Ford did not want visitors or his secretariat on his heels. Sometimes he would come in and go out a back way—maybe just step out a window. When he was bored by a caller, his secretary knew the symptoms. He would begin to pick imaginary lint off his clothes, stare bleakly out a window, straighten out nonexistent wrinkles, slouch deep in his chair. He never seemed in full command at these trying moments and could not bring himself to say that he now regarded his visitor as an unmitigated donkey and would he please get out.

The secretary would enter the breach and say there was a long-distance call waiting. Ford would look with an air of apology at his guest over the interruption. He would rise and say he was sorry about the diversion.

"But you stay here; I'll be right back," he might say before dashing out.

He would keep right on dashing, and there always was the possibility that a credulous visitor would die of famine if he waited in the fatuous belief that Ford meant what he said and ultimately would come back after he answered a purely fictional telephone call.

A family crest or a massive record of achievement was no better guarantee than a social security card that Ford would keep an appointment. Your importance or the fact that you had gone through the prescribed channels and had been assured that at a set hour on a set day Henry Ford would see you was no irrevocable insurance policy that it would turn out that way. He allowed few appointments to interfere with his exercise of free will.

I remember three writers who came by appointment and he had exchanged only a few words with them when he left the room. He did not reappear for an hour, and when he returned he wore a turtleneck sweater, stocking cap on his head and over his arm a pair of skates. He had been out for a few turns on the frozen pond. It apparently had flashed on him at the beginning of the interview that what he really wanted was a little skate instead of strangers breezing questions at him.

On days when visitors were scheduled he was followed and his exact whereabouts telephoned at intervals to the nervous executive whose job was to establish liaison. Guards at the gates flashed word if he left the grounds.

The system saved headaches and enabled many a caller to converse with Ford who otherwise might have been sitting on his deflated rump in the Dearborn lobby for days. His forgetfulness was not hard to explain in view of his broad interests but it was surprising in one who in some ways was a stickler for punctilio.

A letter from the State Department in 1930 said that Prince Louis II, sovereign head of the House of Monaco and in the United States incognito, had expressed a desire to visit the Ford plant and chat with its owner.

"Yeah, I'll be here," he said when told. "Tell him to come along."

A response was sent in the more urbane language of diplomacy. Mr. Ford was charmed. Mr. Ford was looking forward with great interest to the coming of his excellency. Men dogging the motormaker reported him in the experimental machine shop when the Prince arrived, and two of us walked out to tell him the guest was waiting.

"The Prince of Monaco is here, Mr. Ford," the company executive said.

"Heh? Oh, yes." He lifted his eyes from a cam on a machine. He looked slightly misty. "Where in hell is Monaco?" he asked. He was told.

I chipped in, encyclopediacally, that in the year 1863 when Ford was born, the Prince's grandfather had sold to François Blanc the concession to run the Monte Carlo gambling casino in Monaco for a period of fifty years. Ford evinced no interest in the historical tip and turned back to the cam.

"Well," he flung over his shoulder, "bring him out here."

The executive told His Highness he was to have the privilege of meeting Ford as he was working at the machinery he loved. The Prince, in kind, said he was enchanted by the prospect. Ford fell swiftly into the vernacular of the shop and they conversed until the host noticed that while the Prince was nodding agreeably at what was being said, he had heard a limpid overtone above the shop sounds around him and was looking for its source.

"That's an orchestra I have to play for old-fashioned American dances," Ford explained.

"One instrument is a dulcimer, isn't it?" The Prince seemed quite interested.

"Yes, it is." Ford wiped his fingers on some waste and took his visitor by the arm warmly as if mutual knowledge of a dulcimer established a closer bond.

We strolled down the laboratory to the dance floor.

"This gentleman is the Prince of Monaco," Ford announced.

The orchestra rose and bowed. The Prince inclined.

"Play his national anthem," suggested the host.

The musicians looked blank. They knew by heart *Grandpa's Favorite,* the *Seaside Polka* and a good rye waltz, but they were short of anthems, especially Monaco's.

It was a difficult situation—almost an incident.

"I would like to hear the *Marseillaise*." The Prince saved it.

The orchestra obliged and a strain on international good will was relieved.

Ford was adept in saving a situation himself upon a visit of Queen Marie of Rumania when one of his own staff was accidentally overlooked in the introductions by her American consul.

"Queen," said Mr. Ford, "meet our Mr. Black."

He would not be pinned down at home or abroad by unattractive diversion, and his extrications were no different than those of other men. He ducked a house-party in the war to spend an afternoon with two young, obscure New Zealand mechanics, down from a Canadian training field on a two-day pass, whom a newsman guided to his gate.

He said in parting, "If you write your folks you had a good time with Henry Ford, tell them he said he had a great time, too."

An Associated Press man who went to Ford's Huron Mountain Lodge found himself implicated in one of the efforts to wriggle out of an engagement distasteful to his host.

The bureau man spent a couple of interesting days and decided to return before the head office accused him of making a holiday of his work.

"You couldn't go back tomorrow instead of today?" asked the world's wealthiest citizen, anxiously. "Wish you could?"

In a sheepish burst of confidence he said that there were a lot of women coming to the lodge that afternoon but he had pleaded to Mrs. Ford he could not possibly be around to meet them because he had an important appointment with his newspaper friend. The newsman stayed over a day.

But when Ford wanted something very much for his wife he was hard to put off. They visited an English castle which had become a national monument and were delighted by some of its furnishings. Mrs. Ford was especially enamored of a piece of porcelain.

"This, Henry," she said, lingering over it and picturing it in her own home, "I would like to own."

Ford was undaunted by the fact the porcelain was part of the national treasure. It was enough that Callie wanted it and that her birthday was only a few weeks off. Very well, he would not say anything to her but he'd get it. He hunted up Sir Percival Perry, his

English representative, and told of Mrs. Ford's desire. He said he wanted her to have it.

"You buy it for me," he said coolly. He would have asked for the Kohinoor in the Tower of London with the same casualness.

The blanching Perry was thoroughly indoctrinated in what could and couldn't be done in the kingdom, or considered that he was.

"Mr. Ford," he said, hesitatingly, "there really are things which are considered sacred in England and cannot be bought." He said this was particularly true of museum pieces.

Ford dismissed it as probably propaganda kept alive by Crown or Commons. Had not his son found a few grandees not ashamed to turn an honest pound? Edsel obtained a lovely staircase from Lyveden Hall in Northhamptonshire, a pine panel from Spitalfields, and for his dining room some eighteenth century paneling from the Clock House in Upminster. The senior Ford guessed he could have a little bowl for his wife. He often said himself he would sell anything he owned but Mrs. Ford and the plant.

"I know few things money won't buy," he said. "You will find you can get that porcelain."

Sir Percival winced. His face was redder several days later. He discovered he was able to buy the porcelain and reported the fact with some chagrin. It was not true that some of this treasure could not be bought—or the British government made an exception in Ford's case in return for his gifts to the empire's economy. Mrs. Ford had a happy birthday—Fair Lane a new and desirable decoration.

The only adjective continuously true of him was "unpredictable," although he also said consistency was a hobgoblin of little minds, even if his respected Ralph Waldo Emerson said it first.

The late Albert Kahn, distinguished American architect, asked if I would come to see him in the Twenties. One of his major clients was Henry Ford and the relationship was of long and cordial standing. Kahn gave credit to Ford for a great number of major improvements in industrial building design. The conception of an entire plant under one roof with no open courts or division walls was his. Ford also was first to use steel sash.

The architect told me that he had met that morning with Soviet engineers and Amtorg representatives and signed a contract to make plans and supervise construction of a series of manufacturing buildings on the American model at the mouth of the Volga. The initial contract was for a $4,000,000 tractor plant. The total work probably would run into several hundred millions. In all Kahn and his staff were to build more than 500 buildings for the Soviet.

I knew Kahn well and asked what he thought Ford would say. His eyes twinkled.

"You tell me," he said. He promised to let me know what happened.

Ford telephoned next morning when the story was published and asked if the architect could come to Dearborn. I thought it wise to be on hand also for any possible repercussions. The United States had not recognized Russia. Moneyed people in the country were in the main unfriendly if not hostile. Ford might take the same line.

"Glad to hear of your new business, Albert," he said. "We'll give you every help we can."

He bustled about his car loading bags for a motor trip.

"You tell those fellows," he said, "they can have our patterns, models, anything they want and we'll send some fellows to Russia to show them how to make cars." He said he'd take 500 Russian engineers into his own plant, if the Soviet wished, and let them see close up how the place was run.

Ford had pushed the apple-cart over on one wheel again. He said prosperity for any country meant more prosperity for all. Kahn went to Russia and although born there, thought the Russians slightly nuts. They demanded extra heavy foundations and extra steel in the construction because they said it got awfully cold there. He said the lighter construction would not be affected no matter how cold it was but they had their way. Even then they were thinking in terms of war.

Kahn need not have worried, if he did, over what Ford might do. Several years before, Ford representatives in Denmark had contracted with Russia for delivery of 18,000 cars a year, and the same year Ford announced shipment of 900 tractors to the Soviet, plus extension rims, fenders and pulley attachments. As a compliment to him and for his criticism the USSR shipped him one of the first it made when its own tractor plant got going.

Yet when Samuel Crowther wrote a life of Ford in collaboration with him, the Soviet made sixty omissions and changes in their edition. It would not permit Ford to say for Russian consumption, "There are entirely too many attempts at reforming the world. Reformers and reform are nuisances. The man who calls himself a reformer wants to smash things. He would tear up a whole shirt because the button-hole did not fit, instead of enlarging the button-hole."

Blue-pencilled, also, was the paragraph:

"Russia is at work but it counts for nothing. It is not free work. In the U. S. a workman works eight hours a day—in Russia 12 to 14 hours. In America he lays off if he wants to—in Russia he goes to work whether he wants to or not."

Three easy lessons in how to deal with people who think every man has his price and who may be coming up your walk now with some such fancy offer.

CHAPTER XXII

BILLIONS

HAD A HIGH WIND blown away his last penny one never could imagine Henry Ford stepping to a window and jumping out, unable or unwilling to face a life capitalized at less than a billion dollars. It was easier to conceive of his packing his lunch box and reporting to another powerhouse to make a fresh beginning, perhaps pinning a badge on his shirt as he required other men to do for him. From nothing to a billion and back—well, maybe he could make the summit a second time.

He spoke of money disrespectfully, if at all, in imposing contrast to those who develop vertigo or whose palms grow wet at mention of profit. It could have been the surfeit of a man working on his fortieth clam or wheatcake. It might have been a pose and a prerogative of the very opulent, but the indifference was Ford's even in the early days when the landlord was not sure when he called for the rent—$16 a month for the mechanic's half of the double house—whether it would be waiting or he'd be put off for a couple of days. The indifference was equally strong in him when he refused three cash offers of a billion each in successive years for the company.

Seven words turned down the first billion, "I'd have the money but no job." His son, Edsel, waving off two similar offers, took a cue in brevity from the father and said, "What could we do with the money?" The answers are well to note. It is possible that no one ever again will have occasion to reject a billion.

Long before he became stuffy with money he had $150,000 in one bank and smaller amounts in others. He walked up to a paying teller with a check for all he had in his principal account. It was paid him and he stood about and held the bills in his hand for a moment in some surprise, as if he had half expected to catch the bank off guard and unable to respond to such a demand. He even thought the place might suspend and bolt the front door but people kept going and coming just the same.

He sat down and counted and recounted the money slowly. The total always came to $150,000, all right. He had not wanted to deposit the money in the first place. Always thought it would be better to have the cash in some kind of a safe place at the plant where he could go in and look at it and feel it every five minutes, if he wanted to, and be certain no banker was up to any hanky-panky with it. Never trusted the general run of bankers too much.

He stepped back to another teller four windows from the one who had paid him and pushed the money through the grating.

"I want to deposit this," he said. "Yes, Mr. Ford, good morning." The teller was unaware that ten minutes before the customer had drawn out the same money he was now turning in.

Ford only wanted to know the $150,000 was there. Ten minutes did not convert him to the side of bankers but it proved at least that his funds were still shipshape. Yet it was not the money itself that worried him. If the bank had not been able to pay off he would not have raged over the loss but at being outfoxed and yielding his judgment to that of those who got him to put money into the bank in the first place.

He bristled in later years when someone tried to pin him down on the exact extent of his fortune, as he was nettled when asked what would happen to the company when he was gone. To the first I remember his growling, "Damn it to all hell! I don't know or care!" To the second he responded brusquely but with less temper, "If we keep the place up someone will be able to use it."

His billion gave him power and he never was contemptuous of that. It enabled him to play the grand monarch. With it he could try the thing never done—and even that which never would be. He could be a Samaritan. He could win or lose with no emotion except as his pride might be bruised by failure.

For years Ford Motor topped Wall Street's shopping list. Rejection of staggering offers got commonplace for the man who tramped the streets with his wife the night before Christmas of 1895 and found no one willing to trust them for a chicken for their holiday dinner.

William C. Durant, promotional fireball and one-time president of General Motors, had a vision, in 1908. To begin with, he would consolidate four automobile companies. They would be the rock on which he'd build.

"Very well," said Ford, a little tempted, "our price is $3,000,000."

But if Ford got that much, Ransom E. Olds wanted the same for his company—and the Durant plan collapsed.

The determined promoter did not give up. He acquired Oakland, Cadillac and Olds and was back in a year fishing for Ford again. The telephone rang in a New York hotel room. Ford had lumbago. He had had no luck in finding a restful position on the bed and was testing the floor for comfort. Couzens, his general manager, answered the call. Durant was in the lobby and wanted to come up. Ford didn't want to see him. He did not want to talk to anyone until his backache left him.

"I'll come down," Couzens compromised. "Henry's not feeling good."

He was back in an hour. Durant wanted Ford Motor—for $8,000,000 this time.

"Tell him he can have it if the money's all cash," Ford shouted from a shaving operation in another room. "Tell him I'll throw in my lumbago."

"He's gone. He's coming back tomorrow for an answer," Couzens walked over to the bathroom door. "You want to let it go for that?"

"What do you think?"

"I'd say 'yes.'"

"If we get cash," Ford reminded.

"Cash or the answer is 'no.'"

It seemed a gold strike for both. Five years before they had been nervously debating whether $3,000 a year salary for Ford and $2,500 for Couzens would be too much to ask of the stockholders. Couzens, the ex-car checker, would come close to clearing a million on the Durant deal and he had started on $900 of his own, $100 borrowed from his sister and a note for $1500.

Ford would get between four and five millions. He'd be far better off than most inventors. Durant would inherit the headaches of the Selden patent suit brought against Ford for alleged infringement in engine design. Ford could wash his hands of worry and be the country squire. Couzens told Durant what Ford had said and the promoter flew to his bankers.

Ford Motor wasn't worth it, they decided—and recorded an all-time peak for short-sightedness. But if Ford would take some cash and the rest in stock? Ford would do nothing of the kind. It forced him into the world's most successful parlay. It was the last time he was in a mood to dicker. He got over his lumbago, won the Selden suit, the Model T caught on, and in 1914 the company had net sales over $200,000,000 and a surplus of $110,000,000.

He rejected one unique bid that year. Employees made it. Must have been radicals, everybody said, because only a few months before he had instituted his $5 minimum wage. They asked him to loan them the plant for a month so they could make cars for themselves and families. They set a reasonable maximum—one car to a family—and they said as well, "We agree to pay for all raw materials, maintain all existing departments and return the plant in even better condition than it is now."

Ford did not loan the plant. Model T's sold as fast as they popped off the assembly line. He even rebated part of the purchase price to buyers when sales topped a prescribed figure.

It was hardly the moment for the senior partner of a New York brokerage house, acting for unidentified principals, to visit Dearborn. The House of Morgan was the rumored backstage dickerer.

John W. Prentiss, of Hornblower & Weeks, was in the office of C. Harold Wills, one of Ford's top command, when Ford himself bobbed in. He got around, after a few amenities, to asking Prentiss what business he was in and what brought him to Dearborn. The visitor said he dealt in stocks and bonds.

"One of those Wall Street fellows, eh?" Ford put up a hand with palm toward Prentiss as though to ward him off. He had fixed notions about stock market rascalities.

The broker said if Ford would recapitalize the motor company for $500,000,000 his house was prepared to take all or any of the stock issue. Ford asked why he should do anything of the sort and Prentiss argued there were advantages to a free and open market.

"And some moderate distribution of stock," he added, "will not endanger your control in the slightest."

"Not for me," Ford said. He moved toward the door. "I guess we'll go along as we are, Mr. Prentiss."

Another offer of $200,000,000 for a quarter interest was made through Stuart W. Webb, New York manufacturer representing other interests in 1923, but Edsel Ford, with whom he lunched, "did not think much of the idea."

Webb was back a year later for another lunch and with a second proposal—this one designed to break down the defenses of any person in his right mind. "How would you like it if I should take a billion in cash and swap it for stock of the Ford Motor Company?" Now it was a billion for what three million could have had 16 years before. Ford still was not impressed.

"What," asked Edsel, "would we do with all the money?"

"But you have it now, Mr. Ford, except in a different form."

"We couldn't do it; we're having too much fun as it is." The junior Ford dropped the subject.

Once a hardware dealer put a $15 credit limit on Henry Ford's purchases. Now he could say a curt "no" to a billion. The last laugh seemed to be his. *Judge* had once quipped, "A fool and his flivver are soon carted," and the *Life* of Charles Dana Gibson, not Luce, had jibed, "The five-day week is in force at Ford's because it takes the sixth day to get the darned things started." Pretty comical, but the magazines, not Ford, folded.

The offer was renewed in 1926, and in 1927 the grapevine had it that now the Fords positively were thinking of recapitalization and a Detroit representative of a Manhattan banking group was instructed to see how much truth there was to the report. Model T had been abandoned. The accouchement of the new car seemed prolonged. Maybe in a disheartened mood Ford had softened and would step down.

There was nothing to it. The senior Ford had said that if he sold he'd have the money but nothing to work at. Besides he didn't have lumbago any more. He hardly needed money. A study of the wealth of the world's twenty richest men by Stuart Chase for the New York *Times* in 1927 lumped the fortunes of Henry Ford and son at $1,200,000,000 and John D. Rockefeller and son at $600,000,000. The Fords, said the *Times,* were the richest men on earth.

Others listed—and only four are alive today—were Richard B. Mellon, banking; Edward S. and Ann Harkness, oil; Sir Basil Zaharoff, munitions; the Gaekwar of Baroda, whose Indian courtyard guns were said to be gold and who possessed a single tapestry valued at a million; Payne Whitney, real estate; Thomas B. Walker, Minnesota lumberman; Duke of Westminster, owning about a third of the 2,300 acres between London's Fleet Street and Kensington, Oxford Street and the Thames; Baron H. Mitsui, Japan, shipping; Simon I. Patino, Bolivia, tin; and Alfred Loewenstein, Belgium, mines, steel and shipping, the latter dead in the English Channel in a mysterious fall from his plane a year later.

Experts sparred over the claim that the Fords were wealthiest of all. The past was explored for parallels.

What sort of man, it was asked, was this Pythias who gave $25,000,000 to Xerxes I as a token of esteem?

Had not some Lydian Croesus spent $200,000,000, at today's rates, on a propitiatory pyramid of golden brick to the Delphic Oracle and capped it with a solid gold lion?

Did not Solomon have an income of $20,000,000 a year—and no taxes to shrink it?

Cheops had pulled 100,000 men and women from the fields and used them in three-month shifts on the Great Pyramid for twenty years.

Rameses III was Exhibit A. He had $500,000,000, the space-writers said, or relatively $10,000,000,000 in buying power, if one took into account the cost of living and materials today and 3,000 years ago when a fat ox brought only a dollar, wheat was 12 cents a bushel and 12 to 20 cents was a day's wage.

The researchers dug up lesser prototypes—the Medicis and Fuggers, Cleopatra and the Queen of Sheba, Herodotus and Plutarch—and thought that some of these might not have been so very far behind the Fords.

Ford understood quite well that he was rich and that there had been rich men before him, but was disinterested in all the speculation about his money and theirs. Once walking along the River Rouge with him I got out a newspaper clipping in which his probable financial standing was set down against that of early ancients.

"Know what would make a better article?" he asked when I had read a few of the more pertinent paragraphs.

I asked what would improve the newspaper story.

"A comparison of the life of an automobile worker at $7 a day and a fellow on the Pyramids at 10 cents," he said. He had another thought. "I wonder," he chuckled, "if Cheops could stand up to me in a 50-yard dash?" Was Rameses good at pitching hay? Could those ancients read blueprints? Ford looked off to the orchard. "I'd like to have Solomon here now and see if he could chin himself on one of those trees." He thought he could beat Solomon's pants off at the exercise.

"Could Cleopatra polka?" I tried to play up to his mood.

He looked interested. "Do you suppose she could?"

"How would I know?"

"Yes, that's right; how would you? Well, she probably couldn't hold a candle to Mrs. Ford." We moved up the bank and over to a field where a half dozen reapers were starting on the wheat. The tops shone golden and Ford's eyes traveled satisfiedly down them.

"You'd never think food would ever look so slick, would you?" he said, pressing against the fence. The lady of the asp and her probable clumsiness at the polka had been instantly wiped out of mind at sight of the ripened grain.

The public turned from guessing how much money Ford had to describing some of the things he could do with it if he took it into his head. The old New York *Evening World* printed an unguaranteed list of possibilities in the Twenties:

He could buy absolute control of General Motors and U. S. Steel, and have enough left to buy New York Central.

He could buy the gold reserve of the twelve federal banks against their outstanding bank notes and still have a balance of $350,000,000.

He could acquire the wheat, oats, potato and tobacco crops of the United States in 1925.

He could pay for the total imports of Canada in 1926.

Three per cent on his capital, if he was able to get such a return, would give him an annual income of $36,000,000.

But Henry Ford's principal purchase was almost complete independence to do as he liked, and there are many proofs of his disaffection for pomp and custom and riches and games of men who amassed fortunes before him. There was so much proof of his disdain for ceremony that critics came in time to ask if the amplitude of evidence was not in itself a sign of ostentation and if the role of shrinking homespun citizen was not a carefully planned way to mellow a public to an indubitable autocrat.

On a war visit of the Duke of Windsor and Lord Halifax an office boy upset a tray of mail a few yards from where the guests were talking. Ford got to his knees and helped pick the letters up. The Duke and the ambassador waited without hint that this might breach the usual protocol. Edward even recaptured a couple of letters which fell his way. The mail back in the receptacle, the host got to his feet and without comment resumed the conversation where he had left off.

President Harding once let him out a basement door of the White House so he might escape interviewers. When he was asked to dinner by the Franklin Roosevelts to meet England's king and queen in 1939, he said he could not make it—Mrs. Ford was having a meeting of her garden club at the house that day!

In England he bought a Rolls to tour but the elegance drew attention to him and his wife, and Mrs. Ford authored what may or may not have been her only Ford joke.

"Next time we come we'll travel in a Ford car and no one will notice us," she told him when the tenth levée of villagers had dissolved.

A child was killed by one of his trucks on a town-line road feeding into an expressway from Detroit to the Willow Run bomber plant, during World War II. The death shocked him. He telephoned the county road engineers. Where the accident occurred, the highway jogged and the child had not seen the oncoming car until too late.

Couldn't the road be straightened so that children attending the new school he had built could have a clear view of traffic? Several crooks in it would have to go. The commission would look at it right away.

"I'm a little tired," Ford announced to his own deputy and the highway engineer when they joined up at the scene. He was in his late seventies. "I'll wait here while you see what can be done." He threw himself on the grass and the others went up and down the road to estimate the necessary changes.

Upon their return they found Ford had taken off his coat and shoes and was on his back between two trees, his stockinged feet pressed against the trunk of one about a couple of feet up from the base and his head cushioned against the second.

"This," he remarked, "is an awfully comfortable position. Why don't you fellows try it for a few minutes?"

The two companions found birches in similar juxtaposition, took off their coats and shoes and obligingly copied Ford's relaxed position. Yes, it was a good way to stretch out, they conceded. "Well, what can be done about the road?" asked Ford from the comfort of his leafy couch.

The recumbent conference seemed to set a new mark in informality. It was decided right there in "the awfully comfortable position" that it would be easy to uncurl the road and reduce future trouble. The conferees, that settled, put their respective dignities and shoes back on and adjourned *sine die*.

> Paris, Aug. 26, (1933)—Sixteen men alive today could lump their fortunes and pay the debts of the world. In a special number of Paris *Vu,* Richard Lewinsohn presents the list as follows, ranking them in order of wealth:
>
> Edsel Ford, Henry Ford, Baron Edward G. Rothschild, Duke of Westminster, former Kaiser Wilhelm of Germany, Gaekwar of Baroda, Basil Zaharoff, Simon I. Patino, Ruppert Guinness, Ireland, second Earl of Iveagh and manufacturer of Guinness Stout; Aga Khan III, Georges de Wendell, French industrialist; John D. Rockefeller Senior and Junior, Louis Louis-Dreyfus, French industrialist; Andrew Mellon, and Fritz Thyssen, Germany.

Ford played the billionaire in line with expectation at times and seemed to be fouling up the part at others, but the uneven performance should have surprised no one. No standard script existed. Being the first supposedly to amass such money, he had to write his lines as he went along. There were no precedents, no listed cues and stage business by which he could govern his actions and feel he was enacting Dives in historic tradition.

If it had been Hamlet, he would have had Gielgud and Maurice Evans to consult, Sothern and Barrymore and Forbes-Robertson to study. If it had been a matter at court, any law library would have told him how a judge had once ruled in such a case as his, but being Billionaire No. 1 there was nothing to do but go it alone, playing some scenes in the grand manner and muffing his lines in others.

All he had to go by was a record of poorer contemporaries, unattractive to him. The Vanderbilts had sailed a hundred yachts. An Astor wore a dog collar of pearls with diamond pendant attachment, a stomacher of diamonds, a massive tiara and the royal purple of a French queen to her annual ball. Henry Frick, steel tycoon, favored Titians. Madame Rejane had acted at Sherry's amid 3,000 white roses for a multimillionaire's well chosen guests.

So-and-so took unto himself a beloved wife, his sixth; William K. Vanderbilt's silks were up at Longchamps; Mrs. Horace Dodge Wilson, widow of Ford's old-time partner, gave her daughter an $800,000 necklace in which Catherine of Russia had once dressed up. None of the divertissements tempted Ford. None of these people seemed to be going his way.

The golden age at Newport ended with a dinner on horseback. The favorite steed fed upon flowers, and champagne and cigarettes were wrapped in $100 bills. Ford preferred the lunch the wife of his friend, Tom Edison, packed and which he ate coming home in the car through the Delaware Water Gap.

J. Pierpont Morgan passed the plate at St. George's; young Rockefeller taught a Bible Class at the Fifth Avenue Baptist, but Ford had no wish to do either. It is doubtful if he understood the broader relaxations of Morgan. He was more partial to the junior Rockefeller saying to a classmate at Brown, "Old man, don't you think you're smoking too much?" or to a member of the Bible Class, "Self-help is the only thing in the world."

Astronomical fun, Ford style, was to buy an old and shabby grist mill—some fossil eligible as a set for an O'Neill play. A quick operation would be performed. He would tidy it until not a speck or leaky vent was left. He would build a power-house just as immaculate. A pond would be dredged or created and a fine new dam put in to contain its water. Last would be the omnipresent water-wheel.

In one hamlet the work on such a plaything had been apparently completed when he thought of the good miller and of the fact there was no accommodation for him. Now where would he live?

"How about that house over there?" A villager pointed to a frame place on a nearby hillside.

Ford looked askance. It was a dwelling of recent vintage and his mill was of another century.

"It won't do," he said, determinedly.

He spent the next day roaming the roundabout country and at sundown had the answer. Only two miles away he had come upon a house of the right period, so within the week it was on skids, and tractors dragged it across the fields, sections of fence being set aside to give it a clear right of way.

It was placed by the site of the mill, and there the miller should have lived happily ever after, as many millers did in such Ford-created harmony, for a maintenance crew went to work upon it and gave it white paint and green shutters and a picket fence and fine inner habiliments. Ford wanted no mill on canvas, no matter if Raphael did it—no painted cow in a painted meadow, when he could look out an upstairs window, as he said, and see a live one.

But the Japs dived on the Pacific Fleet and Hickam Field and Ford turned from consideration of millers in correct surroundings to airplane engines, and the miller's trim house went tenantless and, eventually, on the block when the war ended.

> *Commerce and Finance,* American magazine, named in 1934 the following as the ten richest men in the world: Edsel Ford, Baron Rothschild, Duke of Westminster, ex-Kaiser Wilhelm, Gaekwar of Baroda, Zaharoff, Patino, Lord Guinness, Aga Khan III and his Exalted Highness, 60-year-old Sir Mis Osman Ali Khan, principal Moslem ruler of India.

Because he forgot to open mail, his first secretary was hired. A secretary could only slit the envelopes and could not insist on his boss reading what was in them. Ford continued to cram mail into his pockets. The secretary was a step forward, but a crumpled $85,000 check tumbled out of Ford's work suit one day when he was looking for a piece of blue crayon, and the story is that a valet came upon another tattered slip for $125,000 in a suit being sent to the cleaners. Neither time was Ford more than mildly interested.

"What's it matter whether it's in my pocket or a bank?" he was supposed to have said. "It's still our money, isn't it?" Nothing but silly book-keeping, he thought.

An incident in the early relationship of Ford and his chief engineer, William B. Mayo, seemed to bear on this reputed unconcern over money. Mayo, who was to enjoy unique freedom under Ford, worked in those days for an Ohio firm. When an assistant failed to get a bite on a visit to Highland Park, the engineer stuffed his bag and made for the battlements himself to sell the motormaker a power-house installation for which Ford was reported in the market.

He and Ford got along splendidly and they were so companionable that days elapsed before Mayo managed to squeeze in a word about the purpose of his visit. Mayo was in love with the magnificent experiments Ford was making; Ford was delighted to find someone who clearly spoke his language. But as for the power-house—"Forget it; I don't want to talk about it right now," said Ford. He said to come back next week.

This went on for six months. Then without preface Ford said Mayo could go ahead with the power plant.

"Will you have the contract written up?" the engineer suggested.

Ford said for him to write one. Mayo did. Ford said it was too long. The engineer boiled it. Ford said there was still too much wordage. "We don't need all that between us, do we?" he protested. Mayo got the third draft down to acceptable shortness. Ford signed without reading it.

Mayo protested, "Don't you want to see what it's going to cost you?"

"Would you sign it if you were me?" asked Ford.

The engineer thought he would if the same proposition was put up to him.

"That's good enough," Ford said. He didn't ask the cost.

When Mayo went to work for Ford, he was told to draw up a contract that suited him. It was a unique agreement in one respect and gave Mayo greater independence than any other man in Ford service. He was an exception to the general rule among Ford executives: he was a made man when he joined the organization; the company did not make him. He reserved the right in his contract to continue as a director of several companies with which he was then connected. Ford signed the agreement again without reading it and Mayo got the same answer as before when he inquired if Ford did not want to know the terms.

"Would you sign if you were in my shoes?" the motormaker asked.

Mayo said he thought the contract a good one both ways.

Ford finished the signing and put down the pen. "Now you're working for us," he said.

He horrified the banking district by saying that saving was an overpraised virtue—just at a time when some institution was offering college scholarships for essays on thrift.

"No successful boy saves money—money is just a tool—bank accounts give boys a wrong idea of how to get ahead—buy an old engine, take it apart, learn how the wheels mesh and work—buy a book, read a writer's conception of things and put your own thinking on top of his . . ."

The son of Ford's tire-making camping crony, the late Harvey S. Firestone, boasted as a boy to Mr. Ford of a small sum he had saved.

"That's hind end to." Ford sat down and told the heir to the rubber millions how the thing to do was just the opposite of what he was doing. "Spend it for tools and make something—create something." Boys and girls who learned to spend money would be the ones to make a better world. He used Thomas Edison as Exhibit A. The inventor, he said, never had any money until he got so much he could not spend it all.

Of course Mr. Ford confused one a little by this accent on spending and de-emphasis on saving. When he put in his $5 wage minimum, an employee had to save regularly to draw full benefits under the plan, and in 1920 he instituted a workers' saving plan. It had a high of 32,000 depositors and the company paid some $20,000,000 in interest during the life of the program. Left the entire period, $100 got an employee $219.50 in interest alone as against $65 at usual bank rates.

Edwin C. Hill, in *Scribner's* Magazine (1937) submitted a list of the world's richest men in which the Fords were ranked seventeenth. First was the Nizam of Hyderabad, second Aga Khan III, and third the Bolivian Patino. Fifth and sixth were Georges de Wendell and Louis Louis-Dreyfus.

The steward of his yacht *Sialia* quarreled with him in vain about making his own bed. During his cruises, Ford disappeared on shipboard as he vanished from his office in the plant. He would slip into any one of several cabins and since there were many he was fairly sure of not being disturbed unless there was good reason. After his daily mid-morning or mid-afternoon nap he fixed the rumpled linen himself and straightened the room generally.

The steward took him to task several times for this domesticity but it did no good. "That is what you have a staff for," he'd say to Ford with his best officer-to-owner tact.

"I can make a bed and tidy up a place as well as any of them," was all the steward got. Ford continued to smarten up staterooms after he used them.

There was nothing orgiastic about life aboard. They poured tea at parties, not cocktails, although bumboats at Havana had a way of getting rum to sailors in harbor. He did not like the yacht much—too much confinement in walking only around the deck or port to starboard rail. He got most fun in a chair in a passageway from pantry to dining room. One entire side was glass and he could look down on a radiant engine room.

Mr. and Mrs. Ford would see a deserted beach which promised sea shells and quietude. The yacht would move inshore, drop a small boat and it would take the couple through the breakers. The launch would turn about and go back; the yacht would stand to while the Fords rested contentedly in their isolation or explored the sands for shells. There was nothing especially giddy about it, but the effect was the same as daiquiris on other yachtsmen.

He was never able to overcome the handicap of a tattling radio. If the yacht was coming into port it was necessary, of course, to ask ahead for a place to berth and, invariably, the recipient of the message would notify the town that Henry Ford was docking. The *Sialia* would come in to crowded piers; in one case the port declared a half holiday.

He complained of the *Sialia* growling, sawed it in two, and a lot of things happened. Marine engineers advised against the operation and said the cut would spoil the boat but Ford had it sliced in two, a twenty-foot bay added and an ethyl engine installed. The boat cost $500,000, and more than that to lengthen it, but it strained the ship's caulking so badly there were leaks later all over the place.

The bill for the bay, the removal of the steam turbines and installation of new motors cost a million, according to its ex-Captain Walter McLean, and on the test run the *Sialia* was slightly slower than her original sixteen knots. A Model T could go four times as fast.

In tearing out the galley he decided to replace an old stove with a modern electric range and it was thrown out and tossed on the dock. The plan was upset by an incident aboard the flagship of his merchant fleet while the yacht was in drydock. Ford, sailing on the freighter, ordered cocoa for his grandchildren one morning and after a long wait, demanded to know what kind of service he was getting.

"With electricity it takes longer to heat, Mr. Ford, you know," the steward reminded him. He had forgotten that. The day he got back to Detroit he hustled to the shipyards where the *Sialia* was being worked on and asked for the old stove. Thinking it was to be junked, the shipyard workers had pretty much demolished the stove in wrenching it loose.

"Forget about the electric range," said Ford. "Send this stove back to the Rouge and tell them to rebuild it. I'm going to put it back in the boat."

The range came back remade in ten days but the Ford miracle-workers had not been able to get Humpty-Dumpty together again with the original pieces. They practically had to make a new stove except for the oven doors and original lids, but it would bring cocoa to a boil fast—and that's what he wanted when the grandchildren asked for cocoa on the yacht.

He did not have much fun out of the *Sialia* (Indian for bluebird). He was not a good sailor and the confinement of a small deck was not to his liking. He really needed the promenade decks of several Normandies pasted together to be happy. The ship was Mrs. Ford's entertainment more than his. In the Gulf on a return trip from Cuba he really had it in a hurricane, for the *Sialia* was none too easy riding.

Ordinarily, he spent most of his time reading in the sunroom or being read to, napping, watching the engines or playing an electric phonograph. Mrs. Ford kept her housekeeping eye on spots of spray on the sunroom glass and the panes had to be gone over twice or three times daily. The music room was seldom used and there was no fishing gear aboard. Just as he learned of scallops on his yacht, he also saw his first porpoise on a run to Havana. He was at dinner when he caught sight of them tumbling, and carrying his napkin with him he ran to the rail cheering and waving his handkerchief in the direction of the porpoises.

He had his moods at sea, too. Coming north he swung in once at Boco Grande on the Florida Coast. Customs and immigration officials were on duty but the medical examiner was missing and Ford was informed that until he could get medical clearance he could not go ashore. This meant staying another restless night on the ship and Ford was in a dudgeon. After two hours of fruitless waiting, he radioed the White House and asked the removal of the medical examiner.

But his early ire was forgotten an hour later as music curled up from the forecastle. He quietly sat down on the top step of the ladder leading below decks, and the steward found him there.

"Don't tell the boys I'm here," Ford whispered conspiratorially.

The steward sat on a chest near him and the two listened to a sailor with a saxophone and another with an harmonica play and sing a sweet and ribald program. Ford said that when he got back to Detroit he was going to get that deck-hand over to his dance floor and "if he had some real music in him we'll get it out of him."

The sailor with the saxophone appeared at Dearborn by royal command several weeks later and gave a two-hour performance for Ford in the laboratory. Technicians outside the canvas wall, accustomed to novelty, never batted an eye as the note of a saxophone rose above the plant noises.

The press of crowds wore him down. Many a huckster of Dearborn would come upon Ford inspecting a bush that needed attention or stepping out lightly for an early-morning bracer alone and before the house staff was up.

More than most tourists he knew newsboys and lamplighters, homegoing charwomen and milkmen on the Continent without their knowing him, for to be alone and unbothered he would get up at dawn and stroll out into the awakening streets to window-shop. Once he found himself drawn by the odors of baking into a Paris *boulangerie* and watched for a half hour a surprised baker at his tarts and *croissants.*

In Oberammergau he routed the late Anton Lang, Christus of the "Passion Play," out of bed so they could wander unmolested in the fields on the edge of town and see a new sun come over the highlands and out upon the Ammer valley.

I was walking with the Christus a few years later and he remembered Ford well.

"He was an early riser." The eyes of the Christus twinkled. "He will always be young," he said on second thought.

When Ford left the Bavarian village, he told Lang to visit his company branch in Munich and pick out any automobile he wanted for himself in remembrance of the good time they had had together.

Right over there it was: Anton pointed to a sedan with Bavarian plates and a man beside it who looked singularly like pictures of St. Peter. The man beside the car had played the apostle in the "Passion Play." He and one who had been Judas had borrowed the car the day before to go to Mittenwald, and apparently were just back.

Peter was waiting now, a little depressed, beside the car for Anton.

"Grüss Gott," said Peter.

"Grüss Gott," said Anton. "Did all go well?"

The actor-apostle stared at a tire of the car.

"We had a blowout near Garmisch," he reported. "Lucky we had a spare." He was reproachful, though. "You had let the pressure in the extra tire get down to 15 pounds, Anton," he said.

The Christus and St. Peter, except for the *"Grüss Gott,"* might have been two men talking of road trouble in Ford's Dearborn, U.S.A.

Paris alerted all *dépôts sûreté* between the city and the Channel one year when Ford dropped out of a party on the way up from Havre and did not reappear until long after schedule.

In a field outside Rouen he espied a piece of antique farm machinery such as he never had known before. For the next two hours he examined closely the way it worked and tried, without any French, to get information from a peasant who knew no English and had no idea what the foreigner was so gabby about. Ford wanted to buy it but he finally gave up when he drew a continuous blank and went on, defeated, to the Crillon.

The game of estimating Ford wealth, infeasible as it was, remained popular. Periodically appeared an article couched in tones which suggested that its composer had completed a world trek and had been privileged to peek into the bank books of the financial plutocracy.

It was whispered in 1940 that Ford was no longer at the top of the league. He had abdicated, it was said, to the Nizam of Hyderabad definitely—a name mentioned only casually in earlier forms which showed how millionaires were running. The Prince had been listed only tenth in the 30's but had seemingly hit a phenomenal jackpot, although his state finances were once described carefully by the *Encyclopædia Britannica* as "unhealthy."

A 1940 list prepared by a writer for Hearst did not explain what had become of the $1,200,000,000 accredited to Ford in the *Times* of 1927. It simply gave the palm to the lucky Nizam at an even billion dollars. Next:

Aga Khan III	$800,000,000
Simon I. Patino	700,000,000
John D. Rockefeller, jr.	700,000,000
Henry Ford	500,000,000
Duke of Westminster	400,000,000

Presumably the most authoritative index of Ford family wealth was made public the same year by the Securities and Exchange Commission. It revealed that thirteen American families, headed by Ford, controlled $2,700,574,000 worth of securities in 200 of the nation's leading corporations.

The report submitted to a Monopoly Investigating Committee declared the Ford family had a $624,975,000 stake in the sprawling motor empire, and graded other dynasties in this order:

Dupont, chemicals	$573,690,000
Rockefeller, oil	396,583,000
Mellon, banking, aluminum	390,943,000
McCormick, harvester	110,000,000
Hartford, A. & P.	105,000,000

As a gauge of total wealth the SEC figures were short of perfect. The study was limited to corporate holdings and to the top twenty stockholders in each corporation. Thus, if the Rockefellers, for instance, owning 25,000 shares of I. T. & T., ranked twenty-first among the shareholders, the value of their interest was not contained in the government tabulation.

When a correspondent of the Associated Press traveled out from Bombay in 1944, the Nizam was still going doubly strong. The roving writer was appropriately stunned by a throne in such technicolor and a man upon it who, like Ford, did not play the part the way of mad Ludwig.

By stick-to-it-iveness and cutting corners and apparently a lucky flyer, the Moslem ruler had added vast bays in four years to an already transcendent fortune, making two billion grow where only one had bloomed before.

"The Nizam of Hyderabad," all AP subscribers were advised by prompt cable, "is known as the richest man in the world, but he wears shabby clothes, rides from palace to palace in an old car and watches his rupees carefully. The bookkeeperish monarch has been absolute ruler for 35 years of 16,000,000 persons in an Indian state about the size of France. Estimates of his wealth range up to two billion dollars."

The large total of Mr. Ford's fun, his bedmaking and shell hunting, the enthusiasm for foot-races, and the climbing to locomotive cabs to ride the engineer's seat, a certain shyness and desire for solitude and remarks on money's inconsequence seemed to make him one, in homespun simplicity, with the poorly clad Nizam in his unpretentious car.

He quoted McGuffey. He played on a fiddle as Thomas Jefferson did. He danced the polka and preferred a Corliss engine to any foal of Man o' War, a turning water-wheel to rubies. At seventy he read Jiggs and skated on the pond in front of the laboratory. He resuscitated the school house of Mary and her lamb, built a village and Edison Museum, and favored children's voices raised in chapel to the most robustious Caruso.

These were his race horses, his figured goblets, his diamond stomacher and gallery of Ghirlandaios and, while each enterprise might be trumpeted as a gift to the commonweal, they were basically Ford's way of amusing himself. He took little warm-ups and long runs at many avocations—and on each he spent without parsimony.

When he was building his home and the press whooped it up as a $2,000,000 blend of Versailles and Sans Souci, he told his architect to figure on $250,000, or about half what he originally meant to spend. When his son was about to build a home, it was falsely reported that a moat would surround it. The word "moat" seeming to have an aristocratic connotation, a denial was issued that any such feudalistic throwback was in anyone's mind.

When the senior Ford put a new washer on a leaky faucet himself or took care of most of the mechanical repairs when the annual camping party was rolling, it was not the sign of the democrat so much as an enthusiasm for working with his hands. He arrived at his upstate farm one day to find an old-fashioned threshing rig broken and an irritated manager waiting for a repairman to come out from town.

"I know something about these engines," said Ford, shedding his coat. "Let's you and I tackle it." He got off his coat, got under the machine, ripped off the balking ejector and soon had the rig running.

But Mr. Ford, standing or prone beneath a thresher, was still the exacting and mercurial grand duke. He owned no elaborate townhouse because he did not like towns but he, like the Nizam, could drive from one sumptuous house to another—the place in Florida, the 7,000-acre plantation in Georgia, the inn in Massachusetts. There was an establishment outside London, the quondam manor house of four Lord Kenyons; a place one time in Jersey, the estate in Dearborn. He bought so many farms in Michigan one was seldom out of sight of his holdings. He collected them—and lakes, forests, mills—as another might stamps or mustache cups. He was no monastic figure partial to humble lean-to, and the fact should be stated not because anyone expected him to be but because many thought he was. His protestations of indifference to money were ringed with fine exhibits of what he could do with it.

The business of having no small change on him and having to borrow a dime or a dollar now and then became almost a standard act. After a while one began to suspect this was not *ad libbing* but part of a well planned script, especially written for reporters.

If he'd had a pocketful of small coins there would have been no news, but a busted billionaire borrowing a nickel always was clean publishable fun. The country smiled. It felt one with him in what must have been a pretty embarrassing moment, as he fumbled. When he forgot to pay a hotel or restaurant bill, no one pursued him down the street or posted him as a dead-beat; a boniface of any brains ran businesslike, instead, to his publicity department. Ford, unable to muster a quick dime or dollar, made a three-column cut; walking out absentmindedly on a hotel bill was good for a waggish note in any column.

Under Henry Ford's inkwell was a constant $200. It was checked each morning before he arrived, and if any had been removed the previous day the difference was made up so there always would be that amount to draw on. A few feet away was his private vault and there was $1,744,500 to the penny in it when its custodian was fired and as his last act checked the contents with the records. Twenty years before the jocular Henry said he was glad to get three dollars I paid him for golf balls—said he had come away from home without a cent on him. It pleased me to find he was all fixed in 1944 against the day he would ever be so remiss again.

Predicted battle of the century is a wet firecracker when Ford, capitulating, says yes to everything including demands made only for trading purposes.

CHAPTER XXIII

LABOR DEALS ITSELF IN

Because we thought ourself thy lawful king:
And if we be, how dare thy joints forget
To pay their awful duty to our presence?
If we be not, show us the hand of God
That hath dismiss'd us from our stewardship.

—*Richard II.*

HENRY FORD refused to acknowledge there could be two points of view with merit to each. Men who differed with him were wrong and if something did not agree with what he thought it wasn't true. He had a serene, imperial confidence in his judgment and except in rare instances complete distrust of the views of others. In this he did not consider himself bullheaded but rather Messianic, his wisdom confirmed by what he had done and become and what was said of him, but in his last battle the crystal ball cracked and betrayed him. He thought trade unionism a phenomenon that would pass. The drums would die out.

He was gradually sold on the idea there were little groups misleading the general run of workers. He did not believe what men said on the outside was representative of what his employees thought, and some men fed and fattened his belief, because they believed so, too, or because that was the way he thought.

When Chevrolet sales jumped ahead of his the figures had been doctored. Polls and surveys which did not bear out his conclusions were faked. By a somewhat specious reasoning he decided that actually his competitors were responsible for his troubles. When General Motors and Chrysler made peace with organized labor it was a trick to put him in a hole. Well, he was not afraid of the trackless forest or of walking alone in it. He'd go on as he had. But when he did surrender he went all out, granted a union shop and check-off, or more than they, and he smirked as he looked cross-town at his rivals' roofs. Out of defeat he would salvage a meed of triumph. His generosity put them in a boat, didn't it, and now the union would go away from his place and over to theirs to nag for a matching liberalization?

He was plaguey as a boy and always under foot, as his Aunt Ella said herself, and "plaguey" he was. She used the word when he sent a photographer to take her picture at eighty-three and told him to hang around until he got it, and at Christmas he delivered twenty-five prints in person. "What in the world, Henry, am I going to do with that many pictures of myself?" And in a second breath: "You're still a plaguey boy." When she died there were still twenty pictures of her in the trunk undistributed. Long before and after she was gone he was plaguey to Walter P. Chrysler and Alfred P. Sloan.

If his competitors had treated their employees as well as he had his he believed the black cloud of strikes and sit-downs and slow-ups would never have blown up. Backward management had asked for trouble by failure to subscribe to his principles.

No one was more crestfallen than he, therefore, when 97.3 per cent of his River Rouge workers in a National Labor Relations Board election in 1941 stated a preference for union representation despite his averments, neither true, that his men were not sold on unionism and were not interested because they knew there was no sense in paying dues to get out of him what he was perfectly willing to give.

His words were: "The union says: 'There are 100,000 jobs at Ford's. If you want one, you must pay us a registration fee and so much every month, and we will pass you in and you will work as long as you pay us.'" He always had thought of labor in terms of obedience. I remember his saying long ago: "I have a thousand men who, if I say, 'Be at the northeast corner of the building at 4 o'clock,' will be there at 4 o'clock. That's what we want—obedience."

His views were disavowed in the government booths. Notice

was served that his men would be at the corner of the building at 4—only conditionally. The vote was a conclusive 72,230 for a union and only 1,958 against. It exposed for the bosh it was the constant reiteration that of course any Ford worker who wished to belong to a union was free to do so, whereas the odds were that the new brother, and particularly if he were an eager beaver, would last on the job only until the plant police heard the news and got him out of the place before he defiled others. The new unionist could also be transferred to a job so unpleasant he'd prefer to quit, thus relieving the company of any suspicion that he had been discriminated against for union enthusiasms.

The complete belief of the senior Ford in the perfection of his system was such that had he been still alive at the time, he probably would have been equally set back, as he was by the NLRB vote, by a letter transmitted by Henry Ford II, his grandson, appealing to 3800 striking company foremen in 1947 to return to their jobs. One paragraph was particular proof of reversed philosophy.

"I agree with those of you who have expressed the opinion that the Foremen's Association grew out of past injustices and the failures of past management, but we are trying hard to make things different around here."

The mettlesome dean of global mass production might have been piqued to know he had left rubble around and to hear his eldest grandson admit publicly he had found it, was sorry it was there and was trying his best to clean it up. The grandson had no trouble discovering what his grandfather said wasn't there. A thousand firings and "resignations" and retirements were proof of more than a young enthusiast's fancy for new faces.

It was not unnatural that the padishah of Dearborn regarded union labor an unworthy trespassing force. So that no one could cross him he gave his minority stockholders some $100,000,000 in 1919 for their holdings. Having paid so handsomely to disengage himself from interference in that quarter, it was hardly to be expected he would let down the bars voluntarily to any second filibusterous group, armed with graphs, wage tables, cost of living figures and other such modern luggage certainly strange to a Ford who wouldn't have even an organizational chart in the place. These new intruders boldly said in advance if they ever got in they would want more money and improved shop conditions, two matters on which he believed his record unassailable.

He had no intention of making such a forfeit without a struggle. He had dumped by purchase the shareholders who told him or might have wanted to tell him what to do; he eliminated by firing executives who expressed some doubt at times of what he proposed. He got rid of William S. Knudsen, brilliant production man and later president of General Motors, and later said blithely, "I'd rather argue with him outside the company than in it." Ford went on prospering without them, which to him was the proof of the pudding.

For a time he thought the marching men might not turn down his street. They would go straight past and let him alone. They must recognize and appreciate that his orchestra never would play as sweetly for a mess of shop stewards as when led by the proven top-most conductor. Certainly there could be no more than one baton going at a time. He knew what was to the worker's advantage. Papa knew best. If there was a better way to run his place than the way he did, or any machine to lessen backache, his men knew they could rely on him to change methods sooner and improve machinery faster than could any mouthy agitator waving handbills at the gate.

Why should they think otherwise? Had not a whole body of favorable literature grown in praise of his philosophy of good pay, short hours and low prices? He was on their side, wasn't he? Go to the record! Hadn't he summed up this whole question of high wages in a few crisp sentences?

"The progress of this country was not accomplished by impoverishing workmen. What good is a man who just makes a living—he isn't a market for anything. When a man has only enough to buy bread he is a poor member of society and the worst kind of a customer."

His head was always stuck through the hole in the canvas for anyone to toss a ball at. When he opened his stand, and for years after, he was a favorite target of the wellfed, those who wanted to run the economy their way and who saw something disruptive in Ford's system. They had ideas about paying a worker as little and charging a customer as much as possible.

The carriage-trade changed its tune, however. Putting down the balls with which they used to pelt him, the occupants began to say even in the Twenties that perhaps he was a jolly good fellow and a fine example of the American way and that possibly he had something in his theory they were first so skittish about. The new marksmen who picked up the balls to throw at him wore overalls and spoke of speed-up and technological displacement, time studies and wage differentials and espionage and of drained men going home on street-cars hardly able to lift their eye-lids. Papers which had once made love to him printed villification; some which once looked his way fretfully and prematurely tried to measure him for quick oblivion now turned to sonnets and made his every vocal bead a pearl.

A seminarian writing in *The Christian Century* said Ford was a symbol of America which had risen almost in a generation from an agrarian to an industrialist economic order "and now applies the social intelligence of a country village to the most complex industrial life the world ever has known." Ford was undisturbed. Criticism only honed his saber.

When Henry Ford established his $5 day minimum, the well-fed men trotted out the full crew of scarecrows except one. It was impossible for them to say his plan was the impractical dream of a visionary who never had to meet a payroll.

When the motormaker introduced the five-day week, John M. Edgerton, then president of the National Association of Manufacturers, gripped his Bible with a firm hand and wailed that the Fifth Commandment had for sixty centuries been the perfect and divinely presented basis of human toil and social contentment, and most of Mr. Edgerton's members thought he put it very well.

"Ford may try to amend the Decalogue," he prattled despondently, "but any general acceptance of a five-day week means a surrender to easy and loose living."

The shortening of the week, men of Edgerton's mind shuddered, would create a craving for additional luxuries to occupy the additional time, would be against the interests of those who wished to work and advance, and mean a trend toward the arena. There was a solemn shaking of forefingers.

"Rome did that—and Rome died," said a gentleman who suddenly became sad over good old Rome and what had happened to it. The ranking officer of Westinghouse Air Brake said he felt the average worker would not like being coerced by Mr. Ford or any one else into curtailing his work hours.

The volatile Ford had raised his minimum to $6 a day in 1919 to anguished cries from the conservative benches. Maybe he did not do it for humanitarian reasons and possibly only because it seemed good business, but those who worked for him cashed their profits whichever way it was. No law forced him to give the original $5 minimum, the $6 or the later $7. Moneyed Europe quailed in 1929 when he asked the League of Nations for a survey of Continental wages and announced he had in mind a plan to pay the workers in his 20-odd factories abroad the equivalent of what he was paying in the United States. Those who owned the check-books of Europe moaned that this would be a terrible thing to do and that *le fordisme* would tip the whole economy. In Russia he was Mr. Big and his tractors beloved. Metal workers of Berlin struck against an 8 per cent cut in 1930 and Ford, in Germany at the time, promptly announced a 10 per cent increase in his Berlin assembly plant.

Herbert Hoover, in the growing panic of the stock market collapse of 1929, asked him to do something to brace public confidence and Ford walked out to the press room and announced he was returning to Detroit to raise his basic wage from $6 to $7. "You don't wait for people to create prosperity and then give them back a little of it in their own pay envelopes." The company paid the emergency dollar for 22 months at a total increased cost of $35,000,000 to the company, and dropped it only when Ford found himself virtually the only one with a finger in the dyke.

The volume of evidence of Ford's willingness to spend on wages is a record of voluntary action, however. He liked to play Santa Claus but when he put on the red suit and white beard he did so because he wanted to. He never anticipated a day when a valet in the form of a trade union would lay out the suit and beard on the bed, saying, "Henry, put these on," and then force him into them.

It was one-man rule, unquestionably. He summoned his production and cost men in 1921 and told them to set new prices that would move cars in face of a deepening depression. Then he drifted away, leaving them to figure and only putting in his head occasionally to see how things were going. At 5 P.M. they submitted the price schedule.

"Get them lower," he barked, flintily, and left them with the puzzle.

They shaved a little here and there and finally got to what they regarded irreducible bedrock. Ford again shook his head. He reached into his own pocket and pulled out a single sheet of paper on which he had pencilled some figures.

"Here, gentlemen, are the new prices!" He handed the sheet to the nearest man.

The table was in immediate pandemonium. They said it couldn't be done. They squalled the company would go broke. Ford gathered up the listed figures and made some changes—not up but in two cases down. "There they are," he said and left his brass hats in an unbecoming fit. The couldn't-be-done price slashes ushered in the greatest era of profit the company had.

Ford's self-esteem swelled naturally as he grew in the public eye and he became a one-man brain trust listening to an inner voice but no other. The only thing unshaken in the times of storm was Mr. Ford's belief in himself as paramount. It was an understandable confidence since it constantly was being pumped by witless eulogy.

He promised to address a New York group in 1938. On his way he had an unencouraging talk at the White House and by the time he reached Madison Avenue and The Ritz had changed his mind about the speech. He would not make it.

A former Detroit newspaperman in New York, Frank D. Webb, got a frantic call from an automobile editor of a Manhattan paper who had obtained Ford's promise to speak in the first place. Would Webb intercede and see if the motormaker could be talked into getting on his feet and saying something—anything?

"I'm certainly on the spot," grumbled the distrait editor, and said he was bound to catch a spanking from his boss if the curtain went up and no Ford.

The Detroiter said he would see what he could do. He agreed dubiously to talk to William Cameron, Ford's editor, who was accompanying him on the Eastern trip. Cameron listened. Yes, Mr. Ford and he were going over to the Waldorf for dinner but the boss would not talk.

"But Charlie here is right on the spot, Bill," wheedled the Detroit interventionist. Charlie agreed he definitely was and headed for a pack of trouble. "Everybody has been promised that Mr. Ford will talk. Originally he said he would. Can't you get him up on his feet for just a stickful of wisdom?"

The Ford editor said he was not so sure he could do much about it. The boss had expressed himself pretty definitely. Well, he'd see what he could do about it.

Cameron apparently won Ford's consent before he went into

the dinner for when the motormaker got to his feet co-operatively to say exactly thirty words as a favor to the automobile editor, the opening bars of his sparse speech were strangely reminiscent. They ran:

"Ladies and gentlemen: We are certainly all on the spot. (The automobile editor's plaint had stuck in Ford's head.) Stick to your guns! I will help you, with the assistance of my son, all I can. I thank you."

The words were hardly exciting, as dinner speeches go, but they were to one New York newspaper. It seemed that Mr. Ford had delivered a second Gettsyburg address. It was little wonder he became sure of his almightiness. The sponsoring journal gurgled in reporting its guest of honor:

"These thirty words pack all the wisdom and encouragement necessary. They mean: 'This is a tough country. Here's a prediction that it will beat the New Deal before the New Deal beats it.'"

The paper, happy with its paraphrase, called what Mr. Ford had said "the soul of true Americanism."

He put up only one new lightning rod not on the barns of those who otherwise thought of the labor movement as he did. *Collier's* sent Charles W. Wood to ask him in 1923 what he would do if elected President of the United States, and Ford's offering on trade unionism was:

"Unions are organized by Jewish financiers, not labor, as a scheme to interrupt work." (At the time the motormaker was riding herd against international bankers.) "They speed up loafing. A union is a neat thing for a Jew to have on hand when he comes around to get his clutches on an industry."

When he approached the crucial test with the Congress of Industrial Organizations, he discussed with F. Raymond Daniell, of the New York *Times,* another theory.

"Those movements supposed to serve the workingman," he put it to the *Times,* "are simply pulling out chestnuts of the financial interests and dividend school of business. The control high finance wants is not complete with the control of management—it must have absolute control of labor, too. It is doing its level best to get it. I think, though, that labor will prove too smart for that."

Stock-jobbers and finance, he said, were trying to raise prices and cut wages by obtaining control of labor as well as management. Did he have any objection, as an industrial principle, to labor organization?

"Most of the business men of this country come out of labor. Where else could they come from?" he asked. "I belong to 'labor.' It is all I've done all my life.

"Where does collective bargaining begin? Not with the manager and his men but between the manager and the public. He must produce an article the public will find useful and at a price the public will pay. If the quality is low or the price too high, or for any reason the public does not find it as profitable to buy as it is to sell, there is no bargain. Consequently there is no business and no wages and no field for that specialized 'collective bargaining' we hear about today.

"If the producer is successful in making an article of a quality and price that interests the public you will find he has not accomplished it by maintaining bad working conditions or low wages in his shop. If things are not right in the shop they cannot be right outside.

"Irresponsible parties undertake to force a manager to do more than he can, but if he succumbs he is on the downgrade just as if he sold his goods at half cost. There is a balance that represents progress and prosperity. Destroy it at the behest of some special interest and you are through. Some men succumb to this pressure and try to make the extra cost out of the public. The public stops buying and the business is through. There certainly is such a thing as killing the goose that lays the golden egg, but nobody has to be goose enough to let that happen to him."

He told James I. Kilgallen, a Hearst writer, at his Georgia estate that he knew positively a big industrial combination was behind the unions and its one purpose was to put him out of business, raise prices, cut wages. Asked to name the merged conspirators, he wouldn't or couldn't.

His company had had collective bargaining for 20 years, he said, and had forgotten more about it than a lot of people ever knew. He tied a set of Fordisms to each time card a few days before the decisive NLRB voting:

> A monopoly of labor in this country is just as bad as a monopoly of bread!
>
> Union organizers ask us to sit still while they sell our men the jobs that have always been free.
>
> What was the result of these strikes—merely that numbers of

> men put their neck into an iron collar. I'm only trying to show who owns the collar.
>
> I have always made a better bargain for our men than an outsider could. We have never had to bargain against our men and we don't expect to begin now.
>
> There is no mystery about the connection between corporation control and labor control. They are the two ends of the same rope. A little group of those who control both capital and labor will sit down in New York and settle prices, dividends—and wages.

"The Ford Motor Company has had its own Labor Relations Act for years, and I'd be ashamed to have anyone tell us our conditions and pay were wrong," he insisted.

If, he asked, union leaders thought they could manage an automobile factory better than he and pay better wages under better working conditions, why didn't they build a factory of their own and "show us up"?

Always The Job was the thing to Ford—the job and the speckless plant. The living of a country, he'd say, is not where men trade but where they work . . . every man can find a job either by discovering or creating it . . . the finest thing in the world is a good job. Work was a cure-all. Those who did not work as constantly or intensely as he did were lazy. He worshipped work and the machine on which it was done. He had a compulsion neurosis. He said the chances to do things were wasted for takers and that too much could never be produced because human want was limitless. He worked for play. "Let's have a Do-Your-Best Day, not a Do-Your-Most Day."

Thomas Edison unexpectedly slipped his hand into Ford's hip pocket on one of their camping holidays in the Smokies and the motor-maker looked at him in surprise.

"What are you looking for?"

"I figure you always carry a lighted bunch of firecrackers in your clothes somewhere," said the inventor. "Slow to a walk for a while, will you? I get tired of motion pictures."

The patriarch of the electric light would relax beside a stream, gazing into space; the gentleman from Dearborn would race up and down the bank, measuring the fall of water. He saw no fish in the brook or cooling shade under cooling tree but only the energy if the stream was harnessed.

James Sweinhart, a Detroit *News* veteran who enjoyed Ford's confidence, answered the telephone beside his bed at 1 o'clock one morning. If he would come to Dearborn immediately Ford said he had a story to release on some experimentation on cheap alcohol devised from vegetable waste. "Come right out to the laboratory to the Fair Lane garage." Sweinhart took a taxi to the estate. He arrived at 2.45 A.M. The laboratory was ablaze with lights. An odd engine stood on a chassis to one side of the room. Ford was at work on it—had been since mid-afternoon the previous day. He was bare to the waist, his white trousers smeared with grease and oil. He hadn't taken time out for dinner. To another side of the laboratory a chemist had been working earlier on some food concentrates and had left a quart of milk. Sweinhart and Ford took a swig out of that and got down to their business.

He sloshed through a driving storm into the plant one night in high rubber boots and coat and ordered the place closed for 48 hours for cleanup. Said he found dirt in a dozen places.

"I knew there was something wrong when he came in," an old watchman told me. "It was the first time in six years he didn't say 'Hello, Tom.' He was pretty mad."

Activity is life . . . idleness was what got the world into trouble . . . hard work in the physical sense was out of date . . . Man was better than a beast of burden . . . The fist as a hammer and the arm as a lever were no longer practical . . . it was a badly managed shop where a man did what a machine could do . . . we must lift the burden off flesh and blood. His idea of good, said one analyst, was work; his idea of life work, and undoubtedly his idea of death was something that plunged man into interminable toil.

Round and round in his head always went the same song—a full belief, despite the coronary tables and rising consumption of bicarbonate, that hard work never killed anyone. Yet Ford himself loved only particular kinds of work. The farm lost him when he was a boy because he didn't like that kind of labor, although of course this was later to be made into a virtue and explained by a story that he went to work in an urban machine shop really to find some way to make a machine that would lighten toil on the farm. It is more likely this account is apocryphal. Moreover, he moved swiftly from one piece of work to another; he was not out on a press in his plant, hour after hour, putting a piece of metal into process and 11 seconds later taking a bored piece off and lifting a new piece on. Certainly he would not have been interested in doing for long the repetitious operations evolved by him for others to do.

The misbegotten impression was created that before he came and took all the gimp out of men at forty that toil was heavenly and man lived a larkish life singing each day away. In July of last year when announcement was made jointly by the company and the UAW-CIO that agreement had been tentatively reached on the first retirement plan for hourly rated employees in the automotive industry, a plan later rejected by the union rank and file, one minor point in the bargaining was whether the average age of Ford's workers was forty-six, as the company said, or forty-seven, as the union said. It disposed of the long-lived charge that the pace burned automobile workers out by forty.

Not being afraid of work himself, he asked that those on his payroll give him a full day of it, too, since that was what he paid for, and even if there was a slight difference between Ford's check and that of Joe Doakes, the foundry hand, Ford, in fact, didn't ask any more from Doakes than he would have been willing to give Doakes if their positions had been reversed. One trouble was not peculiar to him. When he started he had fifty or so employees whom he knew by their first names. When he left off, he had 100,000, all numbered. No one could remember that many numbers.

The plant was his baby and he looked after it as if it was one. Everything pertaining to it had to be on a strictly business basis. He went to Europe with a friend, a man of decent fortune himself. The wives went along and the quartet covered a lot of ground, drawn close in the weeks of touring. The friend, who had a company in a non-competing line, began to experiment with carburetion after he got home and when he stumbled on a process which seemed applicable to motor cars he thought of his fellow voyager. If what he had turned out worked as he thought it would, an automobile owner would be able to get many more miles per gas gallon. He'd better tell Henry about it, certainly—let him have it. He arranged a luncheon.

Ford asked a great many questions but chilled eventually. He went on with his eating and seemed to have lost interest. His companion wondered what had gotten into the moody man across the table. Then he found out.

"Just one thing," Ford broke out of his sheath. The guest looked up, glad of explanation for the silence. "This must be handled on a strictly business basis, with no account of our personal relationship."

The surprised friend had only one answer for that—the answer he had had from the beginning.

"Why, I brought it out to give it to you, Henry," he said softly.

Ford tended the plant closely. A superintendent tells of a time when Ford had given an order to mend a machine. A shield had broken and hung out in an aisle. Whoever was instructed to do the job apparently forgot to pass the word along that the assignment was sacred cow—that the boss himself had ordered it. The motormaker came back in three hours and the shield still protruded. He walked away and returned in five minutes with a sledge. He disposed of the damaged equipment himself with a few devastating blows which ruined it completely.

The company got complaints when the one-piece block of the V-8 first appeared. Some cylinder walls were too thin. For some reason the motormaker's orders to get busy on the problem immediately were not carried out promptly. He impatiently put on overalls the third morning and walked out onto the floor of the shop to make certain the error was corrected.

Early clues to the reason for labor turning on him are possibly provided by Dean Samuel S. Marquis and E. G. Pipp, two top-ranking Ford officials who resigned in the Twenties. Marquis headed the sociological department; Pipp edited Ford's weekly at its start. Both were in positions to observe and both wrote books on what they did observe.

The Marquis work, *Henry Ford—An Interpretation,* was dismissed by Ford himself as "about the parson, not me." It became more or less a collector's item and copies stocked by the Detroit Public Library disappeared strangely and with such rapidity that there was much wondering as to whether the plant service men had withdrawn them and forgotten to bring them back. So many vanished in such a short time that the library retired remaining copies to its non-circulating shelves.

One excerpt:

"The old group of executives, who at times set justice and humanity above profits and production, were gone in 1921. Then came to the front men whose theory was that men are more profitable to industry when driven, that fear is a greater incentive to work than loyalty . . . and who felt the one sure way to get production and profits was to curse, threaten, drive, insult, humiliate and discharge labor on the slightest provocation; in short, to use a phrase much on the lips of such men, to 'put the fear of God into labor.'"

Pipp wrote in *Henry Ford—Both Sides of Him,* in 1926:

"As time went on I learned Ford had an inclination to use the lash of his power more and more upon those who opposed him. There also grew the desire to produce more and more at less and less cost, to get more out of the men and machinery than ever had been gotten out of them. The idea that Ford was adored by his men has certainly never existed except outside Detroit. It was the son Edsel who enjoyed universal respect." [1]

The senior Ford indicated himself some change of heart from what he professed when the $5 day went into effect. In his *My Life and Work,* done in collaboration with Samuel Crowther, he said:

"Some organizations use up so much energy and time maintaining a feeling of harmony they have no force left to work for the object for which the organization was created. The only harmonious organization that is worth anything is one in which all members are bent on one purpose—not to get along with itself but to get along to the objective. I pity the soft and flabby who must have an atmosphere of good feeling before they can do their work." [2]

Ford became a chronic critic of the Roosevelt administration. He bought for himself a growing opposition in the shop in the Thirties when presumably embittered and unforgiving after his first joust with the New Deal, as represented by the National Recovery Act, he grew prolific in fault finding. He joined the "That Man" club.

Once when he got home after a visit to the White House, a news bureau chief asked what he and F. D. R. had talked about.

"Well," he said, "he took up the first five minutes telling me about his ancestry." The motormaker said he did not know why this was "unless Roosevelt wanted to prove he had no Jewish blood."

Crop control was worse than common thievery. The NRA was a scheme to turn industry over to labor unions. The terms of the Wagner Act were dictated quite likely by Wall Street. He got to saying

[1] *Henry Ford—Both Sides of Him,* by E. G. Pipp, *Pipp's Magazine.*

[2] *My Life and Work,* Henry Ford and Samuel Crowther, Doubleday.

such things as "the world always has been ruled by mediocre men" and "an expert is a man to tell you only what was being done down to closing time day before yesterday" and "the United States will be in good shape when Santa Claus puts on his pajamas and goes back to bed," and "the New Deal is the handmaiden of international financiers" and "to hear a lot of people talk the greatest object in life is to achieve unemployment." These economists were not doers. He said it was no more fun to be rich and idle than poor and idle but when he said it the company surplus balance never had fallen, even in the worst years of the depression, below a half billion dollars and dividends were passed only in 1929 and 1932.

Here is a striking personality, said *The Christian Century,* who has made more than ordinary industrial success, with humane impulses now slightly corrupted, with a social philosophy not advanced beyond the doctrinaire individualism of the nineteenth century, and yet the world believes he expresses something new in industrial ethics.

Advisers tried to dissuade him in his fight with NRA and Gen. Hugh Johnson, its administrator, when he refused to be a signatory to the automobile code. He wouldn't change—said if he put his name to the code he'd have to live down to it, said it was a conspiracy to sell him down the river. Some executives argued the national stress was such the company's position might alienate the public.

Johnson tried to bully. Ford didn't scare. He said signing a code wasn't in the law. "The Blue Eagle isn't the law. The General's daily expression of opinion isn't the law." He said he'd wait until the final terms were made and then go them one better. He did as he said. After the industry, exclusive of him, agreed to a 35-hour week and a minimum of 40 to 43 cents, he set a five-day, 40-hour schedule with a 50-cent minimum. No union, he said, could give his men anything they did not already have.

He did not say much about the President himself but his editor maintained a steady cannonading and spoke sarcastically of men "piecing new paper worlds together out of fragments of ancient fallacies."

Out in the shop men grumbled. Washington could not be 150 per cent wrong as its opponents made it out. Ford might not like what was being done, but Wayne county, Michigan, voting residence of the bulk of Ford workers, gave Roosevelt an edge of 100,000 over Hoover,

200,000 over Landon, 175,000 over Willkie. Ford's political influence, if there ever had been any, over the boys in the shop waned and it is not impossible the sharp pronouncements of his proxy alienated many of them.

Labor leaders? His editor explained who they were:

"The title 'Labor Leader' given anyone whose influence is toward idleness by strikes is assuredly a misnomer. Men who through initiative lead their fellows to work, and through work lead them to wages, and through wages to higher standards of personal and family life, these are the men who rightfully should be known as labor leaders. They multiply opportunities for work. No one calls them Labor Leaders, yet they alone have led labor in its rise and labor has followed them more than it has followed any other."

It was charged that service men hid behind posts to catch workers at some violation of safety rules; that workers were framed so they could be fired. There were complaints of discriminatory layoffs, a blacklist, espionage, production schedules unrelated to human endurance, blistering speedups, the monotony of repetitious operations, wage rates not in line with the rate for the work done, transfers to unbearable jobs to get rid of recalcitrants, foremen and superintendents as afraid of losing their jobs as the men they supervised, discharges for emery dust under a bench, for failure to tighten correctly one nut in, say, a fender on a pick-up truck.

It was complained that espionage prevailed from roof to basement, that in a labor demonstration company pictures were taken and Ford workers identified in the crowd discharged; that lockers were searched for union literature. How many of the whispers were true and how many weren't was anybody's guess, but they crowded the air and men believed them.

Discipline was declared so severe that it was not unusual for some foremen to hide behind machinery at the approach of certain overseers. It was not unusual for a stool to be kicked from under a worker; it was said that service men, unannounced, were stationed as spies in departments pretending to be regular workers. Some held that the union was not organizing the plant but that the company was organizing the union by its own policies. Workers said: "Some of Ford's trouble is not due to his own uncertainty what he wants but to an inability to make clear to other men what he has in mind." Others said the senior Ford was well aware of what transpired and that the system had his consent.

The question remained unanswered how Ford could know the frictions in a place so big, of what was going on among or being done to 100,000 men.

And then the day came when the provocateurs, a token group, were there—two men on an overpass leading from a streetcar loading platform above a road into the fenced Rouge grounds. One was Walter P. Reuther, now international president of the UAW, and then head of a Detroit local who had been exceedingly vocal in a General Motors sitdown in Flint, Michigan, a year before. The other was Richard T. Frankensteen, organizational director. They were looking over the ground preparatory to circularizing employees.

A decade later Henry Ford II, intelligently abreast of his times, would seek out Reuther at union headquarters, and the two would sit in friendliest fashion for an hour across the table from each other looking to narrow the field of future disagreement.

Attacked as they reached the top of the overpass, the coats of Reuther and Frankensteen were jerked over their heads to pinion their arms, and the two men were then kneed in the groin, kicked, slugged and eventually kicked from the bridge. Their some 25 companions below got a lighter mauling, but the resultant picture shots of press photographers who managed to get away with unsmashed plates were reminiscent of a gangster film in the best tradition. Company spokesmen said, among other things, that the disturbance had been whipped up by newspapers which for six months "had cried for a Ford strike story."

There followed specious argument for weeks revolving whimsically around the question whether those who administered the beating were service men, as the union claimed, or just righteous "loyal" employees, indignant at invasion, as the company said; lies and counter-lies, truths and counter-truths, firings, hearings, court actions. Bennett, chief of the plant police, said he was lunching with two newsmen a good distance from the entrance when the row started and had said when telephoned by an aid: "Let them peddle if they want to." He added: "Nobody is going to storm Mr. Ford's gates!"

Ford went to the Circuit Court of Appeals in Cincinnati to dispute an order of the National Labor Relations Board, following examination of 150 witnesses, which directed the company to reinstate 22 discharged employees, cease discrimination. The Appeals Court refused to change the order, and the company went on to the United States Supreme Court, which upheld the NLRB except it supported Ford's right to express in print his views on union organization by any legitimate means he chose.

The fight on the overpass touched off trouble which spread through subsidiaries from California to Texas to Massachusetts.

Violence at Kansas City. Trouble at Buffalo. Five NLRB charges against unlawful labor practices at Chicago. A strike at Edgewater, N. J., and Ford workers sit masked at a Jersey CIO convention bearing a banner, "We'll take these masks off when Ford obeys United States laws." NLRB orders 975 employees reinstated at Kansas City with back pay. Dissolution of an alleged company union is directed. A charge that after one plant closed, rehiring was based on membership in a blue-card shop organization. Union buttons torn off work shirts. NLRB charges discrimination at Somerville, Mass. The Liberty Legion of America forms. Sixty unionists arrested for alleged assault on St. Louis workers. The Buffalo management accused of ten unfair practices. Arrests for distributing handbills. Ford Brotherhood members offer to buy a car apiece in exchange for a $1,500 guaranteed annual wage. A witness testifies Bennett paid a former union official $3,500 in $20 bills. Government orders reinstatement of 450 discharged workers at Long Beach, California.

Tactics at Dallas, Tex., build into a *cause célèbre*. An NRLB examiner takes a million words of testimony of alleged high-handedness —tapped wires, beatings, tar and feathers, men in company cars spotted throughout the city kicking up trouble, a new contribution to the industrial arsenal in a whip formed by pleating electric light wire and rubber stripping. An Illinois organizer sues for a million and claims he was taken from a municipal park, coated with tar and feathers on the outskirts of town, beaten unconscious and thrown in front of a newspaper office where a photographer was waiting.

An assistant foreman of Kansas City passing through on his way to Galveston with his wife testifies he was ordered to get out of his car and into another, was driven to the city limits, finally persuaded his captors of the truth of his statements, was released with the warning, "Don't join the CIO or you'll get what the rest got." Another

Kansas City Ford employee tells of being halted in Dallas on a visit with his wife to her grandfather, being knocked down and beaten with switches, and his wife told: "If you love your husband, get him out of Dallas." An employee of 18 years' service swears he was flogged for a quarter hour. A national convention of the CIO threatens a boycott of Ford products if the Dallas management persists.

The company held it was a spontaneous explosion of company employees against being forced into the CIO, and laid the blame on "a fratricidal war between two unions." The government examiner, however, accused the company of deliberately applying a program of terrorism.

"The company gathered and financed," he said in his findings, "the most vicious and experienced thugs in its employ who accepted an opportunity to indulge sadistic desires in lieu of additional compensation upon any person pointed out to them as a CIO organizer, member, advocate or sympathizer to be beaten, whipped, tarred or feathered.

"In 1937 the company decided the only way to defeat the workers in their organization efforts was to sow seeds of distrust of unions and fear of reprisals for followers if they joined the union. The NLRB examiner knows no other case in which an employer has deliberately planned and carried into execution a program of brutality with blackjacks, loaded hose, cat-o'-nine-tails and of rubber stripping and electric light wire." At Dearborn the claim the Ford workers were still free to join a union was repeated.

In April, 1941, the company fired eight men in its Rouge rolling mill for alleged union activities within the plant. Other workers took up the cry of "Strike! Strike!" and ran through the plant. Shortly after midnight on the darkened roads countless cars drew up, as many as ten abreast, fender to fender, shut off engines and traffic. A voice from a sound truck shouted, "We are striking Ford Motor Company! Form your picket line!"

This was no minor thrust, as the smaller group's checkered visit had been four years before. This was IT, the sally in force—iron bars, clubs, solemn pronunciamentos, scuffles, knockdowns, name-calling in the press, skirmishes, signs, "Chrysler gives $40 Christmas Bonus; Ford Gives Layoffs," appeals to the Governor, to the White House, government observers, Civil Liberties Union observers, movietone, strike editions, city police, state police—the whole book.

They had come to play rough as the service men or indignant "loyal" employees had played in '37. They also had come to get if they could what Ford never had been willing to yield—some say about their pay and working conditions, a word as to the pace of the assembly lines, an agreement on some curtailment of plant police activities. He was to be forced to bargain since he would not do so voluntarily. The unions already had filed with the NLRB a request for a plant election. It also had given under Michigan law a 30-day strike notice.

Ford was mad and grim. Outside his fences were thousands who were as inflexible as he—mad themselves and mad for others at Dallas, Texas, Kansas City, St. Louis, Edgewater, N. J., and other Rouge assembly points. They had come to water his power, strip some of the ermine. He had no desire to have his one-man Supreme Court expanded, but here they were with a list of new associate judges. He, they said, was a great Samaritan—with a blackjack.

The magazine, *Time,* quoted Bennett as saying that if the CIO won the company would bargain until it froze over "but they won't get anything." Bennet said he had been misquoted and that what he said was Ford would bargain until hell froze over—"but bargaining doesn't mean you have to say yes." Michael F. Widman, jr., union organizing director, chirped: "GM and Chrysler said they'd bargain and not give. Like them, Bennett will bargain—and he'll give."

A missing page of the book was the failure of the strike to measure up in violence to forecasts. It had been luridly foretold that when this one came, it would be a bloody transcript of Homestead and Gastonia and the Ludlow massacre rolled into one superpackage, that it would be transcendentally brutal and the land would be drenched by a crimson tempest, that Ford had a Maginot line and sprinkler pipes were loaded with tear gas, that the service department had at hand a murderous band of ruffians and was importing Negro strike-breakers from St. Louis. He had repeatedly said he would never do business with a union. The union was here to see if he was drawing to a belly straight.

The horoscope must have had a thick film of dust. The forebodings came to naught. There were one or two hard but brief fracases, but no one bobbed up from the fictional defensive labyrinths under the Rouge grounds. The plant closed down the third day. Philip Murray came in for a conference. A formula was found for reopening. The NLRB set a time for an election. The Rouge vote was:

CIO	51,866
AFL	20,364
No	1,958

Management and union negotiated. The union was granted its first union shop and checkoff in the industry.

The union granted permission to stamp the union label on its product, the first time any such privilege had been accorded in the industry. At Washington, when the contract was signed, an enormous debate developed over where the label should be placed and finally an onlooker, who had sweated out the days of battle, disgustedly inserted himself into the squabble.

"It might be possible," he mocked both sides, "to persuade Mr. Ford to make a radio standard equipment. The label could go on the antennae."

As part of a behind-the-scenes deal, NLRB complaints and pending hearings involving Ford were dropped, and three arbitrators, mutually agreed to, sifted a list of 2600 employees claimed to have been fired for union activity, weeded out questionable cases, ordered the company to rehire 1,400 and reimburse them $923,999.75 for lost pay.

The elder Ford remained silent about the NLRB election but his cohorts took the result without grace. They called it a "so-called" election. They declared it a triumph for the Communists, the Governor of Michigan and the NLRB. It was said that unless something was done about the Wagner Act, industry would be sovietized. The whole movement was inspired by greed of certain union leaders for an additional million in dues. Discontent among workers had been stirred up by scurrilous handbills and falsification by the press. There was no admission of the barest possibility, in view of the one-sided vote, that neither Mr. Stalin nor Mr. Roosevelt nor anyone else but Mr. Ford and the temper of the times were responsible—or that 72,000 workmen, instead of not knowing what they were doing or of having been coerced, merely had decided that between them and Mr. Ford was an executive wall they could never get over to make themselves heard without the help of someone who knew about such ramparts and had the proper scaling ladder.

For weeks the orderly plant was a bedlam. A 50-gallon vat was filled by commercially minded workers with victory beer and sold openly. Crap games flourished. Safety rules forbade smoking—cigarettes were defiantly lighted. In November, 1945, the company announced a four-year record of 773 work stoppages since the first contract terms were agreed upon. Three months later the union agreed to inclusion of clauses providing a two-week penalty for participation by a UAW member in a first wildcat strike, extended layoff or discharge for a second offense. For a third, he would be labeled an instigator and be fired.

It is pure speculation why Ford gave up but the most favored guesses are:

1. The company was turning to war work and had a pride in efficiently doing its share. Conversion to war goods was difficult enough without seething labor unrest.

2. The NLRB had turned up a considerable amount of evidence the company did not care to have aired. Unpleasant headlines over a period would be bad public relations.

3. A realization that some retroactive reimbursement of employees discriminated against was inevitable. Each day of unsettlement increased the bill.

4. Mr. Ford was sold the idea that he could place himself in a preferred position, solidify the shop behind him and embarrass his competitors by going whole hog and granting the union more than it had won from General Motors and Chrysler.

5. He could not stand seeing the plant idle.

6. He always had a surrender point—a point where the seemingly hard tire blew out.

7. If unionization was a good thing, as the men seemed to think, Ford wanted the place unionized. It could not be determined without trial.

8. The law of the land and mood of the day were against him.

It may have been that the dramatic pandemonium at the Rouge plant died a little too soon for a man who loved to play cops and robbers. Ford did not read blood and thunder novels but he liked to live them.

He was extremely chary of a New York industrialist who dropped in to chat when he was busy on a new model. The Dearborn nabob suspected a fishing expedition. In the usual procedure he would ask a trade visitor of importance if he'd care to step out to the laboratory and "see what we're doing." In this case he sent out word to fake a show—get up a display that would reveal no secrets.

"Well, sir," he said cannily in telling about it afterwards, "we went out into the shop but he was wise right away. He saw he wasn't getting the real thing and that we were on to him, and finally he said, 'Well, Mr. Ford, I guess I'll have to run along—of course, I'm really a financial man and all this is out of my line.' " Ford wasn't fooled; no, sir. He said later, "He knew we had rigged things up and knew exactly what he was up to—going to steal our stuff if we had anything new."

A newsman was present in the plant protection office one morning with Ford when a worried man in research telephoned. He said he was a little suspicious of a fellow put to work a few days before. The new man was just too good. Bennett told the boss and the motormaker had an idea.

"Here's what you do—put that fellow to work on some of those perpetual motion drawings," Ford plotted. "See if he can make head or tail of them. If he's so smart he'll soon know we're onto him."

The blueprints referred to were a decade's accumulation. Men who thought they had stumbled on the secret of perpetual motion were constantly sending Ford their prescriptions.

The newsman recalled the incident a couple of weeks later and asked Ford for the sequel.

"He was a spy from another company all right," Ford responded. He chuckled over what had really happened. "He wrestled with those crank drawings for a few days and then he said, 'Well, I see I'm not fooling you as to who I am,' and he got out."

At that point you had to make your mind up whether what you were hearing was sheer guff and strictly E. Phillips Oppenheim, born in a head that delighted in plot and counter-plot, or a true report of expected trade villainy.

Edsel Ford and Walter Reuther, UAW chieftain, sat on government war boards together and became friendly but Reuther never met the senior Ford until an inspection trip to the Willow Run bomber plant a few months after the union contract was signed. Edsel asked him if he would like to meet his father. Walter said he would, very much.

The senior Ford delighted in dead-pan joking. It was often impossible to tell when he was in earnest. Col. Charles Lindbergh had found that out—now Reuther did. When the motormaker was eighty he wanted a five-cylinder engine and put it up to his "dream" department—a room of experimental engineers who were encouraged to play with hallucinations, since nearly everything man has evolved has come from scrambled pieces that some one man finally fitted together.

The idea was not commercially practical for automobile use without balancing devices of prohibitive cost, his experimenters thought. The sales department would be cold to it since the public had been sold on sixes and eights. Make it anyway! The engine was delivered in due time to the dynameter for testing, and Ford, Lindbergh and an engineer who had worked on it stood by. The engine was revved up to 4500 rpm and the high frequency had about the same effect on the spectators as a blow on the funny-bone. Then it was shut off.

"Isn't that the smoothest thing you ever heard?" Ford said to his companions. They had no answer for him. He was probably joking but no one could tell. Work on the five-cylinder motor was one of the first experiments dropped after Ford's death.

The senior Ford and Reuther chatted about plane-making for a few moments after a handshake. Nine years before the labor spokesman had been bounced from the Ford plant, where he was working at $1.10 an hour as a tool and die leader, for openly holding an organizational meeting, and five years before, about to pass out union pamphlets, he had been inhospitably booted from a plant overpass.

"You know, Mr. Reuther," the senior Ford finally said, "it was one of the most sensible things Harry Bennett ever did when he got the UAW into this plant."

"Well, I think so but I didn't think you did, Mr. Ford," smiled Reuther. "How do you figure it?"

Ford pursed his lips. "Well," he said, "you've been fighting General Motors and the Wall Street crowd. Now you're in here and we've given you a union shop and more than you got out of them. That puts you on our side, doesn't it? We can fight General Motors and Wall Street together, eh?"

Reuther said it was an interesting theory. He still doesn't know if Ford was serious or having his fun.

A tired old man dies at 83, the age he said he'd settle for —$5 a day had not evoked Utopia; did anyone think nuclear fission would?

CHAPTER XXIV

THE LAST BILLIONAIRE

AND THEN the golden bowl was broken. A cerebral hemorrhage ended the success story of the unconventional architect of an industrial revolution in a cold room lit by oil lamp and candle. Flood waters of the River Rouge had cut off electric power and telephone, and the room in which he died was not unlike in inconvenience the one in which he was born by a midwife's ministrations in the third year of the Civil War. A chauffeur had to go to the plant to get through to a doctor, but before medical help arrived, Henry Ford, fairy-tale American, was dead.

He had lived, strangely enough, the exact number of years he wanted. When he was unable to attend a reunion in 1940 of those who were left who went with him to Europe on his peace argosy in 1915, the hope was expressed that he would be able to be present on the golden anniversary.

"Why, I'd be 102 then, wouldn't I?" he calculated. "I won't live that long." He said he'd settle for eighty-three.

So eighty-three it was. He was born July 30, 1863, and died April 7, 1946, after a dazzling and unflagging performance. With 34,000,000 people to choose from in the United States the year of his arrival, Fate singled him out, kissed him on the cheek, and said, "Son, step into my office!" He made almost as many motor-propelled vehicles as there were Americans when he was born, and when he died one of every seven persons in the United States was employed in the motor car industry and allied businesses.

* * * * *

If William and Mary Ford, bride of a year, had time that morning in 1863 for their newspaper, they found Madame Sparr, *soi-disant* doctress, promising to cure cancer clairvoyantly in 48 hours; a dramatic critic, smitten by a lady singing at a local theater blubbering in print, "Oh, were those eyes in Heaven they would through the airy regions stream so bright that birds would sing and think it was the morn"; Col. John Morgan and twenty of his raiders were locked safely in an Ohio penitentiary, and lightning which struck a school was reported as "playing the dickens with the girls' hoops."

William Makepeace Thackeray died in London during the year. C. Aubrey Smith and John Bunny of the movies, Sir Austen Chamberlain and the Brotherhood of Locomotive Engineers were born. It was the year of the Emancipation Proclamation and Stonewall Jackson's accidental death by the muskets of his own men. Erie was $140 a share, the Union consisted of 35 states, dawn was coming up on the era of industrial capitalism—and in a crib in a Michigan farmhouse dozed its classic exponent. Farmer Ford and his wife noted the date in the family Bible and had their separate dreams for him, but not one measured up to the ultimate in magic he was to perform as the most controversial figure in industrial history.

Longfellow published the *Tales of a Wayside Inn*—the boy in the cradle bought the Inn sixty years later and added a sheen the original probably never knew. Jacob Grimm died in Germany—the eight-pound boy in Dearborn would live a fairy story superior to any he wrote. Gordon took Soochow, a French gravel-pit yielded the Abbeville jaw, and the New York *Times* published police news under the restrained head, "The Metropolitan Police—Their Services During the Past Week."

The farmer's son of 1863 would build the greatest single concentration of wealth in the world on a foundation of ideas which at the turn of the century were regarded as crazy. Men would grow glib in the use of such words as carburetor and fuel pump and fan belt. He would pay no attention to Beadle's Pocket Library or Eliot's five-foot shelf but would do and dare, work and win, without them. He would run after a will-o'-the-wisp—and catch up with it.

He became a world figure. He helped men to conquer space, remade transport, and billowing clouds of persuasive publicity so implanted the idea of his primacy that one came near to forgetting other sculptors who contributed vital tidbits to the reshaping between Gettysburg and panic in Hiroshima. Such nowaday fixtures as telegraph, telephone, incandescent light, lawnmower, talking machine, typewriter, fountain pen, electric trolley, torpedo, dynamite, rayon, linotype, cream separator and adding machine had not been born when he was, but they were before he was 25. Other men were refining the world, also. Before Ford Motor Company produced a single car, Dunlop stumbled upon the pneumatic tire, Welsbach produced the gas mantle, Roentgen the X-ray and Lake the submarine.

The mythmakers were to make him all white or black. Critics dissected him and told with aplomb what he was "really" like and what he "really" believed. He was called the billionaire Utopian, the Great Humanitarian, the Mechanical Wizard. He was given statuettes, plaques, honorary degrees and ebullient citations enough to fill a thousand walls. Man who had once been cheered to travel by floating log, graduated to a steering wheel. Ford made Caspar Milquetoast into a lot of fellows bawling out the car window, "Get the hell over to your own side of the road, Bud!"

One group proved his system incomparable and Ford a supreme lesson in what faith and enterprise and willing hands would do. He was the radio beam other men rode, the Horatio Alger romance in elegant color. They said his greatness was inseparable from his willingness to see new things. One declared that if it were possible to preserve alive for the interest of history one man from each century and country —the one who represented not necessarily the best or wisest but the one who typified most thoroughly the hopes, crudities, background and achievements of his place—no one could better stand for his time and the U.S. than Henry Ford.

But he was reviled as well as lauded. Ah, they said, he was an ignorant idealist and anarchist, a slave-driver bossing a treadmill no different from Cubitt's except in bigness. The machine was making artisans obsolete. They were becoming hostlers to rods and bolts and moving conveyors. He had fixed his mind too hard on one idea after another to understand the proper relationship of all things. It was lack of the General Idea of life, said another, that made him seem bleak and erratic when he was only puzzled.

A monomania consumed him—a love of machines. He had an instinctive affinity for them. A moving part fascinated him. When boys of his age were usually pushing little girls in blue hair-ribbons into snowbanks or shining at shinny, he fixed watches. He walked nine miles to his first job—in a machine shop at $2.50 a week. Long before he contrived his automobile engine he got kicked out of a lot of shops for just standing around, uninvited, looking to see what was new he ought to know. In later years he claimed he could tell in what country a machine was made by the sound of it.

He started to put down his vague ideas of a combustion engine in 1889 on the back of a sheet of music his wife let him have (and Hitler was born at Braunau). His first engine clicked four years later, based partially on a thought he got in watching water being pumped to a rooftop at the Chicago World's Fair to fight a fire. (The wife of the German consul-general to Haiti bore a child they christened Hermann Wilhelm Göring.) Ford rode out in his first car in 1896, and when he drove to his birthplace an ashamed father and the neighbors looked grimly at Henry as if he had done something disreputable. (Guglielmo Marconi was in London at the time taking out the first patent ever granted for wireless telegraph based on use of electric waves.)

The wiry, determined little man from Dearborn made two false starts before he got under way. The first stockholders threw in the sponge after putting in more money than they thought they would have to. The second time a company terminated his contract before the end of the year for which it provided, the directors having in mind one kind of car and he another.

He began manufacturing in 1903 and struck gold five years later. He made a car he called the Model T and it put him into possession of so much money he could afford to speak of gold from then on as something seoond-rate and meaningless, and of so much fame and authority that if he recited *London Bridge is Falling Down* there were those who made out it was a pivotal event. Beside the River Rouge he carved a principality. He transfigured some marshy flat-land by building a mastodonic plant beside which the Wonderland of Alice was Mauch Chunk, Pa. It was his art gallery and opera house, high school and university, his Bible and betrothed. Work was his religion, experiment and efficiency an obsession.

* * * * *

What was so magical about this tin Pegasus, object of wheeze and jingle in which the world once rode and on which the maker waxed richer than any man before him? A traveler in Georgia reported seeing an object half in and half out of familiar wrappings being unsealed in 1945 in front of a barn. It was a new shiny Model T, and the tourist, being from Detroit, stopped. The explanation: "It's the last of three I bought when Ford stopped making them. Used two and kept the other in the barn in the same paper it was shipped in." The farmer slapped the radiator as he might a prized but unruly heifer. "Never'll get as good a car again," he said with positivism, "or one I'll get as much out of." The Model T won such fealty for its manufacturer.

World production of the model in nineteen years at the Highland Park and River Rouge plants, scattered assembly plants in the United States and in thirty foreign operations—plants either owned by Ford or partially owned through stock interests—was exactly 15,456,868. It sold for as high as $900 and as low as $265.

It was introduced at the Chicago Automobile Show in December, 1907, and went into production immediately. It became the nation's workhorse. It was familiar from Saskatchewan to Sydney, Cape Town to the Place de l'Opéra. Through it, men who never heard of Lincoln knew of Ford. Men crossed oceans to toil in his plant, get a nest-egg and go home to preside in distant villages as the only skilled mechanics on the premises.

We were prowling after dark in the Haitian bush in search of voodoo when our car balked. We had forded two streams tumbling with recent heavy rains and were at a turbulent third. The native driver disappeared. He emerged shortly from a thatched hut, barely visible in the black island night, dragging another native of the same complexion as the night itself who raised the hood and went to work as if he knew exactly what he was doing.

"Ford worker," said the driver, a trace of pride in his voice. "He was in Detroit three years."

Whatever was wrong, the repairman found it, and at the end flipped his hand to say all was well again and we could safely tackle the freshet ahead.

On the Moselle one summer the village handyman also proved an ex-Ford worker. GI's were to be there ten years later, but then the only harbinger of what was to come were strutting villagers lifting arms in Nazi greetings. The handyman appeared indifferent to the saluting lodge members—he wanted to know instead how things were going at Dearborn with Herr Ford.

Other men had made gasoline engines and installed them in a

variety of rigs but most of them expired in the fierce battle for survival. Ford grew stronger with each stride. He doubled his workers' wages when there was no competitive necessity and cut the price of the product when he could have gotten more. If the assembly-line was a Tyrian galley, as some men said, many went back to the oar-locks, year after year, apparently content.

The little man, who was in a class by himself in fortune, became the most advertised Croesus of his day and he was largely unenvied because it was regarded as clean money, free of stock-jobbing and illicit shenanigans and pompous use. No two-cars-to-a-garage nonsense—one apiece to a family was good enough for him and the longer they lasted on the road the more pleased he was.

In his drive to lower the price he was smart at trimming corners. His foremen were delighted when they made a machine which would finish the base of a motor block in one-third the previous time but he mocked it—and got an idea.

"Why have we been doing that at all?" he challenged them. "The underside of the block doesn't need finishing!" He threw out the whole operation as unnecessary.

The Model T swarmed over the land. It was virtually a stripped car. If doodads were wanted he did not supply them. He provided transportation, and gimcracks were not necessary to get over the ground. For years he did not add an accessory he did not have to, and the policy enabled him to make a low retail price as against a manufacturer who put on all the gadgets and had to establish a higher price to get his money back.

The car was light and therefore did not use as much gas and oil as heavier vehicles. It was known as a utility car because of the various uses to which it could be put. Being light, it did not require good roads as did weightier makes. Parts were standard. Practically the same cam and crankshaft were on the car when manufacture ceased as when the first Model T rolled out. The parts business in 1913 amounted to $800,000; six years later it was $80,000,000.

At conventions, dealers used to get up on the floor and say, "We understand the Ford car is thrown together." Parts had to be properly machined so they could be thrown together. There was no vise in the place—if a part did not fit it was scrapped.

From a manufacturing standpoint there was no need to toss out a slew of machines annually, and install new ones since the car remained basically the same. Special machines could be set up, built especially to do certain things. It was said, too, that seventy per cent of the workers could be taught the operations required in less than two days and they did not have to read, write or speak English.

From a selling standpoint there were numerous advantages. The man who came into a salesroom did not have to make a choice. There was only the one model on sale. There could be no obsolescence. Some banks would loan money against Ford cars when they were more reluctant in the case of a company constantly shifting models.

From the buyers' standpoint, no car was close to the Model T in price, and it was considered simple to operate and repair.

Ford was master of the fixed idea and he allowed no one to divert him. When he began making T's, Ford Motor Company's surplus balance was $2,156,625; nineteen years later when he came with distaste to the conclusion that the idea of one model had been wrung dry and the last Model T off the line became a museum-piece, the balance was roundly $673,000,000.

* * * * *

The aromatic horse-barn disappeared. The deep rutted road was rolled and widened and surfaced and gave way to the four-lane highway. Garage replaced woodshed and wheel-barrow slunk off before the self-dumping truck. Ford pulled the oceans closer together.

The press was filled with his mixed thoughts: Surplus never could be evil . . . war was due to international financiers and too many diplomats . . . those who believed in high taxes should be run out of office . . . there would be no wars if kings and presidents and some employers were sent to the trenches . . . the labor movement was a plot of rivals to undo him . . . virtue and vision resided largely in the cornstalks—almost all great men were farmboys.

He liked old machines and old furniture, said you couldn't tell much about either until they were old—and affronted antiquarians by taking fine pieces, their wood mellowed by time, and refinishing them until the experts could see their petrified faces in them. He was in the desirable position of being able to tell anyone to go to hell—if there were answering barbs they glanced off his assurance. He yipped for standardization—and in his own life was a non-conformist. He said books mussed up his mind—and collaborated in three about himself. He said absurd things and perceptive things—and he represented thousands of inarticulate Americans who thought as he did and to whom nobody paid any attention. In him they saw themselves, with a bit of luck. What he said often was what they thought.

Diagnosticians were slightly addled by the fact that he did not square with their notions as to how a man with a billion should act. He was considered a queer duck because he said history was bunk, preferred a photograph to a Whistler, ran away from the farm as a boy because he did not like it and flew back later, as fast as his legs would carry him, to reconstruct the homestead just as he remembered it down to the last gravy-boat.

A born adventurer, he constantly rocked the boat, going his way undaunted by any suggestion that what he was doing or planning to do violated some basic principle. He conceded nothing to be fundamental until he tested it for himself—and, doing this, found he could do many things that *couldn't* be done.

He banged away sharply, and often intemperately, at bankers and economists, Jews and the New Deal, the money system and man's unfortunate unwillingness to love work as he did, but he went on changing the world, too, putting it on rubber tires, making it mobile as never before, turning manufacturing into a machine operation, and applying the assembly line principle to production on a scale unmatched by any other entrepreneur. He became the venerated drum-beater of a cult. His methods were a religion. Where man, without them, had made a unit an hour, now he could make a hundred or a thousand under new astonishing techniques. He bobbled some jumps but seemed to land right side up, firmly rooted in the stirrups. If he miscalculated, it seldom got into the publicity.

He went ahead transforming prairie into village, village into town, town into city, and then despised what he had created and said the days of the unlovely city were numbered. A British journalist, after watching the assembly line in its obstetrical labors, reported to his English readers that it would not be surprising if the private home was eventually abolished in the United States in favor of a residential car "in which Americans will be born, live, wed and die."

* * * * *

He thought patents choked competition and hamstrung progress, and executives clipped anything supporting the view and made sure he saw it. It was an attitude that possibly developed in his fight over the Selden patent years before, but he seldom would buy one until it was adjudicated to the last ditch. Some said it was a giant's way of squeezing an inventor who might be in no position to fight back; others declared it originated in Ford's distrust of patent claims and a belief that many existing patents are based on old discoveries.

Inventions, he insisted, were often matters of long evolution. He patented one part for the Model T only to find that a piano-tuner had done the same thing eighty years before. He patented a magneto device—then discovered that Michael Faraday had produced one like it. He took out a patent on a universal joint inside a ball-and-socket joint —and later came upon the same arrangement on a forty-year-old steam engine.

"I'm not so sure there's a new thing on a Ford car despite our hundreds of patents," he once told me.

If he had been given the plans for the first Model A at the time he made his first car in 1896, he said he couldn't have made it. The art of manufacturing had not developed far enough and the right materials were not available. Carrying the idea further, he said if he had the plans of the Model T, begun in 1908, when he began manufacturing in 1903, he could not have built it for the same reason.

"A lot of things on cars were tried years ago and didn't work," the lecture on patents went, "but they could be made to work now. Something that was on the car in 1915, for example, and was unsuccessful, now is feasible because of new alloys or better manufacturing methods."

A Detroit manufacturer of shock absorbers and a patented lubricating system paid a good price to a Moline, Ind., inventor for a patented automobile shackle and imagined he had a good thing. It was installed experimentally on a number of Fords and reports from the engineering department were encouraging. He met Ford at a party and was asked to drop in at Dearborn for a talk. He felt happy about it.

Ford said, "I want to save you some money."

What was meant wasn't quite clear, but the smaller manufacturer chose to think it encouraging. Ford might be going to bid for the shackle patent. He went to see the motormaker next day.

The vast Ford collection of antiques was in the making but he had no idea at the time what he was going to do with them and much of the accumulating old-time machinery was piled outdoors. It could have been mistaken for a junk pile when he led his visitor out to it.

"I get many wonderful ideas out of old machinery," he confided on the way. "I'm never surprised to find something we think new is pretty old." Ford said the other man would be astonished at the number of modern manufacturing patents issued on little gadgets that actually were in use a generation or more ago. "Take those antique steam-fittings from pipes used in Michigan mines! With a little imagination they could be motor car valves, eh?" He asked the guest to name another machine alongside.

"It's an old scale, isn't it?" The small manufacturer looked closer.

"To weigh tanbark," Ford nodded. "Remember how heavy trucks used to drive on for weighing? A heavy load would have broken the platform so it was hung on shackles." He pointed out the ancient shackles. "See what I mean," he said. The shackles were the same type which the caller's recently purchased patent was presumed to cover—and the scale equipped with them bore the year date 1860.

Ford patted the visitor's shoulder sympathetically. "You thought you had something because the government granted your inventor a recent patent. I asked you here to show you the shackle was discovered by another man more than sixty years ago. It isn't really patentable."

Ford talked freely but seldom listened, or if he listened often did not seem to hear. He would be at your side, going through the gestures of sociability, and be a thousand miles away.

He said he wouldn't give a nickel for any painting, but engaged an artist to re-create on canvas the scene when his first engine was born. He made a sandwich of weeds but decided, after one bite, that he had made a mistake; declared that what the U.S. needed was water with a kick in it, tried to make fertilizer of tree stumps which cost him $1,000 to uproot in some cases, and when his son said, "I'll bet that's a profitable operation," looked stony-eyed at such skepticism.

He mixed bosh with cogency. The depression was wholesome because it taught Americans a needed lesson. Most people wouldn't work unless you caught and made them. He had the idea, incidentally, of spending oneself into prosperity long before it became a New Deal tenet. One year his advertising men submitted a slogan, "Buy a Ford—SAVE the Difference." He changed a word, making it, "Buy a Ford—

SPEND the Difference." Prosperity lay in spending, not saving; in the velocity of money, not in its idleness.

Marry young. A good mother-in-law is important but a good father-in-law does not matter. Those who wait and marry calculatingly do not fare so well. Don't drink! Alcohol has better uses. Women who wear short skirts will come to no good end. Don't smoke! Hard work is the answer to most problems.

He could be vindictive, but he was deeply sorry in one case. Beaten in a Senatorial contest by Truman H. Newberry, wealthy Detroiter, he was successful in having his victorious opponent indicted with 133 Republican party leaders on a charge of criminal conspiracy with intent to violate the Corrupt Practices Act. The Newberrys and Fords had visited at each other's homes, had been friends of twenty years' standing, and the junior Ford and one of Newberry's sons were intimate friends.

A Federal judge sentenced some dozen of the defendants to Leavenworth but on appeal the United States Supreme Court declared the statute unconstitutional.

The conviction was set aside. Newberry was seated but resigned shortly.

Nine years later Ford sought out his opponent, apologized and declared his action had been due to bad advice and erroneous information. When the overtures were made through a mutual friend Newberry laid down only two conditions: The meeting was to take place in his office or home and there was to be no publicity. The motormaker agreed and walked into the Newberry office the day before Christmas, 1927. It was the first time, he said, he had been above the ground floor of a modern office building. The apology was extended and accepted; the two talked for a half hour and parted with an exchange of wishes for a merry Christmas.

* * * * *

Ford did not belong to the Automobile Manufacturers' Association. The National Chamber of Commerce did not speak for him. He was not a joiner. He did not sit in with the business oligarchy. A man of inexplicable moods, he gave irregularly to the Detroit Community Fund. Frequently at campaign time the steering committee, shrinking at the memory of previous rejections and at the prospect of approaching him again, would suggest to the co-operative Edsel that he intervene. Sometimes the son would talk to his father; sometimes, if he did not give, the son would increase his own subscription to offset his father's refusal; again he might say, "Father is in such a state at the moment that I'd be afraid to tackle him. There is no telling what he would do."

Yet the senior Ford did not object to his radio spokesman promoting the cause and urging national backing for the 400 chests of the country, and soon Cameron would be saying, "Shall we wait for Providence or be Providence?" or "The glory of the modern community chest work is that it does more than a bucket of water to a fire; it makes the structure fireproof against future mishap." Despite the importunation, Ford usually elected to be his own almoner. He had the money and time and staff. Once when publicly solicited in a New York theater after Al Jolson called attention to his being in the house, Ford rose and stomped out angrily.

His mail, two-thirds begging, once ran 8,000 communications a week. Read these verses! Help their author. Examine this invention! Let me have $3,000,000 to buy a silver mine, four dollars for an unpaid grocery bill. Gimme, gimme, gimme! A wheel chair. A pair of crutches. Fare to a dry climate, passage to America, a ticket to romantic places. European youth bombarded him for backing in university study. Thousands of associations and clubs and missionaries wrote for free cars. One woman said it would be very nice if he would lend her a thousand dollars. He need not send it but if he would just keep on investing it until it reached $100,000, he could then recapture the original thousand and mail her the balance. A count one year showed that $400,000,000 would have been required to do all the letter writers asked.

Nevertheless, he could be wetly sentimental. He found work for drug addicts and prison parolees and had hundreds of old employees around the place who were untouchable even when they were unproductive. He would place at the disposal of sick people he hardly knew the facilities of his hospital without charge and was a push-over for any newspaper sob story. He was not reached so much by distress in the mass as he was by a single misfortune. Volume misery seemed harder for him to grasp or to do anything about, but an evicted family, pictured in its woe on the sidewalk and the photo-page, was likely to be dumfounded by the ensuing largess if Ford happened to pick up his paper that morning and notice its dilemma. One family of eight was moved with celerity into a house specially painted and papered and fenced with pickets in five hours. He set an army to decorating on that rush job.

A friend who lived at a Ford inn began to lose his sight and Ford was so distracted he dropped in daily to chat, but he felt he had to offer some excuse for calling so often. The daily visits might intensify his friend's worry, otherwise, so he used to say he was there to get a shave or haircut and when the two were talked out the sick man would escort Ford to the barber-shop and see him into the chair. Unprotestingly the motormaker got a hundred unnecessary shaves and surplus haircuts so there would be no suspicion that what really brought him to the tavern so regularly was his friend's dimming vision.

A mechanic fitting some boilers for the Detroit Illuminating Company in the 90's had six feet of tubing left over when his job was done and he said to the company engineer, "Can you use this stuff, Ford; if you can I'll leave it?"

In the 20's he got to thinking of that fellow who had given him the tubing which went into the first Ford cylinder. Dillon, wasn't it? He had been with a Buffalo company. Find him! A couple of old-timers thought Dillon was dead but that a daughter lived in a small town in Pennsylvania. The village police chief was chatting with the postmaster when the Ford inquiry arrived. Neither could remember any Dillon.

"Hold on, now," said the chief, "wasn't that the name of Mrs. Collins before she married?"

Mrs. Collins was invited to Dearborn. She and Ford lunched together, tramped through the plant and museum, were photographed and she stayed over for an old-fashioned dance in the evening as the belle of honor. Next day she motored home in a new automobile in appreciation of the six-foot piece of tubing her father kindly left behind thirty years before.

* * * * *

He was sure that airplanes, radio and automobiles existed in civilizations so ancient that historians had no record of them. The globe, he argued, had been inhabited by intelligent peoples millions of times. He called history bunk, and captivated by the inches of space the statement got, repeated it in later years and added an extra flounce by branding it "bunkety-bunk."

It was summer of 1919. The Chicago *Tribune* editorially had called him an "ignorant idealist" and "anarchist," and Ford sued for a million dollars. The litigation engaged the finesse and theatricalism of seventeen lawyers, cost the parties concerned $1,400,000 and the judgment was six cents in Ford's favor, an award each side translated as a victory.

This particular morning the *Tribune* was bent on trying to prove the soundness of its name-calling. The man on the stand did not look to be damaged a million dollars worth but did seem baffled. He knew all about brazing furnaces, slides and rollways, core-bonds and burring machines, valves and monorails, but the man talking coldly in front of him was not interested in what Ford knew of these matters, for this would have proved Ford a supremely intelligent man, within particular boundaries, and *Tribune* counsel was trying to show he was a knucklehead.

"You know of Benedict Arnold, Mr. Ford?" "He was a writer, wasn't he?" "Ever read any of his writings?" "Don't believe I have." "Are you not aware that the action of Arnold constituted one of the first incidents of treason in American history?" "I don't remember."

Did the witness know of a revolution in the United States? "I understand there was one in 1812." (The press seats emptied in a race for telephones.) "Any other time, Mr. Ford?" The witness said he did not know of any. "Don't you know this country was born of a revolution in 1776 and that there wasn't any revolution in 1812?" Ford said he didn't know—hadn't paid much attention to it.

The questioning veered. "Men like Pershing are murderers—is that your idea, Mr. Ford?"

"I guess the general will admit committing many a murder. Killing anyone is murder."

"How about Ulysses S. Grant?"

"Yes, I think he said war was murder."

The lawyer said, "I think you are wrong there, Mr. Ford. General Sherman said war was hell but neither he nor Grant said it was murder that I ever heard of."

"I think General Sherman said it was murder," said Ford, confidently.

In a book the motormaker had said that advice of militarists on the need of a vast army and navy was about the same as the advice of a group of gamblers would be in the framing of civil laws—"the only difference is that the military man gambles with human lives and pleads for national honor when he means personal glorification or blood money."

"You put the soldier below the professional gambler, Mr. Ford?"

"Yes. One gambles with lives. The gambler does not do any harm."

"You prefer the professional gambler to the soldier?"

Ford said he thought he did.

In an anti-preparedness advertisement use had been made of the word "ballyhoo." He was asked for a definition.

"A blackguard, I guess," ventured the witness.

His counsel suggested "barker." *Tribune* counsel snorted, "A shouter to sell his wares."

Ford, helpfully: "At a peanut stand or something? There's a lot of blackguarding there."

Tribune counsel, curtly: "I don't know. I am not in that business!"

He was questioned about a preparedness speech delivered by the late Henry A. Wise Wood, inventor and writer, prior to World War I and a subsequent talk Ford had with Wood at Dearborn in which Ford was quoted as saying that perhaps when the war was over the American flags over his plant would come down never to go up again. He might put up an international flag.

"Mr. Wise was a gentleman, wasn't he?"

"He did not look free."

"What was there about him? Did he look like a slave?"

"A slave, yes—a slave to the financiers. I judge so from the things he said."

"What did he say?"

"I don't remember now," said Ford, "but I think he was trying to trap me into saying things."

The examination tacked anew. This was to be the capsheaf. It was led up to with bogus gentleness since the question might boomerang.

"Mr. Ford," said the *Tribune* attorney, "I have some hesitation about the question I am about to ask but in justice to you I will put it." He said the impression had been created that Ford could not read because of his refusal to read any of the printed material handed to him at various times in court. "Do you want to leave it that way?"

"Yes, you can leave it that way," Ford said, and added:

"I am not a fast reader. I have hay fever and I'd make a botch of it."

"Are you willing," the examiner persisted, "to have that impression left?"

"No, but I'm not a fast reader."

"You can read?"

"I can read."

"Do you want to try it?"

"No!" Ford didn't raise his voice.

"You would rather leave it that way?"

"I would rather leave that impression," the galled motormaker said stiffly.

Counsel rubbed his hands slowly. Reporters disappeared again into telephone booths. The witness smiled upon the jury and the farmer jury smiled genially back. Out the windows they could see the Fords rolling north and south on U.S. 25, bumper to bumper, and they knew who made them. Jurors Nos. 3 and 7 never had heard of Benedict Arnold either and wondered if it made them anarchists.

* * * * *

Ford found fault with the American school system and introduced his own. He did not think education should begin with words and end with words. Man risked, thereby, becoming a parrot. He thought too many adolescents and their parents had their eyes on white shirts, shiny desks and gold letters on the door and that if they continued to center on such things, they would be poor prospects to do the world's work.

As the elder Morgan delighted in reference to himself as the American Lorenzo, Ford tired in late years of being called the Great Industrialist and preferred a good word for his work in education. He launched a school for apprentices in 1915 when he heard a group of employees was paying one of its number for instructions in shop mathematics at his home after working hours. He opened a trade school for boys 12 to 15 the next year, which probably reflected Ford's own table of values. It emphasized Safety, Orderliness, Accuracy and the Time Element in that order.

The school began with six pupils and wound up with 1,500 students, 600 acres and 125 full-time instructors. He preached that there was no system of government or scheme of life which would relieve youth of doing its own tasks. The master of the machine was sure that handiwork would remain basic. However much critics talked of automatons of the assembly line and spoke slightingly of the need of skill required, Ford was positive that changing conditions of manufacture, mass production, and closer limits of measurement and increasing importance of the time factor intensified the need for training.

He opened a third school, for high school boys, in 1936. He developed others in Greenfield Village, three in Sudbury, Mass., two in England, others in Brazil and Georgia. A school official once complained it was illogical for him to finance the industrial training of such an army and permit business rivals to snap up its graduates.

"They're good mechanics, aren't they?" he retorted. "Let them work where they want to."

Girls were taught not only academic subjects but how to keep house, plan meals, shop and meet guests. On top of academic subjects for boys Ford piled training in the skills of the machine shop and sank two million dollars in machinery to implement the spoken word. At Greenfield enrollees learned of rocks and trees, clouds and flowers, and there was even a class to encourage good conversation and manners. Many children were registered at birth for later entrance.

Not long after the trade school opened he asked for the number enrolled and was told 400, with 4,000 waiting.

"Reverse it!" he ordered.

He was never able to bring it off. When enrollment reached 2,800, the waiting list was 15,000. To him it proved that boys still wished to make things. Parents were wrong in assuming that diplomas and degrees would insure success. The youngsters had to be taught in such a way, he said, that when they graduated they would be in demand. It was not enough if the boy or girl could only say he or she was a graduate of a certain university.

When anyone said differently it surprised him as much as Billy Sunday did. In behalf of God and temperance, Sunday, a retired baseball player, slid across stages sown to sawdust several decades ago and unexplainably by his paroxysms won converts and enriched the American language. Conversion by the Sunday recipe came to be known as "hitting the sawdust trail." The athletics also were referred to as "muscular Christianity."

On a visit to Detroit he had an audience with Ford and in a rapturous private showing Mr. Sunday climaxed an appeal for funds by leaving his feet and sliding magnificently the length of the Ford private office. Either bowled over by the thud of thighs or possibly to avert an encore with spikes, the motormaker grabbed money from under his inkwell and pressed it on the evangelist before he fully got himself in hand.

* * * * *

The adventure was about over. Ford was no longer at concert pitch. He was brought home on a stretcher in mid-war from Georgia and he never rallied wholly after that, although it was said there was nothing wrong organically. But newsmen did not see much of him thereafter. Only infrequently was he in the headlines—a tribute by his home town, a ceremonial honoring pioneers of the industry on the fiftieth anniversary of the time when first his friend Charles B. King in 1896 and then he, three months later, drove their first cars on the streets of Detroit. He resisted all reminders that it was late and to remember his rest and stayed until midnight, chinning exuberantly with men like him who were present when hill-climbing was a feat and a car was a back number without a wicker basket for the umbrellas.

He warmed himself in the sun of the back veranda overlooking the River Rouge and occasionally warmed others by descending unannounced on the plant, almost as brisk as ever, and going on a rampage in the old commanding way. He had withdrawn so definitely, however, that a contretemps was narrowly avoided. A guest speaker on a program in Ford's honor luckily submitted to the Ford News Bureau a script in advance of presentation. It was written in the past tense and there was a frantic changing of verbs to make it sound less as if the flivver king had passed away.

He remained a fun-loving man. It was during this tapering-off period that he walked down the aisle of a church after a wedding ceremony. His steps were much slower at the time, and guests made way for him so he could reach his car without being jostled. He seemed to be paying no attention to any one but he stopped to speak to a man and his wife who had not left their pew. The woman's face had been scratched by briars in her rose garden. Ford bent over and whispered softly to her husband, "Now you're getting to be a man, Ed! Treat 'em rough! It's the only way to keep a wife in line." He straightened up, unsmiling, and continued to the exit, looking neither right nor left.

City rooms of Detroit newspapers were their usual orderly madhouse one April night last year. A state election was in progress. Old leads were being killed, new ones written, as late scores rolled in. A new voice broke in on the telephone shortly after 1 A.M. It said, "This is the Ford News Bureau. Mr. Henry Ford died at 11:45 P.M. of a cerebral hemorrhage. We haven't many details but will call back as soon as we have." A short time later the bureau began reporting the details on a special telephone hookup which tied up the offices of the three Detroit newspapers and the three national wire services.

If Ford was right in his philosophy the saga did not really end in the candlelight. It will have a sequel which unfortunately will not be available to press associations. When William McKinley, third President of the United States to be assassinated, was buried in 1901, a friend gave Ford a small book, the work of Orlando J. Smith, Civil War general, Mississippi cotton planter and editor who set up and named William Jennings Bryan's *Commoner* and was first to distribute newspaper boiler-plate on a large scale. When Ford finished it he had an answer that satisfied him as to the meaning of life. There had been a life before he came into this one—there would be another when he left it. The soul was eternal.

Man went on endlessly gathering enriching experience from one life to another. This one was but a short act in existence which had no beginning or end. He told associates he felt there was nothing in the world he had not seen in a previous life and also that work would be futile if it was impossible for man to use the experience collected in one life in the next.

If he was right about the use he would make of his encyclopedic experiences, it is reasonably sure he is going about with his inquisitive eyes appraising all before him, already dissatisfied with some things he has found, planning refinements, suggesting ways of cleaning up some dark corners, clocking operations to see if things where he is are one-two-three with the storied Rouge.

The king is dead and there will be none like him for a time or ever. Apprentice critics who had not opened their eyes when his first car was made, have fobbed off his passing as though years before he had not stood at a fork in the road and turned the world's march in a new direction. Peasants of Russia once scheduled fetes upon arrival of his tractors; *Pravda* said only, "A correspondent of Reuter's reports from Detroit the death of Henry Ford, well known owner of automobile plants." Men more constant in their affections and sounder in their perceptions, wrote, when he died, as if an age had ended.

He was at his zenith the world's richest man. The tax tables being what they are and implicitly promise to be, he was probably America's last billionaire.

INDEX